MICHIGAN
❧ IN ❧
LITERATURE

GREAT LAKES BOOKS

*A complete listing of the books in this series
can be found at the back of this volume.*

PHILIP P. MASON, EDITOR
Walter P. Reuther Library, Wayne State University

DR. CHARLES K. HYDE, ASSOCIATE EDITOR
Department of History, Wayne State University

MICHIGAN
❧ IN ❧
LITERATURE

CLARENCE ANDREWS

 WAYNE STATE UNIVERSITY PRESS   Detroit

96 95 94 93 92   5 4 3 2 1

Library of Congress Cataloging-in-Publication Data

Andrews, Clarence A.
  Michigan in literature / Clarence A. Andrews.
      p.   cm. — (Great Lakes books)
  Includes bibliographical references and index.
  ISBN 0-8143-2368-5
  1. American literature—Michigan—History and criticism.
  2. Michigan in literature.   I. Title.   II. Series.
PS283.M5A5   1992
810.9'32774—dc20   91-31020

Designer: Elizabeth Pilon

Human beings produced that [fiction] at a certain time in a certain place under certain conditions. Literature may or may not reflect life, but life determines all about the character, theme and scope of literature.

—John Theodore Flanagan

CONTENTS

PREFACE

Fictional work about Michigan follow[s] a pattern that [i]s similar to novels about American life in general. Romances, frontier life, historical sagas, novels of the great outdoors were replaced with the new realism of the twentieth century. Life on the farm, once supposedly a thing of beauty and a joy forever, soon became just plain drudgery as the sons of the soil left the farms for the big city. The grim portrayal of city life, factory towns, depressions and war all find their place in Michigan fiction as they did universally.
—Francis X. Scannell, "The Novelist and Michigan"[1]

Much of Michigan's lengthy and colorful history—from its Indian through its British and French periods, from its brief territorial status through its century-and-a-half existence as a state—has been recorded in its newspapers and other state periodicals; in the *Michigan Pioneer and Historical Collections*; in *Michigan History*; in a wide range of general and specialized histories; in biographies; and in primary materials stored, for example, at the state of Michigan Archives and Library in Lansing and the state's universities, colleges, county courthouses, museums, libraries, and depositories, especially the Clarence M. Burton Historical Collection housed in the Detroit Public Library.

This book expands those records by offering a catalog of literary and dramatic works set in Michigan over the years, places them in a significant context, evaluates them, and furnishes information about their authors. It also shows how novelists, short story writers, dramatists, and poets created their particular images of Michigan, either as foreground or background, by utilizing and interpreting its history—land and waters; people; year-by-year events, both major and minor; ideas, philosophies, and policies—sometimes as factually as possible; sometimes distorted, changed, or modified; sometimes fancied or imagined.

Michigan, with its 96,675 square miles of land and lakes; its forests and mines; its cities, towns, and farms; its factories and businesses; its colleges and universities; its diverse populations; and its rich history, has proven a fertile soil for over a thousand novelists, short fiction writers, poets, dramatists, and filmmakers. The state as literary subject encompasses the New Holland of the southwest to the Arbre Croche area, Mackinac Island and The Bridge to the Soo, and the Detroit megalopolis.

In many ways the Michigan Upper Peninsula, familiarly known as UP, is a world unto itself, like the Old World of the nineteenth century. On its village streets, one may still hear the accents of England's Cornwall and Italy's provinces as well as the dialects of Sweden, French Canada, and Finland. Its remote towns and villages, with their Cornish, Finnish, French, Indian, and New England names, have a pretwentieth-century appearance and atmosphere. Its cutover vastness, second-growth forests, abandoned railroad right-of-ways, weed-covered slag heaps, and mining camp ruins tell of a more prosperous, more heavily populated past.

Such unique aspects of the two peninsulas and their adjoining lakes and islands have furnished the action, tone, idiom, characters, and settings for a large quantity of imaginative literature—folktales, poetry, short fiction, novels, plays, pageants, and films.

My criteria for selecting the works discussed are: Is the work, or a significant part of it, set in Michigan? Is it fiction, verse, or drama in which the action or plot takes place within the state? As a consequence, some works by authors who were either born in or were longtime residents of the state are not discussed. For example, Rex Beach's novels set in the northern frontiers of North America are omitted, even though he was born in Michigan. On the other hand, some books by non-Michiganians are included—for example, *The Oak Openings; or, The Bee-Hunter* (1848) is set in Michigan during the War of 1812 by New Yorker James Fenimore Cooper (1789-1851), who visited Kalamazoo in 1847; and *The Primitive* (1949) by Iowan Frederick Manfred (1912-) who used the pseudonym Feike Feikema, is based on the author's four years of study in the 1930s at Calvin College in Grand Rapids.

The complex body of material herein required difficult, often arbitrary, decisions of organization. To me, the reader's convenience was best served if literary works were placed and described according to the major themes identified in my chapter titles—Indian life, farms, the mining industry, colleges, and the like. If a work has two or more subjects, the book's major theme dictates its placement in a specific chapter.

Within a chapter, the major subject may be divided into sections. Thus, the chapter on settlers begins with the Dutch, one of the first large group of settlers in the nineteenth century; this is followed by a discussion of blacks in Michigan literature, because of an early novel and the number of works about blacks.

When, as is often the case, the subject matter ranges over time, the book that begins earliest is discussed first, even though it was published after other books that cover the same subject but that begin at a later time period. Thus, Marion Schooland's *A Land I Will Show Thee* (1954), which is based on the first Dutch migration to Michigan, is placed before J. Keuning's translation of *The Man in Bearskin*, which was published earlier but is based on a later Dutch migration.

When two or more books are based on the same general subject, they are discussed in order of publication: Jean Hoyt's *Wings of Wax* (1929), which is about a troubled university, is discussed before W. Stock Hume's (pseudonym of William Hume Stockwell) *Rudderless: A University Chronicle* (1930), which is about the same troubled university. Works on a specific or limited subject—such as French explorer La Salle—are listed in order of publication.

Sometimes a book's placement depends on other circumstances. For instance, novels about Pontiac that refer to Indian-white conflicts as the Pontiac Uprising—in other words, as having some political or military unity under the direction of Pontiac—are grouped together. Later novels that reject this concept and describe Indian attacks on whites as being tribally conducted, perhaps owing to Pontiac's influence, form a second group.

In cases where an author has published works with varying subjects—Mary Frances Doner's romances, for example—individual works will be found in chapters appropriate to their subject. All works by these authors can be found in the index under the author's name.

Information about authors is presented when the first work by an author is discussed. The published opinions and judgments of reputable critics and scholars are also presented.

ACKNOWLEDGMENTS

To Keith Rageth and his staff in the Inter-Library Loan Department of the University of Iowa, and to the public, college and university libraries in Michigan and elsewhere who made it possible to examine most of the books and periodicals discussed in the following pages.

To the members of the University of Iowa Library Information staff who time and time again solved problems in locating hard-to-find information.

To David D. Anderson, who helped expand my knowledge of literature set in the Peninsula State.

To the Society for the Study of Midwestern Literature and its members, whose scholarship and research have been utilized in my efforts.

To the Michigan Technological University whose generous research grant led to the realization that there is a substantial body of literature set in Michigan, and to the accumulation of information about that literature.

To all the scholars whose earlier research in Michigan literature and subsequent publications proved invaluable in identifying, locating, and evaluating both primary and secondary resource materials.

Grateful acknowledgment is made for permission to reprint or quote from the following:

"The Novelist in Michigan," by Francis Scannell, from *The Detroit Historical Society Bulletin* (November, 1964). Reprinted by permission of the Detroit Historical Society.

Come and Get It by Edna Ferber. Copyright © 1935 by Edna Ferber. Copyright © renewed 1962 by Edna Ferber. Reprinted by permission of Harriet F. Pilpel, as trustee and attorney for the Ferber Proprietors.

Parti-Colored Blocks for a Quilt (1982) by Marge Piercy. Reprinted by permission of the University of Michigan Press.

The Conquerors (1970) by Allen Eckert. Reprinted by permission of Little, Brown and Company, Publishers.

A Treasury of American Folklore (1944) by B. A. Botkin. By permission of Crown Publishers, Inc.

Northwest Passage (1937) by Kenneth Roberts. By permission of Doubleday, a division of Bantam, Doubleday, Dell Publishing Group, Inc.

Ballads and Songs of the Shanty Boy (1926) by Franz Rickaby. By permission of the Harvard University Press.

"Lumberjack Ballads" by James Cloyd Bowman, from *Michigan History Magazine*. By permission of *Michigan History Magazine*.

"Paul Bunyan: Ecological Saint or Villain?" by Arthur Coleman. By permission from *The Old Northwest*.

They Knew Paul Bunyan by Earl C. Beck (1956). By permission from the University of Michigan Press.

The Indian Drum by William McHarg and Edwin Balmer (1917). By permission of the copyright holders, Putnam & Grosset Book Group.

Soo Canal! by William Ratigan (1955). By permission of the copyright holder, Mrs. Pat Ranger.

The Country Kitchen (1935) by Della Lutes. By permission.

The Middle Western Farm Novel in the Twentieth Century (1965) by Roy C. Meyer. By permission of the University of Nebraska Press.

The Hero as Vegetable by John Brooks. Copyright © 1969 by The New York Times Company. Reprinted by permission.

Midwest Miscellany for permission to quote from "New Dimensions in Recent Michigan Fiction" by Douglas A. Noverr.

Excerpt from *Even Tide* by Larry Woiwode. Copyright © 1970, 1971, 1977 by Larry Woiwode. Reprinted by permission of Farrar, Straus and Giroux, Inc.

Excerpt from *Freaky Deaky* by Elmore Leonard. Text copyright © 1988 by Elmore Leonard. By permission of William Morrow and Co., Inc.

Excerpt from "Dum-Dums in Detroit" from *Newsweek* (October 14, 1974, p. 118) by permission of Newsweek, Inc.

Excerpt from *Contemporary Authors*, Volumes 29-32. Edited by Ann Evory. Copyright © 1972, 1978 by Gale Research, Inc. Reprinted by permission of the publisher.

Excerpt from Hal H[orace] Smith (1873-1944), *Three Essays: On the Gathering of a Library; A Detroit Literature; The Bibliophile* (1945). Used by permission of the Detroit Public Library.

Excerpt from "The Sweet Singer of Michigan" in *The Papers of the Bibliographical Society of America*, 29 (1945) by permission of The Bibliographical Society of America.

Excerpts from "You Can Have It" in *Selected Poems* (1948) by Philip Levine, used by permission.

Excerpt from *5 Detroits* (1970) by Philip Levine, used by permission.

"The New Affluence," by Alice Fulton, in *Contemporary Michigan Poetry: Poems from the Third Coast* (1988), used by permission of the copyright holders.

"I Want to Go Back to Michigan Down on the Farm," by Irving Berlin. Copyright © 1914 by Irving Berlin. Copyright Renewed. Used by Permission. All Rights Reserved.

CHAPTER I

MICHIGAN IN LITERATURE

Non-Michiganians, if they give the Peninsula State a thought at
all, picture it as little more than a snowy waste sprinkled with
pines, sand dunes, Indian wigwams, small inland lakes and
automobile factories all lying somewhere in the wilderness
north of Toledo and South Bend.

—Edna Ferber, *Come and Get It*[1]

When we think of Michigan we are likely, as Kalamazoo-born
Edna Ferber suggests, to create certain verbal or mental im-
ages: Detroit and automobiles, Grand Rapids and furniture, Kala-
mazoo and stoves, Battle Creek and cornflakes, Midland and salt,
Ann Arbor and football, Holland and wooden shoes, Mackinac and
the Grand Hotel, the Straits of Mackinac and THE Bridge, Sault
Sainte Marie and the Soo Canal, Marquette and iron, the Copper
Country and long snowy winters, and Calumet and Hecla. Such
names as Henry Ford, Walter Chrysler, Lee Iacocca, W. K. Kellogg,
Father Charles Coughlin, Benny Oosterbaan, Walter Reuther, and
Gerald Ford slip trippingly from our tongues.

We may acquire some of our images of the Peninsula State by
being born or growing up there or by becoming a resident. Others we
may acquire by working, touring, camping, fishing, or hunting in the
state—or even flying over it on our way to Bangor or Seattle. Still others we may acquire from magazine articles or from newspapers, such
as the *Detroit Free Press*, the *Houghton Mining Gazette*, the *New York
Times*, or the *Chicago Tribune*.

We may further acquire or reinforce our images from the written word in such books as Prentiss Brown's *The Mackinac Bridge Story* (1956) or Philip V. Stern's *Tin Lizzie: The Story of the Fabulous Model T Ford* (1955) or Howard Peckham's *Pontiac and the Indian Uprising* (1947) or Willis F. Dunbar's *Michigan: A History of the Wolverine State* (1973)— moving backward and forward in time as we choose. For visual images we may turn to the books of photographs, ranging from that deluxe, full-color, folio-sized volume of text and pictures, Charles Steinhacker's *Superior: Portrait of a Living Lake*, to those equally colorful books produced by the versatile Avery Color Studios of Au Train in the Upper Peninsula.

But there are also verbal or visual images we may acquire or reinforce by reading the state's imaginative literature, verse, and fiction or by watching a play or a motion picture set in Michigan. To quote Marge Piercy, "[F]iction is a way of inducting [us] into the [places] other people know; people who are poorer or richer than [we] are; people who speak another language; people who construct the world of different forces and different necessities and different desires; people who live down streets [we] fear or streets who fear [us]."[2]

New and old images of Detroit are found in such imaginative literature as *The Little Girl in Old Detroit;* of Grand Rapids in *Cast Down the Laurels;* of Ann Arbor in *Ann Arbor Tales;* of Holland, Michigan, in *Bram of Five Corners;* of Mackinac Island in *Anne;* of the Straits of Mackinac Bridge in *Songs of a Bridge Builder;* of Marquette, Michigan, in *Anatomy of a Murder;* of Sault Sainte Marie and the Soo Canal in *The Invasion;* of the Copper Country in *When Copper Was King;* of Henry Ford in *The Flivver King;* and of Father Charles Coughlin in *The Hate Merchant.*

These and other book-length works like them are the subject of this study: the imaginative narrative, dramatic, and lyrical creations with Michigan settings characters, subjects, and themes that have been produced through the years—from a time before Michigan became a territory until the relative present—and the images of Michigan that we acquire from them.

Other writers, historians, critics, and scholars have at one time or another noted or described or reviewed such works. The most significant of these is Kathleen I. Gillard (?–1956), first in her George Peabody Institute dissertation, *Michigan as Recorded in Its Writings* (1950), and then in *Our Michigan Heritage* (1955), published shortly before her death. Gillard states her purpose as,

> [T]o describe those writings which have their origin in what is known today as the State of Michigan, or which record the landscape of the

state, the history and the traditions, the ideas and ideals, the interests and way of life of the people who have dwelt there, and to present through this record the development of the state from the period of exploration to the present position of industrial and cultural achievement.[3]

Insert the word *imaginative* before the word *writings* in the first line of this quotation and you have a statement of an important goal of the present work.

Gillard's study opens in the fall of 1534 with Jacques Cartier's description of what he had been told about "the great wide seas" to the west and of copper deposits in that area—perhaps the first European inkling of the magnificent Peninsula State. Her four lengthy chapters discuss, in turn, the Indian, the French, the British, and the American in Michigan historical writings as well as some eighty imaginative works. Gillard's book has a bibliography, but it lacks an index.

An earlier, less-comprehensive document by Alice Laurine Pearson, *The Upper Peninsula of Michigan in Literature* (1939), was written as a master's thesis. Pearson's categories are "Legendary Literature," "Fiction with Settings before 1880," and "Fiction with Settings. . . 1880–1918." Her thesis statement reads, "[I]n the development of northern Michigan, *what personalities and philosophies have manifested themselves* as judged by the plots enacted and the characters revealed [in the Upper Peninsula's literature]?"[4] The added emphasis demonstrates that Pearson was interested in the local images a reader might acquire by reading fiction set in Michigan's Upper Peninsula.

Pearson's work discusses about two dozen titles; it provides story lines in most cases and some critical comment is appended. In 1940, she drew on her master's thesis for an article titled "The Upper Peninsula in Fictional Literature."[5]

Articles, Bibliographies, and Books

Here are brief reviews of earlier significant materials about literature with Michigan settings, themes, and characters. Where annotations are included that fact is noted.

Russell, Hattie Sanford. "A Group of Michigan Women Writers." *Midland Monthly* October 1896): 327–36. Russell's authors are mostly persons with minor publishing records. She identifies the only significant author, Mary Hartwell Catherwood, as an Illinois author, but does not refer to Catherwood's Michigan books.

Lamport, Warren W., and Floyd D. Raze, comps. *Michigan Poets and Poetry: With Portraits and Biographies* (1904). The compilers, a

North Dakota teacher and a Michigan minister, respectively, note that the book's collection of work by sixteen poets (including themselves) is not intended to be comprehensive. Of the eight poets born in Michigan, the most significant, Will Carleton and Ben King, are discussed in chapter 15.

The book's preface has an apologia that later commentators either echo or quote, "Michigan has been somewhat backward in the development of her literary genius. Her forests, her lakes and streams, her vast inland seas rich in thrilling incident, and the romance of her early history, should appeal most powerfully to the poetic sense of her sons and daughters. But that they have not done as they might is evident from the very limited number who have attempted to celebrate them in song or prose."[6]

Mulder, Arnold. (1885-1959). "Michigan as a Field for the Novelist." *Michigan History Magazine*, 6, 1, 1922: 142–55. Mulder says "there is no reason why great art should not be produced in Michigan" and complains that "people think of New York or Boston as the place where the real writers live." He adds "the real writers today live in the Middle West or hail from it." He notes the advent of realism as a replacement for romanticism in the novel and suggests topics for Michigan writers—the state's geography, the Great Lakes, the Upper Peninsula, Michigan's cities, the automobile industry, business, and the state's resort areas.

Foster, Bernice M. *Michigan Novelists* (1928). This pamphlet is useful as a finding list.

Goodrich, Madge V. *A Bibliography of Michigan Authors* (1928). Much more complete than Foster's pamphlet, this work cites 114 novelists and the titles of their books. Of these authors, 55 are discussed in the present book; the rest are either not authors of book-length fiction set in Michigan or else authors of works not located geographically.

Stace, Sister Frances. "Michigan's Contribution to Literature." *Michigan History Magazine* 14 (1930): 226–32. Stace opens with a lament that Arnold Mulder would echo just nine years later; she has difficulty finding Michigan books "[in which] moral truth and human passion are touched with that largeness, sanity and attraction which are the marks of true literature." She then quotes from Lamport and Raze's preface cited earlier.

Mosher, Edith R., and Nella Dietrich Williams. *From Indian Legends to the Modern BookShelf: An Anthology of Prose and Verse by Michigan Authors [With Prices]. Prepared Especially for the Youth of the State* (1931). The book has 395 pages of biographical information and samples of the published work of some seventy-five authors. Appended is "a limited list of books [with prices] by Michigan authors." Mosher was an author of scholarly books on trees, Williams a librarian and author of school textbooks.

Mulder, Arnold. "Authors and Wolverines: The Books and Writers of Michigan." *Saturday Review of Literature* 19, No. 9 (March 4, 1939): 3–4, 16. [One of a 1939 series on the status of midwestern literature.] Mulder emphasizes the unsatisfactory quality of Michigan literature, "Michigan has put the world on automobile wheels, [but] Michigan novelists are still jogging along in one-hoss shays." Mulder would trade "the whole caboodle of them" for a single Theodore Dreiser or a Sinclair Lewis, or an Ellen Glasgow or a Ruth Suckow— all non-Michigan authors. But Mulder does not discuss Caroline M. Kirkland, Mary Hartwell Catherwood, or Constance Fenimore Woolson—authors at least the equals of Glasgow or Suckow—among others.[7]

To his remonstrances, Constance Rourke (1885-1941), a Michigan author, responded, "Another author, a Michigan writer, as it happens, has sadly discovered that literature doesn't flourish among us; that our novelists write one novel and stop under a blight; and that we have no poetry except for the crude rhymes of the 'Sweet Singer,' to whom he devoted a considerable space as our most considerable literary figure."[8]

Michigan Writers' Project. *Michigan: A Guide to the Wolverine State* (1941): 145–51. In the 1930s Eleanor Roosevelt, wife of President Franklin D. Roosevelt, helped persuade her husband to include writers, artists, playwrights, and actors in the Works Progress Administration (WPA) program, which had been designed to provide productive work for the unemployed or for men and women employed inappropriately—unable to exercise their creative talents. One result was a series of state guidebooks that included descriptions of guided tours, data about major cities, maps, photographs, and general state information.

Author Harold Titus saw the Michigan guide to a successful conclusion. In a mere seven of its seven hundred pages, the Michigan guide provides the best summary of Michigan literature to date. Some fifty books and about the same number of writers are discussed.

Ellison, Elizabeth Love. "The Literature of the Upper Peninsula." *Michigan History Magazine* 30 (1945): 509–17. A better summary than Pearson's 1940 article, in part because it is updated.

Mulder, Arnold. "Michigan's Writing Men." *Michigan History Magazine* 35 No. 3 (September 1951): 257–66. Mulder begins by apologizing for the unfortunate title—"Michigan Writers" would have been more appropriate. The essay covers a half-century of Michigan literary history in ten pages. Mulder expresses his conviction that there was no reason why "letters should not flourish in Michigan as anywhere else in America," but he opposed a provincial Michigan literature.[9]

Hilbert, Rachel M. *Michigan Authors* (1960). Publication data and brief biographies of one hundred "Michigan" authors, not all of whom wrote imaginative literature. Includes Rex Beach (1877-1949), who, though born in Michigan, moved away when still a child; and Ringgold (Ring) Lardner (1885-1933). Lardner grew up in Niles; later he became a Chicago journalist, a New York playwright, a Hollywood scriptwriter, and a major American fiction writer. But he is barely a Michigan author as defined herein. "Haircut" with a slender reference to the Northern Peninsula could be set in Niles; "Anniversary" alludes to Niles; and the couple in "Reunion" grew up in Buchanan. A 1923 nonfiction sketch, "What I Ought to of Learnt in High School" refers to Lardner's schooldays, in Niles.

In 1980, a second edition of *Michigan Authors* was published by the Michigan Association for Media in Education. It lists alphabetically some four hundred authors, with brief biographies and titles of their publications. Its criteria was birth or extended residence in Michigan. The publications of those who wrote book-length fiction set in Michigan are discussed in the following pages.

Black, Albert G. *Michigan Novels: An Annotated Bibliography* (1963). The most ambitious project of its type to date, with 303 titles.

Scannell, Francis X. (1917–1988). "The Novelist and Michigan." *Detroit Historical Society Bulletin* 21 (1964): 4–12. In this essay—presented earlier in 1964 at a conference titled "Michigan in Perspective"—Michigan State Librarian Scannell's most significant contribution is his annotated list of eighteen Beadle and Adams dime novels with Michigan historical backgrounds, most of them by Michigan authors. Scannell also wrote "Michigan in Fiction 100 Years Ago" and a World War II novel, *In Line of Duty* (1946).

Andrews, Clarence A. (1912–). "A Bibliography of the Literature and Lore, Together with Historical Materials of the Upper Peninsula of Michigan." *Great Lakes Review* 3, no. 1 (Summer 1976): 37–66. Contains over six hundred items, including titles of imaginative literature and supporting materials. Andrews is also the author of "A Bibliography of Fiction and Drama by Women from Iowa and Michigan." *Great Lakes Review* 6, no. 1 (Summer 1979): 56–68.

Taylor, Donna, ed. *The Great Lakes Region in Children's Books* (1980): 104–141. Lists 226 Michigan titles by 172 authors, with brief annotations of subject matter. Still, the material is incomplete. A number of the titles are nonfiction. (In later chapters of the present work, some young people's books are described, but by and large I have omitted discussion of books for children.)

Tipton, James, and Robert E. Wegner, eds. *The Third Coast: Contemporary Michigan Fiction* (1982). Actually, this work contains short fiction or excerpts from longer works by authors with Michigan connections. Not all of the fiction is set in Michigan, and one story was originally published in 1943.

Goldstein, Laurence. "The Image of Detroit in Twentieth Century Literature." *Michigan Quarterly Review* 25 (Spring 1986): 269–91. Goldstein concentrates on the work of novelists Harriette Arnow and Joyce Carol Oates and on poet Philip Levine.

Lee, Dorothy H. "Black Voices in Detroit." *Michigan Quarterly Review* 25, (Spring 1986): 313–28. Article discusses poets, novelists, and playwrights—excellent but brief.

Massie, Larry B., ed. *From Frontier Folk to Factory Smoke* (1987). This illustrated anthology contains sixteen selections from sixteen works of fiction that set in Michigan from pioneer times to the early twentieth century. Each selection has a useful introduction to the book and its author.

Michigan Council for the Humanities. *The Michigan Connection* (1987). A folio-sized booklet that has four interesting and insightful articles about Michigan literature by a free-lance writer and documentary producer, a skilled poet, a librarian who specializes in midwestern and Michigan bibliography, and a free-lance historian who specializes in Michigan history. The respective authors and their articles are:

LoCicero, Thomas. "Michigan Screenwriters." Pp. 1–2.
Scott, Herbert. "Contemporary Poetry in Michigan." Pp. 2–4.
Beasecker, Robert. "The Michigan Novel Since World War II." P. 5.
Massie, Larry B. "Michigan Authors and Their Novels, 1832–1941." P. 6.

In 1988, these were enlarged and issued by the Council under the title *Literary Michigan: A Sense of Place, a Sense of Time*. This work includes an introduction by Richard J. Hathaway; a section on "Michigan Literary Magazines," by Leonard Kniffel; a selected bibliography of secondary sources by Robert Beasecker; a checklist of Michigan authors and poets by Cory Retzke; an article, "Michigan Poets and

Their Poetry Prior to WW II," by Larry B. Massie; and a concluding section "Let's Talk about Michigan: The Literary Connection."

Smith, Thomas H. "Michigan Upper Peninsula Literary Traditions. . . ." *Midwestern Miscellany* 16 (1988) 52–58.

Three other works are of interest: Arnold Mulder's essay "Michigan as a Field for the Novelist,"[10] Lawrence H. Conrad's essay "Michigan as a Literary Opportunity,"[11] and Hal H. Smith's monograph *A Detroit Literature* (1953).[12]

From 1958 to 1984, the Michigan Department of Education published a quarterly catalog titled *Michigan in Novels;* later it was renamed *Michigan in Books*. The first editor was Rae Elizabeth Rips (1914–1972). It ceased publication in summer, 1984.

Michigan in Novels discussed only fictional works, catalogued according to area and city settings. *Michigan in Books* reported both fiction and nonfiction, the latter catalogued by subject matter such as "Architecture," "Detroit," and "Law." These issues also had articles such as "Michigan Literature in the Sixties" or "Michigan Memo— the Underground"; the latter focused on the countercultural movement of the 1960s as it pertained to Michigan.

Another source is the *Michigan Library Bulletin* (January 1910 to April 1938), a rich source of information for the 1920s and most of the 1930s.

The *Michigan Alumnus Quarterly Review* in its sixty-seven volumes often carried verse, short stories, articles, and book reviews pertinent to the subject of literature set in Michigan. It ceased publication in 1961 and was succeeded that year by the *Michigan Quarterly Review*, a periodical that focuses on literature.

Pageants

From time to time, Michigan towns, cities, and other areas have presented pageants that reviewed their past history. One example of this quasi-dramatic form is *The Pageant of Escanaba and Correlated Local History* described in the second volume of *Michigan History*, pp. 334– 80. This essay presents a review and a detailed outline of the pageant as well as photographs. The script was written by F. E. King, then superintendent of schools in Escanaba.

The Jule and Avery Hopwood Award

A number of novelists, playwrights, and poets are identified herein as winners of Hopwood awards for distinguished literary achievements while they were students at the University of Michigan.

Avery Hopwood (1882-1928), from Cleveland, Ohio, graduated from the university in 1905. In New York City, he became a writer of plays that, although not critical successes, became immensely popular. By 1922, following a season in which he had had five plays on Broadway at the same time, he was, as the *New York Times*, quoted by Arno L. Bader in *The Michigan Alumnus Quarterly Review*, said, "almost unquestionably the richest of all playwrights."[13] In 1928, he drowned while swimming in the Mediterranean at Juan-les-Pins, France.

Hopwood bequeathed a sum of money to the university to found the Jule and Avery Hopwood Award for students at the school whose on-campus writing was of high quality or showed promise of future literary or dramatic success. (Jule Hopwood was his mother—Hopwood never married.)

Since the school year of 1930–1931, Hopwood awards have been conferred annually, biennially, or triennially on a great many University of Michigan students, both undergraduate and graduate, for plays or novels or collections of essays, poems, or short stories. The judges at first were prominent Michigan and American authors, some of whom had been Hopwood winners. In more recent years, the judges have been faculty members, among them Arno L. Bader.

Winners of the Hopwood awards include playwright Arthur Miller, novelist Harvey Swados, and poets John Malcolm Brinnin, Robert Hayden, John Ciardi, and William Brashear. (Other winners whose works used specific Michigan settings, characters, or events are discussed at appropriate places herein.)

The Hopwood estate was substantial. In 1987, almost sixty years after Hopwood's death, approximately $30,000 was awarded to some thirty University of Michigan students. Materials related to the awards, past and present, are maintained in the Hopwood Room in Angell Hall at the university.

Beadle and Adams

In chapters dealing with Michigan history through the nineteenth century, occasional books are identified as Beadle and Adams publications. These were inexpensive volumes, many selling for only ten cents, published in New York City by Erastus and Irwin P. Beadle, first as Beadle & Co. and later as Beadle & Adams. Many were written by Michigan writers.

Characteristics of Beadle and Adams romances include a pattern of paired hunters, of whom the elder always speaks in a noticeable dialect, whereas the younger (who usually wins the heroine) speaks in "normal" English. The stories often feature mysterious events in which the main character or those allied with him seem trapped or doomed but always manage to escape. Often, the authors withhold information from the reader until it suits their purpose to disclose it.

A new Beadle and Adams novel was published every week. The publishers demanded that, however fantastic some incidents might be, the stories had to be based on knowledge of the historical setting, such as the War of 1812 and related events.

Francis X. Scannell said, "[T]he Dime Novelists of the House of Beadle and Adams added little of significance to the literary heritage of Michigan [but] were of tremendous interest and popularity in their day and they helped fill a vacuum in the history of the Michigan novel for the second half of the nineteenth-century."[14] Scannell does not mention that many nineteenth-century readers, particularly young ones, received a significant impression of Michigan history from these books.

CHAPTER II

INDIANS, FRENCH, AND BRITISH

Brothers! These Englishmen are not as the French who are our
friends. The Frenchmen wished to be our brothers, to live with
us in peace, but not the English. No! The French wished to do
business with us and provide for us what we needed in ex-
change for what they wanted but not the English. No! Yet now
the French soldiers who protected us have been driven away
and the English soldiers have taken their place and our lot
grows unbearable.

Allan W. Eckert, *The Conquerors*[1]

When the French came to Michigan in the seventeenth century—the first whites to arrive in numbers—there were an esti-
mated 15,000 Indians in six nations or groups in the state: Chippewa
(Ojibwa), Wyandot, Miami, Ottawa, Huron, and the Potawatomi.[2]

In a Beadle and Adams novel set in this early period, *Weptono-
mah, Haunted Wolf of the Wyandots; or, The Renegade's Prisoner, a Tale of
the Lake Country* (1871) by Thomas C. Harbaugh (1849–1924), the Wyandots are fighting with the Chippewa in the area that became eastern Michigan.

Beginning about 1620, French explorers, seeking to expand
French domains, followed a route from Montreal directly west to
Michigan's Upper Peninsula. French Jesuits came soon after; their
goal was to win Indian converts to Christianity. Later, traders and
trappers came seeking animal hides, particularly beaver skins, which
were in great demand in Europe because of the vogue for broad-
brimmed beaver-skin hats in the seventeenth century.[3]

The French established several forts and trading posts on
the perimeter of Michigan's Lower Peninsula, from southwestern

Michigan to Michilimackinac (now Mackinac) to Detroit, the latter under the direction of Cadillac.

Of those early French in Michigan, the first to be given heroic stature in literature are Jacques (Pere) Marquette (1637–1673) and Charles de Langlade (1729–1800) in Nellie Wildwood's (pseud. of Mrs. Elizabeth Farnsworth Mears) "Voyage of Pere Marquette, and the Romance of Charles de Langlade; or, the Indian Queen: An Historical Poem of the Seventeenth and Eighteenth Centuries" (1865), a long narrative poem in decasyllabic couplets. De Langlade was a significant figure in Michigan's French period.

The more common literary treatment of actual French, Indian, British, and American figures in the Michigan scene was the historical novel, a genre that sometimes emphasized the major figures of history but at other times placed them in the background and focused on lesser actors in actual historical events. Jesuit Charles Corcoran's *Blackrobe* (1933), celebrating the three-hundredth anniversary of Marquette's birth, is an example of the former approach. As such novels often do, there is an added imagined romance, this one between a young voyageur and a French noble's daughter.

Jim Kjelgaard's *The Explorations of Pere Marquette* (1951), written for elementary school children, contains a strong fictional element. Robert Stern's *Pere Marquette*, a pageant, stays closer to historical fact; it was staged at Saint Ignace in 1962.[4]

The second French explorer to be given heroic stature in literature, René-Robert Cavelier de La Salle (1643–1687), appears in William Dana Orcutt's *Robert Cavelier: The Romance of the Sieur de la Salle . . .* (1904); [Horatio] Gilbert Parker's *The Power and the Glory: A Romance of the Great La Salle* (1925); Maurice Constantin-Weyer's *The French Adventurer: The Life and Exploits of La Salle* (1931); Jeannette Covert Nolan's *La Salle and the Great Enterprise* (1951); John [William] Tebbel's first-person narrative, *Touched with Fire* (1952); Merritt Parmalee Allen's *The Wilderness Way* (1954); and *The Golden Torch* (1957) by Iola Fuller (Goodspeed McCoy). These novels show La Salle landing at the mouth of the Saint Joseph River, traveling across the state to the Detroit River, building the *Griffon*, and voyaging on the lower Great Lakes. The novels by Tebbel and Fuller are the best of these, in part because they reflect later research and have less of a tendency to romanticize.

Tebbel (1912–), a descendant of the Johnston family into which brothers Henry and James Schoolcraft had married, was born in Michigan and graduated from Central Michigan University. In 1961, he delivered the Clarence M. Burton Memorial Lecture, "Fact and Fiction: Problems of the Historical Novelist," at the eighty-seventh annual meeting of the Historical Society of Michigan. Tebbel's theme was the necessity for historical novelists to give Americans a true story and word picture to make them conscious of their great heritage.[5]

Iola Fuller (Goodspeed McCoy), born in 1906 at Marcellus, Michigan, received a 1935 bachelor's degree and a 1940 master's degree from the University of Michigan, where she was elected to Phi Beta Kappa and became a Hopwood Award winner. Fuller credited Roy Cowden, a University of Michigan English professor, with being her greatest writing influence. She later became a school librarian and teacher.

A lesser novel, *The Last Fort: A Story of the French Voyageurs* (1952), relates the fictional journey of Alexis Picard, son of a French Canadian farmer. It presents "a good picture of the French voyageurs and Indian life."[6] The author Elizabeth Jane Coatsworth (1893–1986), a Maine native, was a poet and the winner of the 1931 Newbery Medal (awarded to authors of distinguished children's books).

Daniel Greysolon Duluth (also Du Luth, Du Lhut or Dulhut, 1673–1710), who explored Michigan's Lake Superior coast, is the subject of *Daniel Du Luth* (1926) by [Henry] Everett McNeill (1862–1929). Minnesotan John T[heodore] Flanagan (1906–), a major scholar of midwestern historical fiction, says that although Du Luth is "pictured as a paragon . . . he is not made real."[7]

In 1694, Antoine Laumet de La Mothe sieur de Cadillac (1658–1730), the founder of Detroit, came to Fort De Buade (on the site of present-day St. Ignace). Trading for furs, he became wealthy, but he angered the Jesuits who opposed trading whiskey and rum to the Indians. Seven years later, Cadillac established a trading post and fort at Detroit's strategic location.

Mary Catherine Crowley's *A Daughter of New France: With Some Account of the Gallant sieur Cadillac and His Colony on the Detroit* (1901) was the first of three historical romances to be set in the area. Cadillac takes the novel's fictional narrator, young Denys Norman Guyon, with him to Detroit. They endure Indian attacks, a fire, and Guyon's romantic problems. The novel ends with Guyon happily married and Cadillac in a French prison.

Crowley (?–1920), a native of Boston, while living in Detroit from 1893 to 1903, researched local materials related to the French history of the city. G. Harrison Orrians, an Ohio scholar, says that she "made a thorough study of potential martial episodes and gave fairly accurate descriptions of the events included" in the novel.[8]

In Alice Prescott Smith's romance, *Montlivet* (1906), Cadillac is at Michilimackinac. Her book, *Kindred* (1925), focuses on Charles De Langlade at Michilimackinac. Both novels end at Green Bay.

Documents given by Clarence M. Burton to the Michigan Pioneer and Historical Collections made possible two Cadillac books in the 1930s: Agnes C. Laut's (1871–1936) 1931 biography, *Cadillac: Knight Errant of the Wilderness;* and Arthur Pound's 1939 novel, *Hawk of Detroit*, which shows Cadillac and his nephew, Jules, building Fort Pontchartrain on the Straits of Detroit, thus stopping the westward and northward British advance despite opposition from enemies in Paris and New France.

Arnold Mulder said that Jules, whose romance with a young Indian woman receives as much attention as Cadillac's efforts, becomes the prototype of future American push and drive—even "the spiritual ancestor of Henry Ford"—as he deserts the world of politics and manners to build a farm and a mill in order to raise grain and to grind flour.[9]

Arthur Pound was born in 1884 in Pontiac (a place he later called Paradise),[10] was educated there, earned a B.A. degree from the University of Michigan, and was awarded honorary degrees by that school and Union College in Schenectady, New York. He wrote for several newspapers, became associate editor of the *Atlantic Monthly*, New York State Historian and Director of Archives and History of the State University of New York at Albany, and a research professor at the University of Pittsburgh. Pound died in 1966.

Green Pavilions: A Novel of the French and English Wars (1978) by Helen E. Muse (1917–) is set on the straits in the old French city that became Detroit.

Marie Caroline Watson Hamlin (1850–1905), a descendant of an early French settler in Detroit, and James V. Campbell (1823–1890), a Michigan poet and historian, collaborated on *Legends of Le Detroit* (1884). There are thirty-two legends, each related to a particular event in Detroit history. In almost every case, the legends report superstitions and the usually fatal consequences to those who fail to take them seriously. Thirty-one are by Hamlin; the thirty-second, "A Legend of L'Anse Creuse," a long narrative poem by Campbell. Like Hamlin's second legend, it tells of the building of La Salle's *Griffon* and its ill-fated first voyage. In 1890, the poem was reprinted.

The Indians and the British

Fort Michilimackinac, built by the French at the water's edge on the Straits of Mackinac at the northern tip of the Lower Peninsula, fell into the hands of the British at the conclusion of the French and Indian War. In May 1763, in response to a message from Pontiac, Minivavana, a Chippewa chief, deceitfully proposed that a celebration of King George III's birthday be held at the fort on June 2. For their part, the Indians would demonstrate *baggataway*—a game of American Indian origin later called lacrosse.

As the game began outside the fort British soldiers and French traders lolled about watching the game through the fort's open gates. A group of Indian women, each concealing a rifle under a blanket she had wrapped around herself, stood near the entrance. At a signal, a ball was seemingly accidentally tossed into the fort. As the Indians chased after it, the women handed them the rifles. In the melee that followed, the soldiers, mostly unarmed, were killed or taken prisoner. The French inhabitants were not harmed. Charles de Langlade, who lived there, managed to conceal Alexander Henry, an English fur trader, in his attic, thus saving his life. Henry later told the story in his 1809 nonfiction work, *Travels and Adventures in Canada and the Indian Territories between the Years 1760 and 1776.*

Caribou Zip; or, The Forest Brothers (1874) by Illinois author Joseph E. Badger (1848–1909) uses Michilimackinac's fall in a tale whose central character is Joseph Brant, "an educated Mohawk."

Mary Hartwell Catherwood's "Fort Michilimackinac," the first section of her historical romance, *The White Islander* (1893), also offers a fictional account of these events. In her novel, Wawatam, a Chippewa, joins de Langlade in saving Henry's life.

Catherwood (1847–1902), who was born in Illinois and reared in Ohio, spent the last ten summers of her life on Mackinac Island. She is often credited with initiating the vogue for the historical romance in which the romantic developments are set against historical backgrounds. In such novels, the latter were often distorted to accommodate the romance.

However, reviewers of later historical romances argued that such carefully detailed books were a waste and concluded that authors might write equally interesting romantic novels without the authentic backgrounds, most of which were lost on their readers.[11]

The British Take Charge

Despite the disaster at Michilimackinac, the British retained order over Mackinac Island, Fort Detroit, and the area between.

The first eighty pages of *The Colonials . . .* (1902) by Allen French (1870–1946) are set in the "thumb" area of Michigan; the balance takes place in New England. The Michigan segment presents an intriguing picture of non-British whites trying to survive on a lawless frontier prior to the American Revolution.

William Cyrus Sprague's *Felice Constant; or, The Master's Passion* (1904) is set in Fort Detroit at the time of the British occupation. Sprague (1886–1922), a Detroit lawyer, founded the *American Boy* in 1899; it continued long after his death as one of the two leading periodicals for boys.

Almost three decades passed before the next novel about the British. Thomas Boyd's *The Shadow of the Long Knives* (1928) demonstrates the fluid situation in the Old Northwest when those seeking control of the area recognized no state or territorial boundaries but, instead, were restrained by lakes, rivers, streams, and by forts, such as the one at Detroit. Angus McDonald, the chief character, who has been reared by Indians and sympathizes with them, is forced to decide where to place his loyalties. He finally rejects the British and becomes an American.

Boyd, born in 1898, was a friend of novelists Sinclair Lewis and F. Scott Fitzgerald and of historian of the Old Northwest Grace Flandrau. He was married to novelist Margaret Woodward Smith, who wrote as Woodward Boyd. His promising career was cut short when he died in 1935.

The first third of Minnesotan Neil Harmon Swanson's (1896–1983) carefully researched *Forbidden Ground* (1938)—one of the half-dozen completed novels of some thirty in which he had proposed to cover all of American history—is set in "De Troit." The place is in Indian hands and the English and Indians are enemies. The novel's particular interest lies in the details of the Old Northwest's fur trade, the attitudes of the English, and the role of the Indians in the uneasy changing social, political, and economic situation.

Three decades later, Allan W. Eckert's *Wilderness Empire: A Narrative* (1969), in a series of dramatic tableaux set in the years 1730 to 1774, focused on Sir William Johnson at Detroit and Michilimackinac in the 1760s. Once more Alexander Henry is seen escaping death with the help of de Langlade and Wawatam.

Colonel Russell Potter ("Red") Reeder (1902–) set his 1959 *Attack at Fort Lookout* in a half-finished fort on Lake Huron in 1806. Like his other books, it is written for teenage boys.

The Pontiac Uprising[12]

By 1760, Pontiac, an Ottawa chief, "one of the ablest Indians ever to contest the white man who had intruded upon the Indian hunting grounds,"[13] had come to hate the British so much that he persuaded several Indian groups to attack British-controlled forts in the Great Lakes region. As a result, the British "were compelled to meet the most formidable Indian uprising in American history."[14] Early historians and novelists described this uprising as being led by Pontiac, but later research has indicated that he was more likely only an instigator.[15]

Pontiac's first literary treatment came in a 1766 play, *Ponteach; or, The Savages of America*, supposedly written by Major Robert Rogers (1731–1795). But large portions of it seem to have been composed by a collaborator more familiar with the conventions of English drama than with the Old Northwest.[16] Kenneth Roberts (1885–1957) in *Northwest Passage* (1937) shows Major Rogers reading portions of the play, then turning the script over to his secretary, Natty (Nathaniel) Potter, for further work.[17] The play asserts that it's no crime to cheat the Indians, who are "savage beasts," and "don't deserve to breathe Christian air."[18]

Subsequent literary efforts focus on Pontiac's 1763 siege of the fort at Detroit, which the British had named Fort Lernoult. In May, Pontiac, apparently imitating the trickery that had led to the killing of British troops at Michilimackinac, asked the fort's commander, Major Henry Gladwin, for a parley in the fort. But a French woman, Angelique dit Beaubien Cuillerier, who was in love with James Sterling, a Scotch trader at Detroit, told Gladwin that the Indians would have weapons concealed under their blankets; thus the trickery failed.

The earliest fictional uses of Pontiac's career are Canadian Major John Richardson's *Wacousta; or, The Prophecy* . . . (1832), which also depicts the Indian attack on Michilimackinac; General Alexander Macomb's three-act play, *Pontiac; or, The Siege of Detroit* (1835); and Osgood Bradbury's *Pontiac; or, The Last Battle of the Ottawa Chief* . . . (ca. 1845).

Pontiac is almost lost in the story of attempted revenge in *Wacousta*. John T. Flanagan calls it "a nightmare of the improbable . . . an absurdity."[19] Macomb's play is the first literary work to use Pontiac's ruse to enter the fort.

Later Pontiac romances identify a variety of fictional characters as the actual informant. From 1851 on, these books seem to have been influenced by *The Conspiracy of Pontiac and the Indian War after the Conquest of Canada*, by Francis Parkman (1823–1893). The publication of this book also led to the reissue of Richardson's *Wacousta*. (The novel was again reissued in 1906.)

Six Beadle and Adams novels are set during Pontiac's siege of Fort Lernoult: J. Stanley Henderson's [pseud. of Edward Willett,

New York journalist] *The Trader Spy; or, The Victim of the Fire Raft* (1869); Thomas C. Harbaugh's *Silver Rifle, the Girl Trader; or, The White Tigers of Lake Superior* (1873); Frank Webber's [pseud. of William H. Bushnell (1823–1909?)] *The Beautiful Scout; or, The Indian Maiden's Sacrifice* (1868); Lewis J. Gardner's [pseud. of Andrew Dearborn] *Scarred Eagle; or, Mooroine, the Sporting Fawn, a Story of Ship and Shore* (1870); and William J. Hamilton's [pseud. of Clark C. Dunning] *Red Lightning; or, The Black League, a Tale of the Trading Posts* (1872).

A novel by Kirk Munroe (1850–1930), *At War with Pontiac; or, The Totem of the Bear, a Tale of Redcoat and Redskin* (1895), went through several American editions and a London edition.

Colonel H. R. Gordon invented a married Pontiac who kidnaps a young English woman intending to add her to his harem in *Pontiac, Chief of the Ottawas* (1897). Gordon was the pseudonym of Edward Sylvester Ellis (1840–1916), an Ohio native and a prolific author of juvenile novels.

In 1902, Mary Catherine Crowley (?–1920) turned to the Pontiac siege for her *The Heroine of the Straits*, basing it on materials in the Burton Collection, and on a "time-faded diary," written in French, which had "lain unvalued in the garret of the old St. Aubin house" in Detroit for fifty years (p.viii). The 375-page novel begins with the arrival of Gladwin at Detroit and continues until the cessation of hostilities, but its focus is on the real-life Angelique and her romance with Sterling. John T. Flanagan says the novel "sketches with considerable charm the life of the habitants—those French-Canadians who were torn between the dispossessed Indians and loyalty to the whites even though [the latter] wore the hated British uniform." But, he adds, "Crowley's characters do not breathe life; even Pontiac is little more than a [historic but] sinister name."[20]

The prolific, usually pseudonymous, Edward Stratemeyer (1862–1930) wrote *On the Trail of Pontiac* (1904; reissued 1923) under his own name. The only Michigan event in *A Sword of the Old Frontier: A Tale of Fort Chartres and Old Detroit* (1905) by Iowan Randall Parrish (1858–1923) is the defeat of Major Robert Rogers in the disastrous Bloody Run battle of July 31, 1763. The rest of the novel is set in Illinois.

Will Ludlow Cumback's *Onawago; or, The Betrayer of Pontiac* was published by friends in 1911 four years after the author's death at age twenty-two.

In *Hatchet in the Sky* (1954), a five-hundred-page novel by Margaret Cooper Gay (?–1957), a jealous Indian woman murders Pontiac at Detroit. But he was actually assassinated by a Peoria Indian in Cahokia, Illinois.[21]

Richard Clyde Ford, historian and novelist (1870–1951), had two degrees from Albion College and a 1900 Ph.D. from the University of Freiburg, Germany. In 1913, he translated a French-language "Journal of Pontiac's Conspiracy" (1763) into English. This effort led in 1915 to a juvenile work, *White Captive: A Tale of the Pontiac War.*

Ethel Claire Brill (1877–), who wrote books about Boy Scouts under the pseudonym, Edwin C. Burritt, and other books under her own name, was a native of Minnesota who spent her summers at Tobins Harbor on Isle Royale, a place closer to Minnesota than Michigan. She once said, however: "I am deeply in love with the wild country of Northern Michigan and much interested in the history of the Upper Peninsula."[22]

Ethel Claire Brill's *White Brother: A Story of the Pontiac Uprising* (1932)—set on Mackinac and at the Sault—is a book for juveniles.

Black Forest (1937) by Meade Minnigerode (1887–1967), focuses on a Scotch trader and his wife caught up in the Pontiac uprising.

Merritt Parmalee Allen (1892–1954), a Vermont native, in his 1939 *Black Rain* changed one historical fact: Captain Donald Campbell survives the Bloody Run massacre.

Only the last seventy pages of Canadian Army officer Norman Tucker's *The Years Ahead* (n.d.) are set at Detroit during the Pontiac siege.

War Belts of Pontiac (1943) by William H[arvey] Bunce (1903–) focuses on a boy who acts as an emissary between the British and Pontiac. Two *Library Journal* reviewers differed in their opinions of the book, one calling it "unimportant," the other recommending it particularly for its use of Rogers' Rangers and for its Great Lakes background.[23]

Harry Hamilton's *Thunder in the Wilderness* (1949) focuses on a young French-Indian boy from Kaskaskia, Illinois, who, along with Illinois Indians, joins Pontiac's forces.

(Richard H.) Dirk Gringhuis (1918–1974) set his best-known book, *The Young Voyageur: Trade and Treachery at Michilimackinac* (1955; reissued 1969), in 1762. A boy voyageur from Fort Detroit accompanies a French trader to Fort Michilimackinac and manages to survive capture by Pontiac's Indians. Gringhuis also illustrated the book.

Gringhuis, born in Grand Rapids of Dutch ancestry, was also a college teacher, museum curator, television producer and director—roles in which he could express his genuine interest in Michigan's past. He has over twenty books to his credit and has produced murals for both forts Mackinac and Michilimackinac.[24]

Howard Peckham—whose *Pontiac and the Indian Uprising* (1947, plus later editions) offers the presently accepted version of Pontiac's role in attempts to defeat the British—wrote *Pontiac, Young Ottawa Leader* (1963). Wilma Pitchford Hays's *Lion in the Forest* (1965), John William Tebbel's *Red Runs the River: The Rebellion of Chief Pontiac* (1966), and Clide Anne Hollman's *Pontiac: King of the Great Lakes* (1968) are later juvenile versions of this oft-told tale.

The War of 1812

From June 18, 1812, to December 24, 1814, America was at war with Great Britain. A consequence was a number of novels set during the war. Some of these have events set in Michigan.

Canadian Major John Richardson drew on his army service for *The Canadian Brothers* (1840), a novel that uses events on and around the Great Lakes in the war. His 1851 American version, *Mathilda Montgomery*, eliminates some Canadian material and focuses on the renegade Simon Girty and the massacre at the Raisin River south of Detroit.

Ann Snelling's *Kabaosa; or, The Warriors of the West, a Tale of the Last War* (1842) begins with Tecumseh as a youth on Lake Michigan and follows his career until his death. Snelling, daughter-in-law of Colonel Josiah Snelling (for whom Fort Snelling in Minneapolis is named) and sister-in-law of author W. J. Snelling, focuses her novel on the Indians rather than the whites, although she uses her family's military experiences as resource material. G. Harrison Orrians says, "The work is a lament for the injustice of the white man to the red and a heavy sigh for the passing of the noble Indian."[25]

Fanny Woodville's *Edward Wilton; or, Early Days in Michigan* (n.d., but probably after 1851) tells of a boy captured by Indians who fights in the War of 1812, then, despite pleas from his former Indian comrades, gives up tribal life to return to his family.

Emerson Bennett (1822–1905), a poet and novelist from New York and Philadelphia, set his *The Refugees: An Indian Tale of 1812* (1856) south and east of Detroit just after the surrender of "the cowardly General Hull" to the British at Detroit on August 16, 1812. A young couple flee to safety down the Detroit River on a barge. The "tale" was published in the *Detroit Daily Advertiser* in late 1856 and the *New York Ledger* in early 1857.

Joseph Badger's Beadle novel, *The Border Renegade; or, The Lily of the Silver Lake* (1872) is set near Lake Saint Clair during one week in June 1812. A young woman and her father disregard an old hunter's warning that there are warlike Indians in the area, with tragic consequences.

Among Beadle and Adams novels by Iowa-born Oliver (Oll) Coomes are three that use the war as a background: *One-Armed Alf, the Giant Hunter of the Great Lakes* . . . (1874); *Long Beard, the Giant Spy; or, Happy Harry, the Wild Boy of the Woods* (1881), both set in the Muskegon area; and *Happy Harry, the Wild Boy of the Woods* . . . (1875) set on Lake Saint Clair. Long Beard was also a character in Beadle and Adams novels by other authors.

Victor La Tourette (1875) ("by a Broad Churchman") by Edward Augustus Warriner (1829–1908) tells of a Frenchman who becomes a missionary to the Indians and marries a Detroit woman. With the help of friendly Indians, they survive the war.

Among numerous books by Ohio attorney and author Albert Gallatin Riddle (1816–1902) is *The Tory's Daughter: A Romance of the Northwest 1812–1813* (1888). Set around Detroit, Frenchtown (modern-day Monroe), Fort Malden on the Canadian side, the Thames River, and Put-in-Bay, the story sympathizes with the British.

Hans Leigh's novelette *Heroine of War: A Tale of Detroit* was published in two installments in the *Detroit Times* (January 18 and 21, 1892). A woman attempting to frustrate an imaginary scheme by General William Hull to turn Detroit over to the British, is captured by British soldiers and falls in love with their captain.

Annetta Halliday Antona's *Captives of Cupid: A Story of Old Detroit* (1896) is a complex tale that leads readers through a tangled web of romances, murders, burnings at the stake, and Tecumseh's death at the battle of the Thames.

James Otis [Kaler] wrote *Toby Tyler; or, Ten Weeks with a Circus* (1880), a novel that American juveniles were still reading in this century. In *At the Siege of Detroit* . . . (1904) Otis places two fifteen-year-old boys at Detroit with General Hull.

Mary Catherine Crowley's third novel, *Love Thrives in War: A Romance of the Frontier in 1812* (1903), begins with the Detroit fire of 1805, then presents a romance in which even Tecumseh takes a part; the conflict among French, English, and Americans as the war comes to the city; and several superstitions based on the 1811 Comet and ominous specters and apparitions that appear in the nighttime skies.

Crowley's work has not been nearly as well received by literary historians as the work of Mary Hartwell Catherwood, a contemporary writing in the same general area. Nowadays, Crowley is simply lumped with other forgotten novelists of romanticized history.

The title poem of John Couchois Wright's *Pe-tah-se-ga and Other Poems* may owe its source to Frederic Alva Dean's 1889 *The Heroines of Petosega*. Wright was also the author of *Ella: A Story of White Slave Traffic* (1911), set in part in Harbor Springs; a volume of verse, *Northern*

Breezes (1915, reissued 1917); *Stories of the Crooked Tree* (1915); and *The Crooked Tree: Legends of Northern Michigan* (1917). The latter two utilize tales and stories told to Wright by his French-Indian grandmother who could remember hearing sounds of the battle between the Americans and British at Mackinac Island.

Wright's *The Great Myth* (1922) is a story of Nana Bosho, the miracle man of the Algonquins.

Henry James O'Brien Bedford-Jones (1887–1949)—one of Michigan's most prolific authors in the twentieth century (although he set few of his stories in his native state)—was born in Ontario, educated in Michigan and at Trinity College, Toronto. His more than one hundred novels and numerous short stories (some written under pseudonyms or in partnership with Donald Friede or Kenneth Fearing) won him wide acclaim during his career. Several novels, none set in Michigan, were filmed.

His early short novel *Trails Chivalrous* (1915) is set in the northwestern Lower Peninsula, Mackinac Island, and the nearby Canadian area. There, in September 1814, American soldiers under Colonel George Croghan and Captain Arthur Sinclair were surprised and captured on the *Scorpion* and the *Tigress*, leaving the British in command of the northern Great Lakes. "The period," said Bedford-Jones, "marked the end of Michigan's old romance, before the smallpox had quite swept away the [Indians], and when Mackinac was still the meeting place of Mohawk and Chippewa, French voyageur and British redcoat."[26]

Hearts Undaunted: A Romance of the Four Frontiers (1917), a novel by Eleanor (Stackhouse) Atkinson (1863–1942), focuses on John Kinzie, an actual fur trader at Mackinac and Detroit, who became a prisoner of war at Fort Malden during the War of 1812. Lennox Bouton Grey says that the shift in this novel from a "plot-romance" to the "biographical romance" is a significant move toward the truer concept of frontier life that was to lead to such epics as Julia Cooley Altrocchi's *Wolves against the Moon.*[27]

Atkinson was a Chicago teacher and writer.

Anna Van Noorden's *The Backwoodsmen, a Romance of the War of 1812* was published in 1926.

Francesca Falk Miller's lengthy *1812: The Story of the War of 1812 in Song and Story* (1935) versifies such topics as "Women of 1812" and "Land Battles of 1812."

The next 1812 War novel was Julia Altrocchi's 572-page epic, *Wolves against the Moon* (1940), based on the adventures of an actual person, Joseph Bailly, a fur trader. The novel is set in Bailly's trading post, Baillytown, a few miles east of present-day Gary, Indiana; the Lake Superior region; and on the Saint Joseph and Little Calumet rivers. Bailly survives the 1805 Detroit fire, the War of 1812, and the massacres at Fort Dearborn and the Raisin River. Although the book's numerous reviewers found faults in the complex tale, they also found much to praise. (The novel was reissued in 1951, 1969, and 1974.)

Altrocchi, born in Connecticut on July 4, 1893, was educated in Chicago and at Vassar. She had a summer home near Warren Dunes State Park, close to the homes of Joseph Bailly and Simon Pokagon. "I . . . [love] Michigan's scenery, history, and general magnificence," she once said.[28]

Louis Zara's 750-page historical novel *This Land Is Ours* (1940) is the tale of Andrew Benton and his family who leave Philadelphia in 1755—hard upon General Edward Braddock's defeat at Pittsburgh—and between that time and 1835 manage to be in Detroit and everywhere else that battles raged.

Robert Harper, Ohio author and Civil War expert, set only the first quarter of his 1940 *Trumpet in the Wilderness* in Michigan. The time is the beginning of the War of 1812, the setting between Lake Erie and Lake Huron. Ralph Beebe's 1941 *Who Fought and Bled*, after an Ohio segment, focuses on General William Hull's surrender at Detroit and the resulting battle at Frenchtown on the Raisin River. Both novels present Hull as "old, fearful, vacillating, soft, inconsistent and lacking in intrepidity, valor and basic military judgment."[29] One critic thought Beebe's novel had too much of "the tinge of the textbook."[30] In contrast, a second said, "Beebe writes with the gusto of an action writer who knows his craft. His characters are well defined and the account of their exploits holds [the reader's] interests to the end." In particular, this critic thought that Beebe had done a fine job of showing the officers as superannuated, bungling old men who were not equal to the courage and devotion to duty of their soldiers.[31]

Other Michigan Indians in Verse and Prose

In the mid-nineteenth century, Levi Bishop set the twenty-eight cantos in his *Teuchsa Grande: A Legendary Poem* (1869, reissued 1870 and 1872; also found in his *Poetical Works*, 3rd ed. [1876], and later editions). Its locale is an Indian village, Teuchsa Grande, which stood on the site of present-day Detroit from the mid-sixteenth to the mid-seventeenth centuries, but it had disappeared by the time the French arrived. Other poems are "La Ville Du Detroit," "River Raisin Battle," and "Pioneers of Detroit."

Captain Henry Whiting (1788–1851), who Professor R. Lawrence Dawson says is "Michigan's first poet,"[32] published his lengthy poem *Ontwa, the Son of the Forest* in 1822—a narrative poem about an Erie-Iroquois Indian battle. It antedates Henry Schoolcraft's *Algic Researches . . .* (1839) and Longfellow's *The Song of Hiawatha* (1855). Whiting's *Sannillac, a Poem . . .* (1831) is set on Mackinac Island two centuries before the white people came. The poem's purpose, Whiting writes, is "to exhibit manners and customs, which are generally characteristics of the scene of the forest."[33]

Whiting is also the author of "The Emigrant" (1819); "The Age of Steam" (1830), a playful satire on the dedication of the steamboat *Henry Clay* in Detroit; and "A Retrospect; or, The Ages of Michigan." The latter is published in Henry Schoolcraft's *The Rise of the West . . .* (1830).

Emma Carra (pseud. of Avis J. Spenser)[34] set her *Viroqua; or, The Flower of the Ottawas* (1848) in 1762–1763 Detroit. Wampanoag, an Indian living near Detroit, hates the whites even though one of his two supposed daughters is a white girl. However, in the course of the novel, he overcomes his hatred. Emma Carra was also a pseudonym for other authors.

J. L. Gordon's *Legends of the Northwest* (1881, in verse) includes "The Sea Gull," an Indian legend set at the Pictured Rocks area on the Lake Superior shoreline northeast of Munising.

Marian Austin (Waite) Magoon (1885–?), a New Yorker with M.A. and Ph.D. degrees from Ann Arbor, was a teacher in several Michigan schools and at Eastern Michigan University. She based her *Ojibway Drums* (1955), a book for middle-school children, on summers spent on an island in Georgian Bay, where she was surrounded by an Ojibwa Indian reservation. The book tells the story of Little Half Sky who waits for the time when he will go to Dreamer's Rock, meet his manito [spirit or force underlying life], and then become a warrior in his tribe. Magoon said she based this book on stories she had heard from the Indians.[35]

A reviewer in the *Saturday Review of Literature* wrote, "What sets this [story] off from all the rest is the almost slangy familiarity with which it is written. . . . There is a boisterous humor about the story that has a ring of authority."[36] Magoon was also the author of *Little Dusty Foot* (1948).

Flavius Joseph Littlejohn (1804–1880), who as a young surveyor and geologist became acquainted with "many tribal bands"[37] and their legends, published nine legends, ranging in time from 1800 to 1811 in *Legends of Michigan and the Old Northwest . . .* (1875).

Frederick Russell Burton (1861–1909), who was born in Jonesville, Michigan, published *Redcloud of the Lakes* in 1909. The setting is ca. 1800; the story tells of Megissun, an old Indian, who had had a youthful vision of a strange white monster that destroyed a buffalo, his tribe's symbol. The vision is fulfilled in the lifetime of his grandson, Redcloud, as white men come to the tribe's hunting and fishing grounds and begin to convert young Indians to the ways of the whites. Redcloud has an affair with a white girl but marries his Indian sweetheart.

Mrs. Alden Chamberlin's *White Wing: An Indian Story*, published at Charlevoix, Michigan, in 1911, is a romance based on a tradition in the author's family of a white boy and girl who are reared by an Indian woman after their parents have been scalped and slain.

Joseph E. Badger's Beadle novel, *The Indian Scout; or, Crazy Slack, the Whiskey Trader* (1871)—attributed to Harry Hazard—focuses on the erosion of the Indian character as a consequence of the whiskey and fur trade in the late eighteenth century.

An early work, Charles Scates *Scenes of Lake Huron: A Tale Interspersed with Interesting Facts in a Series of Letters* (1836) is a loosely structured, often anecdotal, tale of an Indian, Magilverie, the chief of the Chippewa tribe at Keweenaw Bay.

Margaret Isabel Ross's *Kaga's Brother: A Story of the Chippewas* (1936) tells how fourteen-year-old Matthew (Matt) Steele in the spring of 1826 accompanies the U.S. Commissioner of Indian Affairs on a long boat trip. At Sault Sainte Marie, Kaga, a Chippewa boy, educates Matt in Indian lore and Old Northwest history. The novel's events are told in a series of letters from Matt to his father, making this one of three Michigan epistolary novels.

In 1843, Louis Legrand Noble's (1811–1882) long semidramatic, seminarrative poem, "Ni-Mah-Min," was published in installments in *Graham's Magazine*, a literary periodical. Three long-dead Indians relate their stories of love, sorcery, murder, and revenge through a young white man acting as a medium. Professor Carl (Ed) Burklund, University of Michigan, believes that Noble's poem has little aesthetic appeal to modern readers: "It takes its place in that list of ambitious failures—before 'Hiawatha'—to give poetic form to Indian materials."[38]

Solon Robinson (1803–1880), a northern Indiana merchant and author, in 1867 published *Me-Win-O-Toc: A Tale of Frontier Life and Indian Character: Exhibiting Traditions, Superstitions, and Character of a Race that Is Passing Away. A Romance of the Frontier*. It is a long tale beginning in 1834 and set in the Indiana-Michigan dune country. Me-Win-O-Toc, a white man who lives with Indians after the death of his wife, discovers that a young white woman, who is being burned at the stake by Indians, is actually his long-lost daughter.

In the 1830s, Father Frederic Baraga (1797–1868), following in the tradition of earlier Jesuits, came to the south shore of Lake Superior. During the next thirty-five years, he labored among the Indians and founded churches that still exist. *By Cross and by Anchor* (1946), by James K[nox] Jamison (1887–1954), although purporting to be a factual biography of Baraga, is, as one Catholic critic has noted, more of a "story" with a number of authorial embellishments, one of which shows Baraga in a birchbark canoe surviving a Lake Superior storm of the type that often has sunk eight-hundred-foot-long ore boats (pp. 93–98). Despite all his efforts, at the end of his life, Father Baraga's Indian protégés tell him "he is a failure . . . that [the Indians] owe their sordid condition to him."[39]

William Bushnell's [pseud. Frank Webber] *Ah-Meek, the Beaver; or, The Copper Hunters of Lake Superior* (1867) begins at Sault Sainte Marie. Ah-Meek, a trapper-hunter who detests white people for despoiling the land by mining, takes a job as a guide for a white man who seeks mine sites. Bushnell was, in turn, a lawyer, a civil engineer, and a Chicago newspaper editor and publisher. His wife was also an author.

In Harry Dean Hildreth's *Wauneta: An Indian Story of Happiness as a Mental Condition* (1894), Wau-Neta, the titular subject of the novel, almost disappears in a maze of seemingly unrelated events.

Reverend William Edgar Brown (1866–?) is the author of *Indian Legendary Poems and Songs of Cheer* (1912) and *Echoes of the Forest: American Indian Legends* (1918). Brown, who the Indians named Nwah-ke-nah-go-zid, was assisted in his research by members of the Michigan Historical Commission and the University of Michigan faculty.

Henry Rowe Schoolcraft

In 1820, Michigan Governor Lewis Cass and Henry Rowe Schoolcraft (1793–1864), on an exploratory mission to the Sault Sainte Marie area, met John Johnston, an aristocratic Irishman trading in furs; his Ojibwa wife, Woman of the Green Glade; and their daughter, Jane, who, with her sister Anna Maria, had been educated in Europe. Schoolcraft became the Indian agent at the Soo, and in 1823, Jane and he were married. Anna Maria married Schoolcraft's brother, James.

Jane Johnston and her mother taught Henry Schoolcraft their language and the lore and beliefs that Jane's Ojibwa grandfather, "the greatest poet and story-teller of his tribe,"[40] had taught them. In

1839, despite Schoolcraft's concern that "incredulity will start up critics to call [my] discoveries in question,"[41] he published his first investigations as *Algic Researches, Comprising Inquiries Respecting the Mental Characteristics of the North American Indians*. This was followed by *Oneonta; or, The Red Race of America: Their History, Traditions, Customs, Poetry Writing* . . . (1844–1845). Schoolcraft acknowledged Captain Henry Whiting's primacy in this area in the book's dedication, "My attention [to Indian lore] was first arrested by the fact of the existence of such tales among the Odjibwa nation inhabiting the region about Lake Superior in 1822."[42]

Janet Lewis's *The Invasion* (1932) tells the story of the Johnston family in "hushed unaccented prose"[43] that reads as if it were fiction. We see John Johnston sympathizing with the British in the War of 1812; Henry Rowe Schoolcraft learning the Indian language and lore that he was to transmute into several books and that was to form the basis for Longfellow's *The Song of Hiawatha*; the mysterious murder of James Schoolcraft; the building of the Soo Canal; and the growth of Sault Sainte Marie. The book ends with the death of Anna Maria Johnstone (Red Leaf), daughter of James Schoolcraft's wife, in 1928. *New York Times Book Review* critic John Chamberlain found pleasure in Lewis's novel and wrote, "the genesis of [*Hiawatha*] forms some of [the book's] most interesting pages."[44]

Janet Lewis was the daughter of Edwin Herbert Lewis, a University of Chicago professor and author. She published her first poem in *Poetry* in 1920, the year she graduated from the University of Chicago; she married poet Yvor Winters in 1926.

Her *The Indians in the Woods*, a volume of verse about the Ojibway, was published in 1922 and reprinted in 1980. *The Friendly Adventures of Oliver Ostrich* (1923) is set along Saint Marys River, where in the summers of the early years of the twentieth century the Lewises stayed, either on Neebish Island or Saint Joseph Island. There, they met Anna Maria Johnstone who rented cabins to summer visitors and told the Lewises the Ojibwa legends and lore that she had heard as a child.

Henry Wadsworth Longfellow
and *The Song of Hiawatha*

Henry Wadsworth Longfellow (1807–1882), one of the country's most respected nineteenth-century poets, had become interested in Indian lore and was influenced by Schoolcraft's books. In 1854, flushed with the success of *Evangeline, A Tale of Acadie* (1847), he wrote his epic poem, this one about Indians—*The Song of Hiawatha* (1855), set largely on the Upper Peninsula shore of Lake Superior. In this poem, he acknowledged his use of Schoolcraft (Nadawatha)[45] materials:

> Should you ask me whence these stories?
> Whence these legends and traditions . . .
> With the odors of the forest . . .
> I repeat them as I heard them
> From the lips of Nadawatha,
> The musician, the sweet singer.

Hiawatha's theme "is the history of a people from their nomadic stage as hunters and fisher-folk, through primitive stages of agriculture and community life, the attainment of cultural solidarity as manifested in a common religion and a common fund of legend, until finally becoming an oppressed people, their fortunes decline, their songs become a memory, and their natural heroism departs as Hiawatha (the central character) disappears into the sunset."[46]

In the years after its publication, the poem became one of Longfellow's most popular works, going through some 125 editions, including translations into almost every European language. It was dramatized by Charles M. Walcot in 1915; set to music by Benjamin Britten; became the basis for a pageant, Constance D'Arcy McKay's *The Passing of Hiawatha* in 1915; was parodied by Lewis Carroll and others; acted out by schoolchildren; and the movie *Hiawatha* was made in 1952.

Frederick Russell Burton was primarily a student of Indian music and a composer. At Harvard, where he graduated *summa cum laude* in 1882, he used Indian melodies as the basis for a musical background for Longfellow's *Song of Hiawatha*. In 1898, Burton also wrote a cantata, *Hiawatha*, for the Yonkers, New York, Choral Society, which he had organized. To make his music authentic Burton used an Indian melody, perhaps the earliest such use of Indian music.[47] In 1902, he supervised the music for the Indian dramatic production of *Hiawatha* that was annually presented on the Ontario side of Lake Huron.[48]

Richard Mercer Dorson (1916–1981), a member of the History Department at Michigan State University from 1944 to 1957 and one of this country's most distinguished folklorists, said, "Michigan has a special interest in America's best known poem, *The Song of Hia-*

watha. . . . [The poem emphasizes] an awareness of Indians as sentient human beings who possessed traditions of artistic and cultural merit."[49]

The best and most objective short study of Longfellow's epic is Stith Thompson's "The Indian Legend of Hiawatha."[50] A much longer study, *Schoolcraft—Longfellow—Hiawatha* (1942), was written by Chase Salmon Osborn (1860–1949)—explorer, prospector, and the only governor of Michigan from the Upper Peninsula (1911–1912)—and his adopted daughter (later his wife) Stellanova. It includes chapters on *Hiawatha* and the *Kalevala* as well as the Hiawatha country, a long section that relates Longfellow's text to Schoolcraft's source material, a Schoolcraft biography, and a bibliography.

Osborn earned an LL.D. degree at the University of Michigan in 1911. After a brief career as a newspaper reporter and editor, he became a publisher in Florence, Wisconsin, and later in Sault Sainte Marie, Saginaw. Concurrently with these roles he was a state game and fish warden, a postmaster in several towns, a commissioner of railroads, and a regent of the University of Michigan. His discovery of an iron range in Canada in the late nineteenth century made him a wealthy man.

Osborn also was the author of eight other books, including his autobiography *Iron Hunter* (1919). Stellanova in addition to collaborating occasionally with Osborn wrote eight other volumes, including verses about the Indians and the lake areas.

In 1964, Michigan native Alida Sims Malkus (1895–?), influenced by the poem, published a fictionalized biography (for children twelve to fifteen) of a eighteenth-century Iroquois sachem of the New York Onondaga nation entitled *There Really Was a Hiawatha*.

Later Works about the Indians

Chief Simon Pokagon (1830–1899), the Longfellow of the red man, was born in Berrien County, Michigan. At fourteen he enrolled in a South Bend school where he learned to speak English and then took three years of college work.

In 1893, he published a birchbark booklet, *The Red Man's Greeting* for the World's Columbian Exposition held in Chicago. "[This] cry of an Indian's heart for the woes of his people [is] [p]itched in a minor key [;] its plaintive sadness voice[s] without any note of vindictiveness the outraged spirit of his race."[51]

Chief Pokagon's posthumously published *Queen of the Woods* (*O-Gi-Maw-Hwe Mit-I-Gwa-Ki*) in 1899 includes a "Brief Sketch of the

Algaic Language." It is a semifictional romance based on Pokagon's courtship of his wife.

In the first decade of this century, dramatist William C. DeMille (brother of Cecil B. DeMille, the Hollywood film producer) produced a Broadway play, *Strongheart*, about a Michigan Ojibwa Indian by that name who matriculates at Columbia University, becomes a star football player, and romances Dorothy, a white coed. But at play's end, out of consideration for Dorothy (and also for the feelings of playgoers of the time, no doubt) Strongheart, in a "noble redskin" gesture, withdraws his suit in favor of a fellow student.

Frederick Russell Burton, whose long association with the Ojibwas of the Lake Huron and Lake Superior areas flowered into his *Songs of the Ojibway Indians* (1903)—later expanded to *American Primitive Music* (1909)—rewrote the play in 1908 as *Strongheart*, a novel of nearly four hundred pages. The book's dust jacket has a stylized drawing of a Plains Indian tepee and the question, "Would you let your daughter marry an Indian?" Unlike the play, the novel's answer is "Yes": Strongheart and the young woman marry. In Burton's novel, Strongheart rescues a Columbia University student from drowning in a northern Michigan river; as a consequence, he enrolls at Columbia so that he can learn "white man's ways" and deal with the whites who are taking over the Ojibwa land.

Twentieth-Century Indians

Frederick Burton's Redcloud and Strongheart were end-of-the-nineteenth-century Indians who were changing under the influence of the white man. Florence McClinchey's *Joe Pete* (1929) and John Moore's *Indian Paul* (1945) bring that change full circle with differing consequences for their twentieth-century Indians.

McClinchey's novel focuses on an Ojibwa boy and Mabel, his mother, after the father deserts the pair. They live on Sugar Island in the Saint Marys River, an island that is being logged by Uno Jaakola, a "black Finn." Mabel degenerates physically, mentally, and socially, but Joe Pete, rejecting the white man's ways, models, and traditions, plans to go to an Indian school.

The novel instances ways in which whites brutalize, cheat, or degrade Indians—and ways in which the Indians seek revenge. The story's conflict between Indians and Finns anticipates the theme of Sharon Dilworth's short story, "Mad Dog Queen" in *The Long White* (1988).

Chase Osborn—who appears twice in the novel and was a neighbor of McClinchey's on Sugar Island—called *Joe Pete* "one of the best books ever written by a Michigan author."[52] Henry Seidel

Canby said it was "a simple but moving story of Indian life in our day . . . a novel with a cutting edge [whose] theme might be described as the inevitable pressure of white supremacy upon Indian mores."[53] Canby thought that Mabel, not Joe Pete, was the true protagonist of the book.

A *New York Times Book Review* reviewer wrote, "[I]t is impressive in the end because of the evident authenticity of the material and the sincerity with which it is presented, because of the depth and reality of the feeling which emerges from its pages of rather awkward prose, because of the honesty and fidelity of the characterizations."[54]

McClinchey later became an English instructor at Central Michigan College of Education (now Central Michigan University).

John Moore's *Indian Paul* is set in an Upper Michigan resort town over the Labor Day holiday after the summer visitors have left. Indian Paul, an alcoholic, murders his mother with an axe. Lodged in jail, he is seized by indignant townspeople intending to vent their built-up anger toward summer visitors by lynching him. A sensible country doctor persuades the mob to take him back to jail. That night some young hoodlums haul Paul off to the woods intending to lynch him, but their false courage fails them. As they discuss their next move, they discover that Paul has cut his own throat.

The novel was not as well received as *Joe Pete*. Reviewers thought that Moore had not developed in depth his theme of man's inhumanity to man.[55] The book did not "find a point of view which would carry the reader beneath the surface of events and provide a meaningful continuity of experience;"[56] and it left the reader "with an impression of divided aim or intent."[57]

Moore was born in Kalamazoo in 1913, earned a bachelor's degree at the University of Michigan in 1936 and a master's degree in 1937, taught at Western Michigan College in Kalamazoo from 1939 to 1942, then moved to Montana. He coauthored a textbook on writing, *The Exposition of Ideas*, with Baxter Hathaway, another Kalamazoo novelist.

Stellanova Osborn's 1955 *Polly Cadotte: A Tale of Duck Island in Verse* is a lyrical narrative. It tells an all-too-familiar story: a young French-Indian woman becomes the mistress of a coarse brute she both fears and hates. She finally leaves him and moves in with a man with a kind heart, a man she can trust.

R. Ray Baker's (1890–?) *The Red Brother and Other Indian Stories* (1927) is set in the Straits of Mackinac.

Arthur G. Kerle's *Whispering Trees, a Tale of Michigamaw* (1971) is a book for young people. It tells of a young Indian in Michigan in the 1880s who wants no part of the white man's culture and who watches in anger as the white pine forests are cleared and the streams become fouled. His anger intensifies as he sees a young white friend become a logger.

Artist Earl H[owell] Reed wrote and Illustrated books about the dune country of northeastern Indiana and southwestern Michigan. His *The Silver Arrow and Other Indian Romances of the Dune Country* (1926) has five romances and four tales, all attributed to the "Ancient," an aged man who lives near the dunes and has a "white unkempt beard [that] reache[s] almost to his waist."

Most, if not all, of the contents of Reed's book are of the species that Dorson and others have labeled fakelore. For those confused about the difference between folklore and fakelore, here is Dorson's explanation: "The folklorist is interested in all forms of what be called the underculture, in contrast with the elite, the uppercrust, the official, the formal culture. He studies folk literature as compared with art literature, folk history as against documentary history, folk arts and not the fine arts, folk religion rather than theologies, folk medicine and belief as against medical science."[58]

Fakelore is literary material that resembles folklore, but it is actually a creation—fanciful or imaginative—of one or more persons.

Poet Lew Sarett (1888–1954) is claimed by Illinois, Wisconsin, and Michigan as a native son. He was born in Chicago; reared in Marquette and Benton Harbor (both in Michigan); educated at the University of Michigan, Beloit College (Wisconsin), the University of Illinois, and Harvard; and he taught at the University of Illinois, Northwestern University, and the University of Florida. Alma Johnson Sarett, his third wife, said in 1977 that "even though Lew was born in Illinois, he thought of Michigan as his home state."[59] But Sarett attributed some of his nature and Indian poetry to Wisconsin, saying his fourth volume, *Wings against the Moon* (1931), was rooted in the years when he was at Beloit.[60] His poetry may be fully examined in *Collected Poems* (1941) in which the northwoods are treated with sympathy, understanding, and respect.

Leo Shapiro said Sarett was "primarily a poet of nature" and noted that Sarett's fine reputation as a poet had deteriorated owing to a change in the attitudes of literary intellectuals. He quoted Joseph Warren Beach: "[I]n twentieth-century poetry the term and concept of nature have virtually ceased to appear. One main reason for this is that the religious elements in the concept—purposiveness, benevolence, etc.—are no longer assumed to be true, and so the word 'nature' has lost most of its emotional force. . . . The romantic concept of nature . . . has not been able to withstand the impact of modern critical thought."[61]

Two Tall Tales about Michigan's Past

Frederic Alva Dean's 1889 novel, *The Heroines of Petoséga*, is based on the premise that in 1100 B.C., thirty centuries before the book was written, there was a kingdom and a city of Petoséga— where modern-day Petoskey is—and an island, Effelda—present-day Mackinac Island. The kingdom was inhabited by whites of Grecian origin—it was much like ancient Rome or Athens. Long before, it had been destroyed by the whirling, revolving monster called the Floating Mountain—much like a glacier but moving with the speed of an express train—and then rebuilt. In the novel, the Floating Mountain again appears overnight, and only a few people, including the heroines, escape. These fortunate few make their way to an island like Tahiti.

In *Viking Mettles* (1924), Johann Baner, an Ironwood newspaper publisher, used verse to relate a tale (one he apparently accepted as factual) that, combining Swedish and Ojibwa legend, reports Swedish explorers met Ojibwa Indians near the western end of Lake Superior in A.D. 1010. Baner based his narrative on an account he heard from an Indian near Ashland, Wisconsin, in 1891. The Indian had a Swedish name but, nonetheless, spoke Swedish with some difficulty.[62]

Summary

Many of the books discussed in this chapter dramatize the years of conflict between French traders and Jesuit missionaries, between British and French, and between Europeans and Indians that finally resolved the tenancy of Michigan. For too long these conflicts made the Indians subservient, second-class citizens of the land that had once been theirs. Others have examined the problems of Indians adapting to a white-oriented materialistic society whose beliefs and practices contrast with—or even oppose—those that were the way of life of Indian society, a way of life much more in harmony with the natural world of lakes, rivers, and forests.

Of the many writers who have used the Indians, French, or British in Michigan as subjects for literature, only a few—Henry Rowe Schoolcraft, Longfellow, Catherwood, Sarett, and Cooper—have attracted the attention of literary scholars.

Indians still remain in Michigan, some on reservations in both the Upper and Lower peninsulas, others in rural areas, towns, and cities.

CHAPTER III

SETTLERS COME TO MICHIGAN

My eastern friends who wish to find
A country that will suit your mind,
Where comforts all are near at hand,
Had better come to Michigan.
We here have soils of various kinds
To suit men who have different minds,
Prairies, openings, timbered land,
And burr oak plains, in Michigan.

—*Detroit Post and Tribune*[1]

In the eighteenth century, there were French in Detroit, Sault
Sainte Marie, Saint Ignace, and other points; British at Mackinac
Island and elsewhere after 1760; and itinerant traders and trappers everywhere. American migration to, and settlement in, Michigan on a
large scale, however, did not really begin until after 1825. This chapter discusses imaginative literature about migrants and settlers, their
settlements, and their adventures and misadventures.

May Pettit Hay was a descendant of Michigan pioneers, the earliest of whom had served in the War of 1812. *The Last Best Hope* (1972),
based on her family's history, poses its events against the larger
Michigan scene and frames the whole within a modern setting.

James Fenimore Cooper (1789–1851), a major American author
of the early nineteenth-century scene, in *The Oak Openings; or, The
Bee-Hunter* (1848) tells of the consequences of the outbreak of the War
of 1812 on a small group of whites on the lower Kalamazoo River. The
two characters of Benjamin Boden (*Le Bourdon*), the bee-hunter—
an American who tracks bees to their honeycombs to collect honey,
which he later sells in far-off Detroit—and Gershom Waring, a trader,

presage the coming of American entrepreneurs. Other characters include Dolly, Waring's wife; Margery, Waring's sister; Corporal Flint; and a missionary named Parson Amen. There are also Indians: Pigeonswing, an "O-jib-way," on his way to Fort Dearborn (at Chicago) to warn the fort commandant of an Indian uprising, and Elksfoot, a Potawatomi. Later, a third Indian, Onoah (Scalping Peter), comes on the scene. In the conflicts with Indians that follow, Elksfoot, Pigeonswing, Flint, and Amen are killed.

Iowan Dorothy Dondore (1894–1946), author of *The Prairie and the Making of Middle America* (1926, reissued 1961), says that Cooper's "mastery" of the novel deserted him in *Oak Openings;* although it presents "such vivid pictures as the midnight council in the wood, or such significant revelations of early thought as [Parson] Amen's theory of the Lost Tribes of Israel, or [the bee-hunter's] effective use of . . . necromancy."[2]

Ohio historian G. Harrison Orrians argued that "the whole narrative is skillfully projected against the events of the first year and a half of the war. . . . Historically [Cooper's] novel is significant in conveying the terror felt by isolated whites in Michigan Territory after the fall of [forts] Michilimackinac and Dearborn, . . . and in dramatizing the plight of the Indians trying to hold back the hordes of the whites debauching upon their hunting grounds."[3]

Two useful discussions of the novel are found in "James Fenimore Cooper and Michigan: His Novel, Visits, and Attitude" by Lawrence R. Dawson, Jr., and in "James Fenimore Cooper and *Oak Openings*" by Kate Russell Oakley.[4] Larry B. Massie's comments in *From Frontier Folk to Factory Smoke* are also interesting.[5]

Dawson reports that Cooper's visits to Michigan in the 1840s resulted in some Kalamazoo fakelore. Albert G. Black, for instance, writes in his *Michigan Novels* that "various [Kalamazoo] families" claim to have "ancestors who were the models for several of the characters in [*Oak Openings*]."[6]

Lulu J. Dickinson dedicated her 1959 novel, *Table in the Wilderness*, to a family member "whose pioneer life and witty homespun philosophy" form the basis for the novel. It tells of Lucina Lemm of Vermont whose husband builds a home for her in 1818 in Michigan's Livingston County, a land of malaria, ague, swamps, Indians, and snakes. Lucina lives to be almost a hundred years old. The novel's point is that it is the women who endure, who build the schools and the churches, and who raise the families, whereas the men go off to work or fight.

Harry Sinclair Drago (1888–1979), an Ohioan, wrote over seventy novels, mostly Westerns. His *Where the Loon Calls* (1928), published early in his career, is set along the marshy coast of Lake Erie between Detroit and Toledo in the early nineteenth century. It features French Canadian 'Toinette Chevalier and her romances with three men: the son of a rich village merchant, a young blacksmith, and a man who smuggles whiskey and wool from Canada to 'Toinette's grandfather. Reviewers liked the locale but were unhappy with the author's manipulation of the action.[7]

Orlando Bolivar Willcox (1823–1907), using the pseudonym Walter March, set his *Shoe-Pac Recollections: A Way-Side Glimpse of American Life* (1856) in the 1820s in Detroit, the city where he was born. The story, narrated by Walter March, focuses on the March family after the father, an agent at Detroit for fur trader John Jacob Astor, dies and the family has to struggle to survive. In 1857, the book was republished as *Walter March; or, Shoe-Pac Recollections* by Major March. Willcox was also the author of *Faca; An Army Memoir* (1857–1858).

In 1953, Columbia Pictures set its last Gene Autry film, *Saginaw Trail*, in the Michigan of 1827. Autry, a captain in Hamilton's Rangers, must deal with Eugene Borden, a fur trapper who has hired renegade Indians to attack settlers trying to settle in woods that he regards as his own territory. Autry resolves the problem with only two songs and a minimum of gunfights and barroom brawls in just fifty-six minutes—and that includes a three-cornered romantic affair in which Borden's son is the loser.

In his novel *The Wolverine: A Romance of Early Michigan* (1904) Lansing native Albert Lathrop Lawrence (1865–1924) begins in the early 1830s in Detroit. Perry North, a New England Puritan and land surveyor, is involved in the "Toledo War" of 1835, a brief, sometimes bitter debate between Ohioans and Michiganians over the inclusion of the Toledo Strip in the newly forming state of Michigan; it also depicts the hero's long drawn-out romance with a French Catholic woman. In spite of Michiganians' efforts to the contrary, Toledo and the Toledo Strip are awarded to Ohio, and Michigan, as a consolation prize, is given the western three-quarters of the supposedly worthless Upper Peninsula.[8]

Helen Topping Miller (1884–1960), "daughter of a literary mother,"[9] was born in Fenton, Michigan ("the Argentine"), which is the setting for the only one of her thirty-three novels set in Michigan. *Born Strangers: A Chronicle of Two Families* (1949), based on Helen Miller's own family history, is a "frame"novel—beginning and ending with the wedding of Augusta Maria (Pet) Chipman and Isaac Wallace (Wally) Lawrence, descendants of the Riggs and Wixom families, respectively, whose history from 1829 to 1949 is traced in the novel. There is no story line—there is simply a sequence of events as the years pass.

The author spent a year at Michigan State College, then married Roger Miller, a Tennessee newspaper editor.

Ray [Costelloe] Strachey (1887–1940), an English feminist author, set the first 150 pages of her *Marching On* (1923) in the northwoods of the Lower Peninsula in the 1830s. The novel has two themes: feminism and the abolition of slavery.

Strachey's heroine, reared in a log cabin, manages at first to escape the traditional roles of farmer and housewife that her parents want her to have. She enrolls in a primitive northern Michigan college and gives birth to a child out of wedlock. Finally, settling on the raw plains of Kansas, she adopts the married lifestyle of her parents.

Merritt Greene (1897–) was the author of three novels set in southern Hillsdale County in the years from 1832 on: *The Land Lies Pretty* (1959), *Curse of the White Panther* (1960), and *Forgotten Yesterdays* (1964). The trilogy begins with Martin Langdon's arrival in 1832 and continues with the development of the Great Sauk Trail from Detroit to Fort Dearborn, the establishment of state government in Michigan, the "Toledo War," and the takeover of Indian lands by the U.S. government. Langdon comes to have compassion for the Indians and marries a half-Indian woman. *Michigan in Books* says that the books' characters are believable and that the trilogy presents an "unforgettable pageant" of the area's history.[10]

Greene lived in Hillsdale County from 1900 on and became a playwright and actor for traveling dramatic troupes, a teacher, and a local reporter for several newspaper organizations.

By far the best author of Michigan pioneer novels is Caroline M[atilda Stansbury] Kirkland (1801–1864). She has drawn more critical and scholarly attention than any Michigan writer except, perhaps, Joyce Carol Oates. The current emphasis on women authors is adding to this interest.

Kirkland's reputation rests on three books, the result of her sojourn in Michigan from 1835 to 1843 with her husband, William, principal of the Detroit Female Seminary and, in 1837 (the year Michigan became a state), the founder of Pinckney, Michigan, about a dozen miles northwest of Ann Arbor: *A New Home—Who'll Follow* (1839), published under the pseudonym of Mrs. Mary Clavers; *Forest Life* (1842); and *Western Clearings* (1846), a collection of Michigan-based essays and stories that had previously been published in periodicals.

Kirkland's first book made her immediately famous in the East. Edgar Allan Poe, who more often impaled authors on the point of his critical pen, called the book "an undoubted sensation," and said that Kirkland stood "at the head of American female authors . . . to Mrs. Kirkland alone we [are] indebted for our acquaintance with the *home* and home life of our backwoodsmen."[11] But James Hall, whose *Legends of the West* (1832), was based on his experience in Illinois, said that Kirkland's books were "a wretched composition—a vile humbug," and he doubted whether Kirkland had ever seen the West.[12]

In her preface to *Forest Life*, Kirkland outlined the thesis of her three books: "What I profess to delineate is the scarce reclaimed wilderness . . . the forest . . . the pioneers . . . the settlers . . . the people who, coming of their own free will . . . each with his own individual ways of profit or advancement . . . have, as a mass, been the mighty instrument in the hands of Providence of preparing the way for civilization, for intelligence, for refinement, for religion."[13]

Kirkland's forte—the characteristic that has endeared her most to the twentieth century—is her realism and, more important, her humor. Both in her books and in her later career as a magazine editor, she rejected nineteenth-century romantic fiction—in particular that of Major John Richardson. She rejected the kinds of characters later favored by Beadle and Adams —Indians, desperadoes, romantic heroines—and wrote about pioneer housewives, speculators, beehunters, and pedagogs. Her influence was to be strong on later local-color novelists, particularly on her son Joseph Kirkland. He, in turn, was to influence Hamlin Garland and through Garland many other regional writers.

Caroline Kirkland came to Michigan expecting—because of her reading of romances—to find a "Florida clime." Instead, she found only trails through the woods with unbridged streams and swamps, settlers whose future homes were still only visions in their heads, and gnats, mosquitoes, and rattlesnakes.[14] In Michigan, Kirkland also discovered new interpretations of democracy. The social level was always at its lowest, and it was assumed that those who had plenty were obligated to share with those who had less.[15]

The first thirty-five chapters of the 1839 *A New Home—Who'll Follow* along with the last three chapters of that book were combined in 1953 with some twenty chapters of *Forest Life* and issued as *A New Home: or, Life in the Clearings*, with an excellent introduction by Henry Nerber. *A New Home—Who'll Follow* was also reissued in 1965, edited and with an equally excellent introduction by William S. Osborne.

Roy W[illiam] Adams's *Peg Leg: A Tale of Pioneer Adventure in the Grand River Valley* (1950) was dedicated to Mrs. Franc L. Adams, author of the *Pioneer History of Ingham County, Michigan* (1923). The preface states that the story is an imaginary one but that some of the characters are real.

In 1835, "Peg-Leg" Hamilton, who lost a leg because of poisoning, has several adventures as he travels from New York to Michigan. There, when intoxicated, he buys a piece of rural Michigan land that turns out to be bog—an incident reminiscent of Herbert Quick's *Vandemark's Folly* (1922) in which a Dutch boy from New York is similarly cheated. But "Peg-Leg's" purchase, like Vandemark's, also turns out well—his "bog" has forty acres of mature black walnut trees.

A Caroline Kirkland contemporary, but quite unlike her, was Metta Victoria Fuller (1831–1885), who, as a Beadle and Adams writer, used several pseudonyms assigned by the publishers. First married to a Doctor Morse of Ypsilanti, she later married Orville J. Victor, an Ohio newspaperman, also a Beadle author.

Fuller's two Michigan titles are *Alice Wilde, the Raftsman's Daughter: A Forest Romance* (1860) and *The Backwoods Bride: A Romance of Squatter Life* (1860). In the first, a New Yorker, "the elegant and cultivated Philip More," in the imaginary town of Center City, Michigan, falls in love with Alice, the plain daughter of a raftsman. In the second, set in the late 1830s, another "elegant and cultivated" easterner, Henry Gardiner, loves Susan Carter, the daughter of a squatter on Gardiner's land. But this is a romance and all ends well.

Teddie: A Simple Little Out-of-Door Story . . . (1910) by Frederick Britton (1910–1960) tells of an eight-year-old boy in 1847 whose widowed mother sends him to live with an uncle sixty miles distant. He travels by himself, meeting along the way, Indians, rattlesnakes, a dog named Epaphroditus (for Epaphroditus Ransom, governor of Michigan from 1849 to 1850), and James Fenimore Cooper!

James Milford Merrill (1847–1936), another popular Beadle author, set his *Cloudwood: Daughter of the Wilderness* (1871) in the fictional town of Wilton, Michigan, in the 1840s. The author seemingly based the details of this romance on the pioneer and Indian life he had observed in Bridgeton on the Muskegon River a few miles northeast of Muskegon.

Henry Hiram Riley (1813–1888), an attorney, studied law in Kalamazoo for six months before moving to Constantine, Michigan. From there, under the pseudonym Simon Oakleaf, he contributed articles set in the fictitious Michigan town of Puddleford to *Knickerbocker Magazine*. These articles, which Larry B. Massie says were based on the town of Constantine,[16] were later gathered in *Puddleford Papers; or, Humors of the West* (1854) and enlarged in *Puddleford and Its People* (1859).

Puddleford's name is an obvious playful reference to Oxford, England, with its reputation as a seat of learning—a state Puddleford will never attain.

Caroline Kirkland is acerbic in her books; Riley is satirical. The reader is left with the impression that if Puddleford and its citizens were representatives of the settlers in Michigan, then education, politics, justice, society, commerce, and the state's future were in trouble and that, for the most part, the East was better off without these migrants.

Benjamin Franklin Taylor's *Theophilus Trent: Old Times in the Oak Openings* (1887) is set in the remote frontier town of Bodkins on the Raisin River in southeast Michigan at a time when pork is a penny a pound, wheat forty cents a bushel, and eggs five mills each—and cash money is hard to come by.

Taylor (1819–1887) taught school in Michigan for several years in the early 1830s, then moved to Chicago. He was also the author of a half-dozen volumes of verse, travel narratives, essays, and the like.

Eleanor Gage Babcock's *Absalom* (1955), set on the Michigan frontier in the 1840s, is, in a sense, a nineteenth-century version of the biblical story of David and his treacherous son—a point emphasized in the first chapter of the novel.

Jerome James Wood's *The Wilderness and the Rose* (1890)—dedicated to his mother, "who saw the wilderness of Michigan blossom like the rose"—is set in extreme south central Michigan near Hudson. This romance of a schoolteacher and the daughter of a tavern owner also sketches "the spirit of speculation [that in the 1840s] entered the [area] and produced causes that marked the decay [of one town] and the rapid rise of its rival" (p. 21).

Wood (1846–1903) was also the author and publisher of *A Child of Genius* (1887), a collection of fifteen sketches, including the hoary legend found everywhere in the Midwest about the ill-fated romance between a young Indian "prince" and a young Indian "princess." A second sketch shows the coming of Dutch, Yankees, and Irish to Michigan.

Like Helen Topping Miller, Helen Hull was an author of many popular novels, most of whose readers were women. Hull (1888?–1971) was born in Albion, the daughter of an English professor at Albion College. She earned her B.A. degree at Michigan State University, her M.A. at the University of Michigan, and her Ph.D. at the University of Chicago. Then she became a professor of English at Columbia University and the author of over two dozen books, both fiction and nonfiction. Only three novels are set in Michigan.

Her 1927 *Islanders* is the life story of Ellen Darcey, an "islander," isolated from life's mainstream. Herman Melville had said that "all men are islanders"—here, Hull shows that women can be "islanders" also. Ellen is left alone on a farm near the small fictional town of Coldstream, Michigan, when the men in her family go to California in the gold rush of 1849 and again in the Civil War. Ellen keeps the farm going until her banker son sells the farm without her consent and keeps the money for his speculations. Ellen is finally able to resolve her frustrations through a granddaughter.

William Allen White, "the sage of Emporia, Kansas," said, " 'Islanders' are women, generic women, planted in the current of life and yet not of life, apart from life, washed by the tides and floods of life, yet always outside of life. . . . The new world and its problems working on the old problems of women's physical being and her function as a torchbearer of life have never been better contrasted than in this book."[17]

Helen Hull, in this and her other novels, was a thoroughly professional writer whose work always commanded the respect of reviewers, even though it did not lead to a reputation as a major literary figure.

Charles B. Lewis's 1883 Beadle and Adams novel, *The Island Prisoner*, tells of a girl in the mid-1800s who is kidnapped from a town on Lake Erie, taken to an island in Lake Superior, and then abandoned on a raft that carries her into Lake Huron where she is rescued.

Lewis (1842–1924), an early graduate of the Michigan Agricultural College, was a *Detroit Free Press* writer and editor, better known by his pseudonym, M. Quad.

Oliver (Oll) Coomes set his 1880 *The Giant Rifleman; or, Wild Life in the Lumber Regions* in "the great green woods of Michigan" along the Muskegon River about 1850. This Beadle and Adams novel features Indians, counterfeiters posing as shingle makers, lumbering, mysterious men and women, bee-hunters, and "Old Wolverine, the Wolf-Hunter."

Gustave Beaumont de la Bonniniere (1802–1866), wrote a two-volume book, *Marie; ou, l'esclavage aux États-Unis (Marie; or, Slavery in the United States)* (1835; nine later French and Spanish editions) that is not listed as a novel in the *National Union Catalog*, but Albert G. Black in his 1963 *Michigan Novels: An Annotated Bibliography* calls it a romantic novel, and Stanford University Press's 1958 English translation is titled *Marie; or, Slavery in the United States: A Novel of Jacksonian Democracy.*

Marie, the "tragic heroine" (like the mulatto, Julie, in Edna Ferber's twentieth-century *Show Boat*) has a trace of black blood in her ancestry. When she and a white man are forbidden to marry, the couple go to the Saginaw Valley, then a Michigan wilderness; there Marie dies. Beaumont de la Bonniere (1802–1866), the author of several other books on ethnic relationships in America, seems to have intended this book as an attack on American racial prejudice.

Charles Jay (1815–1884) had been a New Jersey newspaper columnist for thirty years before he wrote *My New Home in Northern Michigan and Other Tales* (1874). The book was written, the author said, in a matter of a few weeks. The first chapter describes the narrator's tedious journey by rail and boat to his home in a fruit-growing area of west central Michigan (Oceana County) where his family awaits him. One chapter, "How the 'Old Settler' Settled My Potato Bugs," is a favorite comic tale.

Another tale offers Jay's version of the oft-told siege of Detroit by Pontiac. An imaginary event in the story shows Gladwin as a prisoner in Pontiac's camp, doomed to be burned to death at the stake. A young Indian girl helps him escape.

Marguerite (Lofft) de Angeli (1889–1987) set her book for young readers, *Copper-Toed Boots* (1939), in pioneer days in Lapeer.

Hal L. Cutler's *Ne-Bo-Shone* (1917), by contrast, is the story of Henry Allen who at fifty-two, after his wife's death, goes into the Michigan northwoods (on the Pine River in Lake County) and settles in a log cabin. Later, although he had once been anxious to get far away from civilization, Allen mortgages his land to help pay for a dam across the nearby river and for a power plant for a new town. Cutler in a preface says his story is based on actual people and events.

Pioneer Stories for Young People

Michigan-born and educated Harriet Helen Carr (1899–) set only one of her nine books for teenage girls in her native state. *Where the Turnpike Ends* (1955) begins in 1835, two years before Michigan became a state. On its way west, the Rogers family stops off in Detroit long enough for a meeting with Stevens Thompson Mason, the "Boy Governor." Meanwhile, young Anne Rogers finds romance with the brother of a friend.

Carr began her writing career with Ypsilanti and Detroit newspapers, then wrote for educational journals. In Ypsilanti, she became the first woman editor of the *Ypsilanti Daily Press*.

Elizabeth Howard Mizener (who wrote as Elizabeth Howard) was born in Detroit in 1907, and except for a few childhood years in Chicago, always lived there. She earned a B.A. degree at Ann Arbor in 1930 and did graduate work there and at Wayne State University.

From her family's history, Mizener developed a strong sense of the past. One ancestor was Henry Rutgers for whom Rutgers University is named. Mizener's paternal grandfather, General Henry Rutgers Mizener, fought on the Union side in the Civil War. Her mother's family came to Michigan in 1815. A great-grandfather built the arsenal at Detroit and served in the War of 1812.

Mizener's first novel, *Sabina* (1941), like all her books, was written for older teenage girls. It tells of a sixteen-year-old girl in Detroit as the 1848 Mexican War begins. Both the *New York Times* and the *Springfield [Mass.] Republican* praised the book.[18]

Her next book with a Michigan base, *Summer under Sail* (1947), focuses on a Cleveland, Ohio, girl who spends a summer on her grandfather's sailing ship in the Great Lakes. *North Wind Blows Free* (1949) tells of a northern Michigan farm family whose home is a stop for escaped slaves fleeing to Canada before the Civil War. *Peddler's Girl* (1951) is the story of a Detroit girl and boy who travel with their uncle, a peddler, around Michigan in the 1840s.

Next in time was *Candle in the Night* (1952), which relates Tamsen's trip from Albany to Buffalo by stagecoach, and then on to Detroit by way of Lake Erie. Complications ensue—her boat is caught in two storms and then is shipwrecked. In Detroit, Tamsen endures the antagonism of a new sister-in-law, the British occupation of Detroit in 1812, and Indian attacks.

In *A Star to Follow* (1954), the three Stacey daughters are left in Detroit in 1875 with an aunt to be "finished" while their father takes charge of an Arizona army post. Julia Stacey's stylish wedding takes place in Detroit but the two younger sisters follow their father to Arizona.

A Girl of the North Country (1957) finds mystery and romance in a tiny cabin in northern Michigan in the 1820s. In *Wilderness Venture* (1973), Delia Clark's mother trades their New York farm for unseen wilderness land in northern Michigan after Delia's father dies. On the boat trip to Michigan, family members are the victims of robbery, attempted murder, perverse weather, and other trials and tribulations. Delia is romanced by a young man who owns a schooner.

Mrs. Howard once said her mission was to give the girls of her own time "a feeling of unity and familiarity with the past. . . . Not that those days were perfect, nor the people who lived in them. But there was about everyday life [in that distant past] a certain sturdy morality, a simple surety of right and wrong, a security in family and home life that is good to think of and draw upon in these [latter] days."[19]

Miriam E. Mason's two children's books about pioneer life in Michigan are *Caroline and Her Kettle Named Maud* (1951), which tells of an eight-year-old girl who finds a copper kettle (more valuable than a gun on the Michigan frontier), and its sequel, *Caroline and the Seven Little Words* (1967), which contains this speech, "They're real mean kids on account of living in such a desolate land as Michigan. . . . We're going back to Ohio [where women wear silk dresses and eat with silver spoons]. We hate Michigan. . . . Michigan is nothing but a great big woods full of snakes and spooks and wolves and wildcats and horsethieves."[20]

In contrast with the children in that story, the eleven-year-old heroine in Myna Lockwood's *Delecta Ann: The Circuit Rider's Daughter* (1941), set in 1844, would rather stay in Detroit than go with her father who was to become a circuit rider in Iowa. After all, Detroit had "a theater, a fire-brigade and seventy miles of railroad running clear to Jackson. There was [Mrs. Scott's] female seminary on Franklyn Street right where old Pontiac, only a short time before, tried to drive every white man back across the Alleghenies. Detroit had culture and her father was minister of a church with stained glass windows."[21] Although Elvah, the heroine's older sister went to Philadelphia, Delecta Ann Farrar went to Iowa with her family where she was to have many adventures.

Myna Lockwood said that many of the Detroit people named in the book were actual people and that Delecta Ann Farrar was the actual name of her grandmother, a Detroit native, daughter of Captain John Farrar who lived in Detroit from 1817 to 1874. Moreover, although her story was fictional, it was based on the real Delecta Ann Farrar's move to Iowa as the wife of a Universalist clergyman.[22]

Frances Margaret Fox's (1870–1959) *Little Mossback Amelia* (1939) is set in 1879. Amelia and her parents and other settlers in the Michigan backwoods are called "mossbacks," a derisive term, because, theoretically, like the forest's mossback turtles, their backs are covered with moss from life in the deep forests.

Summary

Michigan's history from 1815 on has attracted a great many novelists and poets, some good and some indifferent, and resulted in a great many books.

The best are Caroline Kirkland and James Fenimore Cooper. Of the two, Kirkland, in this instance a better writer than Cooper on the subject of Michigan, has received the most attention from modern critics. The most prolific writers discussed herein are Helen Hull, Helen Topping Miller, Henry Bedford-Jones, and Elizabeth Howard, the latter an author of books for young girls. An English author, Ray [Rachel] (Costelloe) Strachey, set a novel of pioneer life in Michigan.

To those who question the value of the historical novel—such as those discussed in several chapters in this book—Paul Leicester Ford, a turn-of-the-century historical novelist, observed in 1897 that in fiction an atmosphere could be as historical as an event. He attributed the popularity of historical romances up to that time to the conviction of truth that the mention of real persons, places, and events conveyed to the mind of the reader.[23]

By the end of the nineteenth century, the scope of the historical novel was no longer limited to the handsome and chivalrous hero. Novelists no longer felt constrained to subordinate everything to the narrative. It was more and more possible to present a picture, to report the minutiae of life, to study the locutions and inflections of speech, the inhibitions and ethics of society, the foods eaten, the education demanded, the values recognized, and the institutions founded or subverted.[24]

In 1938, Bernard DeVoto observed that the historical novel had begun following "the preference of the times for realistic writing, psychological inquiry, and social judgment in fiction."[25] Such characteristics can be found in the Michigan historical novels already noted and others to be described in the following chapters on diversity among ethnic groups and logging in Michigan.

CHAPTER IV

DIVERSITY IN THE PENINSULA STATE

Of the 20% of Michigan's population in 1860,born outside the
United States, 60,000 came fromthe British Isles, 39,000 from
the German states,36,500 from Canada, 6,500 from Holland,
and fourcame from the "Sandwich Isles."
—Willis F. Dunbar, *Michigan: A History of the Wolverine State*[1]

In Michigan, as in other states, immigrants settled in rural areas or
in small towns, in mining camps or in city neighborhoods. Later
arrivals sought out those whose language or religion or cultural attitudes were like their own: Poles in Hamtramck, Dutch in Holland,
Frisians in Friesland, Germans in Frankenmuth, and Cornish,
Swedes, and Finns in the Copper Country. Some immigrant groups
tried to retain their ethnic and religious identities; others lost their
ethnic or religious identities in the larger population—the melting
pot concept. At times, there was friction between members of ethnic
or religious groups and the societies in which they located.

As the years passed, writers in Michigan, both members and
nonmembers of ethnic groups, began to write imaginative literature
based on their observations of ethnic behavior, attitudes, and envi-
ronments. In Michigan, the largest number of these novels at first focused on the Dutch and Frisians who, just before the mid-nineteenth
century, emigrated from several regions of The Netherlands to southwestern Michigan. But in the latter half of the twentieth century,
blacks began to get more fictional attention.

Marion Schooland's *A Land I Will Show Thee* (1954) depicts the first emigration taking place because of the loss of The Netherlands potato crop in the 1840s and the state-fostered religious intolerance to a new church that competed with the official state-controlled one.

In Schooland's novel, the leader of these first immigrants and the central figure is the actual Albertus Van Raalte, always referred to as a saintly, godlike dominie. The Dutch people come to southwest Michigan after rejecting areas in neighboring states. The novel focuses on the Berghuis family and the romance between young Anton Berghuis and Anna, who is left behind in The Netherlands. The settlement is made in swampy forested land and for a time the settlers endure hunger, severe winters, and disease. But sawmills and houses are built, and the actual Michigan towns of Holland and Zeeland are founded.

Schooland (1902–), a native of Grand Rapids, earned a B.A. degree at that city's Calvin College in 1934 and an M.A. degree at the University of Michigan in 1943. She is also the author of several books for children and a 1951 biography of Van Raalte.

A novel originally published in The Netherlands in 1898, then translated into English as *The Man in Bearskin* by John H. De Groot in 1925 and by J. Keuning in 1946, is part fiction, part religious tract. Gerrit Kolf, a fictional member of the second Dutch group to settle near the area that later became the site of Holland, is aided by a mysterious figure who turns out to be Gerrit's brother, Dirk. Back in Holland, Dirk had stolen a large amount of money from Gerrit and fled. Eventually, the brothers are reconciled and Dirk becomes a religious convert.

Keuning (1902–) was a professor at Hope College.

Bastian Kruithoff's *Instead of the Thorn* (1941) is, says its author, "an attempt to trace the history of an ideal in the lives of a great people," a small group of settlers in the Holland, Michigan, area from 1840 until after the Civil War. The novel focuses on a couple's relationships from adolescence through parenthood that survive gossip, quarrels, and community dissension. In the background is the endless struggle to convert forest and swampland into farmland, recurring illness and disease, birth and death, love and hate, crime and punishment.

Dirk Gringhuis's *Hope Haven: A Tale of a Dutch Boy and a Girl Who Found a New Home in America* (1947) with illustrations by the author, tells of the founding of Holland, Michigan, in the 1840s. It was not reviewed nationally.

The title of a novel by Mrs. Georgia Atwood (1896–1957), *Free as the Wind* (1942), written under the pseudonym of Dascomb Atwood, comes from an ancient aphorism, "A Frieslander must always be as free as the wind out of a cloud."

The three-generation novel chronicles the Zuppans who emigrate from The Netherlands in 1850. Enduring the usual hardships, family members achieve success in manufacturing and shipping enterprises through hard work and thrift. In 1938, two of the characters visit The Netherlands and run afoul of the Nazis. As a consequence, a third family member changes his mind about U.S. intervention in Europe.

Critics liked the novel, but one, Richard A. Cordell, wondered, "[T]here [are] so many good things in the book . . . [why then is] the general impression not more powerful and stirring[?]" Still, he liked "the sharp portraiture, the accurate historical and geographic sense, and (the best part of the book) the exquisite sketches of The Netherlands landscape and Vermeer-like interiors."[2]

Arnold Mulder (1885–1959) was born in that area of Michigan where towns named Zeeland, Friesland, Holland, Graafschaap, Overisel, and Drenthe speak of the Old World origins of the settlers. He was a newspaper and magazine editor, then from 1929 to 1953 head of the English department at Kalamazoo College. Mulder was the first Michigan novelist to make use of a Dutch background, beginning in 1913 with *The Dominie of Harlem*, a tale of conflict that arises when a city-bred minister comes to serve a rural Christian Reformed Church whose members are bound by traditions and customs brought from the Old World. However, all ends well in this "pretty tale," as a reviewer for *The Nation* called it: "To many readers it will be news to be told of Dutch peasants in twentieth-century America. Their squabbles, social and religious, their condemnation of the use of English as the worst of sins, their struggle against progress and colleges and fresh air, make a pleasant if not a startling narrative."[3]

In *Bram of Five Corners* (1915)—quite possibly an extension of the author's first novel—Mulder introduces a new area of intellectual conflict. In 1902, in a poor rural settlement in southwestern Michigan, five-year-old Bram Meesterling, a sensitive and intelligent boy, dreams of becoming a poet. But at the insistence of an uncle who writes essays for a Dutch-language religious paper, Bram goes to college to "larn for Dominie." Once on the campus, Bram is stirred by secular ideas—evolution; the new humanism that stresses women's rights; and in particular, heredity—the latter deriving from reading

Henrik Ibsen's *Ghosts*. His changing attitudes lead to Bram's *censuur* by his church, and he becomes, like his creator, a newspaper writer.

In Mulder's *The Outbound Road* (1919) Teunis Spykhoven, an illegitimate child, is placed with a couple who hold that cardplaying, dancing, and the theater are sinful, a notion that Teunis cannot accept as he grows older. He fails as a newspaper reporter but eventually emerges as a famous American playwright and poet—a possible projection of Mulder's dream for his own future.

His fourth novel, *The Sand Doctor* (1921), set in the Michigan dune country near the areas of Mulder's other novels, focuses on personal disagreements between Dr. Brian Quentin and his young wife Hallie, and between Dr. Quentin and his wife's brother, a man who preaches the gospel of success so prevalent in the United States in the 1920s. Dr. Quentin takes both a personal and a medical interest in young Barry Larramore, the only son of an iron magnate (a character possibly suggested by Chase Salmon Osborn's *The Iron Hunter* [1919]). Barry has a dual personality—that of a seventeen-year-old and that of a twenty-five-year-old. In the latter personality, he makes love to Quentin's wife. The novel's issues are resolved during a Lake Michigan storm that strikes as Dr. Quentin assists his "old medical prof" in an operation on Larramore's brain. All ends well.

Mulder's nonfiction *Americans from Holland* (1948) earned him a decoration from the government of The Netherlands. He also wrote *The Kalamazoo College Story* (1958).

Joan Geisel Gardner's *Desires of the Heart* (1934) reads more like a religious tract than a novel. It begins like so many motion pictures of the 1930s with a boy meeting a girl and instantly falling in love with her. Complications ensue—she is a deeply religious member of the Christian Reformed Church; he likes movies and dances. However, after an injury blinds him, he joins one of the Dutch-denomination churches. Then, through some improbable coincidences, the two are reunited.

The most significant Michigan writer who used Dutch themes (and an important author on the American scene as well) is David Cornel DeJong (1905–1967). Born in Friesland in the northwestern part of The Netherlands, he came with his parents to Grand Rapids in 1913—a move paralleled by the immigration of the Idema family depicted in his first novel, *Belly Fulla Straw* (1934). After grammar school, he worked for six years to help support his family, then completed high school in two years. He attended the universities of Michigan and Wisconsin, then took a bachelor's degree from Calvin College. He began writing verse during his college years, some of which appeared in *Poetry*. His graduate education at Duke and Brown ended when *Belly Fulla Straw* was published. Of this early period, novelist Alvah C. Bessie wrote, "Astonishingly fertile for so young a writer, DeJong has appeared in almost everyone of the 'little' magazines. He was known through them before the larger magazines accepted him."[4]

Belly Fulla Straw is set in Grand Rapids. Harmen Idema; his wife, Detjen; his two daughters, Ka and Ger (later Americanized to Katie and Gertrude); and his two sons, Rolf and Dirk, do not find the New Jerusalem, which is what local residents call their town. The children, in particular, are taunted by their non-Dutch peers:

Dutchman, Dutchman, belly fulla straw—
Can't say nothin' but "ja," "ja," "ja."

Surviving early personal and financial problems, the family prospers. In the 1930s, but following his wife's death, Idema returns to The Netherlands.

DeJong continued writing poetry and short fiction for *Esquire*, *Harper's Bazaar*, *Redbook*, *Virginia Quarterly Review*, and *Yankee*. In each of the years 1937, 1939, and 1941, one of his stories was selected for the O. Henry Memorial Prize Award volume. His 1940 *Light Sons and Dark* is set on a run-down Michigan farm. Davis, the owner, is shiftless, trivial, and hypocritical. His oldest son, Ben, is a "light" son—affectionate and imaginative like his mother. Sutton, Marius, and Bruce are "dark" sons—cruel, insensate, and cloddish like their father. Joel, another "light" son, comes back to the farm from college determined to help his mother and Ben. But Ben, who has married and become a spendthrift alcoholic, kills himself. Joel goes back to his college town; the father, mother, and Marius leave the farm.

Roy W. Meyer says, "[I]n its stress on the characters' inability to communicate with one another, [the] book resembles [Sherwood Anderson's] *Winesburg, Ohio*," although it is "far inferior" to Anderson's novel.[5] Richard Cordell wrote that the novel reveals "DeJong's true stature as a novelist." Although commenting that the book is "emphatically not for readers who seek a facile cheer as the answer to life's problems," he praised the book as a "haunting novel of human compassion, written with gifted and disciplined craftsmanship."[6]

DeJong returned to his immigrant experience in his third Michigan novel, *Two Sofas in the Parlor* (1952), in which a family has problems adapting to its neighbors. Renzel, a quiet sensitive boy in his thirteen year, is caught in the middle between his mother's Old

World moral standards and those he finds outside his home. Johannes, the more interesting character, changes his name to John, falls in with a gang of unprincipled youths, becomes involved with a married woman, and finally leaves home for the wild West. Edward J. Fitzgerald said DeJong's "deeply moving re-creation of [the children's] development adds depth and meaning to a delightful picture of family life in the misnamed 'melting pot' that was America early in this century."[7]

Except for *Somewhat Angels* (1945)—discussed later (see p.238)—DeJong's later novels are not set in Michigan. He has said that his "first books were mainly about [his] native Holland [The Netherlands], only because [his] publishers insisted on a Dutch theme."[8]

DeJong is also the author of *With a Dutch Accent* (1944), an autobiography of his first sixteen years; a volume of short stories; and two volumes of verse. DeJong's work is evaluated in Cornelius John Ter Maat's University of Michigan doctoral dissertation, *Three Novelists and a Community: A Study of American Novelists with Dutch Calvinist Origins* (1962).

A 1942 film, *Seven Sweethearts*, utilized a tulip festival in a Michigan Dutch community and a slender plot: the youngest of seven daughters of a hidebound Hollander wants to marry a newspaper reporter covering the festival, but family tradition says she must wait until her eldest sister has wed. Despite a number of complications, the film managed to solve her dilemma in ninety-eight minutes.

Fiction about Other Ethnic Groups

Cecile Hulse Matschat's *Preacher on Horseback* (1940) is based on events in an ancestor's career as a circuit rider in the Mohawk Valley of New York (where she was reared), and in Michigan after the Civil War. Most of the novel is taken up with the problems faced by a preacher, a Hungarian, Janos, and Rica, his Dutch wife, in the logging area northeast of Muskegon.

Matschat (1895–1976) was also an artist and the author of fifteen non-Michigan books. One, *Suwannee River*, won a 1938 Literary Guild Award.

In June 1938, Vivian LaJeunesse Parsons, a French Canadian student at the University of Michigan, received an Avery Hopwood second prize of $1,000 for her *Lucien* (1937), which is set in Trois-Rivières, Quebec. A second novel, *Not without Honor* (1941), set in a mining town in the Upper Peninsula in the 1890s focuses on racial tensions between French Canadians and Italians.

Ann Pinchot's *Hour upon the Stage* (1929), set in the fictional Lake Michigan town of Muskenaw, is primarily a chronicle of Jewish immigrants from Poland in the 1890s. A second theme is the town itself as it grows from a logging camp to a full-fledged city at the end of the 1920s owing to the enterprise of a young man who builds an industrial empire.

Pinchot was born in New York City in 1910, grew up in Muskegon, and married Ben Pinchot, a civil engineer, who often collaborated with her on her fiction.

Karl Edwin Harriman (1875–1935), born in Ann Arbor, worked for the *Detroit Journal* for a year, matriculated at the University of Michigan in 1896, then left to write for the *Detroit Free Press* and the *Detroit Tribune*. In 1903 he became a founding editor of *Redbook* and an associate editor of *Pilgrim*. By 1900, his short fictions were appearing in *Era*, *Lippincott's*, the *Arena*, and *Harper's Weekly*. Six of these stories, which focus on working-class Detroit Poles struggling to survive in Detroit, were collected in *The Homebuilders* (1902).

Dr. Newton G[eorge] Thomas's *The Long Winter Ends* (1941) is set in the Copper Country in the winter of 1900–1901. Jim Holman, a Cornishman (like his creator), has come to work in the Michigan copper mines because the Cornwall mines of England are no longer profitable. As "the long winter" of his first year ends, Holman learns that his wife, left behind in Cornwall, has given birth to a son. The novel has a fine display of the Cornish idiom and customs.

Caroline R. Stone's *Inga of Porcupine Mine* (1942) tells of a girl whose mother is Finnish and whose father, an iron miner, is Cornish. Inga makes and sells pasties, a Cornish staple, and picks and sells wild berries to earn money for tuition at an art school. But when her father develops an eye infection from working underground, Inga gives the money to pay for a needed operation.

Norman Matson's *Day of Fortune* (1928) is a semiautobiographical novel of a Norwegian family in Grand Rapids based on Matson's own boyhood. Novelist Alice Beal Parsons called the book "the most interesting novel I have read for many months [written by] a new writer with major possibilities."[9] At the time of writing the novel, Matson (1893–1965) was married to Susan Glaspell, author and playwright and an important person in the development of the theater in America in the twentieth century.

Johann G. R. Baner and his daughter Skulda (1897–1964) were minor literary voices for the Upper Peninsula and their old country Swedish culture. In 1923, Johann published a collection of verses,

Namesakes, his purpose to "associate legend with his region." The influence of Longfellow's *Song of Hiawatha* is obvious.

Skulda Baner, though blind from glaucoma, wrote verse as Asabard, taught in a rural North Dakota school, worked in radio, and wrote several other books. Of these, the best is *Latchstring Out* (1944), whose heroine is Stumpastina, a Swedish-American child of seven or eight living in a Swedish mining camp in Michigan's Upper Peninsula. Carl Wittke said that the book, although "not great literature is a charming tale about Swedes who live in a [grim iron] mining town in Upper Michigan at the turn of the century. . . . It is full of good-natured nostalgia for old Swedish customs and traditions imported by the early immigrants."[10]

Robert Gessner (1907–1968) was born in Escanaba, the model for his Chippewa City in his *Here Is My Home* (1941)—a novel about prejudice that develops from a pioneer logging town to a city—even as America is taking steps to ensure "a world safe for democracy."

Characters in the novel are Bernie Straus, a Jewish immigrant who works in his uncle Jasper Goldschmidt's dry goods and notions store; Jasper Goodman, an ex-logger, now the town's richest man; Alfred Bolitho, angered because Bernie has married his daughter; Ogden Norris, a crusading newspaper owner; and the Ku Klux Klan. Critics gave the book mixed reviews.[11]

Gessner, a 1929 graduate of the University of Michigan with a 1930 master's degree from Columbia University, became a teacher and screenwriter. Neither of his two later books were set in Michigan.

Harold Waldo set *Stash of the Marsh Country* (1921) near Detroit (in the marsh area) and also on the Michigan-Indiana border near South Bend. Stashlaf Plazarski, an ambitious Polish boy, becomes, in turn, a baseball player, an iron worker, a reporter, a playwright, a producer, and a miner. At novel's end, he is in a World War I army training camp.

Novelist Rupert Brooke saw the novel's lack of a smooth narrative flow as an advantage: "The novel is like a kaleidoscope, beautiful bits of glass, suddenly shifting to one astonishing pattern and then another. The people are very real and the scenes shown with a vividness of flashes of lightning."[12]

Leonard Cline (1893–1929) was born in Bay City, Michigan. After graduation from the University of Michigan in 1913, he became a poet, a dramatist, a literary and music critic, and a newspaper reporter. At the *Baltimore Sun*, he wrote a Pulitzer Prize-winning story. Cline died in his early thirties after serving a prison term for killing a man while in a fit of anger.

God Head (1925), the first of his three novels, is his best work. Paulus Kempf, a onetime surgeon and sculptor turned Wobbly (member of the Industrial Workers of the World [IWW]), comes to a Finnish copper-mining community as a labor agitator to foment a strike among socialist-oriented Finnish miners. (Cline's plot has an actual 1913 parallel in attempts of the Western Federation of Miners to unionize underground workers of Finnish and Italian origin on the Keweenaw Peninsula.) Ill and forced to hide in the woods after a riot, Kempf is found by a fellow Finn, Karl, and nursed back to health by Karl's wife, Aino, who tells him folktales of Finnish gods. The tales lead Paulus to think of himself as a Nietzschean superman. He seduces Aino, kills her husband, and carves a singing god from a granite projection on a nearby cliff. Critics liked the novel and the quality of the writing, but were less impressed by Cline's word inventions. One labeled them "verbal exhibitionism."[13]

Virginia Evans's *The Lovely Season* (1952) has three themes—racial, social, and ethnic prejudices—and their somewhat disastrous consequences for several family members. But all ends well in this overly manipulated novel. Evans was a student of Roy Cowden's at the University of Michigan in the late 1940s.

Niven Busch's *The Hate Merchant* (1953) is only in part set in Detroit, but that part is significant. Busch's protagonist, Gaspar D. Splane, recalls Father Coughlin and other rabid merchandisers of racist and ethnic propaganda in the 1930s. The climax of this novel comes on Detroit's Belle Isle when Splane's antiblack demagoguery, supported by a Detroit industrialist, catalyzes a mob into terrorist actions. Busch (1903–), an author of short stories, novels, and a score of film scripts, was not a Michigan native.

Leo Litwak's *Waiting for the News* (1969) is a story of labor troubles in Detroit in 1939. Truck driver Jake Gottlieb, forty-seven years old, models himself on Eugene Victor Debs, Vladimir Lenin, and Judah Maccabeus. Jake's employer, Kravitz, is anti-union, whereas Jake is pro-union. Although Jake knows his haranguing of his employer's drivers will lead to a beating (or, as it happens, his murder) he persists. Eventually, Jake's sons, one a student of the University of Michigan, kill the man who murdered their father.

Litwak (1924–), a Detroit native, modeled the book to some extent on his father's career as a union organizer. He attended the University of Michigan before graduating from Wayne State University and is a teacher of creative writing, the author of one other (non-Michigan) novel, short stories, and journal articles.

Vera Lebedeff, herself a White Russian (an emigré from the Byelorussian Soviet Socialist Republic, southwest of Moscow), set her *The Heart Returneth* (1943) in a White Russian community in Detroit—a close-knit metropolitan colony of pre-Bolshevik immigrants and post-Bolshevik emigrés. A former Russian prince who works in an automobile factory is the central character of Lebedeff's novel. She pictures the conflict between the two groups as the war in Europe begins. Some support the Nazis, hoping that they will chase the Bolsheviks out of Russia so that the old czarist world can return. But as the Nazis seem about to overwhelm the Russians, sympathies change. Mother Russia is more important than lesser loyalties.

Robert Traver's episodic collection, *Danny and the Boys* (1951)—like his *Troubleshooter* (published earlier in 1944), *Trout Madness* (1960), and *Trout Magic* (1974)—depicts a procession of Upper Peninsula characters—Canadians, Cornish miners, Finns, and others—and a fascination with fishing. Whereas the episodes in the last three books cited are mostly factual (though the facts are often shaped to suit the author's purposes in telling a good tale), *Danny and the Boys* seems fictional. Danny and the four "boys" take refuge in an old logging camp where they can do as they please as long as what they do not do is work.

In his preface, Traver apologizes for any "social significance" that has managed to sneak into his book. He need not have—this book, like the others mentioned here, is good reading.

"Traver" was actually John D. Voelker (1903–1991) of Ishpeming. Educated at Northern Michigan College in Marquette, he took a law degree at Ann Arbor, then became the Marquette county attorney and a Michigan supreme court justice (1957–1966) before retiring to write books.

Max Apple was born in Grand Rapids in 1941 and matriculated at the University of Michigan, where he won a minor Hopwood Award for fiction in 1963, then became a college professor. His one Michigan-related book so far—*Zip: A Novel of the Left and the Right* (1978)—tells us more about Apple than it does about Michigan. *Zip* is largely fantasy as it tells how Ira Goldstein, "a nice Jewish boy," first pounds lead from used automobile batteries in a Detroit factory, then becomes a manager of Jesus, a middleweight boxer from Puerto Rico. Jesus is a thoroughly indoctrinated Marxist; Ira ends up in jail. Critics liked Apple's display of comic imagination and his playfulness with language but were not otherwise much impressed.[14]

Vern Sneider's (1916–) *Teahouse of the August Moon* (1951), set on Okinawa, won a Pulitzer Prize and was dramatized and filmed. "Uncle Bosko," the one Michigan-based fiction of this descendant of a century-old Michigan family—published in a short story collection, *A Long Way from Home* (1951)—relates the visit of a Russian to his Polish relatives in Hamtramck, family members he had not seen in two decades.

Ruth Seid (1913–), a Brooklyn-born native of Cleveland, was the author of several novels and numerous short stories and articles, including *Wasteland*, which won the 1946 Harper Award of $10,000.

Anna Teller (1960) is the only one of Seid's books set in Michigan. Anna, seventy-four, is a Hungarian-born Jew who managed to survive the Nazi atrocities. She comes to Detroit in 1956 to live with her son, Emil, and his wife, Abby. Anna—soon called "the General" because of her insistence on European manners, customs, and ways—creates conflicts, but eventually Emil, his family, and friends come to depend on her for solutions to their problems.

With the opening of copper and iron mines in the Upper Peninsula, there was an influx from Europe of Italians, Swedes, Cornish, Croatians, and Finns. A descendant of the Finns, Heino "Hap" Puotinen, was the author of *Kool Kat from Kopper Kontri, and Other Finnish Dialect Verses* in 1968. These verses, poking fun at the Finnish settlers, may have encouraged the efforts of Jingo Viitala Vachon (1918–), who acquired some local fame with stories that first appeared in the *L'Anse Sentinel*. Vachon was reared in a two-story log cabin her father built in the Upper Peninsula woods in 1900.[15]

Her books, *Tall Timber Tales* (1973), *Sagas from Sisula* (1975), and *Finnish Fibbles* (1979) are collections of often earthy homespun dialect tales of life in a small backwoods Finnish community where such town names as Toivola, Elo, Tapiola, and Nisula intermix with Ahmeek and Ontonagon, Houghton and Hancock, Lac La Belle, Bete Grise, and Assinins—names that demonstrate the truly cosmopolitan mixture in a small geographical area.

In 1936, James Cloyd Bowman (1880–1961) and Margery Bianco published *Tales from a Finnish Tupa* using materials taken either from *Fables of a Finnish Nation* or else collected in the Upper Peninsula by Gwinn resident, Aili Kolemainen Johnson, a descendant of Finns. In the 1940s, Johnson published several "Finnish Labor Songs" that she had collected in Finnish enclaves in the Upper Peninsula. One of these illustrates the folklore that led many Europeans to migrate to America:

Over nine seasons
I flew to a strange land

Where the trees are scarlet and the earth is blue;
There the mountains are butter,
The cliffs are pork;
The hills are sugar-cakes;
And the heather is honey.[16]

In 1913, Finnish copper miners (and others) in the Copper
Country struck to force the Boston mine owners to recognize their
union, the Western Federation of Miners. Mrs. Johnson reports that
these "black Finns" were reviled as scabs and worse:

Woodenhead, wretched furry foot,
Woodenhead, trouble on this earth,
Woodenhead, when the backlash sings,
He plods along in all his muck, the Woodenhead.[17]

In 1975, Bowman and Bianco published *Tales from a Finnish Fireside* from materials translated by Aili Kolemainen Johnson.
     In 1970, Lawrence M. Joseph won the major Hopwood Award
for verse. His 1983 novel, *Shouting at No One,* which includes one of
these verses, focuses on his immigrant Lebanese family, living far
from its native hills in a crime-ridden area of Detroit. Joseph, says
Laurence Goldstein, "attributes his awakening as a poet to the 1967
[Detroit] riot [to] his father's later near murder by a thief, [to] the killing of a childhood friend, and [to] all the other psychic desolation of
a Detroit upbringing."[18]
     Harry Milostan's *Folksy Fables* (1984) is a collection of Polish folk-
tales centering on the Great Lakes.

Michigan Literature by and about Blacks

Walter H. Stowers (1859–?) and William H. Anderson (1858–),
using the pseudonym Sanda, published *Appointed: An American Novel*
(1894), a story of black-white relationships set largely in Detroit, "the
beautiful City of the Straits," and Michigan. Seth Stanley, twenty-
seven, makes a friend of John Saunders, an Afro-American who is a
steward and cabin boy on the yacht of Seth's father. Seth later accompanies Saunders on a trip down the Mississippi to see for himself
what the "colored situation" is. But in New Orleans, Saunders is
murdered by an angry mob. The novel has been described as the
"first novel to treat peonage, convict labor, lynching, disenfranchise-

ment and segregation as aspects of a systematic repression."[19] It was reprinted in 1977.

Black As Night (1958) by Chicago-born Daniel D. Nern (1926–) is a story of violence in the lives of a black family who leave Atlanta for Detroit after their daughter, Daisy, is raped and temporarily blinded by three white men and their son, Willie, kills a man in a quarrel. In Detroit, the family faces new problems—race riots and attacks on blacks. But Daisy's eyesight is restored, and the novel ends on the note of the family's determination to survive.

Al Young's *Snakes: A Novel* (1970) is at first glance another novel of adolescence, an all-too-familiar genre in recent years. But this story of "MC"—a boy partly reared in Mississippi, where he comes to have a feeling for blues music, but mostly reared in Detroit by an understanding, well-portrayed grandmother who has taken over for his parents after their deaths in an automobile accident—is more than a novel of adolescence. "MC," an aspiring musician, is contrasted with Champ, a boy on his way to a life of drug dependency and crime.

A distinguishing characteristic of the book is the narrator's two voices: one, black street language that comes off rhythmically and naturally—and with a good deal of humor; the other is a more conventional English. Martin Levin liked the book and its style.[20] But Josephine Hendin thought the novel was an emotionally arid, tepid success story "whose narrator was too thick-skinned to realize how cramped he is."[21] Young said:

> [I] tried to go beyond the old socio-racial cliches and formulae that the average reader has not only come to expect but to *demand* from contemporary black novelists [and] . . . to construct what might be called a prose-movie, centered in the emerging consciousness of a black teenager out of the urban Midwest, Detroit, who is more concerned with the meaning of life than with being either black or a musician or "one of the boys" or "hip." I hoped also to capture some of the more elusive and lyrical rhythms and melodies of Afro-American speech.[22]

Of Young's eight other titles, *Who Is Angelina?* (1975) is the only one with any Michigan background. After a California fortune-teller tells Angelina Green that she is "lost," she goes first to Mexico, where she has an affair with a drug and diamond dealer, then to Detroit, where her father is recovering from a bullet in his lung. Angelina finally becomes a teacher and a believer in transcendental meditation. A reviewer said that Young renovates "urban blues, race, the need for roots and love . . . with a fresh aspect."[23]

Al Young (1939–) was born in Mississippi and spent four years (1957–1961) at the University of Michigan. He has been a free-lance musician, a teacher of creative writing, a poet, and an author of articles and short stories. His home is in California.

Barbara Wilson Tinker's *When the Fire Reaches Us* (1970) was written only a short time after the Detroit riots of 1967. The narrator is Danny Sands, who has a newsstand on Park and Woodward and lives on Pine Street near its intersection with Thompson—an area where only one house survived the riots. The novel begins with a description of Danny's neighborhood as it once was—all black, except for one Chinese woman who owned a restaurant.

"Even in flames," said a reviewer, "Tinker's Detroit is like a quiet Southern town, filled with decent, gentle people. Even Maybelle, the prostitute, is a solid working girl. . . . All of Tinker's characters are ladies and gentlemen who, though they feel themselves victims of white atrocities, never lose their Christian charity [even after a white policeman murders a black child.]"[24]

A reviewer called Terry McMillan's first novel, *Mama* (1987), "a Great Lakes version of *The Color Purple*."[25] After ordering her husband to leave, Mildred Peacock of Point Haven supports her five children by taking factory jobs, doing house cleaning, conducting rent parties, drawing welfare checks, and occasionally prostituting herself. A second reviewer said that the novel "distinguishes itself by its exuberant comic sensibility. When life presses in on Mildred in the form of bill collectors, police and nosey neighbors, she presses right back."[26]

Other novels by or about Michigan blacks are in chapters 14 and 15.

The Black Theater in Detroit

Black repertory companies—the Robeson Players, university theaters, and others—began operating in the 1930s in Detroit. In the 1950s, groups such as the Rapa House Writers and Drama Associates tried to raise black consciousness with plays that appealed to "the rising tide of communal militancy"[27] and that rebelled against the historic depiction of blacks on the American stage. In 1964, playwright Woodie King, Jr., David Rambeau, and Clifford Frazier founded Detroit's Concept East Theater, a center for black drama and arts. Later, Ron Milner opened the "Spirit of Shango," a community-based theater where plays by black writers were produced. Milner said it was "[to] be a theater having to do with love of one's self, and one's personal, national, and international family; with wariness and hatred of one's personal, national and international enemies; with, ideally, points as how to break their grip and splatter their power."[28]

Milner's contributions to this genre include *Who's Got His Own*, in which a black mother learns that her daughter has had an intimate relationship with a well-to-do white man that has led to an abortion; *The Monster, These Three*, and *What the Wine Sellers Buy* (1974), the latter a morality play[29] in which a young black resists the temptation to become a procurer for a black pimp who wants to seduce the young man's attractive girlfriend. This play won national acclaim. Other Milner plays are *The Warning: A Theme for Linda* (1970), in which a pregnant black discovers her own womanhood and the meaning of black manhood, and *Checkmates* (1987), a comedy that contrasts the lifestyles and philosophies of two black couples who inhabit the same house—an older couple downstairs; the younger, "yuppie" couple upstairs.

Checkmates, with playwright Woodie King, Jr., as coproducer, began its career at the Inner City Cultural Center in Los Angeles, moved across the city to the Westwood Playhouse, then played in Chicago, Washington, D.C., Atlanta, and San Francisco before moving to New York City's 46th Street Theater, where it closed in late 1988. Most of the Big Apple's critics praised the play, the direction of Woodie King, Jr., and the acting of Ruby Dee, Paul Winfield, Marsha Jackson, and Denzel Washington, but apparently the play's budget of $100,000 a week was prohibitive. Milner's plays have also been presented at New York City's Vivian Beaumont Theater, in Lincoln Center, and the American Place Theater as well as on European stages.

Ron Milner (1938–), a native of Detroit, has won both Rockefeller and John Hay Whitney fellowships. With Woodie King, Jr., a fellow black playwright, he edited *Black Drama Anthology* (1972). Among the plays in this collection is Elaine Jackson's *Toe Jam*, which dramatizes the changing attitudes of an unmarried black woman toward herself and black men as she learns she is pregnant and has an abortion.

Ron Zuber, also from Detroit, is the author of *Three X Love*, a poetic drama that is a paean to the black mother. Philip Hayes Dean's *The Owl Killer*—set in a small city with an automobile factory—tells of a young man, son of a factory worker, who kills and stuffs owls—and who also murders a man in an attempted robbery.

However, Dorothy H. Lee, in a 1986 essay, said that since the 1970s, "audiences for Black theater have diminished" and that only two of thirteen theater groups active in 1981 had survived. But

Milner, Earl Smith of the Black Theater Program at Wayne State University as well as Von Washington and James R. Faulkner of the Afro-American Studio Theater continued to be optimistic about the future of drama by and about blacks.[30]

Summary

Several Michigan ethnic groups have been the subject of novels and plays by Michigan and non-Michigan authors, including many black authors and playwrights. Of the authors discussed in this chapter, David Cornel DeJong is the most significant to date, but some young black authors show promise for the future.

There are other Michigan books with ethnic or racial elements, but because their primary emphasis is on other themes, they are discussed in other chapters.

CHAPTER V

"TIMBER-R-R-R!"

Some love to roam the dark sea foam,
Where the wild winds whistle free,
But a chosen land in a forest band
And a life in the woods for me.
                    —John W. Fitzmaurice, *The Shanty Boy*[1]

Many of us associate the first pioneers in the Midwest with the log cabin—indeed, the Abraham Lincoln image lingers on. In those Michigan novels of pioneer life discussed earlier, cutting down trees and building log shelters is a frequent topic.

But the log cabin was not a practical concept. Most were too small to provide comfort and—as Caroline Kirkland wrote—were often infested with rodents, reptiles, and insects. Moreover, the westward migration of large numbers of settlers to the treeless prairies led to a need for lumber for stick or frame houses, barns, and sheds.

These houses required long straight boards that could be economically produced; that could be shipped efficiently by wagon, rail, or water; and that could be easily moved about, sawed, and nailed.

In the Middle West, two early major sources of such boards were both the Lower Peninsula (north of an imaginary line connecting Port Huron and Muskegon) and the Upper Peninsula—these areas were covered with a nearly impenetrable forest of trees—the pineries.

In the southern part of Michigan, there were other stands of pine, and also stands of oak and walnut that could be harvested and converted into furniture the settlers needed—many had had to leave much of their household furniture back East.

The popular history of the logging of those vast forests in only a few decades has been colorfully and fairly accurately told in Stewart Holbrook's *Holy Old Mackinaw* (1938), a book as fascinating as many novels. His story begins with the 1837 founding in Kalamazoo County of "the brand new sawmill town of Augusta, Michigan . . . by men of the old sawmill town of Augusta, Maine."[2]

Holbrook also includes logging folklore under such rubrics as "Sin in the Pineries," noting that "the legend of the 'Seney stockades' " would not down but had "appeared only recently" in one of Hollywood's many epics of lumberjacks and of timberlands.[3] He adds that the attitudes of loggers toward the pleasures offered in these "hell holes" was reflected in such loggers' songs as "The Flat River Girl":

Then adieu to Flat River. For me there's no rest;
I'll shoulder my peavey and I'll go out west.
I'll go to (old Seney) some pleasures to find,
And I'll leave my own Flat River darling behind.[4]

The first book-length fiction about logging Michigan forests is John W. Fitzmaurice's *The Shanty Boy; or, Life in a Lumber Camp* (1889), subtitled *Being Pictures in the Pine Woods in Discriptions* [sic], *Tales, Songs and Adventures in the Lumbering Shanties of Michigan.*

In his preface, Fitzmaurice says that he had written the book "to instruct and amuse the" lumberjacks and that "nearly every class of work has been sung and told, except the labor of the pine woods" (p. 156).

Fitzmaurice was an ex-newspaper editor who had been employed by a doctor to work as a hospital agent in lumber camps north of Houghton Lake, a necessary occupation because logging was dangerous work. If loggers survived the long winter lumbering seasons without accident or illness, they were likely to be beaten in brawls or robbed in the sawmill villages' hell holes where they ventured with their pay for the winter's work. One *Shanty Boy* chapter tells of Silver Jack who died in a logjam, leaving behind a pregnant wife and baby to mourn him.

In the evening in the shanties where the loggers slept, those who had any energy left after a long, hard day at work would dance jigs and reels. For those with less energy, there were songs:

This winter in the woods, my boys,
Will be the last for Danny.
I'll build a log house with my "stake,"
And buy a grand piano.
My Kit will sing and play all day,
And I'll rock the baby;
I'll always be a shanty boy,
But Kit will be a lady.[5]

Fitzmaurice does not mention any Paul Bunyan tales or lore.

Ernest J. Petersen's two novels, *North of Saginaw Bay* (1952) and its sequel, *The White Squaw* (1954), both published by the Tall Timber Press in Sandlake, are set in the 1870s. In the first novel, a fourteen-year-old lad, refusing to accept the verdict that his father's death was accidental, sets out on his own to solve the mystery. Francis X. Scannell, Michigan State Librarian, said that the novels present "an authentic portrayal of the people and situations of the early timbering settlements of the Saginaw Valley." E[arl] "Doc" C[lifton] Beck wrote that Petersen might have been "an amateur writer, but he is no amateur woodsman. His commas may not lie in the right spots but his rollways do."[6]

Elia W[ilkinson] Peattie's *The Beleaguered Forest* (1901) is set in the Lower Peninsula's pine forests. Although a logging camp is the locale for much of the action, it is a woman's story, and the often lyrical tone is not well suited to the usual strenuous activities of the camp.

Regina Grey, a "blithe spirit," marries a wealthy lumberman she meets by chance, only to discover that his occasional moroseness is a symptom of a severe mental illness that at times puts her life in danger. At one point, disagreeing with her husband about cutting down the forests, she sounds a note that will occur in later novels about logging in Michigan, "See how [the 'lordly pines'] fall," [Regina] cries. "At this rate, in a little while there will be no trees left!" (p. 263). Her husband dies; Regina survives.

Elia Wilkinson Peattie (1862–1935) was born in Kalamazoo, became a pioneer Chicago newspaperwoman and an author of children's stories and novels. She married Robert Peattie, a fellow journalist, who like her and a number of other Michigan writers had moved to Chicago. They were the parents of Donald Culross Peattie, who, with his wife, Louise Redfield Peattie, came to be well-known American authors, their work often reflecting Elia Peattie's naturalist sympathies. Elia Wilkinson Peattie, her son, and his wife were the authors of more than ninety books.

Stewart Edward White (1873–1946) was one of three popular and prolific authors born in Michigan who began writing novels of outdoor life at the turn of the century. Born in Grand Rapids, he spent his boyhood in a Michigan milltown where his father was a lumberman. After four years in California, White returned to Grand Rapids to complete high school, then took a degree at the University of Michigan.

When not in school, he was in the woods studying bird life or sailing on Lake Michigan. His first publication was "The Birds of Mackinac Island." Following a fruitless search for gold in the Black Hills of South Dakota and law study at Columbia University, he took a writing course from Brander Matthews. A short story, "A Man and His Dog," was the first of many that he sold to magazines of popular fiction.

After writing two novels that used his Black Hills experiences, he turned to the white pine country of the north end of the Lower Peninsula for *The Blazed Trail* (1902). Unlike Fitzmaurice's *Shanty Boy,* which focuses on the experiences of the loggers and logging camp workers, White's novel focuses on the bosses. It narrates the conflict between Harry Thorpe, an honest lumberman, and a group of loggers who are also timber thieves determined to drive him out of the woods, and it also tells of the concurrent romance of Thorpe with Hilda Farrand.

The Blazed Trail emphasizes the themes of the red blood and strenuous traditions of that time as well as of outdoors life. In 1903, novelist F. Churchill Williams defined the term "red blood" as a physical characteristic that separated men from mollycoddles. He noted readers' rejection of "emasculated fiction" and their growing taste for "red blood in fiction," citing in particular the books of Stewart Edward White among writers born in Michigan. This appeal, significant "because it marks positively the beat of a healthy pulse," lay in fiction "which is infused with 'red blood'—the red blood that stimulates men to the vigorous exercise of body and mind in the making of a place for themselves in the working world." Such men were "the measure of the plain, the torrent, the mountain. The length of their stride, the power of their arms, determine their greatness."[7]

The terms *red blood* or *red bloodedness* emphasize the manly qualities of productive workers in contrast with the blue bloods of the nonworking class—the aristocracy or moneyed people, regarded in this context as nonproductive parasites.

Historians have pointed out that these traditions owed much to the popularity of then U.S. President Theodore Roosevelt, an advocate of outdoor life, strenuousness, and red bloodedness. Grant C. Knight said that Roosevelt's "reputation as an outdoor environmentalist was an encouragement to the nature writer and to the novelists [of the Great Outdoors], and it is not merely coincidental that the number of such writers during his presidency was striking."[8]

A second theme in White's novel is that of the relationship between religious faith and financial success, "The duty of success was to [Thorpe] one of the loftiest of abstractions, for it measured the degree of a man's efficiency in the station to which God had called him" (p. 404).

Hilda Farrand, the novel's romantic interest, must compete with this concept for Thorpe's heart, "[T]hough it seems that White intended to show Thorpe's idea of success fused at the end of [the novel] with Hilda's idea of love as the highest human motive, yet the reader cannot but feel that it is Thorpe's creed which triumphs."[9]

For all that, in the end Thorpe recognizes that no man can afford to live for himself and in himself too long.[10] Forced to choose between saving the life of a logger or saving thousands of dollars worth of logs, White makes the humane choice.

An important aspect of this novel is that it is based on White's observations as one of the last naturalists to see the Michigan forests in all their primeval grandeur and to write about what he saw. John Curtis Underwood, a contemporary critic, said, "*The Blazed Trail* . . . chronicles an era and a locale which are passing . . . [and which] embodies a spirit that has not died, and never will, as long as men, like the writer, and the men and women he represents, are born and bred on American soil."[11]

John T. Flanagan admired the novel "despite the author's inability to integrate his exposition and his narrative. . . . The exposition of logging is the best thing in the volume, but it does not contribute materially to the art of the narrative."[12]

The Blazed Trail has gone through nine editions. The last in 1968 was published as an example of "American novels of muckraking propaganda and social protest"—concepts that White probably did not have in mind as he wrote.

In 1903, White collected several of his *McClure's* short stories in *Blazed Trail Stories*. Four of them—"The Riverman," "The Foreman," "The Scaler," and "The River Boss"—describe several specialized occupations necessary for logging a forest. In each story, White's central fictional character must resolve a conflict. "The Fifth Way" has nothing to do with lumbering; it is a tale of poetic justice, a type of short story that O. Henry (William Sydney Porter) was making popular at that time.

In 1908, following several books with non-Michigan settings, White used the Lower Peninsula forests for *The Riverman*, a sequel to *the Blazed Trail*, possibly, an expansion of the story in *Blazed Trail Stories*. The year is 1872 and the central character, Jack Orde, is a species of man that is disappearing.

A young New Yorker, Joseph Newmark, who has witnessed an example of Orde's business abilities, proposes that he and Orde enter into a lumbering partnership. The enterprise prospers and Orde marries. In the wedding ceremony these words are spoken, "There comes a time in the affairs of every household when a man must assert himself as the ruler . . . he may depend on a woman's judgment, experience and knowledge, but when it comes to the crises . . . then, unless the man does the deciding, he is lost forever." White believed in a man's world. [13]

After eight years of partnership, Orde foresees the end of logging in Michigan and decides to move to California. But first he must circumvent Newmark, who is trying to steal Orde's share of the business. Not too incidentally, Orde himself had always been willing to circumvent legal technicalities and overlook shady practices on the part of his subordinates. This had helped him succeed. [14]

White's *The Adventures of Bobby Orde* (1908, with subsequent reprints) tells of Jack Orde's son as he grows up in a Michigan lumber milltown from 1879 to 1900. Bobby has a number of youthful adventures and helps clear a neighbor of a charge of murder.

In *The Rules of the Game* (1909), Bobby begins his lumbering career in his father's Chicago office. Also an outdoors man, he is soon in the woods, where he undertakes the work of cleaning up the Michigan operations. Later, in California, he takes over 400 million feet of timber purchased for him years before by Jack Orde.

Cynthia Dodge Crawford's play, *The Tall Trees*—written for Michigan Week 1956—is set in a Michigan logging camp in the 1880s and includes several authentic old lumberjack songs.

St. George Rathbone (Harrison Adams, 1854–1938), a prolific author of stories for older boys, set *Campmates in Michigan; or, With Pack and Paddle in the Pine Woods* (1913) in the Upper Peninsula. The three campmates are Dolph, son of a Cincinnati millionaire; Teddy, son of an area lumberman; and Amos, "a real Michigan boy" who has been raised in logging camps. They have numerous rough-and-tumble adventures typical of novels of this kind and time period, but they always survive.

For the modern reader, the tale suffers from too much editorializing and sermonizing. Nevertheless, at its conclusion, the author promises the breathless readers that more adventures of the boys are in the works.

William George Puddefoot (1842–1925), an Englishman who had migrated to Tecumseh, Michigan, and Isaac Ogden Rankin (1852–1936), a Princeton graduate, said that their *Hewers of Wood: A Story of the Michigan Pine Forests* (1903) drew on the memory of Mary Jane Dobson Puddefoot, William's mother.

The novel has two major strands: the marital adventures of Albert De Wette, a Dunker minister in a pioneer Michigan village, and those of his motherless niece, Hilda, who angers De Wette by eloping at seventeen with a ne'er-do-well. The latter, of course, reforms.

Two parallel story lines concern Maggie McClean, a young woman much put upon by misadventures and evil men, and "Dare Devil" Kate Deverell, a saloon operator in a lumber town. The novel suffers from obviousness and overuse of coincidences.

Myron D. Orr's *Rubberlines: Mystery Romance of Cass River Valley* (serialized in the *Michigan Farmer* [October 17, 1931 to January 16, 1932]) is set in the southwest part of Michigan's "thumb" at a time when timber barons were disregarding straight property lines as they cut timber, a practice called round cornering.

Orr, from Port Huron, a "fifth-generation Michiganite," was a prolific author and, among other occupations, a lawyer and an English teacher in a college at Alpena.

In Samuel Merwin's 1903 *The Whip Hand* (first serialized in *Success*), an independent Michigan lumberman fights the head of a lumber trust. Merwin (1874–1936), an associate editor of *Success*, was the author of twenty-seven books, three in collaboration with Henry Kitchell Webster.

The Red Keggers (1903) and *The Man from Red Keg* (1905) by New York writer Eugene Thwing (1866–1936) are set in the Midland area from 1870 to 1875—at the peak of logging there. Both derive the "Red Keg" in their titles from an actual Red-Keg Saloon in Averill.[15]

In his foreword to *The Red Keggers*, Thwing acknowledged his indebtedness to John Rhines, a Michigan pioneer, for his personal accounts of the 1870s in mid-Michigan, and to Edwin Burton of the Midland area for making available a memoir, *Green Fields and Whispering Woods* (1886), written by Edwin's brother, Frank. The Burtons's father had managed a logging camp, and Frank Burton had operated a shingle mill before beginning a career as founder and editor of the *Midland Sun*, an early newspaper.[16]

The locale and many of the characters and incidents of *The Red Keggers* are carried over to *The Man from Red Keg*. Sam Hawkins, leader of a gang of bootleggers in the first novel, reforms at the end of that book and becomes an upright citizen in the second. The first novel focuses on the transition from logging to clearing and farming, with the usual romantic complications. A number of social events typical of pioneer societies add interest. The catalyst that untangles the novel's tangled threads is a forest fire, based on the disastrous 1871 fire in the Michigan forests.

In the second novel, competition between the town's newspapers and romantic complications are the important elements. As in Puddefoot and Rankin's *Hewers of Wood*, the discovery of salt in the Midland area is also a factor, although, as Kathleen I. Gillard pointed out, the discovery of salt and its exploitation by the Dow Chemical Company has not "called forth as many stories, tales, myths, or po[ems] as the timber industry."[17]

The *New York Times* reviewer of *The Man from Red Keg* thought, "[T]he characterization would have been better had the author devoted more time to a few persons and given less space to a number who have [too little] to do with the tales in hand and so block the stage by their uninteresting presence that the real actors are lost in the maze."[18]

The *Literary Digest* was enthusiastic about *The Man from Red Keg* saying the novel was "clean, wholesome and upbuilding" and that "strenuous religion is here made more palatable by interesting fiction."[19] The *Digest*'s enthusiasm for this novel might have been influenced by the fact that author Thwing was associated with the *Digest*'s publisher at the time. Jean Laming has discussed Thwing's novels in two 1985 essays, "Eugene Thwing's Red-Keg: Taming the Competitive Spirit" and "The Myths and Realities in Thwing's Michigan Novels."[20]

Charles Eugene Banks (1852–1932), an Iowa-born Chicago newspaper writer, was the author of *John Dorn, Promoter* (1906), one of several novels linking Michigan's Upper Peninsula to Chicago business and commerce. The novel tells of an attempt to develop an enterprise that would log pines on Indian-owned land. Atypically, Dorn plans to treat the Indians fairly—paying each one $50—and to practice conservation by planting new seedlings for each tree harvested. The woman in the standard romantic situation is a successful businesswoman who helps unmask the two villains who are trying to thwart Dorn's plan. The Lake Michigan storm that helps resolve some plot complications has its origins in the same actual storm Hamlin Garland used in his Chicago novel, *Rose of Dutcher's Coolly*

(1895), and that William MacHarg and Edwin Balmer were to use in *The Indian Drum* (1917).

Banks's biographer says that *John Dorn, Promoter* is "a persuasive document in the encouragement of the preservation of American forests."[21]

From 1901 to 1905, Banks toured with Michigan author Opie Read, giving literary readings.

Reverend William Chalmers Covert (1864–1942), an Indiana Presbyterian minister, served for a time in Saginaw, Michigan—a tenure that probably gave him the inspiration and information for his *Glory of the Pines: A Tale of the Ontonagon* (1914). The sentimental story is set during the logging years on the Ontonagon River several hundred miles north of Saginaw. The central character, the Dominee, shocked by the reckless and licentious behavior of loggers, sets out to reform the logging town of Ontonagon. His first convert is a saloon owner, who converts his bar into a sort of YMCA; his second convert is an ex-prostitute.

Covert's *Wildwoods and Waterways* (1914) contains several essays that are set in Michigan.

Clarence Budington Kelland's *The Hidden Spring* was serialized in 1915 in the *Delineator* (a popular monthly magazine of the time) and then published in book form in 1916. A young lawyer, a recent arrival in a lumber town, falls in love with a young woman whose uncle, Quartus Hembly, "owns" the town. The hero takes on a client whose logging business has been robbed of millions by Hembly. It is only after the young lawyer develops the courage ("the hidden spring") to risk death or disgrace from Hembley's machinations that he wins the girl.

The *New York Times* called it "a jolly good story" that "move[d] swiftly, with plenty of incident and several thrilling scenes."[22] The *Bookman*, however, said that "the brave man getting the best of the villain [was] the theme of more than one book being written at the time."[23] It seems obvious that readers of the time must have felt some identification between the themes of such novels and their own situations.

Kelland's *Sudden Jim* (1916) is set in a northern lumber camp.

Clarence Budington Kelland (1881–1964) was born in Portland, Michigan, educated in the Detroit public schools, and in 1902 earned a law degree from the Detroit College of Law. He then became a writer and political editor for the *Detroit News*. His early juvenile fiction led to his editorship of the *American Boy* when that periodical was inaugurated. From 1913 to 1960 he was a prolific writer, producing sixty novels and some two hundred short stories. His best known stories for boys were the Mark Tidd series and the Catty Atkins series. *Mark Tidd in the Backwoods* (1914) and *Catty Atkins, Riverman* (1912) are two among several set in Michigan.

Some of his work was filmed, particularly *Speak Easily* (1932, one of Buster [Joseph Francis] Keaton's feebler films), and *Mr. Deeds Goes to Town* (1936), a fine film with Gary Cooper and Jean Arthur. His most successful adult creation was "the wily cracker-barrel philosopher," Scattergood Baines, the subject of numerous stories and serials in the *Saturday Evening Post*.[24]

George Edward Lewis (1870–?), using the pseudonym "Alaska Blackjack," set his *Nick of the Woods: A Tale of the Manistee* (1916) on the Manistee River. Lewis was also the author of two volumes of verse set in Alaska.

A native of the Traverse City area, James Beardsley Hendryx (1880–1963) was a prolific author of short fiction and novels. Two of his Connie Morgan books for young people are set in the Michigan forests: *Connie Morgan in the Lumber Camps* (1919) and *Connie Morgan with the Forest Rangers* (1925). Morgan is "an enterprising young man whose vision and pluck [a favorite term in the earlier years of this century] have already earned him millions."[25] The former book relates Connie's adventures with an older man, "Pap" Whitlock, as they combat some unscrupulous loggers who are more interested in "getting rich" than in the "constructive forestry" young Morgan believes in. Connie is no superboy, "[H]is ingenuity is that of the average American boy with only such knowledge of the woods as is contained in the Boy Scout manual."[26] As one might expect, Connie always triumphs over the villainous adults who get in his way.

Ralph C. Kidder's *Michigan Stories* (1923) are based on logging history in the area around Mancelona, Charlotte, and Grand Rapids.

Harold Titus (1888–?) was also a prolific writer of short stories and novels, most of which focused on the out-of-doors. His first lumbering novel, *Timber* (1922), is also a well-integrated plea for forest conservation—a favorite topic. *Timber* is the story of the conflict between Luke Taylor, a man who has earned a fortune logging Michigan white pine, and John his son; the dissension begins when Luke tells John he must operate on his own. The inevitable girl is atypical—she is developing a small forest of white pine her father had begun as a conservation measure to compensate for the ravages perpetrated by lumbermen such as Luke Taylor. In the end, the several villains get their just dues, and John Taylor, as we have expected all along, gets the girl and his father's estate.

Timber has one other item of interest. A French Canadian logger tells the first Paul Bunyan story ever to appear in a book—Titus spells the name Paul Bunion.[27]

Timber was filmed in 1923 as Hearts Aflame, the second film with a Michigan setting to be produced. Variety's reviewer called it "excellent melodrama with several splendid thrills, much fine scenery, first-rate comedy, and dramatic interest in spots," including a sequence in which the hero and the girl drive a locomotive through a raging forest fire to save the hemmed-in villagers. The locomotive and the fire were the filmmaker's inventions.[28]

In Titus's Smoke Chaser (1924), "a romance of the northwestern timberlands," Dick Webb, a graduate student in forestry at Ann Arbor, aids Hilda Thornberg, a girl plagued by arson while trying to operate her deceased father's logging empire.

Titus's next lumbering novel, The Man from Yonder (1928, and reissued in 1934) is a story set in the northwoods in the red-blood tradition. There is the usual triangle: Ben Elliott the greenhorn, or tenderfoot; Dawn, who owns a logging camp; and the villain who is trying by any means to take over the girl's property. We know early on how the story will end. For all that and despite routine reviews, the book went through two printings.

Titus was a 1911 graduate of the University of Michigan, an occasional newspaper reporter, and an ardent Michigan conservationist.

George Wallace Skinner's The Axe-Thrower of the Tittabawassee (1935) looks back almost half a century to the time and scene of Fitzmaurice's The Shanty Boy. Daniel Dell, a young, inexperienced logger; a logging camp bully; a logger's daughter; and an Indian are the characters. Dan is the axe-thrower; his skill helps the Indian discover that the bully has murdered the Indian's daughter. A poem, "The Burnings," begins the book, and two poems conclude it. The book is more interesting for its factual descriptions of logging operations and the ways by which Michigan pine woods were converted to barren lands than it is for its story line.

"Dirk" Gringhuis set one of his books for boys, The Eagle Pine (1958), in the woods and logging camps of the Saginaw Valley in the late nineteenth century. The book focuses on a young lad's experiences.

Vaughn Kester's (1869–1911) The Manager of the B and A (1901) utilizes a railroad theme and a forest fire as important elements. Dan Oakley, hired by the New York owner of an Upper Peninsula branch railroad to put it on a profit-making basis, angers both the railroad employees and the editor of the logging town's newspaper who is also competing with Dan for the heroine. When Dan's ex-convict father appears, the editor exposes him. Matters are resolved by the fire, which kills Dan's father, makes Dan a hero, and helps him win the heroine.

A *Dial* reviewer said the novel was a "specimen of crisp and vigorous workmanship, typifying an important aspect of American life."[29] Kester was inspired to write by William Dean Howells, a relative; unfortunately, his novel does not reach Howells's standards.

Glen Rounds's 1906 *Lumbercamp, Being the Life and Good Times of the New Whistle Punk at Camp 15 Up Horn Creek Way* . . . has a title almost as long as the book.

Edna Ferber (1887–1968), a major figure in the twentieth-century popular fiction field, was born in Kalamazoo and spent some of her younger years in Wisconsin. Her only novel of lumbering, *Come and Get It* (1936), is set in the Hurley, Wisconsin area on the Michigan-Wisconsin state line. The central character was said to be based on an Escanaba lumberman Ferber had known. The book was filmed (carrying the same title) in 1936.

George Angus Belding's *Tales from the Presque Isle Woods* was published in 1946.

David Garth's *Fire on the Wind* (1951) is an example of the well-made historical novel, which, like Kester's novel, uses a railroad theme and a fire as major elements. Non-Michiganian Garth (1908–) had already published numerous short stories and ten novels, including *Four Men and a Prayer* (1937), which became the four-star 1938 film by the same title.

He spent two years researching *Fire on the Wind*. The primary setting of the novel is the area midway between Menominee and Escanaba. Some incidents occur in the Duluth–Superior area of Minnesota, and there is a brief incident in Washington, D.C. Rufus Preston has dreamed of building a railroad route across the Upper Peninsula to the mouth of the Mishawaka [Cedar] River in order to carry iron ore from the Gogebic and Brule River iron ranges to Lake Michigan. To raise funds for the project, Rufus's son Wayne, a strong man in the red-blood tradition, proposes logging the stands of pine at the river's mouth. For a time, the Prestons' goal is stymied by the usual villains, but their final defeat comes from a forest fire.

David Garth must have had his hopes set on filming this novel with someone like John Wayne playing the hero and someone like Dorothy Lamour playing Huron O'Farrell (the daughter of an Irishman and As-she-way-go, a Chippewa) whom the younger Preston loves. Although Hollywood had earlier drawn the line at marriages of such "mixed" couples, by the 1950s, this romance could have been tolerated.

Reviewers liked the book, although the *Christian Science Monitor* reviewer thought that the characters were "from the stockpile and insufficiently explored."[30] Historian Walter Havighurst praised the novel for "its feel of the upper Lakes country" and because "it pictures the country with vividness and variety—the bustling posts and the busy landings, the gloom of the woods and the gleam of the water."[31]

Leslie Turner White (1903–), a non-Michiganian who was primarily a film writer, turned to Michigan's logging years for his one Michigan book, *Log Jam* (1959). Its story line seems like a mixture of Titus's *The Man from Yonder* and *Timber* with its old-time lumber baron, a young man who wants to move the baron's logs to the mill, a bully out to circumvent the young man, a young woman, and her weakling brother.

Nancy Stone, a writer of stories for younger readers, set her *Whistle Up the Bay* (1966) in Antrim County along the east arm of the Grand Traverse Bay during the late 1800s. Antrim City, a thriving city that no longer exists, was the port through which supplies reached the area and lumber was shipped. The story tells of three sons of a deceased Swiss immigrant who eke out a living from a small plot of cutover land with the help of a neighbor and a minister and his wife.

Stone's *The Wooden River* (1973) tells how young Rose McClaren, at a lumber camp near Bay City in the 1870s, helps rescue her kidnapped brother and capture one of his kidnappers. These activities take place amid technical descriptions of logging, the shouts of "Timber!," log drives down the rivers, the booming grounds at the end of the drive, and the toil of men engaged in specialized activities. Stone's books were obviously based on thorough research.

Mildred Walker (Schemm) (1905–), a Pennsylvanian, a 1926 graduate of Wells College, New York, and a copywriter for Wanamaker's Department Store in New York City, came to the Upper Peninsula with her husband, Dr. Ferdinand Ripley Schemm, when he accepted a position as a surgeon in a milltown. When Dr. Schemm became associated with the University of Michigan medical school, Walker began studying for a master's degree. In 1934, she won the Hopwood Award for her manuscript of *Fireweed*, a novel of a second generation in an Upper Peninsula lumbering town; it was published the same year. Fireweed is the plant with a purplish flower that replaced the tall pines, just as the second generation replaced the pioneers.

In *Fireweed*, Celie Henderson dreams of leaving the lumber town to live in a city with a young man whose wealthy father owns the lumber mill. Instead, she marries Joe Linson, a working man. Although she tries to persuade him that life might be better away from the dying milltown, they remain, surviving even though the mill shuts down. Gradually Celie comes to accept her situation.

Walker next turned to her husband's profession and situation for *Dr. Norton's Wife* (1938), a story of a hopelessly ill wife of a professor in a university medical school. The book was a 1938 Literary Guild selection.

Jan Wall's play, *Lumbering Love*, set in a Great Lakes community, was published in *Midwest Prize Plays* in 1938.

Patrick O'Callaghan's rhymes about pioneer logging days, *North of Menominee*, appeared in 1958.

Semifictional Narratives

Several Michigan authors have written about Michigan's logging days in books that are partly factual, partly fictional. William Davenport Hulbert (1868–1913) in *White Pine Days on the Taquamenon* (1949) offers an early example. Hulbert was a naturalist who for a time lived in the Upper Peninsula in the Taquamenon River area and wrote short fiction for magazines from the middle 1890s until his death. This collection includes nine short stories—all written in the first decade of the century—and some technical lumbering information; it was edited by Richard C. Hulbert (William's brother). The tone of the book is what one would expect from fiction, "Hulbert is a good storyteller, one who knows how to build suspense into a tale and keep [the reader] wondering what is coming next."[32]

Another Upper Peninsula native, Lewis C. Reimann (1890–1961) produced four books of interest. His *Between the Iron and the Pine* (1951), published in the centennial year of the discovery of iron ore in Michigan, is basically a story of his family and others from about 1890 to 1910. But Robert F. Fries says, "[I]t is not a history book in the ordinary sense. . . . The Reimann family [story] is only a hook from which the author hangs his descriptions" of area scenes, outlines of the processes of logging and mining, recipes for such goodies as a Cornish pasty (rhymes with "nasty") or "dago red" wine. The book is replete with "fabulous characters galore, humorous, pathetic, heroic and tragic. . . . there are anecdotes that sketch in bold strokes the lusty community and its people." Fries adds, "The social historian must approach the book with caution. . . . "[T]he details . . . depend upon the memories of the author and those who helped him. Some of the anecdotes have an almost universal character [and have been reported] as happening on other parts of the midwestern frontier."[33]

A year later, Reimann added a sequel, *When Pine Was King* (1952). Robert F. Haugh, reviewing the book, quotes Ralph Waldo Emerson:

The God who made New Hampshire
Taunted the lofty land
With little men—

But says Haugh, if one may believe Reimann's book, Michigan was treated more favorably by the Creator, "The men who got the timber could not be charged with littleness. They ate hugely, drank hugely, and fought hugely."[34]

Reimann's book includes not only lumberjacks but a supporting cast of bartenders, storekeepers, peace officers, and "fancy women" as well. A country doctor and a circuit rider each receive a chapter. Reimann also mentions the deacon's seat in which loggers sat as they told tales and sang songs for the nightly entertainment of the jacks.

Reimann next turned to *Incredible Seney* (1953) for his third book. (Hemingway aficionados will recall Seney, Michigan, as the town where Nick Adams of "Big Two-Hearted River" got off the train.) Once the "hell hole of the north," in its heyday, it was a rip-roaring settlement of three thousand residents whose ten hotels, twenty-one saloons, four or five blind pigs, three brothels in town and two mammoth bawdy houses up the river were always ready to welcome the "wild men from the woods."[35] Nowadays, Seney is much smaller and tamer, located on a long stretch of lonely highway from which one sees only the pine barrens—endless acres that were once blanketed with massive pines.

Reimann gathered his material from old-timers, about whose reliability he said, "No two alleged witnesses of an incident at Seney will give the same account." Samuel T. Dana in a review said that one of Reimann's stories appeared in a similar version in the September 1953 *Harper's Magazine*, a story that probably antedated Reimann's book.[36]

Reimann's *Hurley—Still No Angel* (1954) is about the town on the Wisconsin border that was central to Edna Ferber's 1935 *Come and Get*

It. Reimann quotes an old legend that "the four worst places in the world are Cumberland, Hayward, Hurley, and Hell (the first three in Wisconsin) and Hurley is the toughest of all."[37] Most of the 125-page book documents the statement.

Martha Mitchell Bigelow (1921–)—a professional historian active in preserving Michigan history—said, "[O]ne puts the book down . . . with the feeling that one knows no more about the real Hurley than the sensational reputation that gave it national fame." But, she added, "Reimann has presented that with gusto."[38]

John J. Riordan's *The Dark Peninsula* (1976) is also set in the Seney area. Riordan was born on Manitoulin Island in the Georgian Bay area of Ontario, but he was reared on Whitefish Bay west of Sault Saint Marie. For years, Riordan was a telegraph operator for the Duluth, South Shore, and Atlantic Railway at Seney.

Lumberjack Songs and Ballads

The lumber camps were often miles from the nearest town and lumber camp owners frowned on such inhibitors of the work ethic as the liquor and licentiousness found in Saginaw, Seney, Hurley, and other lumber towns. So, for entertainment on the long winter nights in their shanties (probably derived from the French *chiente* [doghouse]), the jacks were on their own.

Fitzmaurice noted in his *The Shanty Boy* that the loggers entertained themselves by telling tales, singing songs and ballads, and dancing jigs and reels. Usually the tale teller or solo singer occupied the deacon's seat, where he could be the center of attention.

In his *They Knew Paul Bunyan* (1956) Professor Earl "Doc" Clifton Beck (1891–1977) offers a general picture of these evenings, "The shanty boys bragged about narrow escapes and other adventures, sang old and homemade songs, and danced stag dances. Now and then a camp musician was a master on the fiddle or the dulcimer. He was sometimes helped in making his music by a pal playing a pair of rib bones furnished by the cook or a couple of tablespoons from the kitchen, or maybe an empty beer keg with a skin stretched taut over one end."[39]

James Cloyd Bowman, a former head of the English department at Northern State Teachers' College at Marquette, wrote:

> It is hard for (moderns) to visualize an age in America when men sang at their work. . . . Men were so full of the glamor of the New World that they spontaneously burst into song:

I hear America singing, the varied carols I hear;
Those of the mechanics . . .
The carpenter singing . . .
The mason . . .
The boatman . . .
The shoemaker . . .
The wood-cutter's song . . . [40]

Bowman added that it was natural that during the "golden age" of the lumberjack (1870 to 1900) that "[the jack] should celebrate himself in song: "The excitement of felling towering timber; the glamor of wild nature and the hidden recesses of the forest; the camaraderie of the crew; the aloofness of life from the far-away world of men, blended into an atmosphere, and formed an environment, that freed the fancy and lighted the imagination."[41]

But Bowman's poetic imagination ignored the fact that many of the songs the lumberjacks sang had their origins elsewhere—among them the Maine woods and Europe.

There have been several specific collections of lumberjack ballads, and many more have been included in general song collections, or noted in historical articles. Here are a few sources: Franz Rickaby, *Ballads and Songs of the Shanty Boy* (1926); James Cloyd Bowman, "Lumberjack Ballads," *Michigan History* 20 (1936), 231–45; Lewis Reimann, *When Pine Was King* (1952), 155ff.; Earl "Doc" C[lifton] Beck, *Songs of the Michigan Lumber Jacks* (1941); and *Lore of the Lumber Camps* (1948).

An enlarged revision of the 1941 book, *Lore of the Lumber Camps*, was issued in response to the popularity of the earlier version. Both books are set primarily in the area north of the Muskegon and Saginaw valleys, where Beck—a native of Nebraska—had managed lumber camps from about 1936 to 1956. Only a few pages collect lumbermen's tall tales; 328 of the 348 pages contain songs and verse.

Ivan H. Walton said, "The songs [in the two books by Beck] present the rough horseplay, pathos and frequent tragedy that characterized [lumber] camp life. They narrate the felling, swamping, skidding, hauling, river driving, and milling of the big trees. They also narrate the brawls and tawdry and often deeply sentimental love affairs that developed when the Jacks made their spring descent upon the well-salooned and red-lighted communities."[42]

Carl Carmer's review of Professor Beck's book, however, complained that Beck "included, as if they were folk songs, various literary endeavors by literary ladies and even by such a well-known and sophisticated rhymester as Douglas Malloch. Here may be found side by side with authentic songs of folk derivation . . . a synthetic ballad entitled 'The Red Light Saloon,' which won for its author, Judge George Angus Belding of Dearborn, first prize in the Detroit Writers' Club contest of 1946."[43]

Alan Lomax, also a folklore expert, wrote that the "woods ballads" are almost all "in the come-all-ye style, set to Irish and Scots tunes. This style, which dominated American ballad making, became popular in England during the eighteenth century, ruled the forecastles of the American and British merchant ships, caught on in Nova Scotia where the Canadian shantey [sic] boys made the first lumberjack ballads, [and spread through the American lumber industry]."[44]

Franz Rickaby said of his own 1926 collection, "[T]he ballads and songs in [my] book have been gathered by [me] during the past seven years [1918–1925] from men who worked in the woods of Michigan, Wisconsin and Minnesota, mainly during the Golden Age of American Lumbering."[45] Rickaby also commented, "[S]ongs did not serve in logging as in other gang occupations, such as that of sailors, railroad laborers, etc., where efforts in unison were timed, or the general rhythm of the work was maintained, by the singing of the group or an individual in it. The shanty-boy made no appreciable use of his songs while at work."[46]

One of the songs that appears in Rickaby's collection (and many others) is "Michigan-I-O":

It was early in the season, in the fall of sixty-three,
A preacher of the gospel, why he stepped up to me.
He says, "My jolly good fellow, how would you like to go
And spend a winter lumbering in Michigan-I-O? (p.41)

A more general collection, Emelyn Elizabeth Gardner and Geraldine Jencks Chickering's *Ballads and Songs of Southern Michigan* (1939) contains logging and other songs collected in seven southern Michigan counties—Kent, Ionia, Kalkaskia, Macomb, Arenac, Huron, and Ogemaw—during the Great Depression years. Chickering's 1938 master's thesis at Wayne State University, *Some Ballads and Songs from Michigan*, was an earlier result of her research.

Most of these songs and ballads had their origins in earlier times and other places and were brought to Michigan by settlers and latecomers. Only a dozen, listed under the heading "Occupations," are actually related to Michigan. An important aspect of the songs is their revelation of patterns of immigration into Michigan.

Edith Fulton Fawke's (1913–) *Lumbering Songs from the Northern Woods* was published in 1970.

Summary

Although the Michigan logging era produced many books and stories, its most important author, Stewart Edward White, nowadays is at best a minor literary figure. But the era did produce one major literary figure, a figure who has created a great deal of controversy as to whether the tales about him are genuine folklore or fakelore. He is the subject of the next chapter.

CHAPTER VI

PAUL BUNYAN, MIGHTY LOGGER—IN MICHIGAN

—❧❦❧—

Paul Bunyan was the biggest man
  That ever walked the earth;
He logged off northern Michigan
  For all that it was worth;
He logged the hills and hollers
  Of the Lake Superior land,
And he made a million dollars
  For to have at his command.
   —Stanley D. Newton, *Paul Bunyan of the Great Lakes*[1]

Like other mythical American folk heroes, Paul Bunyan is a complex case. On the one hand, it has been asserted that he is a true folk hero, created by loggers and lumberjacks, the "last of the demigods of the pantheon of American folklore";[2] on the other hand, it has been asserted that he is not a folk hero at all, but simply, fakelore, an invention of people who had a monetary axe to grind. Let us consider the evidence in Michigan literature.

John W. Fitzmaurice in his 1889 *The Shanty Boy; or, Life in a Lumber Camp* does not report that loggers told *any* tales as they sat in their shanties at night—let alone tales of Paul Bunyan. And Fitzmaurice wrote from personal experience in the camps.

Paul Bunyan appears for the first time in print in James MacGillivray's "The Round River Drive" in the *Detroit News* on Sunday, July 24, 1910.[3] However, Paul is but a minor character in this collection of twelve anecdotes.

Four years later, Michigan poet Douglas Malloch (1877–1938), at that time an associate editor of the *American Lumberman*, converted this material to "doggerel couplets" and published them in the April

25, 1914, issue of his trade journal.[4] Malloch, Michigan's Lumberman Poet, was born in Muskegon at a time when that Lake Michigan city was becoming a major lumbering center. While yet a boy, his first poem appeared in the *Detroit News*. From 1890 to 1930, he was an editorial staffer on the *Muskegon Chronicle* and during that time became associated with the Chicago-based *American Lumberman*.[5] He was the author of sixteen volumes of verses including *Tote-road and Trail, Ballads of the Lumberjack* (1917) and *Resawed Fables* (1911).

Also in 1914, W. B. Laughead of the Red River Lumber Company of Minneapolis published a thirty-two-page pamphlet that contained Paul Bunyan stories among advertisements for his company.

Laughead also introduced a second character, "Paul Bunyan's greatest asset was Babe, the Big Blue Ox. Babe was seven axe handles wide between the eyes and weighed more than the combined weight of all the fish that ever got away."[6]

In 1916, K. Bernice Stewart and Homer A. Watt published the first scholarly article on Bunyan, "Legends of Paul Bunyan, Lumberjack" in volume 18 of the *Transactions of the Wisconsin Academy of Sciences, Arts, and Letters*.[7] This essay begins with a claim, "The following study of lumberjack legends has grown out of a little collection of these tales made in the lumber-camps by Miss Stewart, who for years has heard the stories told by the lumberjacks of Wisconsin and [the Northern Peninsula and the Saginaw Valley of] Michigan" (p. 640). The authors also cite three sources: "students in the University, who have recently lived in the lumber districts of northern Wisconsin, and who have heard Paul Bunyan tales from boyhood," (p. 639). And the authors go on "[T]he antiquity of the tales is more difficult to determine than the extent of their distribution. It seems certain, however, from the circumstances that they have been passed down from one generation of lumbermen to another for a long period of time, that these stories of Paul Bunyan date well back into the early days of lumbering in Michigan" (p. 641); finally, the authors quote Douglas Malloch's poetic account of how Paul had solved the problem of a liquor shortage in his camp.

In 1920, novelist Lee J. Smits (1887–?), "who had grown up in the Michigan woods [and] became a newspaper man," began writing for the *Seattle Star*. Recalling "the Paul Bunyan stories he had heard in his boyhood[,] . . . he wrote a news story asking 'for Paul Bunyan contributions'." He received enough to supply the *Star* with a two-week series.[8]

As noted, the first Paul Bunyan story to appear in a book is in Harold Titus's *Timber* (1922). Black-Joe, a French Canadian, tells some of his cronies the tale of Paul Bunyan's cornstalk. A teamster ties his mules to it and comes back to find the mules sky high. Later, the government arrests Paul because the stalk is draining the Great Lakes dry.[9]

Titus in 1925 wrote, "Paul Bunyan . . . is a purely mythical figure, although many an old lumberjack will tell you that he has been in his camps. He will insist on this for a time, but if pinned down, will probably qualify this assertion by saying he once knowed a chore-boy who was in Paul's camp the winter of the blue snow."[10]

There is no mention of Paul Bunyan in Franz Rickaby's *Ballads and Songs of the Shanty Boy* (1926).

For all that, in the 1920s, a number of Paul Bunyan books were published, the beginning of a veritable flood of such materials. Until 1927, none of these had a Michigan setting. That year, Professor James Cloyd Bowman published his *The Adventures of Paul Bunyan* as a children's book, trying, he said, "to sketch [the] beauty [of] the northern woods and hills and Lake Superior."[11]

In 1932, James Stevens (1891–1972), an Iowan who had spent several years in the lumber camps in the Pacific Northwest and who had written *Paul Bunyan* in 1925, brought Paul, his blue ox Babe, Johnny Inkslinger (Paul's record keeper), and the rest of the Bunyan crew to Michigan in *The Saginaw Paul Bunyan*.

But reviewers were not entirely pleased by Stevens's book. John Towner Frederick, an ex-Iowan, whose farm at Glennie, Michigan, still was scarred from logging, wrote, "[Stevens] has prettied up the old stories, doctored and elaborated them, made them literary."[12]

In 1946, Stanley D. Newton (1874–1950), of Sault Saint Marie, rewrote the Bunyan tales in *Paul Bunyan of the Great Lakes*, "a kind of running biography of Paul from his birth, as the son of a Russian father, Ivan, through his most eventful years in northern Michigan, to the moment of his fantastic death and possible return."[13]

Newton, born in Ontario, had been a reporter for the *Bay City Times*, but he was living in Florida in 1946. The volume was reprinted in 1985 and 1987, although no one took seriously Newton's claim that Bunyan was of Russian origin.

Professor Earl "Doc" C[lifton] Beck, a Nebraskan who lived in Michigan from 1928 to 1958, was one of those who avoided the literary treatments of Bunyan (which led Richard Mercer Dorson and other folklorists to label Bunyan stories as fakelore) in his *They Knew Paul Bunyan* (1956).

The ubiquitous William Ratigan (1910–) added to the list in 1958 with an illustrated *The Adventures of Paul Bunyan & Babe*. Ratigan was a fourth-generation Detroiter who, after earning a B.A. at the University of Chattanooga, took some further studies at Albion College,

Central Michigan University, and Michigan State University. He then became a teacher, radio news reporter, author, and, operator of the Dockside Press in Charlevoix with his wife, Eleanor. Mrs. Ratigan is the author of *Deep Water* (1961) and articles using the pseudonym "Eleanor Wharton."

In *A Treasury of American Folklore*, B. A. Botkin asked, "Who made Paul Bunyan, who gave him birth as myth, who joked him into life as the Master Lumberjack, who fashioned him forth as an apparition easing the hours of men amid axes and trees, saws and timber?" Botkin's answer to this "puzzling literary question" was, "The people, the bookless people, they made Paul and had him alive long before he got into the books for those who read. He grew up in shanties, around the hot stoves of winter, among socks and mittens drying, in the smell of tobacco smoke and the laughter mocking the outside weather. And some of Paul came overseas in wooden bunks below decks in sailing vessels. And some of Paul is as old as the hills—as young as the alphabet."[14]

Stories and books about Paul Bunyan have not been limited to Michigan but have represented him as living in all the once-forested areas of the United States and have even transported him to Texas oil fields. He has been described in books for adults and for children like Hiawatha, has been dramatized and set to music. In 1936, along with the real-life Johnny Appleseed, he was the subject of a pageant by Henry Bailey Stevens entitled *Johnny Appleseed and Paul Bunyan*.[15]

A native of Port Huron, Dr. William C[harles] S[mithson] Pellowe (1890–?) in his novel *The Skylines of Paradise* (1941) has a speaker at a Saginaw businessmen's weekly luncheon tell how Bunyan came to the area. However, the long speech adds nothing of significance to the history of the Bunyan legends or to the novel's story line.

Harold W. Felton's *Legends of Paul Bunyan* (1961) contains a generous collection of Bunyan tales by various hands, a ten-page bibliography, and a list of authors, publications, and selections. Included in the list are references to Gladys Haney's "Paul Bunyan Twenty-five Years After," an annotated bibliography published in the *Journal of American Folklore* of July 1942 (pp. 155–67), and Herbert Halpert's corrections and additions to Professor Haney's work published in the *Journal of American Folklore* of January 1943.

In his "Paul Bunyan: Ecological Saint—or Villain?" Arthur Coleman answered his own rhetorical question, "Paul Bunyan comes across as more environmental sinner than saint. . . . [H]e seemed to manifest an insensitive disdain for nature." Coleman added, "Paul, you've done this—you and your men. You cut the big pine. You took the clear logs. You left rot. You dried up the springs, and brung in the thistles. You are responsible for this wasted land."[16]

Daniel G. Hoffman in his 1980 *Paul Bunyan, Last of the Frontier Demigods* argues that the Bunyan tales and legends as they were presented in the collections described here—and in texts not related to Michigan—are mostly "inaccurate as folklore and worthless as literature." He noted that W. B. Laughead "discovered that an urban reading audience requires a fare different from that of an occupational audience listening in the woods." Hoffman added that there were "both strong and weak [artistic] uses of the Bunyan theme." Robert Frost had stayed "within the woodland conception of the lumber hero," but Carl Sandburg "confusedly makes [Bunyan] a symbol of hope for a confused proletariat." Richard Mercer Dorson praised Hoffman's volume, but concluded that further research was needed to define the original folktales.[17]

The first four of the following Paul Bunyan books for the young are set in Michigan: *The Blue Snow* (1958) and *Tiny Tim Pine* (1958) by William Ratigan; *Ol' Paul, the Mighty Logger* (1936) by Glen Rounds; *Paul Bunyan* (1975) by James Stevens; *Paul Bunyan and His Blue Ox* (1964) by Wallace Wadsworth; *Story of Paul Bunyan* (1964) by Barbara Emberley (1964); *A Giant Walked among Them* (1977) by Hazel B. Girard; and *Paul Bunyan Swings His Axe* (1964) by Dell Cormick.

Like Hiawatha, Bunyan has become a cultural icon. Often, in oversized statues and other visualizations, he and Babe have been utilized for publicizing commercial ventures.[18]

Folklore and "Fake Lore"

Joseph M. Carriere's *Tales from the French Folk-Lore of Missouri . . .* (1937) contains material related to the Upper Peninsula.

Richard Mercer Dorson demonstrated his folk interests in three books set completely or in part in Michigan: *Negro Folktales in Michigan* (1956, reissued 1974); *Negro Tales from Pine Bluffs, Arkansas, and Calvin, Michigan* (1958); and *Bloodstoppers and Bearwalkers: Folk Traditions of the Upper Peninsula* (1952, reissued 1972).

The last title has three sections: "The European Tradition," "The Indian Tradition," and "The Native Tradition." Included in the last section is a longish collection of lumberjack folklore. Bearwalkers appear in the Indian section. A bearwalker is a person who has the power to transform himself or herself into a bear or owl, and then, by "walking" against some antagonist make that person ill. Bloodstoppers, described in the European section, are persons who have the power to stop unnatural bleeding (as from a cut or gash) either with prayer or touch.

Dorson was also the author of "Dialect Stories of the Upper Peninsula" published in the 1948 *Journal of American Folklore* (vol. 61, pp. 113–50). His *Folklore and Fakelore* (1976) offers an intelligent discussion of this subject and the distinctions to be made between the two.

An entire 1956 issue of *Midwest Folklore* (vol. 5, no. 1) concentrated on Michigan folklore, including essays on "Finnish Wizard Tales," "Modern Ottawa Dancers," Michigan Indian place names, Czech and Slovak songs found in Detroit, and "Jawinikon's Tale."

In 1910, there was an early example of fakelore, William T. Cox's *Fearsome Creatures of the Lumberwoods*, a set of tales about mythical Upper Peninsula beasties, including the hugag, an animal like a moose, except that it had jointless legs and a long upper lip. In 1969, Walker D. Wyman reprinted these and added tales of his own invention in *Mythical Creatures of the North Country*.

Two minor contributions to the pantheon of Michigan fakelore are: Robert Lyon Stearn of Ludington created the character of Ossawald Crumb as a public relations ploy for the Ossawald Crumb Taproom in the Stearns Hotel in Ludington. Crumb, said his creator, was a "sort of Paul Bunyan person—but—with brains."[19] And Robert H. Wright created Pete Pareau, a semiliterate fictional contributor to Wright's *The Luce County Democrat*, published in the late nineteenth century in Newberry in the Upper Peninsula. Some of Pete Pareau's work is collected in *The Pete Pareau French-Canadian Dialect Letters* (1894).

Wright was also author (and publisher) of *Legends of the Chippewa* (1927), a booklet of twenty pages that related myths about the exploits of Indian demigods in the Hiawatha country—the south shore of Lake Superior.

Summary

The character of Paul Bunyan in all likelihood had its roots in the tall tales tradition of working people—the tendency of such persons to exaggerate or comment humorously on their working conditions and problems during breaks from work—coffee time or lunchtime, evening hours, weekends. In this chapter, we have seen how such material, developing from loggers'and lumbermen's tale and anecdote telling, was formalized, and even transmuted, by a number of authors writing books for both adults and young people. None of these literary efforts produced any major literary work. Eventually, this material was adapted to publicize commercial ventures.

CHAPTER VII

"THE GREAT TURTLE"

Wait till you look out over those straits [of Mackinac] into Huron on one side and Michigan on the other—two oceans set down amid riches beyond the dream of man! . . . [Mackinac's] a fortress between two empires—the white man's to the east and the red man's to the west!
　　　　　　　　　　　　　　—Kenneth Roberts, *Northwest Passage*[1]

Mackinac Island, a crown of rock thrusting itself out of the Straits of Mackinac, is insignificant in area compared to nearby Bois Blanc or more distant Beaver or Drummond islands, but far more significant in the history of Michigan and far more significant in Michigan literary history. The legendary home of the Indians who were there first, Mackinac Island became of military and economic importance to French, British, and Americans, in turn—and finally, one of America's most intriguing tourist and resort attractions.

Its name, deriving from French attempts to represent the name they heard from the Indians, should be pronounced as if it were Mackinaw. Many think the name means Great Turtle, referring to its appearance when seen from a distance. Others think it refers to spirits who once inhabited the island.

Washington Irving, in *Astoria* (1836), briefly shows Mackinac as "a mere village, stretching along a small bay, with its fine broad beach in front of its principal row of houses and dominated by the old fort," and its beach, "a kind of public promenade" with its voyageurs and Indians (p. 211), quite unlike the present vista of fort, shops, homes, and docks.

Through the years there have been many folktales about the island: some genuine folklore, some representing the imaginative or fanciful notions of visitors, some simply fakelore. (Richard H.) "Dirk" Gringhuis, has retold some of these in his *Lore of the Great Turtle* (1970) and *Were-Wolves-and-Will-of-the-Wisps* (1974). The final chapter of the latter tells of voyageurs' songs.

In the first part of her *The White Islander* (1893), Mary Hartwell Catherwood shows English trader Alexander Henry saved from death at the hands of the Indians at Fort Michilimackinac by a French woman who conceals him. In the second part, Catherwood shows Wawatam, Henry's "blood brother," conveying Henry to Mackinac, even though he knows that Henry will probably marry the French woman both men love.

In 1899, Catherwood published her *Mackinac and Lake Stories*. (The two set on Beaver Island are discussed elsewhere.) "The Penitent of Cross Village" takes place on the northwest tip of the Lower Peninsula and "The Windigo" at Sault Saint Marie. The other nine are set on Mackinac; the time ranges from 1760 to 1800. Indians and voyageurs are the principal characters.

Catherwood has been singled out as the initiator of the vogue for historical romances that began in the nineteenth century and continued well into the twentieth. Robert Price has said that her book-length romances "were inspired chiefly by Francis Parkman, were often romantically unreal with plots and characterizations of the merest *pastiche*, and will never regain their initial vogue." But, he adds, "[H]er short stories . . . have lived . . . and are now recognized as an important contribution to American letters."[2]

Surely the best book written about Mackinac and the Great Lakes is *The Loon Feather* (1940, with five later printings), by Iola Fuller (Goodspeed McCoy). A 1939 Hopwood Award winner, the book is the first of Fuller's three novels. Stephen Vincent Benét praised it for "the author's genuine and imaginative feeling" and for her ability "to show history as something lived out in the daily lives of people rather than as a hair-raising succession of escapes and adventure."[3] John T. Flanagan said it "gives an excellent picture of the Indian tribes which congregated on the back of the 'Great Turtle' to fish, to exchange furs, to peddle gossip, to bargain with the whites, and to receive their gold."[4]

The Loon Feather is narrated by Oneta [short for Oneonta, the Indian word for *yes*] Debans, the fictional daughter of Tecumseh, who begins her story with these words: "It was fur that made our lives what they were. Fur, and the people who lived by it. . . . Furs were the means of getting whatever the Indian and the white trapper wanted, for in those days they were the legal tender and there was little that prime beaver would not buy."

The time of the novel is from 1806 until about 1830—the period just before the War of 1812 to the beginning of the so-called Black Hawk War in Illinois. The setting is primarily Mackinac Island, with its fort, its trading post (whose shadow falls over the whole island), its homes of settlers, its fishermen and voyageurs, and its Indian encampment along the beach.

Oneta's later education at a Montreal convent makes her an intellectual. Though still sympathetic to the Indians, she can no longer accept their culture; instead, she sees them as dirty and odorous. She is quite unlike Huron O'Farrell, in David Garth's *Fire on the Wind*, who retains the natural instinctive ways of her Indian forebears. The novel seems to imply that the Indians must give up most of their own culture and adopt the white man's ways.

A common element in both the Fuller and the Garth novels is the white man's despoliation of the natural resources of the Great Lakes area, but *The Loon Feather* also shows the effect of this despoliation on the Indian.

Fuller's novel is dedicated to Professor Roy Cowden of the University of Michigan, who aided many students to become significant writers.

Daniel S. Rankin said, "Henry James praised Constance Fenimore Woolson for her stories of Mackinac Island. He would have richer reason to praise Iola Fuller."[5]

Mabel Leigh Hunt's *Michel's Island* (1940) is set on Mackinac and at Fort Michilimackinac in the days of the voyageurs and fur traders. Michel's mother is Indian; his father a French trader.

Grace Franks Kane's *Myths and Legends of the Mackinacs and the Lake Region* (1897) contains twenty-five brief tales relating incidents that happened (or supposedly happened) at some two-dozen geological sites on Mackinac Island. Some of the tales are of the type that Richard Mercer Dorson has labeled fakelore; some, Kane says, came from "word-of-mouth tales of the Indians of the Lake Region and their half-breed descendants, among whom the greater part of my life has been spent" (p. 7).

Lorena M. Page's self-published *Legendary Lore of Mackinac* (1901) is an illustrated collection of twenty-five "original poems of Indian legends of Mackinac."

Larry B. Massie, in his preface to *Early Mackinac* (1987), identifies two lesser Mackinac books: E. A. Allen's *A Jolly Trip . . .* (ca. 1890), a narrative of a voyage to Mackinac on the *City of Alpena* and a stay at the Grand Hotel; and Frances Margaret Fox's (1870–1959) *Betty of Old Mackinaw* (1901). I have not been able to locate copies of these titles. The *Great Lakes Review* in its spring 1982 issue has an essay on Fox and her books.[6]

Two other small volumes about Mackinac are James Challen's *Island of the Giant Fairies* (1868), verses set on the island; and Peter J. Reardon's self-published *The Island Serf* (1957), a small booklet of "lyrical tales of Mackinac Island."

Historically, the two most significant fur traders at Mackinac were John Kinzie and Gurdon Saltonstall Hubbard—both to be immortalized posthumously as candidates for the title of "Father of Chicago" in a debate that lasted well into the twentieth century. Juliette A. Kinzie (John's daughter-in-law) had both men in mind in her *Mark Logan, the Bourgeois* (written in 1870, published in 1887 after the author's death). Logan, a supervisor for John Jacob Astor, is Hubbard; Mr. Ewing, an emissary of Governor Cass, who is preparing a dictionary of Chippewa words, is Kinzie.

The novel, set about 1820–1821, is mistitled; Logan is always outside the main action. The central characters are Monica (Moniqué) McGregor (daughter of a Scotch trader) and an Indian woman, Madeline (Monica's apparent sister).

The novel begins in Detroit, then a small town, with a number of pages reporting its social activities. From there the McGregors and their party sail for "Mackinaw" on the first steamboat on the Great Lakes. Then they go on to Green Bay and Prairie du Chien (both once part of the Michigan Territory), where Monica's attempts to free an imprisoned Indian, who had once been her lover, end tragically.

Hubbard and Kinzie are also characters in Winifred E. Wise's *Swift Walker* (1937), a book for boys and girls, and in Alfred Hubbard Holt's *Hubbard's Trail* (1952), a fictional biography. Holt was a grandnephew of Hubbard.

In 1944, John T. Flanagan, citing Fuller's two Indian novels and August Derleth's Wisconsin River Valley novels, wrote:

> A considerable improvement is manifest in the middle western historical novel during the last century. . . . On the whole, authors have learned to pay more attention to motivation, plots are simpler and more natural, historical figures are treated more carefully and often more fully. Particularly healthy is the tendency to get away from the fictionized biography of heroes and to democratize the novel by choosing the ordinary citizen as protagonist.[7]

Although Derleth's fifty books are almost entirely set in Wisconsin, the first part of Derleth's 1940 *Bright Journey* is set on Mackinac Island at the time in the War of 1812 when the British attacked the island and forced the American soldiers at the fort to surrender.

The story begins at the moment Michael Dousman—an actual person—learns that America and England are at war—even before the soldiers at the fort hear of it. The loss of the fort to the British, who are in control through 1815, and the second defeat of the Americans as they try to wrest possession of the fort from the victors, who are aided by the Indians, are seen from the Dousman family's point of view. Even though the latter are Americans, they are allowed to continue farming their land on the island.

The capture of Fort Mackinac by the British was the subject of some average verse by Francesca Falk Miller in *1812: The Story of the War of 1812 in Song and Story* (1935).

Constance Fenimore Woolson (1840–1894), a grandniece of James Fenimore Cooper, though not a native of Michigan, spent several summers on Mackinac Island. From these visits, she derived the historical background, characters, and flavor she utilized in a novel and in short stories in *Harper's Monthly*, the *Atlantic Monthly*, and other periodicals. Nine of these were collected in *Castle Nowhere: Lake Country Sketches* (1875).

The story, "Castle Nowhere," had not been previously published, possibly because of its length. Seven of the stories are set in Michigan, six on Mackinac or in the area, one in Detroit. The characters include an escaped murderer who is also a lake pirate; a High Church Anglican minister who is a failure; a French-Indian woman who romances a Mackinac soldier; an old and penniless French soldier; Waiting Samuel, a religious fanatic; and a mysterious lady whose unrequited love for a man leads to tragedy.

The best stories are "Peter the Parson," "St. Clair Flats," and "The Lady of Little Fishing"; Henry James applauded their "minuteness of observation and tenderness of feeling" and William Dean Howells praised the stories in the *Atlantic Monthly*.[8]

Mackinac Island is the setting for the first section and the latter part of Woolson's *Anne*, published first in *Harper's Monthly* then in book form in 1882; some of the later reprints contain eight photographs of Mackinac Island scenes.

Anne Douglas lives in a state of poverty on the island with her father, his second wife, and four siblings. After her father's death, a wealthy aunt offers to pay for a year's education in the East so that Anne will be able to earn her living as a teacher. There, Anne has romances with two men. When the one she marries is charged with murdering his first wife, an old friend and a priest from Mackinac come east to help her find the real murderer.

Miss Woolson's work is discussed in some detail in Alexander Cowie's *The Rise of the American Novel* (1948), in J. D. Kern's *Constance Fenimore Woolson: Literary Pioneer* (1934), and in Rayburn S. Moore's *Constance Fenimore Woolson* (1963). She is also the subject of the second volume of *Constance Fenimore Woolson*—one of three volumes of Clare Benedict's *Five Generations (1785–1923)*—in "scattered chapters from the history of the (James Fenimore) Cooper, Pomeroy, Woolson, and Benedict families."[9]

Myron D. Orr, son of a U.S. Customs officer at Port Huron, Michigan, was an English professor at Alpena Community College and a lawyer. He wrote three novels based on French-British-American political relations on Mackinac Island and on the monopolistic practices of John Jacob Astor's American Fur Company from about 1800 to 1830. *Mission to Mackinac* (1956), *The Citadel of the Lakes* (1952), and *The Outlander* (1959) form a sequence in that order. Murders, political intrigues, Astor's schemes, and romances that involve persons from voyageurs to Lewis Cass (the territorial governor) are at the heart of the three novels, each of which has its own satisfactory conclusion. In an appendix to *Mission to Mackinac*, Orr lists the resources for his books. A planned fourth work apparently was neither finished nor published.

Reviewers gave Orr's books mixed reviews, finding the historical elements in them more interesting than the romantic interludes.[10]

Harold Titus's *Black Feather* (1936), another historical romance, covers some of the same period as Orr's books. The title refers to a black ostrich plume worn as a symbol of leadership and fighting ability. In 1818, Rodney Shaw, a young man down on his luck, comes to Mackinac where he fights and defeats a larger voyageur—thus winning the latter's black feather. Shaw acquires the stock-in-trade of an old woodsman, overcomes a charge of murder, struggles for his right to be a fur trader, and finally woos and wins the beautiful Annette Leclerc.

Reviewers for the *New York Herald Tribune* and the *New York Times* agreed that the novel was "crammed with action and good he-man stuff . . . grim, capably told, tense and primitive, withal offering a historically faithful picture of the life and people of the [Old] Northwest in the early nineteenth century."[11]

Mrs. Cynthia M. R. Gorton's *The Fatal Secret* (1873), one of those sentimental romances so popular with nineteenth-century readers, withholds until the end the secret the author knew all the time: Flora, the fourteen-year-old "wild rose of Mackinaw," is the daughter of a wealthy English couple, not of mixed French-Indian blood (a "metive") that a young lieutenant at Fort Mackinaw thought she was. So Flora and the young lieutenant, who, the author reveals at last, is a nobleman, can marry. Albert G. Black reports, "[T]he incidents of this story [are] based on the experience of [a couple] who were for twenty years in the Mission School service on . . . Mackinac."[12]

Although blind, Mrs. Gorton composed fiction and verse on one of the earliest typewriters; besides her own name, she used such pseudonyms as Ida Glenwood as well as The Blind Bard of Michigan and The Sweet Singer of Michigan, the last a title she shared with a contemporary, Julia Moore. One of Mrs. Gorton's later novels, *Lily Pearl and the Mistress of Rosedale* (1892), was edited by Joseph Kirkland, the son of Caroline Kirkland. One wonders what these confirmed realists thought of Mrs. Gorton's romantic capers.

Two Mackinac novels, Marion Harland's *With the Best Intentions: A Midsummer Episode* (1893, reissued 1901) and Mrs. Edna Willa (Sullivan) Troop's *Blackbird: A Story of Mackinac* (1907) have an interesting relationship.

Harland's novel is set at Mackinac's Grand Hotel, at various scenic and historic points on the island, and briefly at Saint Ignace. A newlywed becomes jealous of her husband's friend and tries to destroy the friend socially, only to discover the husband is trying to help the young woman resolve her own marital problems. When the wife is not attacking the young woman's reputation, she is reading Constance Fenimore Woolson's *Anne*, purchased at the hotel shop.

A character in Harland's novel tells the story of Sophia B., a young Catholic woman buried in the Mackinac cemetery. Troop's pretentious book, published six years after the reissue of Harland's under the pseudonym Scota Sorin, was obviously designed for gift-giving; it is composed of letters by several people from 1860 to 1891. Its story line is precisely the story of Sophia B.: Lieutenant John Beech, whose ancestors came to America on the *Mayflower*, decides not to marry Maraquita Dane of Mackinac when he learns she is not Spanish as her name suggests, but a half-breed.

Was there an actual Sophia B. buried on Mackinac? Or was her story borrowed by Troop from Harland's book? A character in Harland's novel says, "[T]he story is so common that the sequel ought to surprise nobody" (p. 121); but that comment could mean that the story of Sophia B. was not unique. Meade C. Williams's *Early*

Mackinac (1897, reissued 1901 and 1912) does not refer to an instance of this kind.

Each chapter of *With the Best Intentions* begins with a poem about the island, each written by a different author, whose poetical reputation has faded with passing time. The *Nation* called *With the Best Intentions* a "most preposterous book" that was improved by the quotations from Woolson's *Anne*, and the reviewer condoled with Woolson for being "an accessory."[13]

Marion Harland was the pseudonym of Mary Virginia Hawes Terhune (1831–1922), who began writing at fourteen and published more than thirty books. She was the mother of the equally prolific Albert Payson Terhune, author of popular stories about dogs early in the twentieth century. She was not a Michiganian, but she must have been familiar with Mackinac Island.

William C. Levere, the author of books about a fraternal order, Sigma Alpha Epsilon, made one detour into fiction, *Vivian of Mackinac* (1911). It is the amazing tale of several people from the island all leaving at the same time for different destinations—and all coming together at the same house on Chicago's South Side to bring the tale to its dramatic conclusion. Its early chapters are illustrated with tinted photographs of Mackinac Island.

One of Hope Daring's (pseudonym of Anna Johnson of Hastings, Michigan) turn-of-the-century stories about young women, *Madeline, the Island Girl*, set on Mackinac, went through several editions from 1907 to 1923. Daring's *An Abundant Harvest* (1904) is also set in part on the island.

Frances McGuire was the author of a half-dozen books for young people. Her *Indian Drums Beat Again* (1953) is the story of Rockey Matthews who, vacationing with his mother on the island, meets Pete, an older Indian boy who hauls tourists about the island in his carriage. From him, Rockey hears about the island's history, and the Ojibwa Indians who live there. Later, Rockey discovers that an accident involving Pete's carriage was a scheme of two scoundrels to collect a sum of money.

Prior to 1957, anyone wishing to cross from the Lower Peninsula to the Upper, or vice versa, whether by train or automobile, had to take a ferry across the Straits of Mackinac. As one novel relates, the wait for one's turn on the ferry could be hours in length.

But in the 1950s, over the protests, real or pretended, of such Upper Peninsula natives as lawyer–novelist John D. Voelker, the "Mighty Mac" Bridge (some 26,000 feet in length) was built across the Straits from Mackinaw City to Saint Ignace—one of the most ex-

traordinary engineering feats of all time. Of the nonfiction books—
including bridgebuilder David B. Steinman's *Miracle Bridge at
Mackinac* (1957), William Ratigan's *Straits of Mackinac! Crossroads of the
Great Lakes* (1957), and his *The Long Crossing* (1959)—that tell the story
of the bridge's construction, Gay Talese's *The Bridge* (1964) is interesting for its New Journalism approach. This technique employs a
factual base, but with many fictional touches, such as imagined dialog, character development, and descriptions like, "[Bridgebuilders]
drive into town in big cars, and live in furnished rooms, and drink
whiskey with beer chasers, and chase women they will soon forget.
They linger only a little while, only until they have built the bridge;
then they are off again to another town, another bridge, linking everything but their lives."[14] David B. Steinman, the designer and
builder of "Big Mac" and other bridges, was also a poet; his volume,
Songs of a Bridgebuilder (1959) is unique as it probably is the only volume of poetry ever stacked in libraries of engineering books. Steinman is the author of other books and numerous technical articles.

Yale student G. Whitfield Cook's *Saint's Parade*, a play set at
Mackinac's Grand Hotel, although seen in performance at Yale by
representatives of New York theater owners and despite the fact that
Yale's distinguished William Lyon Phelps called it "one of the most
original, interesting, thoughtful and diverting plays produced at the
Yale theatre" seems not to have had a further life.[15]

Far more visible to the American public was Metro-Goldwyn-
Mayer's (MGM's) 1947 musical film, *This Time for Keeps*, with Esther
Williams, Jimmy Durante, Lauritz Melchior and Xavier Cugat and his
orchestra. The setting of this typical Williams opus was Mackinac Island's Grand Hotel, both in summer and winter.

A 1980 film, *Somewhere in Time*, also used the island and the hotel for its settings. In 1980, a young Chicago playwright (played by
Christopher Reeve of *Superman* fame) becomes fascinated by a 1912
photograph of an actress who, as an old lady, has visited him. After
her death, the playwright goes to Mackinac. There (the time is now
1912) he meets the actress as a young woman and they have an affair.
Richard Matheson's novel (*Bid Time Return*), on which the film was
based, was set in California. Matheson also wrote the screenplay.
Both the *New York Times* and *Variety* reviewers thought that the hotel
and the island provided a superb backdrop for the film, but the *Times*
reviewer was not as happy with the production as was the *Variety*
reviewer.[16]

Melinda Pollowitz set her 1981 *Princess Amy (Sweet Dreams)* on
present-day Mackinac. A sixteen-year-old's unhappiness at having to

spend a month's vacation on the island quickly changes to happiness as she is courted by two young men who are unalike.

Summary

Mackinac Island, from its early strategic military and commercial history to its present role as a summer resort and tourist highlight, has attracted a disproportionate share of literary interest. The best literary treatments are those by Mary Hartwell Catherwood, Constance Fenimore Woolson, Iola Fuller, August Derleth, and "Dirk" Gringhuis. The balance of the fiction set on the island is of less than major quality, and too much of the verse is like this:

Of old, strange suitors came in quest of her,
Some in the pride of conquest, some for pelf;
Priests in their piety, red men for revenge—
All seek her now, alone, for her fair self.[17]

CHAPTER VIII

THE GREAT LAKES IN MICHIGAN LITERATURE

Where the forest whispers stories
While the flowers all aglow
Listen to Algonquin legends
From the land of long ago,
Where the waves in watercolors
Paint the portrait of the sky
From the faintest blush of sunrise
Till the school of stars swims by,
Dwell the blue-robed, white-capped maidens,
Dwell the five Great Lakes, the daughters
Of the mighty Mississippi,
Father of Waters.

—William Ratigan, *Soo Canal!*[1]

Because Michigan consists of two major peninsulas projecting into three Great Lakes and has the third longest coastline of the fifty states, it is often called the Great Lakes State, the Peninsula State, or (by some Michigan poets at least) the Third Coast.

The early explorers stayed close to the state's shorelines; Indian camps and the first white settlements were close to the water. As the state was being settled, the lakes continued (as they still do) to serve to transport people and materials, to produce a lake effect on weather conditions, and to provide recreation and food.

The King of Beaver Island

One of the odder bits of Michigan and U.S. history took place in the mid-nineteenth century on Beaver Island, the largest of the dozen or so islands in the northeast portion of Lake Michigan that are part of the state. After the 1844 murder of Mormon leader Joseph Smith at Carthage, Illinois, Jesse James Strang (born in Scipio, Cayuga County, New York in 1813) and his wife Mary established the

Mormon colony of Voree near Burlington, Wisconsin. In 1848, Strang changed his name to James Jesse Strang and moved his colony to Beaver Island. After ousting most of the island's residents, he established the Kingdom of Saint James, with himself as king. In 1852, Strang was elected to the Michigan legislature where he earned the respect of his fellows for his political abilities.

But all was not well on Beaver Island. There were objections to Strang's taking several wives, there were charges of islanders' piracy against passing ships, and of robberies and thefts of property of non-Mormons on the island and of residents of nearby islands. On Monday evening, June 16, 1856, the U.S. steamer *McCulloch* (the first U.S. Navy steel vessel) anchored at Beaver Island, and a message was sent to Strang asking him to visit the ship's commander. As Strang approached the vessel, he was shot and seriously wounded. He was taken across the lake to Voree, where he died.

Strang's story became the subject matter of several short stories and novels as the years passed, beginning with Mary Hartwell Catherwood's "The King of Beaver" and "Beaver Lights" in her *Mackinac and Lake Stories* (1899) and also James Oliver Curwood's *The Courage of Captain Plum* (1908).

Curwood, a native of Owosso, Michigan, and Rex Beach, who was born in Michigan but left at age six never to return, set most of their novels in the seemingly romantic Alaskan and Canadian wildernesses. Their books were widely read; many were filmed. The *National Union Catalog* lists 216 different editions of Curwood's novels in English and in almost every major foreign language. Beach was equally prolific and as widely published.

Curwood—a grandson of a Dutch settler and an Indian girl and a great nephew of Captain Frederick Marryat, the adventure story novelist—was born in 1878; eventually he built a "castle" at Owosso on the Shiawassee River banks where he had grown up. He died in 1927.

Henry Bedford-Jones early became interested in the Strang material. In a 1928 *Michigan History Magazine* article he complained about writers "who indulge in a great deal of [ill-founded] romanticism" in utilizing Michigan history for their fictions. He referred, in particular, to "a poem of a few years back" that purported to recite the death of Strang at the hands of an imaginary jealous rival. But he admitted some delinquency on his own part, "having written, as a boy, some Indian legends about northern Michigan which were published in the old *Chicago Record-Herald,* and which were two-thirds made up out of my own brain."[2] These stories are "Strang's Men," "Blood Royal," "The Convert Goes North," and "The Devil's Disciple."[3]

Later Strang novels are Nehemiah Hawkins's *The Mormon of the Little Manitou Island: An Historical Romance* (1916)—supposedly by The Knight of Chillon of Switzerland and Associates—which included a biography of Strang; and Karl Detzer's *Pirate of the Pine Lands* (1929), which the *Saturday Review of Literature* praised.[4] Harold Titus's *The Beloved Pawn* (1923) echoes Strang's career but it is set on Garden Island and the ruler is King Norman Eldred.

By far the best of the Beaver Island novels is also the last: *The Stranger on the Island* (1933) by Brand Whitlock (1869–1934), Ohio author and politician. On Beaver Island, ruled by one, King Gorel, a romantic quadrangle develops involving Gorel, a fugitive from Mackinac, and a Gorelite elder and his wife. Although reviewers found the novel somewhat naive they still praised it.[5]

Historian's have also focused on Strang. Milo M. Quaife's *The Kingdom of St. James* (1930) is the best study. Others are O. W. Riegel's *Crown of Glory*, Doyle C. Fitzpatrick's 1970 *The King Strang Story: A Vindication of James J. Strang, the Beaver Island Mormon King*, and Roger Van Noord's *King of Beaver Island: The Life and Assassination of James Jesse Strang* (1988).

The Lakes

With John Hoskyns-Abrahall's *Western Woods and Waters* (1864), written in the meter of the *Kalevala*, we move to the lakes themselves. The book tells of a tour made in July 1858 through "that magnificent region, which presents the grandest combination of inland woods and waters that earth can show." Hoskyns-Abrahall and his wife were the only passengers on a mailboat from the Sault to the Lake Superior country.

The book includes a legend about Michipicoten, the floating island, and a fable about the origin of the whitefish at the Sault. An appendix discusses the origins and pronunciation of the name *Mackinac*.

William Pendleton Chipman, author of numerous books for boys, set his *Roy Gilbert's Search: A Tale of the Great Lakes* (1889) on Lake Superior and in the Upper Peninsula.

William Ratigan's 1955 *Soo Canal!* first appeared in a shorter version in the *Country Gentleman* under the title "Gangway for Tomorrow." Ratigan says he wrote the book for "the entertainment of the reader . . . as a love story and a historical romance." But he also wrote it as "a definitive book on one of the most important but least known examples of free enterprise"—the building of the first Soo ship canal at Sault Sainte Marie in 1855 through the enterprise and energy of Charles Harvey, a young salesperson (p. 1).

Soo Canal! is an epistolary novel, the letters passing between a Great Lakes sailing-vessel captain (he claims to be a cousin of Henry Wadsworth Longfellow) and Longfellow himself. The captain taunts Longfellow because the "half ton" of books sent by Schoolcraft to the poet have not as yet produced even a single verse!

Ratigan was also the author of *Young Mr. Big* (1955), a biography of Charles Harvey for young people. Ratigan says his *The Adventures of Captain McCargo* (1956) relates "the adventures (ca. 1856) of a Great Lakes skipper who would commit anything from mayhem to matrimony to round out a quartet" of male voices for his rakish schooner (p. 1).

Actually, the book recounts the adventures of a Captain Thunder Bay McCargo and Old Cap Sparhawk his friend, that "pass[ing] beyond belief . . . had to be recounted as folklore." The adventures, all related with Ratigan's tongue firmly implanted in his cheek, include a battle between fishermen on Whiskey Island (in the Beaver group) and King Strang's supporters, a battle that is settled by McCargo and Sparhawk. The novel was reviewed favorably by Iowa author Phil Stong, who himself loved to write tall tales of the cornlands.[6]

Frederick H. Seymour's *A Canoe Trip; A Lark on the Water, Cruise of the "Ulysses" from Lake Huron to Lake Erie* (1880), a revision of fictionalized sketches originally published in the *Detroit Free Press*, tells of a solo canoe trip down Lake Huron, through the Saint Clair River, over to the Canadian shore, and finally to Detroit.

Non-Michiganian Robert Carse (1902–1971) set one of his many books in Michigan and on the nearby lakes. *Beckoning Waters* (1953) is a tale of logging, limestone mining, and shipping in the years from 1876 to 1932. Alan Kennard, an immigrant Irish sailor, becomes an industrial tycoon, a rival of the Rockefellers and their kind—his rise paralleling the growth of Michigan industry and Great Lakes shipping. Eventually forced to take a stand either with the capitalists who aid him or his sailors who are forming a union, he sides with the latter.

Walter Havighurst, author of expository books about Michigan and the Great Lakes, liked the book, "Alan Kennard is a convincing figure of the generation that produced iron and steel fortunes. . . . [T]he Lakes trade was built by men like Alan Kennard and not all of them died in bed."[7] But Wisconsin historical novelist August Derleth, not so impressed, wrote; "One is left with the inescapable conviction that Robert Carse is much happier at writing the short magazine adventure story than the historical novel."[8]

Alan Sullivan (1868–1947), a Canadian, set *The Rapids* (1920, re-issued 1972) in Sault Saint Marie, Ontario (a much larger city than its Michigan counterpart). But the relations of the two border cities are so intertwined that the novel belongs in a study of Michigan literature.

The Rapids is "[a] thinly disguised interpretative account of one of the greatest entrepreneurial adventures in Canadian history, the rise and fall of Francis H. Clergue's industrial empire at Sault Sainte Marie, Ontario, between 1894 and 1903."[9]

In the novel, Clergue becomes Robert Fisher Clark, a man with a dream of what the energy of the Saint Marys River rapids might accomplish if it were harnessed by a dam, locks, and a power plant. Clark secures financing from American financiers, builds the Clark Industrial Works, discovers a source of iron, and opens an iron mine. But in the end he fails.

Elliott Flower (1863–1920) was the author of two muckraking novels of the type prevalent in the early twentieth century before he turned to the Grand Traverse Bay area of Michigan for his novel *Delightful Dodd* (1904). Daniel Dodd is a former banker who owns a cherry and apple farm on the bay, operating it as a resort in the summer. Regarded as an eccentric by those who know him, Dodd is an intelligent, self-sufficient man whose character seems to be influenced by Edward Noyes Westcott's *David Harum: A Story of American Life* (1898). *Delightful Dodd* is both a character study of Dodd and a simple tale of a romance that takes place one summer on his farm.

In 1903 and 1904, Karl Edwin Harriman published in *Era* a series of short sketches, or stories, set in 1902–1904 on an island that is presumably in Lake Michigan. The central characters are humble Catholic fisherfolk. Several characters, in particular a Father Hennessey, appear in more than one story. A priest, Father Schmid, is a Dutch character in "Conspirators."

"The Lie That Larry Told" is typical of these tales. Larry Gallegher, crippled as a child, has one ambition—to become a man, whole and strong, and to captain his own fishing boat. But then he overhears his father telling his mother that Larry will never become a sailor. One day on the lake, father and son are caught in the worst storm the lake has ever known. As their boat nears the rocky shore and certain total destruction, Larry tells a lie that costs him his own life but saves his father.

James Oliver Curwood's first book, *Falkner of the Inland Seas* (1905) is a collection of short stories featuring Jim Falkner, who, as a boy, saw his mother and father drown during a Lake Superior storm.

When Jim is rescued, he cannot remember his family name, so he is christened Falkner. In "The Law of the Lakes," Falkner advises a sailor who has murdered the man who was about to kill the sailor's wife. The story's thesis, one often found in outdoor stories such as those written by Curwood and Rex Beach, is that natural law should supersede the written laws when the latter seem ineffectual. In "The Christopher Dugan," Falkner hears a story about a boy who comes to the aid of a young girl left icebound in a lumber ship after her father suddenly dies. In "The Frozen Ship," a captain becomes insane on his icebound ship; in "Salvage" a clever woman outwits a heartless salvager, gaining possession of a derelict ship loaded with copper ore for its rightful owner, an impoverished man.

Curwood was also the author of *The Great Lakes: The Vessels That Plow Them, Their Owners, Their Sailors and Their Cargoes, Together with a Brief History of Our Inland Seas* (1909). Critics complained that this nonfiction book had too much of a romantic quality, too much heroism and adventure, too much of "the American dream" of the "boy who starts down at the bottom and rises to do things," or "the poor ten-hours-a-day mechanic of a few years since, whose word is now law in the directing of a hundred vessels, the greatest fleet in the world, [or] the president of five steamship companies who began as a messenger-boy at Lansing, Michigan."[10]

The Merry Anne (1904) by Samuel Merwin (1874–1936) is a predictable adventure story about Great Lakes whiskey smuggling from a Lake Huron town to Chicago at the turn of the century, with the usual romantic triangle.

In a dedicatory note to Henry Kitchell Webster, a coauthor on three occasions, Merwin says, "We grew up together on the bank of Lake Michigan . . . and have not forgotten . . . the miles we have tramped along the beach—nor . . . the grim old life-saver on the night patrol near Ludington" (p.7).

Merwin's novels link Chicago and Michigan, demonstrating that, at the turn of the century, western Michigan with its pineries and lumber mills may have looked to Chicago across the lake rather than to Detroit.

Brothers-in-law William MacHarg and Edwin Balmer (1883–1959), the latter a *Redbook* editor, began their *The Indian Drum* (1917) in "the great storm of December, 1895" on Lake Michigan—a storm also used by several other authors. A "steel freighter," the *Miwaka*, on her first voyage, sinks off the northwest coast of the Lower Peninsula near "a copse of pine and hemlock back from a shingly beach. From this copse—dark, blue, primeval, silent at most times as when the

Great Manitou ruled his inland waters"—there came "a sound like the booming of an old Indian drum, . . . one beat for every life" lost when the *Miwaka* sank (pp. 1–2). But, although the *Miwaka* had twenty-five passengers, the drum beat only twenty-four times. Some eighteen years later, the mystery is solved.

Although part of the story takes place in Chicago, much of it is set along the northwest Michigan coast:

> [A] region filled with Indian legend and with memories of wrecks . . .
> Ile-aux-Galets [Skilligalee], Waugaushance, Beaver and Fox islands—
> [where] on the dark knolls topping the glistening sand bluffs to north-
> ward, Chippewas and Ottawas, a century and a half ago, quarreled
> over the prisoners after [the capture of Michilimackinac;] to southward,
> where other hills frown down upon Little Traverse Bay, the black-robed
> priests in their chapels chant the same masses their predecessors
> chanted to the Indians of that time" (pp. 2–3).

Ohioan Louise Kennedy Mabie's (?–1957) *The Lights Are Bright* (1914) is a tale of intrigue and romance that begins in Cleveland and ends, after a voyage through Lakes Erie, Huron, and Superior in Michigan's iron country. A villainous character, trying to take over a mining and manufacturing enterprise, pretends to be romantically interested in the young heiress to the property. He almost succeeds, but at the last moment the young hero shows the heiress what is happening. She keeps the enterprise and the young heir as well. Reviewers were only slightly impressed.[11]

Louis Arundel's *The Motor Boat Boys on the Great Lakes; or, Exploring the Mystic Isle of Mackinac* (1912) is another in those series of formula tales so popular with young adults in the long, long ago. Jack Stormways, Nick Longfellow—the usual fat boy in such novels—and a companion are traveling on Lake Huron in three "natty" little motorboats (after boating through the Thousand Islands in a previous volume) when they encounter two villainous types: "Crafty Clarence" (also called "Sneaky Clarence") Macklin and "Bully Joe" Brinker. They also have adventures and narrow escapes designed to intrigue housebound readers.

Carroll Watson Rankin (1864–1945), a native of Marquette and a prolific author of magazine short fiction, placed three of her books for teenage girls in a Lake Superior setting: *The Castaways of Pete's Patch* (1911), *Cinder Pond* (1915), and *Gypsy Nan* (1926).

Richard Matthews Hallet, a Maine native (1887–) with a law degree from Harvard, wrote two novels and a number of short stories from 1916 to 1939. None of the latter are set in Michigan, but his

Michael Beam (1939), a story of the Old Northwest about 1832 is set partly in the state.

His *Trial by Fire: A Tale of the Great Lakes* (1916) takes place on the *Yuly Yinks,* a coal-burning steamer that hauls coal, grain, and ore on the lakes. Aboard the ship are Bartholomew Grant, the somewhat un-scrupulous owner, and Cagey, the ship's stoker, who has been of-fered $1,000 by a gambler to see that Rutherford Taylor, Cagey's new and inexperienced assistant, is "accidentally" killed. Taylor is actu-ally Grant's son, Alexander (Alec), who has embezzled money from his father's bank in order to pay a gambling debt and is hiding out to avoid arrest. The ship's cook is Cagey's mother—the senior Grant does not know he is Cagey's father. The book's best part is in those scenes where Cagey and Alec, not knowing they are stepbrothers, fire the steamer in the hell of the furnace room—and Cagey watches for a chance to push Alec into the open maw of the furnace.

James J. O'Brien dedicated his *Best Short Stories of 1916* to Hallett, saying, "[I]t is no coincidence that the finest expression of our na-tional life is coming out of the middle west."

The interrelationships among Michigan's Upper Peninsula, Lake Michigan, and Chicago figure prominently in two solo novels by Edwin Balmer, who knew the areas well: *Resurrection Rock* (1920) and *Dangerous Business* (1927). The subject of the former is crime—some long concealed, some new. The Michigan setting is an old mansion on a rocky isle in Lake Huron near the Upper Peninsula's south shore. Lucas Cullen, who once made a fortune logging the area; his granddaughter, Ethel Carew; and Barney Loutrelle, a man with a mysterious past, are the main characters. *Dangerous Business* (1927) has more of its setting in Chicago, but two of the principal characters are from "Emmet County, Michigan, at the very tip end of the roar-ing, windswept lake" (p. 21).

Edward Alden Jewell (1888–1947), art critic and novelist, was born in Grand Rapids. His *The Moth Decides* (1922), the only one of his three novels set in Michigan, takes place over a period of twenty-four hours at a Michigan beach resort where "the moth," Louise Need-ham, daughter of a clergyman, is spending the summer. During the novel's course, Louise vacillates between two men: Lyndall Barry, who is coming from Arizona to marry her, and a young man she has allowed to fall in love with her—even though he was at first more interested in her younger sister, Hilda. Eventually she chooses Barry.

Reviewers thought the novel seemed like either a revival of the typical Trollopian novel plot, featuring long-drawn-out confusion on the part of its heroine, or else a revival of an early Gilbert and Sulli-van light opera.[12]

The hero of Harold Titus's *Spindrift* (1925) is Carl Garrison, skipper of a private yacht whose owner is murdered aboard the vessel one night. Garrison, charged with the crime, is sentenced to prison at Marquette. But he manages to escape and find his way through the northern Michigan woods to a point on Lake Michigan near the Michigan–Wisconsin line where he assumes a new identity, romances a woman, and finds the actual murderer. Even the casual reader will wonder at the several improbabilities and coincidences in the story.

Clarice Nissley Detzer often coauthored books with her husband Karl, but she was sole author of *The Island Mail* (1926), which ran originally as a serial in the *American Girl* under the title "Secret Cargo." Two girls, who plan to sail from the east shore of Lake Michigan to fictional Four Wind Island are entrusted with a sack of mail. The mail is stolen, and at a lighthouse, the women find themselves involved in one of Lake Michigan's "old mysteries."[13]

A year later, Karl Detzer's second book, *The Marked Man* (1927), featured Lake Michigan fishermen, members of the Coast Guard, lighthouse tenders, and nearby farmers. Its central character, Norman Ericson, the son of a former sea captain, dominated by fear of the water, becomes a lighthouse tender. A Lake Michigan storm and a potential ship disaster finally help Norman overcome his phobia.

Ethel Claire Brill's *The Secret Cache: A Story of the Lake Superior Region* (1926), tells of Hugh Beaupre, who comes from Montreal to Isle Royale's fictional Bay of Manitos (Tobins Harbor) to seek a hidden cache of furs.

In *Copper Country Adventure* (1949), Steve Harlow, in the mid-nineteenth century, takes a pioneer steamship through the Soo Canal to the Keweenaw Peninsula to search for copper, visits Isle Royale, encounters a rampaging moose, survives a shipwreck and a forest fire, and outwits the unscrupulous ex-partner of his dead uncle. Harlow returns East for an education (!) before at last becoming a copper mine owner in the Upper Peninsula.

Brill's *The Isle of Yellow Sands* (1925) is a late-eighteenth century tale set on Isle Royale and Lake Superior. *When Lighthouses Are Dark* (1921) is a contemporary story of three boys and a girl stranded for the winter in a lighthouse on a deserted island. Brill was also the author of *The Boy Who Went to the East and Other Indian Fairy Tales* (1917).

Edwin Herbert Lewis used the family summer home on an island in Saint Marys River as the setting for parts of two novels.

Those about Trench (1916) tells of a Chicago doctor, summering at the Sault, who meets a Chicago woman there. Two Indian women, one of whom is undoubtedly modeled on Anna Maria Johnstone, influence the lives of the two protagonists.

In *White Lightning* (1923), Marvin Mahan, a mutilated World War I veteran, hopes to buy an island in Saint Marys River reputed to contain titanium, an economical source of electrical power. (This is the first novel to use the concept of atomic energy.) But Mahan meets a woman who is more interested in preserving the natural beauty of the islands, one of which she owns. He also faces opposition from Ojeeg (a descendant of the Ojibwas), who tells Mahan that white men are scoundrels who make Indians drunkards and "break three hundred treaties" (p. 222). Chase Salmon Osborn is a character in the novel.

Sidney Corbett's *The Cruise of the Gull-Flight* (1937), although written for younger readers, was recommended by one reviewer as a book any "grownup who likes fast-moving yarns can enjoy."[14]

Incredibly, this story tells of five young people who are taken on a cruise of northern Lake Huron by their Uncle Bill, a secret service agent watching for smugglers operating between the United States and Canada. The children, the reader is told, are taken along as a blind. Complications set in—scarfaced gunmen (no doubt a sideways glance at Chicago gangster Al Capone), Indians, a smuggled Asian, secret passages, gunplay, and even a murder—all this as a Great Lakes storm rages. Reviewers noted that the reader would gain a wealth of information about a sailing ship.[15] *The Gull-Flight Sails Again*, a sequel, appeared in 1939.

Sidney Corbett was a young General Motors executive. With his wife Lucy, he coauthored "Pot Shots from a Grosse Ile Kitchen" for the *Detroit News* from his farmhouse on Grosse Ile in the Detroit River—opposite the Fort Malden historical site—even though he was confined to a wheelchair. His wife shared his *Detroit News* byline. Each of these columns—on such subjects as Detroit history, the War of 1812, Cadillac, and the history of Grosse Ile—included one of Lucy Corbett's recipes, somewhat on the order of Della Thompson Lutes's books (see chap. 9, p. 131). They were collected in *Pot Shots from a Grosse Ile Kitchen* (1947) and *Long Windows* (1948), with the Corbetts as coauthors.[16]

The proximity of Ontario, Canada, and Michigan, particularly in the Detroit and Port Huron areas—where no more than a few hundred yards separate U.S. communities from their Canadian neighbors—means that there are varying political and economic loyalties, even a lingering resentment from both the French and Indian War of the 1760s (when Canadians moved freely about, but Americans who ventured forth were murdered and scalped) and the War of 1812, which found citizens on the two sides of the Saint Clair and Detroit rivers at war with each other.

Moreover, in the 1920s, there were customs officers on both sides to insure that liquor was not smuggled into the United States and that other merchandise was not smuggled into Canada. These officers had their work cut out for them, for industry was booming on the American side and thousands of Canadians daily crossed over into Michigan to work.

Howard Blakemore's *Special Detail* (1944) focuses on the criminal aspects of smuggling. Vera Henry's affectionate *A Lucky Number* (1957) focuses on Mother Tippett, who bought dresses in Detroit and smuggled them past Canadian customs. When her husband complained, she said; "Just show me a place in the Bible where it says a single word about smuggling. Just one word."

A reviewer—noting that Father Tippett grew tomatoes in the bathtub and that "Mother provoked innocently enough the laundry driver's libido, and that their daughters set fire to the house with contraband cigarettes"—thought the book was too much in the tradition of *Life with Father, One Foot in Heaven, Cheaper by the Dozen,* and similar [non-Michigan] books, and that therefore no family archive was safe from one's own flesh and blood who had authorial ambitions.[17]

Jay McCormick was born in Harbor Beach in 1919 and grew up in Detroit. At Ann Arbor he was editor of both the university newspaper and the class yearbook, and he won four Hopwood awards. His *November Storm* (1943) was based on a manuscript that had won a major Hopwood Award for fiction in 1942.

The novel's *S. S. Blackfoot* is a dirty "self-unloader" that hauls coal and limestone among ports on Lakes Erie, Huron, and Michigan. The bunkrooms and pilothouse, the stokehold and messrooms of the ship, are the principal settings. The coming-of-age of young Sean Riley provides the novel's principal theme, although the most memorable part of the book is the all-male crew. At the climax of the novel an early winter storm tests every member of the ship's company.

"My father is captain of a Great Lakes freighter," McCormick said, "which provided much of the detail for my novel. I tried my best to keep the novel out of the local color class, but I will probably be known, if at all, as the 'sweet singer' of the Great Lakes."[18]

"Bay Mild" in Louis Kintzinger's 1945 novel of the same name is not a calm watery inlet but a young fisherman by that name who lives in a fishing hamlet on northern Lake Michigan about 1930. Of the novel, about a romance between the young man and a girl, John T. Flanagan wrote that "neither setting nor characters seem plausible."[19]

Ruth Barlow, for a number of years head of the Children's Department in the Flint Public Library, set her *Lisbeth Holly* (1947) forty years earlier in a cottage on the shore of Lake Michigan during the Holly family's vacation. The book was based on the summer home in the Lake Michigan sand dunes where Miss Barlow had spent her first seventeen summers. Gypsies, a lost dog, wagon trips to town, games on the dunes, and swimming the lake enliven this book for young people.[20]

Mary Frances Doner set three of her romantic novels in the Great Lakes area. *Some Fell among Thorns* (1939) takes place in a town where the men are away on boats all summer. Lyn Farnsworth is engaged to John Bigelow, a ship captain; while John is away, Lyn has a momentary romance with a wealthy young visitor. There's a mystery about Lyn's parents that is resolved and the book ends as we might expect.

Not By Bread Alone (1941) is the story of three generations of women in a small lake town. Part of this novel is set on a freighter that is caught in a storm one winter night. But all ends well.

Glass Mountain (1942) tells of a boy who always wanted to be captain of a Great Lakes ship and a young girl who always knew some day she would be somebody. A Chautauqua forms part of the backdrop for the romance between these two.

In Myron D. Orr's *White Gold* (1936), New York gangsters are ostensibly engaged in the fishing industry off Michigan's thumb area, but they are actually smuggling opium from Canada to Detroit. Seemingly a narrative of a fishing war between rival fisheries, the book quickly turns into an account of a war between the young owner of one of the companies and the gangsters. The woman in this romance at first seems to be allied with the gangsters, but after she's rounded up the evildoers, we learn she's a secret operative for the Coast Guard.

Bernice C. Wexstaff's story for juveniles, *The Black Panther of the Great Lakes* (1957), focuses on shipping.

Helga Sandburg (1918–)—daughter of poet Carl Sandburg and the former Lillian Steichen and niece of Edward Steichen, the American photographer and painter—grew up in southwest Michigan's dune country. Carl Sandburg in his poem "Winter Milk," described the young Helga as a "daughter with milk drops on her chin." Helga Sandburg set her third novel, *The Owl's Roost* (1962), on southeast Lake Michigan and its dunes, near the area where the Sandburgs had their summer resort home.

"The Owl's Roost" is the summer home of Dr. Bill and Elizabeth Olson, their daughter Clara, and their son Gus. These two pairs—the adults and the juveniles—represent the division of activities in the novel. The younger are paired off against the older with their paths crossing at crucial moments, such as when fifteen-year-old Clara unexpectedly stumbles upon her mother in bed with a celebrated visiting journalist. Among other adults are a hard drinker, a lecherous native who rents cottages, and an evangelist. The mystery of a drowning has to be solved.

Reviewers found the book interesting, even if they did not think it as good as her earlier *The Wheel of Earth* (1958), which had been set in Kentucky.[21]

Thomas Rogers's *At the Shores* (1980) is set in the summer of 1948 at Indiana Shores, a resort community obviously modeled on Michiana, Michigan, and Michiana Shores, Indiana—two neighboring communities on the Michigan–Indiana line and Lake Michigan. It is the summer before Jerry Engels's senior year in high school, and this "erotic pantheist" (he is fascinated by both the lake and young ladies, particularly Rosalind) is involved in several adventures, including visits to a house of prostitution and an attempted suicide by drowning. This last event follows his realization that his immaturity has led to his loss of Rosalind's affections.[22]

Stephen Tudor's *Hangdog Reef: Poems Sailing the Great Lakes* (1989), in thirty-nine unrhymed verses, takes the reader on a tour from the Detroit River, along the Lake Ontario shore, through the Sault Saint Marie River, through the Straits of Mackinac, to Beaver Island and along the Lake Michigan shore. The places, incidents, and experiences described are based on Tudor's own sailing experiences.

Summary

Michigan writers, just as many other homefolks and tourists, have discovered romance, mystery, adventure, and excitement in those vast bodies of fresh water that lave the Peninsula State's shores. In their books and tales, they have produced images of the lakes' effects on their imaginations, and they almost always have produced books worth reading—if they have not produced the great literature serious critics admire. And the story has not ended, surely Michigan authors will continue to turn to the Great Lakes for subject matter for future fiction and verse.

CHAPTER IX

THE MICHIGAN FARM NOVEL

From the ceiling hung hams and joints of beef wrapped in muslin. On a zinc-topped table stood pans of milk and cream. Bowls of brown eggs from Rhode Island Reds. Jars of pickles and preserves in rows on the shelves. In bins along the concrete floor were potatoes, beans, onions. In the high, dry garret . . . beans, popcorn, peas, nuts, pumpkin, squashes. Down in the cold cellar were more potatoes, turnips, pumpkins, carrots, parsnips, cabbage. Also barrels of vinegar, cider and homemade wine. Out in the smokehouse hung more.

—Arthur Pound, *Once a Wilderness*[1]

Despite the facts that Michigan State College had the first college-level academic courses in agriculture in the United States[2] and that the nation's best strawberries are grown south of Houghton in the Upper Peninsula; despite the highly visible orchards and vineyards in southwest Michigan; despite Traverse City area's famed cherries; and despite the farmfields everywhere else, Michigan is not ordinarily thought of as an agricultural state. Yet, although the farm novel did not come into vogue until about 1920, decades after Michigan's first college novel, and although it had faded from the scene by 1950, there are twice as many Michigan farm novels as there are Michigan college novels. Most of the farm novels were written by college graduates, and, in one case, by a college professor.

Of Arthur Pound's seventeen books, two—*Once a Wilderness* (1934) and *Second Growth* (1935)—are major farm novels at a national level and significant in Michigan's literary history. Together, they form a history of the Mark family on the "Mark section" west of the present metropolis of Pontiac from about 1840 to 1920. There are so many Marks and related non-Marks in these cavalcade novels that we may find it necessary to consult the genealogical chart at the end of the 1935 book to sort them out.

The novels also depict the evolution of the prairie into settled farmland, of the farm into the city. The automobile, arriving about 1900, contributes to the evolution.

Roy W. Meyer, historian of the Middle West farm scene, writes, "An attitude of *noblesse oblige* characterizes the Mark family, who consider themselves and are considered by others superior to their neighbors. John Mark [the family's patriarch] is one of the best individualized figures in modern farm fiction."[3]

Pound's books were also praised by Kansan William Allen White and by Phil Stong, a novelist of the Iowa farm scene. White said that *Once a Wilderness* "stands up and walks, from the first chapter to the last, from the Civil War to the [first] World War and the crash of the War's third phase . . . [It is] honestly conceived."[4]

Pauline Benedict Fischer's *Clay Acres* (1938) is a novel of the rise and fall of a family farm and its fortunes in two generations. James Gelston, a sane close-to-the-soil farmer, brings his less-than-bright bride, Clarissa, to "Up South" Michigan in 1860. Indoctrinated with the culture of the U.S. East coast, she tries to make him a country squire. After Gelston's death, she stupidly allows their son to dissipate the farm and the family's fortune.

Dr. Henry Ormal Severance (1876–1942) was the scion of a family that had come to Oakland County, Michigan, in 1835. He became a school superintendent, a librarian, and a prolific author.

In 1926, his "The Folk of Our Town" in *Michigan History* described the people of his rural Oakland County community and their varying activities from 1867 to 1880. The area is close to that utilized by Pound for his two novels, but unlike the baronial Marks, Severance's people are plain folk. Four years later, his *Michigan Trailmakers* utilized this material and more (ranging back to 1835) in a fictionlike sociological study of the area, much like Hamlin Garland's books, which Severance both quotes and paraphrases, set on the northeast Iowa prairies in the 1860s. Severance lacked Garland's skill as an author, but his book is a valuable record of pioneer Michigan farm life. For example, Severance shows a group singing the "Emigrant Song":

My eastern friends who wish to find
A country that will suit your mind,
Where comforts all are near at hand,
Had better come to Michigan. (p. 15)

Della Thompson Lutes (1869?–1942) is the most remarkable Michigan recorder of the Michigan rural scene. She was born of pioneer parents in Jackson, Michigan, and become a rural school teacher. Moving to Detroit, she taught school, married Irving Lutes, and wrote her first (non-Michigan) novel, *Just Away: A Story of Hope* (1906). From 1907 to 1930 she lived in Massachusetts where she edited several homemaking magazines, including *Modern Priscilla*.

About 1930, Edward Weeks at the *Atlantic Monthly* began publishing her stories that described nineteenth-century rural life in Millbrook, a semifictional town southwest of Jackson. In 1936, when Mrs. Lutes was sixty-five, this material was published in *The Country Kitchen*. The American Booksellers Association awarded the book its prize for the most original book of the year. Another award winner that year was *Gone with the Wind*. By 1938, Lutes's book had gone through thirteen printings.

Some of the book's popularity may have been due to its title and its cover—a red-and-cream gingham-cloth diagonal checkerboard binding—which made it look like a cookbook. If this were the case, purchasers got their money's worth, for interwoven into the book's narrative are comments on food, and descriptions of such kitchen chores as ways to prepare chicken, marble cake, and fig layer cake, for an auction at a box social.

The book also concentrates on the narrator's father, proud of the fact he was directly descended from one of "Three Brothers [who] Came From England":

> [T]he gathered clan: men with rusty-black best coats and cowhide boots; women in dresses of cashmere, alpaca, or, in the case of Aunt Hanner, a black grosgrain with a huge cameo pin. Aunt Sophrony did not boast so fine a dress, but she had a dark green bombazine with many buttons in which we thought she looked exceedingly elegant. The younger women wore gayer gowns; a certain Annabel, I remember, on this particular occasion, wore a bright red merino trimmed with jet which was severely criticized by her elders as being too gaudy (pp. 6–7).

The story line is a social litany of the seasons—holidays, church suppers, church attendance, weddings, death, and the Jackson County Fair, a big event in southern Michigan in the 1880s.

The *Boston Transcript* called *The Country Kitchen* "a lovely and witty story . . . a wholesome and charming book." Dorothy Canfield (Fisher) said it was "odd, original, with a fresh, honest, old-time gingham charm all its own." The *New York Times Book Review* said it was "a luscious book . . . worth treasuring . . . for its sharp and sane philosophy, its pungent style, its racy reminders of the delights of the simple and richly fed existence. It is one of those rare treats which are priceless."[5]

Lutes's *Home Grown* (1937) and *Millbrook* (1938) continued the narrative of the Thompson family; these works also pleased major reviewers.[6] Lutes's *Gabriel's Search* (1940), telling of the beginnings of a pioneer southern Michigan town, was followed by *Country School-ma'am* (1941), which may have had its inspiration in Edward Eggleston's 1871 *The Hoosier Schoolmaster.*

Her sixth and last book of southern rural Michigan life—what for Lutes were the "Easy Eighties" and the "Edible Eighties"—was *Cousin William*, published in 1942, the year of Lutes's death. (A *New York Times* review of the book was accompanied by a "last picture" of Mrs. Lutes, showing her as a semi-invalid.)[7]

Mella Russel McCallum's *Tents of Wickedness* (1928) chronicles the forty-year marriage of Adam Whitaker, son of a southwest Michigan Methodist farmer, to an equestrienne in a small circus, Bess Marvel, whom he first saw as she performed. The novel is set against a background of Adam's family affairs, small town and rural values, and gossip. Bess, though her heart is always with her circus past, makes the marriage endure. Her reward comes in the discovery that a granddaughter will become an entertainer, though on a higher plane than that of a mediocre traveling circus.

Larry Smith's *The Original* (1972, reissued 1974) is set in the period from the 1880s to World War I, a time when former lumberjacks were turning to farming on cutover land as the forests disappeared. The "original" in the story is Jelm Garrett. One of nine children in a squalid farm family, Jelm is an intelligent boy who leaves home after a quarrel with his father. He moves in with Sary Dawkins, a woman of questionable background old enough to be his mother. With her, Jelm finds a comfortable family life and a satisfactory sexual relationship that comes to a tragic end when, still a young man, he dies of overwork.

Douglas A. Noverr says:

> [This] essentially tragic [book] documents the psychological realities of Midwest rural farm life. . . . [I]n many ways [it] also comments on the diminishing qualities of the American Dream as it was perceived by rural folk. . . . At the end . . . there is a sense that the American Dream of unlimited opportunity and self-realization has imposed a false sense of priorities or created a negative effort. . . . [T]he dream,

however perceived, too often pits men against things or against each other, destroying or denying the expression of human needs. The work and the symbols of the work lock men into the limitations of self-justification and pride.[8]

Larry Smith (1940–) took a B.A. degree from the University of Michigan in 1962.

Bessie Ray Hoover's *Rolling Acres* (1922), set in her home area on the Saint Joseph River, tells of Norman Lybrook, who is closely related to English aristocracy, and his family—his wife, Emily; his eighteen-year-old daughter, Viola; and his twelve-year-old son, Bobby. Lybrook's attempts to live like an English aristocrat get him into financial troubles. Then, voila!—Lybrook's older brother dies in England, Lybrook acquires the family wealth, and his problems end.

Hoover, born in Saint Joseph in 1874, alternated two careers as teacher and writer, using her southwest Michigan area as the setting for her work.

Eleanor Blake's *Seedtime and Harvest* (1935), a story of three generations of an immigrant Norwegian farm family, focuses on Else Martison, the daughter. The Martisons had settled near Traverse City because it reminded them of their native Norway.

Else had hoped to go to California to live with a sister, but her "lapse from virtue" one spring night with her father's hired hand keeps her in Michigan. In the end, though she continues to dream of moving west, her mother, her husband, her children, and the farm keep her in Michigan.

Seedtime and Harvest was widely and favorably reviewed. The *Times Literary Supplement* called it a "sincere and well-told tale"; Roy W. Meyer said it was "a fairly skilled treatment of the changing status of the farm woman."[9]

Blake's 1938 *Wherever I Choose*, a sequel to *Seedtime and Harvest*, relates the degeneration of Else Martison's daughter, Bergit, after she marries a Chicago man and moves to a suburb. Though she seems to have intellectual possibilities, away from the farm she soon falls into a routine of heavy drinking, bridge games, and casual acceptance of extramarital affairs. At the end, it seems that Bergit may mature and change her way of life.

Eleanor Blake [Atkinson Pratt] (1899–) was the daughter of Eleanor (Stackhouse) Atkinson, who used the pen name Eleanor Atkinson.

In that late summer of 1935, which had seen the publication of Pound's *Second Growth* and Blake's *Seedtime and Harvest*, a third Michigan author, Isabel Stewart Way, published *Seed of the Land*.

Her protagonist is Ruhama Robins, a woman with the body and drive of a man. An orphan, Ruhama had been sent west from New York City with one of those trainloads of orphaned children that helped decrease the population of New York City and increase the population of the Midwest.

Ruhama, raised on a farm near Flint by Asa Wyatt, constantly contrasts her plowhorse image with the butterfly image of Wyatt's daughter, Mamie. Through Ruhama's eyes the years unfold—the slow backbreaking process of surviving on a forty-acre farm after her husband dies, paying off the mortgage, and always helping Mamie and her hapless husband.

From time to time the novel sermonizes on the worthlessness of farmers like Mamie and her husband and the worth of farmers who prefer backbreaking drudgery to lives as social butterflies.

In a review of the novels of Blake, Pound, and Way, Gladys Hasty Carroll, the Maine author of a saga of the soil, *As the Earth Turns* (1933), said of *Seed of the Land:* "Reading, it, one feels the book is wanting nearly every quality of power, depth, pride, passion and still serenity which contacts with the earth might have been expected to reflect upon it."[10]

Way was born in 1904 and educated at Albion College.

Clara Dillingham Pierson, a lifelong Michiganian (from Stanton), began writing farm stories for young people before 1900. Her first stories were collected in *Plow Stories* (1923), followed by *The Plucky Allens* (1925) and *The Allens and Aunt Hannah* (1927)—all coming near the end of a writing career that had produced fifteen books. The Allens are four orphaned children—Raymond, Frederic, Eleanor, and Polly dear—who live with a woman they call Aunt Hannah (although she is not their aunt) in a large house on a large Michigan farm. Raymond, the oldest, is twelve when the first novel begins.

Early in the twentieth century, overzealous real estate promoters surveyed the cutover country where the Upper Peninsula joins Wisconsin, saw a potential bonanza in this barren land, and began to promote the area in *Cloverland* magazine, telling the readers that the land was a new Eden that would grow farm crops and green pastures for dairy herds.

Jolie Paylin's *Cutover Country: Jolie's Story* (1976) is the fictional treatment of an Illinois family that was enticed to this area and remained there, even though Mrs. Dan Paylin longed for the past comforts and certainties of the corn-and-hog country. The novel is based on the real life experiences of the author's family.

Jolie's life centers on an orphan dog, Spark, and her Indian pony, Bill. In the background, along with Mama's ever-cherished dream of returning to Illinois, are the Ku Klux Klan and bootleggers smuggling illicit liquor south to Milwaukee and Chicago.

The author, Mrs. Henry (Alice) Behrend, the Jolie of the novel, is a farm wife on the Michigan–Wisconsin boundary; she wrote her novel while maintaining a seven-day-a-week schedule of 6 A.M. to 11 P.M. family chores—including milking cows and driving a farm tractor.

Mrs. Behrend's next, *Nels Oskar* (1979), features a northwoods romance between Nels Oskar Fajlstrom, a Swedish-Moravian farmer, and Amalia ("Molly") Basilivich Sprague. The narrator is Nels, thirty-two in 1918, whose family had migrated to the cutover country from Europe. He meets Amalia during the 1918–1919 influenza epidemic that swept across the United States, killing thousands; in Europe, it infected the soldiers in the trenches.

Mrs. Behrends's *Gill Netters* (1970) is set in the Upper Peninsula from 1860 to 1867. Her "Ontonagon," a story set in the Copper Country, was serialized in a local newspaper in 1985.

Gordon Webber's 1959 *What End but Love,* like Pound's novels, treats to some extent the consequences of change on the land and, ultimately, the coming of the automobile, "The black ash and the pine are timbered away. Another wilderness grows there now: the creosoted poles fling their copper strings of communication across the rutted streets. The timid bittern and coot and the black-crowned heron are gone with their marshes, and the otter and the beaver come no more to the ghosts of the long-ago grassy banks. And Jacob Smith is a metal-finisher in the Buick plant and never dreams of Wayshonono."[11]

What End but Love is set on Memorial Day in 1934 at the farm home of old Hollister (Holly) Zenas Hobart. His family comes home as they have on Memorial Days for years past, but this time they expect to hear that Zenas has completed the sale of his land (on the outskirts of Flint) to an automobile manufacturer. But Zenas has changed his mind—he intends to keep the farm and marry a woman half his age who will undoubtedly inherit the property.

The novel was generally praised by reviewers;[12] Roy W. Meyer writes:

> [T]he significance of the novel lies not in the simple plot but in what the reader learns about each of the characters. . . . [They] represent a wide range of occupational and educational levels, from his sons Randall, Methodist minister and Phi Beta Kappa, and Ripley, an auto executive, to his niece, Dee, whose husband . . . combines pig farming and garbage collecting . . . and Julian, actually Holly's illegitimate son, who has virtually resigned from the human race.[13]

In the end, the issue of the farm is resolved when the barn catches fire and Holly dies of overexertion.

Gordon Webber (1912–1986) was born in Linden and earned a master's degree in journalism at the University of Michigan in 1936; then he became a professional writer and film producer.

The ubiquitous Mary Frances Doner contributed two novels to the fiction of the Michigan farm scene. *Gallant Traitor* (1938) features a romance between Diana Sayre and Michael Ward that is hindered by the feud between their families. When her grandfather dies, Diana finds herself responsible for managing a large dairy farm near the fictional Great Lakes village of Saint Gabriel. With her dream of escape to New York City gone, Diana manages to adapt to her new role, help end the feud, and find romance with Michael.

Cloud of Arrows (1950) uses Michigan's sugar beet industry— from planting to processing—as a backdrop for the romantic affairs of a New York commercial artist who moves to Michigan leaving a lover behind. In Michigan, she marries a man involved in the sugar beet industry, but after he leaves her for another woman, she marries her first love. The emphasis is on the romances: the sugar beet industry serves as background.

Significantly, Roy W. Meyer in his *The Middle Western Farm Novel in the Twentieth Century* makes no mention of Doner.

In reading Middle West farm novels of the first half of the twentieth century, one sees opposing views of farm life. "There have been . . . two popular attitudes toward the farmer: 'God bless him,' and 'devil take him,' " said Nelson Antrim Crawford of the U.S. Department of Agriculture. "On the one hand he was viewed as the romantic pastoral husbandman, on the other as an uncouth boor or a troublesome agitator against the economic and political status quo."[14]

Nowhere in farm fiction are these two attitudes as polarized as they are in Geoffrey Dell Eaton's proletariat novel *Backfurrow*[15] and John Towner Frederick's *Green Bush* (both published in 1925). Eaton's novel represents the devil-take-the-farmer point of view; Frederick's the opposite.

It is entirely possible that the attitudes expressed in the two novels are projections of the personalities of the two men. Says Roy W. Meyer: "Eaton's short and mercurial career included a farm background near Plymouth, Michigan, and [his novel] is reputedly autobiographical. As a student at the University of Michigan, [he] antagonized students and faculty by writing violent letters to . . . the *Michigan Daily*, attacking complacency. Elected to Phi Beta Kappa, he refused the honor."[16]

H. L. Mencken said that "Eaton made a sensation . . . by denouncing the more preposterous jackasses of the faculty, and calling upon God to save him and his fellows from their pedagogy."[17]

Backfurrow is a fictional biography of Ralph Dutton, an illegitimate child who grows up in a harsh rural environment. For a time he lives in Detroit, but economic pressures force him back to the country. While saving his money so he can return to the city, he becomes involved with Ellen Tupper, marries her, and becomes a farmer for life. A series of misfortunes—including illness, debt, and crop failure—leads him to resign himself to a hopeless future.

Frederick (1893–1974), a college professor (totally unlike Mencken's "preposterous jackasses") had already published one of Eaton's poems in his *Midland* literary magazine. He said that "Eaton's novel contains more information about farm life than any other recent novel I have read." In contrast with Meyer's later judgment that *Backfurrow* was "structurally faulty," Frederick said that "it is strongly built, highly unified in its essential nature as a narrative." With respect to Eaton's attitude, he added:

> Mr. Eaton's picture of farm life, true as it is in every detail, is not the whole truth. My own experience of farming communities, which is at least as varied and intimate as his [leads me] to wonder whether Mr. Eaton does not give false impression to the uglier sides of rural life and the worst elements in modern society. . . . My knowledge of Mr. Eaton's artistic integrity leads me to believe that he has made a truthful rendering of the scene he chose.

Frederick concluded: "*Backfurrow* is a novel which I am able to admire if not always to like."[18]

John Towner Frederick was raised on an Iowa farm. In 1915, at the University of Iowa, he founded *The Midland*, a literary quarterly, to promote writing about the Midwest by Midwest writers. His efforts contributed directly to the founding of the University of Iowa Writers' Workshop and influenced the founding of programs for creative writers on other American college and university campuses.

In 1919, along with several other Iowans, Frederick and his family moved to the cutover country near Glennie, Michigan, in Alcona County. It was a semiwilderness area where frontier conditions prevailed:

> I use the word "frontier" intentionally [said one of those who went to Michigan with Frederick]. I know now that the life we saw in those years was the end of the last frontier. The north end of the Lower Peninsula of Michigan was far from the early routes of migration to the

West. . . . The early fur traders in Canada had their own routes north of the Great Lakes. Mackinac had been a fort in the days of the fur trade, even before the Revolution, but the interior of the Peninsula was almost unknown to white men before the logging industry began.[19]

In Michigan, Frederick began farming while continuing to edit the *Midland*. Out of these experiences came *Green Bush* (1925) set in Detroit, Ann Arbor, and the Glennie country.

Green Bush debates—through the personae of Frank Thompson (a projection of Frederick) and his friend, Steen—the relative merits of life on the farm (even a poor one such as those around Glennie); life in Detroit; and life as a student and teacher at the University of Michigan. (Detroit comes off a poor third.) For Frank, the problem is not academic; his father has died and someone must take over the family farm and the weekly newspaper his father had edited and published. Frank goes back to school, taking a job to support himself. But when he is offered a teaching position at Ann Arbor, he rejects it, gives up his city job, and returns to the farm, poor as it is.

Frank tells Steen, "[T]he prolonged contact with the earth has brought [me] finally the power to confront life, fate, and [my]self at one with clearness of vision and with peace of mind" (p. 301).

For his part, Frederick never gave up teaching. He spent twenty-eight years at Northwestern and Notre Dame, during which time he became a book reviewer for Chicago newspapers, radio stations, and other media. At the end of his career, he retired to an Iowa farm.

Roy W. Meyer says that the case Frederick "makes out for the superiority of farm [over] city life is the strongest early presentation of this position and perhaps the strongest case that has been made or can be made for it."[20] N. Brillion Fagin declared that *Green Bush* was "a good novel, a novel with some moments [but] also with disappointing moments. . . . [The] book is greater than its plot."[21] Nelson Antrim Crawford wrote, "So far as interpretation of the deepest aspects of farm life is concerned, . . . *Green Bush* reaches the high point in recent fiction. Here, as in no other American novel, implicit unity with the soil is given adequate and coherent expression."[22]

Gordon Webber's *Years of Eden* (1951) utilizes a set of poetic idylls rather than conventional narrative in its account of the early years of Zenas Wheelock, "a rather neglected small boy on a backwoods farm and in a nearby small town" in the 1920s. Trying to understand his section of the universe, Zenas confronts fields, hills, river, and swamp; farm animals; and people in country and town. As in Jolie Paylin's *Cutover Country*, there are "hooded klansmen cavort-

ing in idiotic white." He also confronts such events as a barn burning, roller-skating in the village, and an accident with a haybaler.

Reviewers were ecstatic. Richard Sullivan called *Years of Eden*
"distinguished fiction." Florence Haxton Bullock said it was "a beautiful little book written with humility and an exquisite sweetness of
spirit." Marion West Stoerr chimed in with, "[Webber] portrayed
boyhood, perplexed, astonished, and being acted upon; the well-
nigh anonymous Zenas ranging the limits of a vast and cruel jungle . . . with wide eyes and slumbering mind." Stoerr then compared
the book, albeit somewhat unfavorably, to Wordsworth's *The Prelude;
or, Growth of a Poet's Mind.*[23]

From 1929 to 1932 three volumes of *University of Michigan Plays,*
edited by Kenneth Thorpe Rowe and printed by that distinguished
printer of Michigan literary materials, George Wahr, were published
at Ann Arbor. Of these, only *The Provider* (1932) by William A. Comp-
ton has an identifiable Michigan setting. It has a rural farmhouse as
its background and presents a negative image of farm life.

Ruth Barlow in *Fun at Happy Acres* (1935), a book for young readers, tells of a long day's visit to a farm.

Glendon Swarthout's *The Melodeon* (1977) was labeled "autobiography" by its publishers, but it strikes the reader as pure fiction.
The time is a Great Depression year, the setting a rural community. A
farm couple decides to give the wife's ancient melodeon—a gift to her
family from her grandfather who had been killed in the Civil War—
to their rural church on Christmas Eve, even though a howling bliz-
zard rages. Then, miracle of miracles. As they struggle to carry the
instrument through the snowdrifts into the church, a horseman in a
Civil War cavalryman's uniform rides up and helps move it into the
building. Reviewers were mildly impressed by the tale.[24]

Swarthout was born in 1918 in Pinckney, took B.A. and M.A.
degrees at the University of Michigan (1939 and 1946,) and became
an author and college teacher. He has won several awards for his
work, but the Avery Hopwood Awards Office at Ann Arbor has
no record of his winning a reported Hopwood Award in fiction in
1948.[25] With his wife Kathryn he has written several books for young
people.

Margaret Isabel Ross's book for young adults, *A Farm in the
Family* (1943), tells of four children of a university professor who take
over a rundown family farm after their father has lost his teaching position. At first their ignorance of farm life and their citified notions of superiority over their new country acquaintances and neighbors cause them some problems. But they learn and change, only to

encounter a new problem. As the farm and the children prosper, several relatives arrive to claim the farm. But all ends well.

David McLaughlin's *Lightning before Dawn* (1938) is set both in a small town and on a nearby farm. When Reen Dorr, daughter of the town sexton, becomes pregnant, her lover, Steve Bierce, flees. Through her father's efforts she marries thirty-year-old Lance Janssen who lives on his family's farm. Lance hires Steve as a farmhand; when Steve accidentally learns he is the father of Reen's son, he tries to blackmail her into more sexual relations. When she rejects his advances, he disappears. Lance has learned who the child's father is and thinks Reen has murdered Steve. Reen thinks Lance has murdered him. Then, Steve's body is discovered in a strawstack. All ends well, however, with Reen and Lance happily married.

Roy W. Meyer said the novel has "a melodramatic plot filled with improbabilities and contrived situations, an undistinguished style, inconsistent characterizations, an emphasis on sex that approaches the obscene" and that "its faults outweigh its merits."[26]

Meindert De Jong's *Wheels over the Bridge* (1941) is one to two dozen books De Jong has written for older children. It tells of the efforts a young couple and their son make to keep a farm they bought from a mean old skinflint, who later decides he wants it back and uses all sorts of dirty tricks to achieve his goal. He has his way, but the young family is on the road to a better farm and a better life.

Reviewers liked the book.[27] De Jong, born in Holland in 1906, but later a resident of Grand Rapids, won a number of national and international awards for his books.

Jim Harrison's *Farmer* (1976) focuses on forty-three-year-old Joseph who resides in a Swedish agrarian community in northern Michigan. A schoolteacher for twenty years, he now lives on a farm. His friend, Rosalee, has for years been expecting him to marry her. But Joseph is having an affair with a teenage student that eventually everyone, including the girl's father, a retired army officer, knows about. At the end of the novel it appears that Joseph may marry the girl.

Harrison, who is both poet and novelist, was born in Grayling in 1937, took a bachelor's degree at Michigan State University and became a farmer near Lake Leelanau.

Allan Seager set his 1956 novel, *Hilda Manning*, on a farm and in a nearby town. Hilda, a 1950s Madame Bovary,[28] has placed her illegitimate son with her sister and has married middle-aged Acel Manning who has been forced to quit farming because of a heart attack. He does not know that he is dying of cancer, but Hilda does.

Impatient, she poisons his coffee one morning and collects $40,000 for the house and farm. But Sam Larned, who is obsessed with Hilda, becomes suspicious and initiates an inquest. In the end, however, Hilda, goes free, recovers her son, and, somewhat improbably, marries Sam.

Seager was born in Adrian in 1906, graduated from the University of Michigan in 1930 with a Phi Beta Kappa Key, and then became a Rhodes scholar. He was teaching at the University of Michigan when he died in May of 1968.

Helga Sandburg's second novel, *Measure My Love* (1959) is set on a farm twelve miles from Lake Michigan. Faith Summers, 27, marries Buddy Bain, 22, an indifferent young farmer. He keeps going by secretly borrowing money from Faith's father, and is shortly responsible for the pregnancies of both Faith and her younger sister, Lacy. After Faith and Buddy quarrel over Lacy's pregnancy, Buddy leaves to cut down some trees. In his anger, he tears violently into a tree; part of it falls on him, and he is killed. Faith takes over the leased farm.

Doris Betts thought that the novel was "one of the finest novels with a rural setting in this generation"; Richard Sullivan said, "In the slowly rising entanglement of [the novel's] characters there is a genuine, captivating power; the story carries a strong charge of primitive passion." But Walter Havighurst wrote, "It is hard for a reader to measure [Faith's] love, or to find in this gray little novel any recognizable love at all."[29] Both Havighurst and Sullivan faulted the style.

Helga Sandburg's children's story, *Joel and the Wild Goose* (1964), tells of a farm boy, lonely for a pet, who in the fall finds a goose that had been wounded by hunters. In the spring, the goose, now recovered, joins other geese flying north. But Joel will always keep the memory of the great wild bird. The book has a warm feeling for farm life.

Katherine Neuhaus Haffner's *Clay in the Sand* (1953) covers the first twenty-two years of the marriage of an unlikely couple, Caroline Crawford, a Catholic, and Jonathan Adams, as Puritan as his name. Although it is the roaring twenties, the couple travels to Adams's farm in northern Michigan's cutover country in a horse-drawn buggy. Before she can get her wedding dress off, Adams has her milking a cow. Somehow the unlikely marriage lasts. At one point Caroline leaves her husband and family and goes back to Indiana whence she came—but there she decides she likes northern Michigan. The priest who married Caroline and Jonathan is a constant character in the novel, a young man at the wedding, gray-haired at its end.

Bess H. Tefft (1913–1977), a 1937 graduate of Hillsdale College and an editor of the *Washtenaw County Farm Bureau News*, published two books about Michigan farm life for young people, *Merrie Maple* (1958) and *Ken of Centennial Farm* (1959). The books are, in turn, about a young girl and a young boy who live on Michigan farms.

Three other juvenile books with rural settings are Mrs. Troy E. Clawson's *McBane's Wolf and the Dutchman's Goat* set in Allegan County (1920), Roy K. Moulton's *The Blue Jeans of Hoppertown, Being Extracted from the News Columns of the Hoppertown Gazette* (1908) set in rural Kent County, and Clara Holton Ulseth's *Sandy Trails* (1947) set in Leelanau County.

Summary

Essentially, the farm novel was an outgrowth of several conditions: the rise of industrialism in the United States, to which the farm seemed an antidote; the encouragement and development of fiction set in the Middle West (including most farm novels) by teachers— among them John T. Frederick and the University of Michigan's Roy Cowden—and in regional publications, such as *The Midland* and the *Prairie Schooner*; in the rise of regionalism as a factor in the production of literature, art, and drama in the several areas of the United States; and in the interest of the Eastern publishing establishment, which found that rural literature could attract an audience, not only of rubes, hicks, and hayseeders but also of more cosmopolitan audiences.

But about the end of World War II, interest in regional writing began to dissipate; there was a concurrent loss of interest in the farm family and its problems among fiction writers, and the farm novel virtually disappeared as a genre.

CHAPTER X

THE MICHIGAN SMALL TOWN

"Yes. . . . Well, I can't talk now. . . . I can't talk now, old
sport. . . . I said a *small* town. He must know what a small
town is. . . . Well, he's no use to us if Detroit is his idea of a
small town . . . "

          —F. Scott Fitzgerald, *The Great Gatsby*[1]

William Wallace Cook (1867–1933) "lived in rural grandeur on a
Kalamazoo Avenue estate at the town's edge," churning out
ten thousand words a day of typewritten copy. "Once a week, he
would be seen in the evening, jauntily swinging his cane, on the way
to the mailbox at the Michigan Central depot" with his weekly contribution to the pulp mills of the Street & Smith Publishing Company.
Marshall "was proud of its author."[2]

But Cook's *Wilby's Dan* (1904), published by Dodd, Mead, &
Co., is an improbable tale with frequent coincidences that would test
most readers' willingness to suspend disbelief.

Dan, a southwest Michigan town boy, age eleven, has the reputation of being the worst boy in town. He lives with his miserly
grandfather, old Mr. Wilby, who, although somewhat well-to-do, has
sent Dan's crippled sister Alice to the county poorhouse. One day,
old Mr. Wilby is shot while counting his money, and Dan's father, an
ex-convict, turns his son in for the $1,000 reward as several coinci-
dental events point to the boy's guilt.

Dan escapes from jail and frees his sister from the poorhouse. The two flee to Chicago, arriving there after several narrow escapes from harm. Other misadventures follow. Alice is accidentally shot and killed, and Dan's innocence of his grandfather's murder is established. He returns to fictional Trueville to live on his grandfather's money.

Arthur Jerome Eddy (1959–1920) of Flint wrote *Tales of a Small Town* (1907) from the viewpoint of "one who [has] lived" in the Michigan "pine lands." The stories focus on a judge with a past marriage he would like to forget; a grave robber (the town bully) and the small boy whose death he causes; some dishonest lawyers, a concurring judge, and the family they ruin; a saloon owner who is almost found guilty of a murder he did not commit; a small boy, accused of a robbery, who, to save himself, commits a robbery; a blind and mute man who unintentionally kills a girl who has been his benefactor; and a self-centered rector whose occupation causes his wife a number of problems. Some tales are simply vignettes, others have O. Henry-type surprise endings. Some have a sentimental tone and some are bittersweet in their conclusions. Eddy was better known as an author of books on art subjects.

Howard Vincent O'Brien's *The Terms of Conquest* (1923) begins in the small town of Coldwater, Michigan, in the late summer of 1892, with one more eternal triangle. Its members are: Homer Gaunt, a "puritan," who was educated in a convent school and now works in a newspaper shop in the town; Eleanor Jessup, a debutante whose well-to-do father kills himself when his investments fail; and Ivy Gossman, whose father, an 1850s fugitive from Germany, hates Gaunt. Homer marries Ivy; Eleanor marries Watson Miner. Both families move to Chicago where Gaunt becomes a successful publisher of school textbooks and Eleanor's lover. After a bullet intended for Gaunt has killed Miner, Gaunt takes Ivy back to Coldwater to die. He intends to return to Chicago and marry Eleanor.

Part of the novel's significance is its portrait of a couple, who like thousands of others in the late nineteenth century and early twentieth migrated from small Michigan towns—where opportunities seemed limited—to Chicago, Detroit, and Toledo and other cities.

Dan Cushman (1909–) was born in Marion, Michigan, the grandson of a Maine man who stayed in Michigan—after he was shipwrecked and became a lumber worker—first in the Middle Branch area and later in the Upper Peninsula. Cushman's parents were graduated from the Ferris Institute (now Ferris State College). His early years were spent in the Copper Country and the Upper Peninsula iron range before he moved to Great Falls, Montana.

Like many writers, Cushman has had several careers—as assayer, prospector, geologist, and then as a magazine and newspaper writer and radio announcer. After 1950, he wrote some two dozen books—one of which was a Book-of-the-Month-Club selection—and founded his own publishing company, Stay Away Joe Publishers (from the title of his 1953 book *Stay Away, Joe,* which focused on American Indian outcasts).

Two of Cushman's books are set in Michigan. *The Grand and the Glorious* (1963) is a story of a Fourth of July celebration in neighboring Red Wing and Altooma and its consequences for the citizens of those two fictional towns. Its characters include a Republican with Catholic sympathies who, while campaigning for the Michigan House of Representatives, works both sides of the religious electorate by attending a Protestant church; the Viking, an aviator who wings in to thrill the crowd with his flying ability in his monoplane and tells tales of worldwide adventures—but who turns out to be plain Oscar Nettles from Minnesota; the narrator's grandfather, who is heavily in debt to banker A. B. Finreddy, a minor-league villain; and several others. The main events are a Fourth of July parade; a ball game between the novel's Red Wing and the Bengtsen Germans; a race between Grandpa's automobile and the Viking's monoplane; a box social; and several romances.

Brothers in Kickapoo (1962, published in England as *Boomtown*) focuses on a "demon insurance salesman," Willard T. Watney, a "re-incarnated George F. Babbit, a Willy Loman who has made it." When the Westboro village idiot—an author whose previous book *The Nymph and the Maniac* was only a modest success—sells his second novel to a motion picture company, Watney, whose schemes for the town have included a tractor assembly plant and a fertilizer factory, persuades the film's producer to make the film in Westboro.

Then an industrial complex that is financing the film decides to erect a chemical plant in Westboro—a boon for business but ruination for the town's character. Next, the tourists flock in and the local Hyenas' Club stirs up the cry for "Growth! Business! Progress!" Finally comes the rude awakening for Watney.[3]

The story line of *Brothers in Kickapoo* is much like the story line of *Looking for a Location* (also 1962), a novel that Sewell Smith, the protagonist of Glendon Swarthout's *Welcome to Thebes,* plans to write about his (fictional) hometown of Thebes, Michigan. Reviewers didn't think *Brothers in Kickapoo* rivaled *Moby Dick* or *The Scarlet Letter,* but it made them laugh more often.[4]

Edmund G. Love (1912–1990), who grew up in Flint, set his autobiographical *The Situation in Flushing* (1965) in a small town just northwest of Flint in the years 1915 to 1924—"a period of profound change in the lives of" Americans. A six-year-old boy, whose father owns a hardware store, is fascinated by the steam locomotives that must climb out of the valley in which the town is located, pulling their heavy trains behind. In the winters, with his friends, he slides down the steep streets in the city. In the summer, afraid that there will not be enough pumpkins for his favorite pie dessert, he plants pumpkin seeds in gardens and flowerbeds all over town. Theodore R. Kennedy says Love's "portrayal of village life during that decade when the automobile worked a profound transformation in American life," is superb.[5]

Russell Kirk, a history scholar and teacher, was born in Plymouth, Michigan, in 1918; although he has taught at colleges and universities in and away from Michigan, he has often given his home address as Piety Hill in Mecosta, Michigan, Mecosta County, west of Mount Pleasant. To friends he is the Wizard of Mecosta, a town one of his great-grandfathers helped settle. Piety Hill, a pioneer structure that was Kirk's great-grandfather's home, was destroyed by fire in 1975.

Of Kirk's more than two-score books, one, *The Surly Sullen Bell* (1962), is a collection of ten tales and sketches the author has described as "unabashedly Gothic." He says that the reader may find in the tales "hints of M. R. James, Henry James, and even Jesse James." A "true" narrative in the volume is "Lost Lake," a descriptive sketch of Mecosta. Of the fictional pieces, one tells of "Skyberia," and its "earthy people and [their] struggles with faith and the soil." "Behind the Stumps" tells of a "seedy old house, strange unneighborly people, and a long-dead harridan—or her ghost." "The Cellar of Little Michigan" is probably based on both Plymouth and Mecosta, although Kirk calls his fictional town New Devon. Some of these tales were later published in *The Princess of All Lands* (1979).[6]

The Mecosta rural area is also the setting for Curtis Stadfelt's nonfictional *To the Land and Back* (1972).

Paul Osborn (1901–), who had previously produced the successful *On Borrowed Time* for the New York stage, wrote *Morning's at Seven* in 1939 about four aging sisters and their husbands, all neighbors in a small town, and the resulting complications when the middle-aged son of one couple brings his thirty-nine-year-old intended wife to his parents' home.

The title is ironic—all is not well in this ménage. But the play's complications are presented in droll fun rather than in a Freudian study of human behavior or a situation where crime is imminent. Brooks Atkinson called it "pure comedy in the vein of American folkways," but he thought it ran twenty minutes longer than necessary.[7]

The 1939 production of the play had only forty-four performances, but a new production in 1980 became a hit, running for 584 performances in New York City and winning three Tony awards.[8]

Born in Evansville, Indiana, Osborn spent his childhood in the first decade of this century in Kalamazoo. He once told a *New York Times* reporter that he created his play from the gossip and arguing he heard in the neighborhood in which he grew up. He earned a master's degree from the University of Michigan and taught there from 1925 to 1927. Then he went east to George Pierce Baker's Dramatic Workshop. His best plays were *On Borrowed Time* (1938), *A Bell for Adano* (1944), *Point of No Return* (1951), and *The World of Suzie Wong* (1958), none with Michigan settings.

Helen Hull's *Heat Lightning* (1932), a Book-of-the-Month-Club selection, is a novel about the disintegration of a Michigan small-town family who became wealthy through lumbering and a farm implement business. The father is dead; his widow, Madame Westover, is the family head.

By 1930, the family is disintegrating, the business is facing bankruptcy, and the family's "movie palace" mansion is now in a deteriorating residential area. In the course of the narrative, some of the family's skeletons emerge from their closets. As their bones rattle, Madame Westover, in a fit of anger, tears up her will intending to write a new one. But she dies during a nighttime summer storm. Her children are left to fight over the estate and to face the consequences of the past errant behavior of their family members.

Such social disorganization is a frequent theme in Hull's work. Critics thought that in *Heat Lightning* the talented Hull had produced her best work.[9] Hull's novel also forecast the coming disintegration of Midwest small towns as farms became larger and the number of farm families decreased.

Edith Elizabeth Kneiple Roberts (1902–1966) set her 1940 *Tamarack: A Novel* in one year of the life of a moribund Upper Peninsula town that had once been a logging center and that now thrives only in the tourist season, except for a tavern frequented by young men from the nearby Civilian Conservation Camp (CCC).

The novel emphasizes illicit relationships among Tamarack's citizens that produce fatherless children, ongoing gossip, hate and jealousy, isolation, and even attempted murder in what must be the bitterest attack on the small American town ever published. (One is reminded of the attitude toward farm life in Geoffrey Dell Eaton's

Backfurrow.) This note of small-town deadliness is reinforced at the novel's end with a character's comment that all small towns are alike in their petty, vicious, character destruction.

In a later novel set in Minnesota, *That Loring Woman* (1950), Roberts again turned to the inflammatory role of gossip in a small lumbering town.

At the University of Chicago, Roberts had studied with Robert Herrick, whose novels were highly regarded in the early years of this century. Bernard Duffey has synthesized Herrick's own attitude, "Chicago was boring, Chicago was vulgar, Chicago was ugly, Chicago was cruel."[10] Perhaps Mrs. Roberts acquired some of her pessimistic philosophy from her mentor.

Allan Seager's *The Inheritance* (1948) presents another negative image of small-town life, "[T]he dark places, the reservoirs where fear, hate, despair collect." The people of Athens, Michigan, "are shown as the inheritors of a tradition of greed and violence that had been useful when log houses had to be built and the forest cleared, when there had been Indians to fight for possession of the land, or even when the coming of the railroad had been a realized dream."[11] This theme is worked out in the behavior of one family.

The Inheritance was one more in a series of attacks on small-town life that had begun a generation or so earlier in a "revolt from the village" on the part of authors, artists, and intellectuals and that had produced a large collection of novels and plays by writers who saw the small town "as a mean, evil, warping influence."[12]

Mrs. Lila M. Burnham's *The White Lilac Tree* (1952) has an unusual narrator—a white lilac tree that narrates neighborhood affairs in Cobb's Corners, Michigan, in the "Arcadian" years before the First World War brought in the age of anxiety. The tree's viewpoint is obviously limited, but it is aided by overheard conversations between two cousins. During the years in which the two are growing up, such simple events are related as the coming of new schoolteachers, graduation exercises, visits to the farm or city, a New Year's Day sleigh ride, a maple sugar party. The novel, said a critic, does not "penetrate very deeply into character" or have much variety.[13]

Mrs. Burnham was born in Byron Center near Grand Rapids, the small town on which the Cobb's Corners of the novel is based; she was a 1909 graduate of the University of Michigan.

Richard Lardner Tobin, son of Ring Lardner's sister, and one of Lardner's close friends, was born in Chicago in 1910 and took a degree at Ann Arbor in 1932. Following graduation, he worked as a reporter in Niles and nearby South Bend, Indiana, then went to the *New York Herald-Tribune*. He later wrote for the American Broadcasting Corporation in both radio and television and was a teacher at the Pulitzer School of Journalism at Columbia.

Tobin's one novel, *The Center of the World* (1951), is set in a town he calls Clearwater, Michigan, but is plainly modeled on the Lardner's home town of Niles. The time is the 1920s, an era when the Stutz Bearcat and the Franklin automobile with its air-cooled engine were replacing the horse and buggy.

The novel's theme is the clash between the old and the new— the old represented by Dr. David Fawcett, son of a former town doctor, and his two neighbor ladies, both quite elderly, both with distinct memories of the town's history from the time when there were more Indians than whites. The new is represented by Geoffrey Householder, who has come to town and acquired one of the town's banks, the paper mill, and the newspaper, and by Ephraim Peacock, the son of a former Clearwater banker, who manages Householder's bank for him. These last two represent the twentieth century with its goals and ideals (or its lack of them) and are the story's villains. Critics were moderately pleased with the book.[14]

In 1962, Glendon Swarthout published *Welcome to Thebes*, which, in its ugly image of a town, parallels Roberts's *Tamarack* and Seager's *The Inheritance*. The setting is Thebes, Michigan, a town of two thousand, at the junction of two rivers, the Ionian and the Button, forty-one miles north and west of Grand Rapids. Swarthout probably chose the location because nowhere in that area is there a place that matches the description of his fictional town.

Thebes has two sets of pillars: the first, the business and professional men who are the town's backbone; the second, three stone columns at the edge of town supporting a Welcome to Thebes sign. Nearby is a Greek outdoor theater built into the hillside.

Sewell Smith left Thebes at eighteen because a boyish prank nearly turned into disaster. He returns at thirty-five, a war hero and successful author, intending to write a novel about Thebes and to avenge his father's death at the hands of the town pillars—the school superintendent, a mill owner, the newspaper editor, a bank vice-president, the town's leading doctor, and a merchant.

In the course of the novel, both sets of pillars are demolished— the reputations of the town's leaders by Smith's efforts, and, in a symbolic parallel, the pillars on the hillside are demolished by a young man with a new sports car. Reviewers had mixed emotions about the novel.[15]

Summary

The Michigan small town, like the Michigan farm, has been treated both positively and negatively in fiction. Such positive and negative attitudes about small-town life were not limited to Michigan authors. In the twentieth century, however, those who wanted to depict the village romantically as Oliver Goldsmith had in "The Deserted Village" were opposed by novelists such as Theodore Dreiser, who, writing about his work as a newspaper reporter at the turn of the century, said:

> You could not write about life as it was; you had to write about it as somebody else thought it was, the ministers and farmers and dullards of the home. Yet here I was busy in a profession that was hourly revealing the fact that this sweetness-and-light code, this idea of a perfect world which contained neither sin nor shame for any save vile outcasts, criminals, and vagrants, was the trashiest lie that was ever foisted upon an all too human world. Not a day, not an hour, but the pages of the very newspaper we were helping to fill with our scribbled observations were full of the most incisive pictures of the lack of virtue, honesty, kindness, even average human intelligence, not only on the part of the few, but of nearly everybody.[16]

CHAPTER XI

THE MICHIGAN CAMPUS SCENE

New Padua is a university town. But let not anyone be
deceived by the name into fancying that New Padua is anything like Oxford, or Bonn, or even for that matter like Cam-
bridge in Massachusetts, where . . . Harvard is situated. New
Padua is the seat of what the people in England would call a
great popular college rather than a university; a college
founded by the State, of which it is the educational centre,
with special reference to the needs of the somewhat rough and
vigorous youth who are likely to pour in there. The city of
New Padua belongs to a State which not very long ago used to
be described as Western, but which the rapid upspringing of
communities lying far nearer to the setting sun has converted
into a middle State now.
—Justin McCarthy, *Dear Lady Disdain*[1]

The relative handful of authors who set novels on Michigan college and university campuses as compared with the much
greater number of Michigan authors with college degrees may be
taken as an indication that authors of Michigan novels found life away
from the campus more suitable to the novel, or it may not. But the
books we do have, with their subjects ranging in time from the late
nineteenth century to some distant future time, indicate that the
Michigan campus scene does have novelistic potential.

The earliest novel set (though only in part) on a Michigan campus, Justin McCarthy's *Dear Lady Disdain* (London, 1875; New York,
1876) was written by a native of Ireland who spent most of his working life in London. However, McCarthy (1830–1912) had made two
visits to the United States in the course of which he visited Ann Arbor—twice—as well as other Michigan towns.

The novel's story line is simple enough. At Ann Arbor, a lower-
class immigrant from England is invited to the university president's
home to meet the wealthy upper-class English girl who had rejected his
marriage proposal. Once again he proposes; once again he is rejected.

The reception gives McCarthy a chance to comment on the faculty of the university at that time:

> The university had gathered a community about it from all quarters. . . . The president . . . came from New York. His wife, still a fine woman, though passing her prime, was from Maryland. Professor Benjamin was from Ohio; his wife had drawn her early breath within sight of the Boston Common. . . . Clinton was a Vermonter, married to a lady from Illinois. The various foreign professors . . . had some of them foreign wives; and the editor of the journal . . . had once been United States consul at Athens, and had brought home to New Padua a countrywoman of Sappho as his wife (p. 319).

The identification of the fictional New Padua and its university with Ann Arbor and the University of Michigan was made clear by McCarthy in a note to a sometime literary collaborator, "Arun-Arbor (sic) is the *New Padua* of *Dear Lady Disdain*."[2] On page 318 of the copy of the novel at the University of Michigan, a penciled note states that the Professor Clinton of the novel, an important character, was probably based on an actual Professor Alexander Winchell of the University of Michigan faculty.

Basil L. Crapster said that the value of McCarthy's novel lies not so much in its literary caliber as in its image of "Ann Arbor and the university as they looked [in the early 1880s] to an informed, perceptive and sympathetic foreigner."[3]

Olive San Louie Anderson, using the pen name of "Sola [from her initials]," was the author of *An American Girl and Her Four Years in College* (1878). Its setting was the University of Michigan.

Stanley Waterloo (1846–1913), born on a farm in Saint Clair County, graduated from the University of Michigan in 1869. He was one of the early Michigan authors to make a name for himself, although that reputation was made after he had moved to Chicago and become a newspaper reporter. In 1898, the University of Michigan awarded him an honorary master's degree, just a year before his Michigan college novel, *The Launching of a Man*, was published.

Waterloo's image of the school as "one of the largest and greatest universities in the world" (p. 13) may not have influenced the university in its award, but it did not hurt his cause any. But Robert Sargent does not spend all his time contemplating the university's status or even sitting at the feet of "learned professors," such as "Old Syllabus." He plays on the eleven in the fall, on the nine in the spring, and entertains a romantic interest in two women, one of whom he marries after becoming a builder of railroads.

Waterloo was the author of many books. His *The Wolf's Long Howl* (1899) is a collection of twenty short stories, of which several are set in Michigan. His most successful book, *The Story of Ab: A Tale of the Time of the Cave Man*, went through sixteen editions from 1897 to 1934.

The third writer to make use of the University of Michigan in the late nineteenth century was Karl Edwin Harriman (1875–1935) in his collection of eight short stories, *Ann Arbor Tales* (1902). These are not the "Hurrah-for-Old-Siwash" type of story so common in the early years of the century but rather sentimental, romantic tales, all probably based on Harriman's college days at the University of Michigan.

"The Making of a Man" introduces the college widow to American fiction—the college-town woman who finds a new romance in each succeeding generation of students but who is always discarded in favor of another girl. Two stories feature running contests that involve one Bunny of '85—probably based on an actual University of Michigan student. Another, "The Kidnapping," is based on the practice of hazing—here, an attempted fraternity initiation backfires on the hazers.

"The Old Professor: A Portrait" is also in all likelihood based on a real person—a southerner who came to Ann Arbor long before the Civil War. When Fort Sumter is fired on and the university organizes a volunteer company of soldiers, the old man's loyalties are severely tested.

"The Day of the Game" features the big game between Michigan and Cornell universities, played on a Detroit gridiron. The focus of the story is on John Adams, the Michigan player who is the game's star. In a hotel lobby after the game, he sees his father, drunk. On the way home on the train, he thinks about his Polish ancestry (his last name is actually Adamski), and he decides to drop out of school and return home where he belongs. (Harriman similarly dropped out of the University of Michigan to become a journalist.) "The Day of the Game" was reprinted in *The Homebuilders* in 1903.

In 1922, George Gibbs dedicated his *The House of Mohun* to "my friend, Karl E. Harriman in appreciation of his constructive criticism and encouragement."

Leonard Cline's *Listen, Moon* (1926), written in a "spirit of sheer holiday nonsense," is a tale of the adventures of an absent-minded professor after his "dull wife" leaves him. His gambols with a "wild flapper" having incensed local Ku Klux Klansmen, he takes to an ancient sailing vessel with a motley assortment of people, all tagged as pirates, for a wild assortment of adventures. At the end, his wife now a ghost, returns to offer him advice about his future.

John T. Frederick, who had not been precisely happy with Cline over his *God Head*, said *Listen, Moon* was a "joyous . . . pagan" book, both "arresting and intensely fascinating."[4]

Dewitt C. Miller used the classic epistolary form for his *The College Cut-Up; or, Letters from Jack to Dad*, set at Ann Arbor. It was published by Wahr in 1927.

Janet Hoyt, a pseudonym for Jean Hamilton, a college Dean of Women, focused her *Wings of Wax* (1929) on a supposedly imaginary president of Woban College, but critics have identified the model for her Victor Marston as former President Clarence Cook Little of the University of Michigan.[5]

President Marston heads his university for only two years. He tyrannizes the faculty, angers the state legislature, and alienates supporters. He is friendly toward the students, but his slipshod administrative tactics at last cause them to burn him in effigy. Although he is married to a faithful wife, he cannot resist pretty women students. When a member of his board suggests that he resign, he contemplates suicide. Then he dies in an automobile accident with his young student paramour. The novel also presents "evidence of [students'] wickedness."[6]

T. P. Brockway took a dim view of the book, calling it "a partisan but thinly veiled depreciation" of the University of Michigan president. "The remarkable coincidence of agreement between the known facts of President Little's life and much of Janet Hoyt's description of President Marston suggests that *Wings of Wax* is something other than it appears."[7]

President Little's brief career had not long to wait for a second fictional treatment. William Hume Stockwell, concealing his identity behind the nom de plume of W. Stock Hume, wrote *Rudderless: A University Chronicle* (1930), a *roman à clef* of a student's four years at the novel's Harcourt University in Belham, Michigan.

This "incredibly dull book about the University of Michigan," obviously written from an insider's view, is dedicated to C. C. L., "The almost insurmountable difficulties which beset him as an administrator, while he was engaged with the problems herein presented in narrative form, do not cloud his recognition as a man of vision, brilliance and sincerity. He had the perspicuity to recognize these problems far in advance of his time, and he dealt with them courageously according to the measure of his ability."[8]

But the major problem delineated in the course of Tom Benham's student years is that the educational program is "superficial," and in the words of one teacher, "rudderless"—it lacks "direction" (pp. 188, 190).

Behnam becomes a fraternity member—football is big business at Harcourt and fraternities recruit potential top-flight players. He writes papers for fellow team members who never go to class and romances a girl.

Frederick Manfred (1912–), under the pseudonym Feike Feikema, set his *roman à clef, The Primitive* (1949), on the campus of Calvin College in Grand Rapids (in the novel Christian College in Zion). Manfred, an Iowan who prides himself on his Frisian ancestry, is one of six major authors who have matriculated at Calvin; the others are David Cornel DeJong, Peter DeVries, William Brashear, Paul Schrader, and Meindert De Jong.

At Calvin, Manfred, probably the tallest of American authors at six feet nine inches, played basketball; joined literary, philosophical, and dramatic clubs; and helped edit several college publications.

Peter Oppewall, a Calvin College English professor, has shown how Manfred uses realistic details, such as names of streets, students, and teachers, as well as his college experiences in the novel. But there are imaginative situations, too, such as the one where the giant Thurs breaks the elfin queen's [ribs] in a moment of passion.[9]

Reviewers had mixed reactions to Manfred's novel. Most readers would agree with George R. Stewart's judgment that, although Manfred "tends to overwhelm the reader by massiveness of design and by a tanklike rush of his writing," he also has "magnificent qualities as a novelist: a fine and basic honesty, tremendous powers of observation, a considerable knowledge both of nature and humanity by which to direct his observation, a Whitman-like enthusiasm for life."[10]

Readers would also agree with fellow Iowa author, Paul Corey, that *The Primitive* is "considerably weakened by [Manfred's] use of such [invented] words as *lornsick* and *stumbered* to get an effect of a "fine" writing style. His trick of parodying contemporary writers' names and book titles [B. S. Idiom, 'The Love Song of J. Freddie Petticoat'] is not really clever, but an annoyance to the reader."[11]

The novel has one other distinction—at 460 pages, it is the longest and most detailed fictional study of the Michigan college scene. In 1962, it was combined with two other semiautobiographical novels, in one volume titled *Wanderlust*.

Manfred's *Winter Count* (1966) is a volume of verse containing "The West Sends a Call," written at Calvin College in 1934.

Kenneth Millar (1915–1983), who later used the pseudonyms John Macdonald, John Ross Macdonald, or Ross Macdonald, set his first novel, *The Dark Tunnel* (1944), on the University of Michigan campus where, in the late 1930s and early 1940s he had received M.A. and Ph.D. degrees as a fellow in English. The mystery story involves an English professor, a respected colleague who is a refugee from Europe, a member of the university's War Board, and Nazi agents. The novel was reissued as *I Die Slowly* in 1955.

Millar's wife, Margaret (1915–), is also a novelist.

Helen Hull used her experiences as the daughter of an Albion College English Professor for three novels. *Quest*, her first novel (1922), focuses on Jean Winthrop, the daughter of a man who is a failure both as a college professor and in business. She grows up in a household torn by differences between her parents, and after college becomes a teacher herself. The novel continues with Jean's quest to make her own life worth living.

Hull's *A Circle in the Water* (1942) is set in a small midwestern college in the "normalcy" of the Harding presidency. Hilary Sedgewick, a young instructor with a wife, a small son, and literary ambitions completes his first novel—a realistic work in the vein of Eugene O'Neill—based on his own Maine youth. He hopes that the novel will be a money-maker and will win him the professorship he seeks. The novel does neither, but the furor it creates costs him his job. He moves to New York.

Hull's *The Asking Price* (1930) is also set in a small college town. It tells of a young teacher with the soul and aspirations of a poet who marries the woman of his dreams, only to discover that her aspirations for him include moving onward and upward on the collegiate ladder—poetry can wait. In the end, his only joy is encouraging his daughter to be the rebel he had not been.

Peter DeVries (1910–) was a student at Calvin College in Grand Rapids from 1927 to 1931. His *Let Me Count the Ways* (1965) has a character named Tom Waltz, an English teacher in Polycarp College in Slow Rapids, a Bible Belt town. Waltz rebels against both his atheist father and his Gospel Mission mother, ending up in a quandary. (As Corey Ford once wrote, the walls of quandaries are slick as glass.) The novel is typical DeVries—puns ("Gladly, the cross-eyed bear"), startling events (a man with his umbrella on fire), parodies (the "Three Little Prigs"), and the like.

Nolan Miller (1912–) came to Detroit when he was eleven. His education was completed in Detroit public schools. At Wayne State University, where he was the literary editor of the *Collegian,* he took a bachelor's degree in 1929—he was seventeen! After graduate work, he taught at a Detroit high school and at Wayne State, then became writer-in-residence and teacher at Antioch College. At the University of Michigan in the summer of 1943, he was presented with a minor Hopwood Award for short fiction.

Nolan Miller's second book, *The Merry Innocents* (1947) tells of the week before Christmas 1946 in the lives of a Michigan family—a professor, who is writing a book; his wife, who has social pretensions; their four children, who range from a graduate student to a young boy; and the black maid Julia. During that week, individual members of the family each survive personal crises—some serious, some comical—usually with the help of Julia. In general reviewers were satisfied with the book.[12]

In 1954, Nolan Miller published his third novel, *Why Am I So Beat*. The novel describes a weekend of parties by four students: the liberal editor of a college literary magazine; a young man unrestrained in manners and morals; a noncollegiate young woman picked up in a park—with her nursing baby; and the narrator, a confused young male student. A reviewer found the book as confused as the narrator.[13]

Virginia Evans's *The Cautious Husband* (1949) is one of several novels that reflect the arrival after World War II of a new type of student on college and university campuses—war veterans, many with wives or husbands and children, attending college under the GI Bill, which paid for tuition and books and gave a monthly stipend as well. These families often lived in student dorms for married couples, which frequently consisted of former Army barracks and Quonset huts. Like Evans's novel, many of the books were written by wives and thus are seen through a woman's eyes.

Lloyd Andrews is the son of a Babbitt-like father and an efficient, but pathetic, mother—both midwesterners. His wife, Caroline, is from Washington, D.C. The school is the University of Michigan where Mrs. Evans herself studied with Roy Cowden in postwar days. The couple's differing personalities lead to strained relations that are resolved by the wife's pregnancy. Of four reviewers, only the *New York Herald-Tribune*'s liked it.[14]

Alma Routsong (Brodie) (1924–), was born at Traverse City and attended Western Michigan University for two years, then she joined the Waves (Women Accepted for Volunteer Emergency Service). After marriage in 1947, she returned to Michigan State University to complete her degree work.

Her *A Gradual Joy* (1953) is set in a college barracks at Michigan State University. A young recently married couple, both World War II veterans, are planning careers—he as a teacher, she as a surgeon. She is not especially attractive; he has proposed marriage to her in a moment of "misplaced sympathy." A reviewer liked the realistic touches:

> Mrs. Routsong captures the essentials of [such] communities, flimsy, crowded, domesticated. There is the [village] office with its bulletin-board where second-hand strollers, cribs and textbooks were offered for sale. There is the laundry where young fathers discussed the "Burma Road" [a heavily attacked World War II supply route in Asia], Thoreau, or whether the colored shirts would run, with equal conviction. . . . Everywhere there were diapers.[15]

Reviewers liked the book, because, as Marjorie B. Snyder, *Chicago Sunday Tribune Magazine of Books* reviewer, said, "it is genuine."[16]

Jeanne E. Wylie (1913–), earned a master's degree at Wayne State University, taught in the Detroit schools, then became a writer. She published some poems before her "A Long Way to Go" won an *Atlantic Monthly* award over 1,116 other short stories and was published in the *O. Henry Memorial Award Prize Stories* of 1942.

In 1952, Wylie's *Face to Face,* set in a university town, focused on five people, two of them World War II veterans, who become involved in a public debate when a black war veteran applies for admission to the university. Before the affair is settled, the man of color and two others are casualties.

Robie (Mayhew) Macauley (1919–) is a native of Grand Rapids with a bachelor of arts from Kenyon College and a master of fine arts from the University of Iowa Writer's Workshop. His professional career has consisted of teaching at the college level, editing, and writing.

Macauley's 1951 *Disguises of Love* is set on a campus in southern Michigan, much like the University of Michigan. The novel tells of a college professor, Howard Graeme, who has a wife and a rebellious sixteen-year-old son. All three take turns narrating the story's incidents from their own points of view. A fourth character, Frances Mitchell, one of Graeme's students, seduces him. But at the airport, where Graeme has come to fly with her to a new life elsewhere, she deliberately leaves him standing at the gate.

Reviewers had mixed responses. One said the novel "speaks with eloquent sadness to everyone who knows that love is never without its limits—and realizes the series of masks it perhaps necessarily assumes."[17] A second said that the reader "doesn't necessarily believe in [Macauley's characters]—the tragic end is implied, but Macauley unfortunately blurs it by understatement."[18] And a third said that people were not likely to take the novel seriously.[19]

Peggy Goodin (1923–) was born in Kansas City, Missouri, grew up in Indiana, and attended the University of Michigan. There she won the 1944–1945 Hopwood Award of $1,000 for her novel *Clementine* (1946) set in a small Indiana town—hers was the only major Hopwood Award winner that year.

Her second book, *Take Care of My Little Girl* (1950), is a satirical novel about college sororities set at Midwestern U—obviously based on the University of Michigan. Liz Ericson's mother had been a "Queen" in her college sorority days, so Liz comes to MU as a "legacy," hoping she also will become a "Queen."

The "Queens" insist that the group is democratic, even though Jewish and Catholic students have no chance of acceptance and girls from well-to-do homes are preferred. Liz at first accepts the situation but in time she leaves the "Queens."

A reviewer for the *Michigan Alumnus Quarterly Review* was concerned that the novel was too one-sided as far as its treatment of sororities was concerned. But he conceded that the image of "student life, with allowance for satirical exaggeration, [was] authentic."[20]

Glendon Swarthout's *Where the Boys Are* (1960) shows a University of Michigan coed from Carter City, Michigan ("the Best Little City by a Dam Site") spending her spring break on the beach at Fort Lauderdale. She has sexual relations with three men, becomes pregnant, and drops out of college for a year. A reviewer called the novel a "highly carbonated elixir of sex, sunshine and beer."[21] It was filmed the same year with the same title. The book, the film, and a song with the same title have been credited with building the popularity of southern Florida beaches during northern college spring breaks.

In 1965, Richard Emmons, poet, and Robert Forman, illustrator, collaborated on *Michigan Memories*, a book of illustrated verse about the University of Michigan campus. Here is a quatrain that accompanied a drawing of Harris Hall:

> The piccolo's delicious trill,
>   The rattle of the snare,
> The trumpet's blat all told us that
>   The Marching Band lived there![22]

Norman Garbo's (1919–) *The Movement* (1969) presents a campus scene that is the polar opposite of both Goodin's *Take Care of My Little Girl* and Swarthout's *Where the Boys Are*. Published as the student protest movements of the 1960s were losing some of their energy, the book assumes otherwise. It is set in a brief span of time on the novel's Chadwick University campus in Michigan, overlooking Lake Huron. The story focuses on three people of the several hundred ultimately involved: a mulatto, Joshua Lecole; his paramour, Karen Jalner, a physically handicapped blonde girl; and Renata Venturi, a wealthy seventy-two-year-old woman with a mystical ability to sway swarms of young people into becoming a part of the Glow movement—a students' rights organization with nationwide goals to give students more control of their colleges and universities.

Chadwick—where the president, Dr. Hadley C. Young, has banned demonstrations—has been selected as the school to inaugurate the reform movement. In a carefully orchestrated scheme, Joshua, Karen, and Renata address ten thousand Chadwick students who have assembled despite the ban and university precautions.

When university police attempt to stop the rally, they are overwhelmed by students bearing military weapons. The Michigan National Guard is called in. At the end of the novel, U.S. Army Air Force bombers and National Guard planes strafe the crowd into submission. Venturi is killed and Jalner is raped and murdered. Lecole survives. Reviewers were not enthusiastic.[23]

Stephen Walton (1945–) was a senior at the University of Michigan when he wrote his futuristic *No Transfer* (1967). It is set on the campus of Modern University, a campus that has only a fifty-story building and a football stadium.

The enrollment is about four thousand. The 1,012 freshmen enrolled each fall are supposedly the cream of the academic crop and highly motivated. But, as the title indicates, once enrolled, they may not transfer from MU.

On Paramours Day, men and women students pair off, and from that time on, couples share the same room and bed.

The student paper is strangely named the *Tumbrel*. The "soul of the University" is its "Self-Discipline Plan." The reader first learns of the significance of the paper's name and the plan on a day that sirens sound for a convocation of students, who then watch a delinquent student guillotined by a fellow student. The ultimate irony comes when a young woman is called on to behead her rival for a man's affections. A reviewer commented, "Walton has created an enclosed, complete, and believable society as a setting for a successful horror story. He has much larger intentions as well—most obviously, an admirably sardonic comment on the insane competitiveness of the American educational system, the dangers of the pursuit of excellence."[24]

Summary

The small number of Michigan college novels has ranged through a social revolution—from the nineteenth-century world of manners and customs to the twentieth-century campus with its student organizations, athletic teams, and for a time its hordes of war veterans and their families and then on to a glimpse of future campuses that during the 1960s seemed entirely possible. In general, these views of the Michigan campus scene have been negative; one might wonder from reading them how it was possible for Michigan colleges and universities to turn out the splendid array of college graduates that they have—among them most of the authors of these works.

CHAPTER XII

BANKS, BUSINESS, AND MINING

> What hardened villains business makes of us . . . it's a shame
> to take advantage of the simple ignorance of that young man.
> The franchise is cheap at half a million, but, alas, business is
> business.
>
> —Robert Barr, *The Victors: A Romance*[1]

Many of the early settlers in Michigan collected in settlements rather than on lonely farms or in the woods. Towns grew around these settlements, at their hearts a tavern, a store, a blacksmith shop, a mill for grinding grain or converting logs to lumber, or a bank to furnish financial services. Some of these settlements became cities; others remained towns, built around a cluster of stores, banks, schools, and churches or near mines or lumber mills.

In this chapter, the focus is on literature that has Michigan banking, business, or mining enterprises as its major subject.

Robert Traver, the pseudonymous author of *Laughing Whitefish* (1965), which is set in the Marquette iron mining area, is John D. Voelker, an Ishpeming attorney, former Michigan supreme court justice, and author of the earlier *Anatomy of a Murder* (1958), whose success surely inspired his later novel. Both works were based on actual Marquette County court cases.

Voelker, in a 1970 "Clarence M. Burton Memorial Lecture," related the historical background for *Laughing Whitefish*. Surveyors, who discovered the first Michigan iron vein in 1844 with the help of

Marji Gesick, an Indian, promised Gesick a small percentage of the mining profits. Some later mine owners, learning that Gesick was dying of alcoholism, ignored him. When his daughter, Charlotte Kawbawgam, showed the owners her father's original contract and asked for a fair share of the astronomical profits, they scorned her. But, wise to white man's ways, she hired a lawyer. Her case went to the Michigan Supreme Court three times before she won.

In Voelker's novel, Charlotte becomes Laughing Whitefish (there is a river by that name in the Upper Peninsula), and she and her lawyer fall in love.[2]

Ralph C. Schoonover's *Pageant: Iron Ore Centennial (1844–1944)* uses the same material that Voelker used in his novel.[3]

Osgood Bradbury's *Manita of the Picture Rocks* (1848) is set near Ontonagon at a time when the first copper was being mined in the Upper Peninsula. A young geologist, Frederick Augustus Copperall, explores the Lake Superior shoreline for traces of either copper or silver and competes with both a halfbreed and a wealthy young Englishman for the affections of a young Indian woman, Stellawagona (Bright Star). Despite obstacles, Frederick discovers a vein of copper, wins the girl, and the two live happily—and wealthily—ever after.

James North Wright's 1905 *Where Copper Was King* is a tale of early copper mining at the tip of the Keweenaw Peninsula. Although it has a unique romantic touch (the heroine rescues the hero who has been trapped in an underground rock slide), the story focuses on three topics:—primitive underground mining techniques, early attempts to secure rights for workers, and nineteenth-century business attitudes.

The mine owners become rich as the Civil War brings them peak prices for copper; once the copper veins are mined out, they sell their mines to unsuspecting buyers. Accidents are either acts of God or caused by the carelessness of the miners (pp. 121, 132). When miners, angry at unsafe working conditions, strike, they are jailed.

A sociologist critic says the novel is "the testament of an old-line benevolent despot who is not on the defensive but to whom that combination of laissez-faire and feudalism once the rule in many mining communities is as natural as breathing."[4] Literary historian John T. Flanagan said, "The book lacks structure and suspense, but as a sketch of early copper mining, it has definite merit."[5]

There was also some gold and silver mining in the Upper Peninsula in the nineteenth century. Before she died, Gertrude Tupala (1922–1981), an administrative assistant at Northern Michigan University, had completed a rough draft of a novel, *There's Gold in Them*

Hills! Gold!, probably based on actual Ishpeming area mines. In 1988, the Avery Color Studios of Au Train, publishers of many Upper Peninsula books, issued a paperback edition of Tupala's novel. Unfortunately, the document was not well edited and is below the superior level of other Avery publications.

Kirk Munroe (1856–1930), a Harvard graduate, set *The Copper Princess* (1898) in Michigan's Copper Country. The title refers both to a mine by that name and to a woman the hero romances.

The story has a rags-to-riches plot. Richard Peverill, a gentleman down on his luck, rescues the son of a Cornish mining captain from under the wheels of a narrow-gauge train and is rewarded with a mining job. From his low status he rises to financial success with the aid of a demented old man who shows Peverill a secret cave originally dug by ancient Indian copper miners.

Social class plays a role in the book. Peverill and a friend are graduates of Oxford University in England. The Trefethens are middle class, quite unlike the miners, who are lower-class "foreigners—Italians, Bohemians, Hungarians or Poles" (p. 41).

Iowan Judson Keith Deming (1858–1952) used the pseudonym Jay Cady for his 1912 novel, *The Stake*, which, although set entirely on the New England coast, features Dick Weston, a young man from the Upper Peninsula, who has come east to settle his uncle's estate, including the affairs of a copper mine. There Weston encounters a Massachusetts state senator who is trying to seize control of the mine and falls in love with the senator's daughter. In the end, Weston gets both the mine and the young woman.

The novel's significance lies in its similarities to an actual case that William B. Gates, Jr., has detailed in his *Michigan Copper and Boston Dollars* (1951, reissued 1969). Alexander Agassiz, the brilliant Harvard scientist and son of Jean Louis Rodolphe Agassiz, the even more brilliant naturalist and educator, came to the Copper Country to seize control of the copper mines at Calumet with backing from Boston capitalists (p. 41). Among the latter is the Lowell family; Amy Lowell, the poet, is reputed to have paid for her black cigars with copper mine dividends.[6]

Jacob Wendell Clark was a company doctor for Calumet and Hecla. *White Wind* (1927), his second novel based on his "scientific" philosophies, is the story of Scottish-born Robert McTish, brought to Calumet where his father became a miner. The time is 1900.

The novel's focus is on the conflicts between Robert and his dour Presbyterian father; between the Presbyterian point of view and the "papist" point of view of the O'Sheas whose daughter Robert

loves; between the Anglo-Saxon property owners and the "dirty" foreigners—men from the south of Europe who are seen as not much
better than animals, even though their semislave labor brings the
mine owners their wealth; and to a slight extent on the philosophical
conflict between capitalism and socialism.

There are good scenes in the novel: the birth of Robert in a Scot-
tish gale; Robert's glimpse of his father catching a carnival dancer's
red slipper that she has tossed into a crowd of men; and a fight between Robert and a miner named Polecheck. But these are offset by
too many badly written scenes. An improbable, one-sided, chapter
tells of the 1913 mine strike.

The strike, which came about because of a failed attempt to
unionize the underground mine employees, is still remembered in
the Copper Country because it led to the 1913 Christmas Day, Italian
Hall tragedy in which more than seventy children and adult members of strikers' families died when someone cried "Fire!" in the middle of a Christmas party. (There was no fire.)

John L. Beem's play, *The Mother Lode* (1974), based on the strike
and the tragedy, was first produced in the Calumet Theatre only a
block away from the Italian Hall. Peggy German's 1984 *Tinsel and
Tears* also uses the 1913 strike and the Italian Hall tragedy as subject matter.

Two books for juveniles are set in Michigan's Iron Range coun-
try. Iron smelting is a theme in the Reverend James Hibbert Langille's
Snail Shell Harbor (1870), set near Escanaba. Betsey Rose's *Uncle Sam's
Star Route* is set in part in the area.

Mildred Walker's *The Brewer's Big Horses* (1940) is a cavalcade
novel that begins in Saginaw, a prosperous lumbering town, in 1882.
As the town's economy shifts from lumbering to industry, the story
follows seven-year-old Sarah Bolster as she develops into one of the
"new women," marries Dr. William Henkel, mourns his accidental
death, takes control of the Henkel family's brewing business, and
eventually has to cope with the Prohibition movement in the first two
decades of the twentieth century.

The novel's theme of intolerance is developed through Sarah's
nontraditional feminine behavior, her marriage to a German Jew, and
her role as a businesswoman. The novel also makes the point that, in
part, Prohibition was an anti-German movement. German laborers,
working six days a week, relaxed by drinking beer on Sunday after-
noons in beer gardens, thus desecrating the Sabbath in the view of
puritanical citizens. Moreover, when America sided with the Allies in

World War I, a strong anti-German feeling spread across the country, much like the anti-Japanese feelings of World War II.

Mrs. Walker dedicated the book to her husband, Dr. Ferdinand Schemm, "who is intolerant only of knaves and intolerance." For twenty-three years, the Schemms lived in Great Falls, Montana. Walker set her later novels in that area.

Robert Barr's *The Victors: A Romance of Yesterday Morning and This Afternoon* (1901) begins near Ann Arbor where two would-be students, peddling merchandise in the rural area, encounter a scoundrelly man. All three become involved in a local election concerning a proposed drainage ditch, then they go on to New York where they enter the political scene. Only the first half of the novel is set in Michigan. In "An Effort at Dedication," Barr said that it was his ambition to associate the book with the University of Michigan . . . "even though such Hitching of my waggon to a Star is entirely unauthorised" (pp. v–vi). However, the university plays such a minuscule role in *The Victors* that there should have been no objection to the dedication.

Barr (1850–1912) used the pseudonym Luke Sharp for many of his forty books. Only one other, *The Speculations of John Steele* (1905) has a Michigan setting. John Steele begins his career as a "man of all work" at a remote point on the Midland Railroad where trains occasionally pass each other. For preventing a disastrous wreck, he is promoted to the novel's Warmington City, a town dominated by the Rockervelts who control a competing railroad. From here on, Steele rises rapidly, becoming wealthy, buying a railroad, dabbling in wheat. Part of this story is set in Chicago.

Barr, from the Ontario region east of Detroit, was a graduate of the University of Michigan.

Chicago author Will Payne (1865–1954) set his business novel, *When Love Speaks* (1906) in fictional Sauganac, on the east shore of Lake Michigan, an hour's boat ride from Chicago. Like his other novels, this one focuses on corruption in business and politics as well as the relationships among men and women.

At stake are the attempts of distillery owners in the novel's nearby Nogiac to monopolize the liquor business by corrupting entrepreneurs, judges, newspaper people, and legislators.[7] A vacillating young attorney—whose moral uprighteousness is encouraged by his girl friend—opposes the distillery's legal and illegal efforts. He is then falsely arrested for his efforts, and he and his friend flee to the western frontier. The novel was widely and favorably reviewed.[8]

Harold Hunter Armstrong was born in Morenci, Michigan, in 1884, graduated from the University of Michigan in 1905, and took a law degree from the Detroit College of Law in 1907. In 1919, under the pseudonym of Henry G. Aikman, he wrote *The Groper*, the first of four novels concerning the business scene.

This is the familiar story of the country boy who goes to the city in search of fortune—in this case, the city is Detroit, the time is 1907 when the automobile industry was just emerging from infancy, and the city's great growth and prosperity are just beginning. Lee Hillquit, a dreamer and idealist like many of his contemporaries who believed the copybook maxims of Horatio Alger's stories, tries his hand at real estate, the motor car business, and the operation of a big department store—with varying fortunes. In the end, he sees himself as a groper—stumbling, floundering, following false lights, only at intervals catching a real glimpse of the truth.

The *New York Times Book Review* saw *The Groper* "as the work of an established author" despite the publisher's statement that the book was a first novel. The *Bookman* said, "[T]he tale is more noteworthy as a discussion of real estate, the automobile industry, and the drygoods business than it is as a novel." The *Nation* called it the best of six current books, all by established authors that it reviewed at the same time.[9]

Armstrong's second novel *Zell* (1921)—also published under his nom de plume—is the best of his four books; it received the most reviews and is the only one of his books mentioned by later historians. It was published by Alfred Knopf in his Borzoi series, which also included books by Carl Van Vechten, Willa Cather, Thomas Beer, and H. L. Mencken.

Zell's three parts begin in 1894 when Avery Zell is eight and dreaming of a career as a singer, and the story follows him through an unsatisfactory marriage. He works in a bank and invests in a petticoat manufacturing enterprise. The business fails although Avery's investment is repaid. But for the sake of the couple's son, Avery gives up a romance with a young woman and remains with his wife. That's his only success—even his banking job is not doing well.

Zell is, in a way, a comedy of manners, but the society depicted is less genteel, somewhat more shabby than the worlds of novelists Edith Wharton and William Dean Howells, the latter Armstrong's second cousin.

The *New Republic* and the *Freeman* praised the book. The *Nation's* reviewer noted "an extraordinarily swift development" in Armstrong's skills over his first book, and then added, "The moral history of America is being written in a series of books (such as *Zell*) that have the virtue of stating all their criticism by implication. They avoid discursiveness . . . and let the operation of the intelligence by coincident with the creative act. Thus, they forego a certain liveliness and nimbleness, but gain in solidity and strength." The *Weekly Review* said that the "protest and revolt" of the years before World War I were "settling into a fiction of discouragement" where the Middle West serves as the ideal scene, "There, if anywhere, dwells the average citizen; there in their perfection are the hubby, the wifie, the front lawn, the terrible infant, the grocer's bill, the other woman, and all. There, in the narrow houses dwell the blind mice, there flourish the tyrannies of dust and sand."[10]

Armstrong published *For Richer, for Poorer* (1922) over his own name to the puzzlement of critics. It is set in New York City, although one reviewer said it was another *Main Street* novel.[11]

Having not fared too well with New York, Armstrong returned to Detroit for his locale in his fourth and last novel. *The Red Blood* (1923), also written under his own name, is a better book.

To emphasize the work's theme, the title page quotes a motto, "We have divided men into red-bloods and mollycoddles." Armstrong's red-blood is Dennis Wellington McNichol, born in an Ontario town, who comes to Detroit with his mind set on fame and fortune. An illegitimate child, he is determined not only to find acceptance but also to prove his superiority over his fellow citizens. He is successful in business, he learns how to manipulate politicians and becomes Detroit's mayor—there is even talk of a future role as governor or president.

But McNichol learns he is dying of cancer and has at most a year to live; his wife learns he had once been unfaithful to her; and he loses out in his fight against those who want to use the streets of Detroit to build a trolley car empire. After his death, a grandson provides a moral, "Nature always frowns upon the idealist—always showers her misfortunes on him. Every statesman has to learn the bitter lesson. And yet this is undoubtedly the finest moment of his life. Men are only great in their impossible aspirations and in their splendid failures."[12]

In his 1951 essay on "Michigan's Writing Men," Arnold Mulder, a contemporary of Armstrong, praised *Zell*, but referred to the author as a member of the "frustration" group of Michigan writers—the others were Leonard Cline, Lee J. Smits, Geoffrey Dell Eaton, and "in some respects" Ann Pinchot.[13]

Kenneth (O'Donnell) Horan's *A Bashful Woman* (1944) follows Sally Evans from 1890 when her Welsh family is suffering from discrimination to the mid-1940s. She marries a wagon manufacturer, takes over the enterprise after his death, and converts it to a successful automobile factory. Along the way she marries Elliott Carstairs, a member of one of those families that had despised the Evans family. The novel failed to arouse any critical enthusiasm.

Dr. Charles A. Cooper (1906–), after taking an M.D. degree from the University of Michigan, practiced medicine in Copper Range and Iron Range towns. His *We Pass This Way* (1950), a fictional record of a doctor's experiences in such places, has little literary value. From a social viewpoint, like other novels set in Michigan mining camps, it demonstrates a bias in favor of the managerial, professional, and property-owning class and reflects a negative attitude toward the miners whose underground labors made the mining camps possible.

Samuel Merwin's *The Honey Bee* (1915) is an unusual novel of business for its time. The honey bee of the novel is a new character in fiction, the woman worker, who, as another character, "Blink" Moran, son of a Michigan beekeeper, says, is "the worker, the unsexed female that does nothing but work." Hilda Wilson, the honey bee, is a Paris agent for the Hartman dressmaking business of Michigan. Moran, a prizefighter, is in Paris to fight Georges Carpentier. (The latter is a real person who was defeated by the American, Jack Dempsey, in 1921.) Moran loses the fight.

The title of Alexander Duffield's first novel, *Any Smaller Person* (1935), refers to a character's statement that "any person who is less than one-fifth accountant, two-fifths lawyer, three-fifths political economist, and four-fifths gentleman and scholar may be a pawnbroker or promoter, but not a banker" (p. 9).

Sam Lorimer's world, in a city, obviously Detroit, is a world of "smaller persons" with one exception—Sam's father, a brilliant lawyer and financier, is one of the city's richest and most powerful men and seemingly determined to keep his three sons "smaller" than himself. Sam, a somewhat frustrated artist, is a teller in his father's bank; William makes a fortune manufacturing toothpaste from inferior materials; Roscoe, a war veteran, becomes a drunkard, loses his job, and forges his father's name on a check.

Then the federal government orders the 1933 bank holiday. The value of Sam's estate diminishes as stocks drop in value. The bank closes its doors and the newspapers attack Sam's father. Roscoe kills himself, and Sam asks a bossy girl to marry him.

Mary Frances Doner's *Ravenswood* (1948) starts in 1940 and ends with the word that Japan has bombed Pearl Harbor. It is another of those complex family chronicles, complete with a genealogical table that, unfortunately, is incomplete.

The St. George family, replete with its share of dark secrets, is in the business of mining and processing salt. The book contains more than enough data about the origin and discoveries of Michigan salt deposits and the financial shenanigans seemingly needed to keep the business of mining and processing salt going.

The novel reads like a radio soap opera of the times—one suspects that Doner had her ears turned to daytime radio as she wrote her books. Like soap operas, there are so many characters involved that readers sometimes must throw up their hands in despair.

Allan Seager's *Amos Berry* (1953), although called by one critic a "fiction of a perfect crime," is in actuality a condemnation of the twentieth-century world of business, commerce, and industry. Berry, a middle-aged man who is divorced and alienated from his son, sees his life as a failure, particularly when he contrasts it with the freedom and vigor of his pioneer ancestors. Trapped in his well-paying but routine job, he seeks revenge by murdering his employer who, to Berry, has become the symbol for all that is wrong with the industrial scene—its depersonalization, its emphasis on efficiency and organization, its confused value systems, and the direction in which it is moving. Berry's crime remains unsolved until a final conversation with his son as they finally are able to communicate with each other. His confession concluded, Berry kills himself.

Some reviewers were dismayed by Seager's novel; one or two were not. All of them, however, disliked the long philosophical discussion between Berry and his son.[14]

Seager later said that he "would have hesitated to say that the novel is the conscience of the middle class but when he remembered *Amos Berry* discovered that [he] believed it."[15]

Seager's *Old Man of the Mountain* (1950) contains eighteen short stories, eight of which had previously appeared in either the annual O. Henry or the O'Brien collections. His autobiography, *Frieze of Girls* (1964), is told in a series of short fictionlike essays. Two chapters, "Actress with Red Garter" and "Miss Anglin's Bad Martini" are based on his university days.

Josephine Winn was a Pennsylvanian who lived in Detroit. Her 1961 *Each Day's Proud Battle* is another of those through-the-years books, which, like a football game in these days of specialized teams, requires a program to help the reader identify and remember the players.

In Pokana, Michigan (read Detroit), there are four dominant families—the Tureks, the Benbys, the Fleurs, and the Manoques—and among them there is a great deal of interaction, romantic and otherwise. The Manoques have a Great Lakes shipping line; Key Fleur owns the *Guardian News;* Wilber Benby is a U.S. senator. The focus narrows a bit to Jerome (Jerry) Turek and his third-generation son, Monroe ("Roney"), the financial speculations Jerry enters into with his Mid-North holding company, and the consequences for the four families and others during the Great Depression.

Winn's thesis seems to be that during the economic downturn of the 1930s even the rich had problems. In this book, they are not alone.

Summary

There are other books in which Michigan business plays a part. A number of these that emphasize the automobile industry are discussed in the Detroit chapter.

It is a curious circumstance that the writers who used the subject of Michigan business as their main topic generally found fault with it. But they were not alone—American business and industry have usually suffered at the hands of American fiction writers despite evidence that the American free enterprise system is, in general, superior to other systems, such as collectivism or socialism.

A second curious circumstance is that these books would probably never have found their way into print had it not been for the American business enterprise system of manufacturing and marketing!

CHAPTER XIII

CRIME IN MICHIGAN LITERATURE

Booker said, "Who's this?" A woman's voice said, "You sitting down?" Booker said, "Baby, is that you?" . . . Her voice said, "Are you sitting down? You have to be sitting down for when I tell you something." Booker said, "Baby, you sound different. What's wrong?" He sat down in the green leather chair, working . . . around to get comfortable. The woman's voice said, "Are you sitting down?" Booker said, "I *am*. I have sat . . . down. Now you gonna talk to me, what?" Moselle's voice said, "I'm supposed to tell you that when you get up, honey, what's left of you . . . is gonna go clear through the ceiling."
—Elmore Leonard, *Freaky Deaky*[1]

Michigan literature discussed elsewhere in this book has often incorporated activities regarded as criminal or quasicriminal, but not as the most important aspect of the work. The books, plays, and films discussed in this chapter are those in which criminal activity is the heart of the story, and all else is subservient.

The earliest crime novel, set in Detroit, is Edward L. Wheeler's *Deadwood Dick, Jr., in Detroit; or, Turning Tables on Satan* (1889), a Beadle and Adams dime novel, the thirtieth title to feature the nineteenth century's most famous crime solver. Deadwood Dick was always dressed from head to foot in black; his face was always hidden behind a black mask.

Harold Payne, using the pen name George Kelly, set two 1895 Beadle and Adams novels of crime in Michigan. *The Man from Mexico in New York: or, Turning Down the Shylock Pawnbroker* tells of Detective Thad Burr who discovers that a supposed bank robbery has been faked and that a Detroit pawnbroker is involved. *The Circus Detective; or, Bareback Billy's Big Roundup* is set in Big Rapids, Michigan, where

"Bareback Billy," posing as a circus performer, breaks up a criminal operation.

E[dward] Everett Howe's (1862–1913) *The Chronicles of Break O'Day* (1894) is set in the frontier town of Break O'Day, and in swamps in Ingham and Jackson counties that are a haven for horse thieves, escaped convicts, and army deserters.

The major characters are farm-owner Major Ratke, a veteran of the Mexican War; his niece, Nora, and two men who want to marry her; a suspected horse thief (whose mother is in prison and whose father is a drunkard but who proves to be an honest man); and an apparently honest man who is found to be a murderer.

The novel, overburdened by endless philosophical debates, is at its best when it describes horse thievery and other crimes in a community where the only law enforcement officer is also the village idiot.

Horace T. Barnaby's *The Decade: A Story of Political and Municipal Corruption* (1908) is a tale of two Ann Arbor graduates who sense in Joseph Leiter's failed turn-of-the-century attempt to corner the Chicago wheat market a route to instant wealth with little effort and other people's money. When the attempt fails, the two men turn to crime to pay back the misused funds. Both men end up in jail.

Although the novel was badly conceived and written, it was reprinted as *Water Scandal* in 1910. Supposedly, the facts of the story were based on an actual case in a town close to Grand Rapids.

Barnaby (1823–1917) was a bishop of the United Brethren Church of Christ. He was born in New York, but from age seventeen on lived in southwestern Michigan.

In 1911, in a northwest Lower Peninsula town, a Catholic nun was murdered and the local priest was charged with the crime. A half-century later, Milan Stitt, a student of dramatic arts at the University of Michigan, began writing a play based on the case. In 1960 and 1962 he won Hopwood awards for his work.

Stitt's *The Runner Stumbles* was to take some eleven years to bring to fruition (including work at Yale with John Gassner) before it opened on Broadway in May 1976. Father Rivard is "a maverick priest who has been relegated to a God-forsaken and largely non-Catholic rural section of Michigan." Shortly thereafter Sister Rita, who is both "lively and impetuous," arrives; she "manages to upset the precarious balance of his personal and spiritual life."[2] Their relationship becomes a love affair and they incur the anger of the priest's housekeeper. Then the nun is found murdered and Father Rivard is accused of the crime. But, as we suspect, the housekeeper killed the girl.

The tightly knit, well-conceived play was selected as one of the ten best plays of 1976 and was published in book form in 1976 together with a long personal statement, "Night Rainbows: An Afterword," by Stitt. In May 1978, it was produced at the Boarshead Theatre in Lansing, a rare play about Michigan by a Michigan native. In 1979, the play was filmed with dancer Ray Bolger as a Catholic dignitary, Dick Van Dyke as Father Rivard, and Maureen Stapleton as the housekeeper. The film was not well received.

Harold Titus's "Sheriff Bob Reaches a Verdict" in the *American Magazine* (July 1924) is a tale of "retrieved reformation," similar to O. Henry's turn-of-the-century story. A Michigan sheriff trails a boy suspected of a Michigan murder to Canada. Although the boy claims self-defense, the sheriff puts him in a canoe to take him back to stand trial. But the canoe sinks and the boy saves his captor from drowning. The sheriff frees the boy and tells him to stay in Canada.

Myrta M. Dreyer's *Beckoning Hands* (1930) shows a mysterious murder taking place in a Detroit motor executive's remote northwoods mansion in a violent snowstorm, followed by more deaths among the snowbound wealthy guests before the police can arrive. Although the novel attempts to build a ghostly cause for the deaths, the reader eventually discovers there was one more person present than the author had revealed. Dreyer's novel is not up to the standards set by those of either Eleanor Atkinson Blake or Jo Valentine.

In the 1930s, Karl Detzer did a series of factual articles for the *Saturday Evening Post* on the then-innovative use of radios by the Detroit Police Department and, as a result, was employed to write a script for a motion picture, *Car 99* (1953), starring Fred MacMurray. An urbane professor, after masterminding a series of bank robberies, paralyzes the police radio system in order to accomplish an even bigger robbery. But the MacMurray character, knowing that the Massachusetts police radio operates on the same wave length as the Detroit system, telephones the necessary information to the Bay State so it can be broadcast to Detroit police cars. Frank Nugent of the *New York Times* thought *Car 99* was "one of the best melodramas to come from Hollywood in many a moon."[3]

Detzer (1891–) became a newspaper writer after graduation from high school in Fort Wayne, Indiana. He wrote several motion picture scripts and was a prolific author of magazine articles and stories, sometimes using the pseudonyms Michael Costello, William Henderson, or Leland Woods. From 1947 to 1951 he published the *Weekly Leelanau Enterprise-Tribune*.

Near the end of his life, James Oliver Curwood—who had acquired an international reputation as an author of adventure novels set in the Canadian northwoods—began *Green Timber*, the first novel to be written about a Detroit gangster. After his death, the novel was finished in 1930 by Dorothea Bryant, Curwood's biographer, from notes he left behind.

When Allan Campbell, a minor Detroit hoodlum, rejects an invitation to join Scarfell's gang, the latter orders his execution. Campbell flees to northern Michigan, where he woos Hilga Novak, an ex-member of the Detroit underworld—until Scarfell discovers them. A final gun battle in the northwoods leads to a happy ending for Campbell and Novak.

Curwood's unfinished autobiography, *Son of the Forests* (1930) was also completed by Bryant.

Glendon Swarthout's *Loveland* (1968) is set in the Great Depression year of 1934. Perry Dunnigan, a high-school boy, playing in an orchestra at Loveland, a summer dancehall at Charlevoix, is attracted to a once-rich, now impoverished girl. When he learns that she is interested in a man with $9 million in the bank and a yacht in Charlevoix Harbor, Perry murders him. Reviewers were not enthusiastic about the book.[4]

Dr. William C[harles] S[mithson] Pellowe's *The Skylines of Paradise* (1941), set in Saginaw, begins with the murder of a labor organizer in the fictional Bristol Hotel. It includes philosophical debates over the roles of labor and capital, a girl's attempted suicide to call attention to her proposed movement for social tolerance, and a chapter that reports a word-for-word luncheon club member's irrelevant speech about Paul Bunyan. The murder is solved by a conversation accidentally overheard in a remote Mexican town. Major reviewers ignored the book.

Pellowe, a resident of Port Huron, was also the author of *Tales from a Lighthouse Cafe* (1960) and the collector of poems by assorted Michiganians under the curious title of *Chuckles in the Cemetery*.

Marian Austin (Waite) Magoon and Elisabeth Carey, using the pseudonym of Carey Magoon, coauthored the 1943 mystery novel, *I Smell the Devil*, set at a fictional Cowabet College in Michigan. When a librarian is murdered, Adelaide Stone, a library patron, is linked to the crime; soon she and her middle-aged friend, Henrietta, are in the midst of the investigation led by a Sergeant Morningstar of the Michigan State Police. Suspects also include an archaeologist and his fiancée, a visiting professor from Egypt, several other educators, and a person who has escaped from the state asylum for the insane. Adelaide helps the sergeant catch the culprit, who, it turns out, is also responsible for other violent deaths on the campus.

Howard Blakemore's *Special Detail* (1944) consists of several narratives of the day-by-day activities of members of the Immigration Patrol stationed at Marine City between Detroit and Port Huron. The patrol's primary duty seems to be stopping the smuggling of Chinese from Canada to Michigan across the Saint Clair River.

One of the narratives is a love triangle involving a school teacher, an immigration officer, and the officer's wife. When the wife learns the officer is planning to divorce her, she kills herself in such a way as to make it appear her husband is the murderer.

John R[ichard] Humphreys' *Vandameer's Road* (1946) is set in a rural community outside Grand Rapids, inhabited mostly by people who work in the city. Among them is Showell Henderson, once a lawyer but now a night watchman, whose secret past is somehow related to the silo in his yard. There is also the unsolved mysterious disappearance of a civil engineer who had been working on a local highway.

Henderson and his wife Ruth have two sons. Jorg, the younger, daydreams about Boga, a courteous ape who talks like the GIs of the early days of World War II; Beulah, a gigantic cat; and Boof, a monster in the shape of a toad.

As the narrative unfolds, we learn that Henderson fled to this community to escape the charge that he had murdered his brother. Ruth Henderson, who has never recovered from the birth of Jorg, dies. The silo is cleaned out and discovered to be the burial place of the long-missing engineer: Henderson, jealous of the man's attentions to Ruth, had killed him. Once again Henderson flees, and Jorg is left to the ministrations of a relative.

Reviewers reacted variously to the novel. Richard Match thought that the inability to solve the mystery of the missing engineer was a reflection on the Michigan State Police. He also thought the interpolation of Jorg's daydreams detracted from the suspense of the novel. James Sandoe said, "[T]he novel as a whole is impalpable and fragmentary. The author raises more ghosts than he lays." Alan Vrooman called it "an unsuccessful first novel." Arno L. Bader said the book had "a peculiar eerie quality," but that the "abrupt breaks and changes of pace necessitated by switching from realism to fantasy to poetic prose [were] ultimately wearing upon the reader." But Phil Stong liked the book.[5]

Humphreys (1918–) won minor Hopwood awards in 1938 and 1939, and a Guggenheim Fellowship. Martha Foley selected one of his short stories for *The Best Short Stories of 1947*. He was the author of *The Dirty Shame* (1955) and *The Last of the Middle West* (1962); in the latter, he narrated memories of his years in Michigan.

Monica Porter (1919–), the granddaughter of a Michigan supreme court justice, was born in Detroit. After two years at the University of Chicago, she became a newspaper reporter, covering country offices, social agencies, and probate courts. A Pontiac murder trial led to her 1955 book, *The Mercy of the Court*. In the novel, a judge who is anticipating appointment to a higher court, faces a dilemma as he tries a teenager who has killed a prominent citizen. His research into the boy's homelife and the circumstances of the crime make him sympathetic toward the young man, but he knows if he frees the accused, his own chance for the appointment is gone. Porter overloads the situation for the judge to the point where there is no way out.

Only the *New Yorker* liked the book, calling it "very readable." The *New York Times* said it was "clumsy" and the *San Francisco Chronicle* said the plot was cut-and-dried, the characters black and white.[6]

Twenty-one-year-old William Wiegand's *At Last, Mr. Tolliver* (1950) won the Mary Roberts Rinehart Mystery Novel Contest Prize that year. Tolliver had once been a gangster's private doctor, but he lost his license to practice and served a jail sentence.

When John Lawson, a bank robber—who lives in the same cheap boarding house as the hero—is stabbed to death, Tolliver hopes to solve the crime and earn a reward. A sadistic police lieutenant tries to pin the murder on the doctor, but Tolliver manages to find the real murderer.

Reviewers disagreed about the book. Anthony Boucher said that "the book was excessively long and largely lifeless" but that it did indicate Wiegand's third book might perhaps be "worth waiting for." The *New York Herald-Tribune Book Review* reported that "the plot is sound and winds up with a twist which ought to satisfy even the most orthodox" and that the "characters defy a lot of the formulas, which in itself is a good thing."[7]

Wiegand (rhymes with seaman) next turned to the prison theme that was popular in the films of the 1930s—but with a difference. Those films had been essentially melodramas, with the bad guys polar opposites of the good guys. But Wiegand's *The Treatment Man* (1959), which Albert G. Black says is "evidently based on the Jackson [Michigan] prison riot of 1952,"[8] is a much more complex treatment of the theme of men institutionalized for criminal behavior. (The novel identifies the institution as the Southern State Prison at Creighton and places it about 200 miles north of St. Louis.)

The novel contrasts the two prison governments: one under the control of the warden keeps prisoners confined, serves some of their needs, tries to rehabilitate them, and governs most of the conditions under which the inmates fulfill their legal obligation to society; the second, a powerful one, conducts bookmaking (gambling), a numbers game, sales of drugs and visitation rights, and the auction of homosexual prisoners.

A riot that erupts viciously on a spring day takes up most of the novel. The prisoners take hostages and retire behind hastily thrown-up barricades.

The "treatment man" of the novel is Deputy Warden Pryor— a hoodlum himself as a young man, now the prison's psychological therapist—who takes control of the efforts to end the riot and secure release of the hostages unharmed. His opposite number among the convicts is Roy Kinney, whose sale of homosexual rights to a new convict, a rebellious nineteen-year-old, is the catalyst for the riot.

The best review of Weigand's novel saw it as a morality tale: the prison stands for the society in which we live and the debate is between Freudian psychology (which Wiegand derogates) and Christianity (by which Wiegand means the Roman Catholic faith). In fact, Daniel M. Friedenberg in the *New Republic*, opines that the hero of the novel is neither Kinney nor Pryor, but Father Carey, the prison's Catholic chaplain.[9]

Wiegand (1928–) has a B.A. (1949) from the University of Michigan and a Ph.D. (1960) from Stanford. After two years as a Harvard instructor, he became a professor of English and creative writing at San Francisco State University.

Horace Lowe Lawson (1900–), who was primarily an article writer, set *Pitch Dark and No Moon* (1958) on Saginaw Bay. A young man in his first year at Point Lookout Coast Guard Station helps break up a smuggling ring and at the same time learns to control his temper. A second title, *The Raider's Moon*, listed in Rachel M. Hilbert's *Michigan Authors* (1960) as a sequel to the first work, is not in the *National Union Catalog*.

Mary Owen Rank's *A Dream of Falling* (1959, reissued 1960), in manuscript, won the 1957–1958 major Hopwood Award for fiction. Rank, who had a 1939 bachelor's degree from the University of Michigan, used this work for her 1958 master's thesis and dedicated it to Allan Seager.

Eleven years after her marriage at seventeen, Jeannie gives Ken Probert, her alcoholic, hypochondriacal husband—who no longer cares for her—an overdose of a sedative he has requested. Then she watches him die. Most of the novel is told in flashbacks as a police captain interrogates her. Muddling along, she reveals her guilt.

Rank has tried to portray a woman who is really three persons in one—the outer Jeannie, the most delicate, a mere thin and fragile shell; a second middle person; and the "inmost Jeannie," a girl whose parents, "blind drunk," had been killed in an auto accident when she was five. She had been raped by a school janitor at eleven, and when a man is making love to her, she dreams that he is the kindly policeman who came to help her after the rape.

Marvin Felheim agreed with other reviewers in calling Rank's novel "respectable, managed with skill and restraint."[10]

John D. Voelker (1903–1991) was sitting on the Michigan State Supreme Court bench in 1958 when his *Anatomy of a Murder* (under the pen name of Robert Traver) was published. (A full-length photograph on the book's dust jacket showed Voelker in his Supreme Court robe. A caption identified his wife [the former Grace Taylor] and stated that he had three daughters, had in 1943 been Marquette County's prosecuting attorney, and was presently a Michigan Supreme Court justice.)

Like others of his fictions, *Anatomy of a Murder* is based on an actual incident, a slaying that took place in the resort town of Big Bay near Marquette, Michigan. In that case, Voelker was the attorney for a young army officer who had emptied a Luger pistol into the bartender at a lodge that had originally been built by Henry Ford for his guests. In the novel (told through the persona of Paul Biegler, a young lawyer in the town of Chippewa in the Upper Peninsula), Biegler defends Army Lieutenant Frederic Manion, charged with the murder of Barney Quill, owner of a tavern and trailer camp.

Biegler dislikes the arrogant Manion and is more or less convinced that the officer's wife may be guilty. Despite his misgivings and the opposition of a hotshot downstate lawyer, Biegler succeeds in having Manion acquitted.

The book was an immediate success, became a best seller, a Book-of-the-Month-Club selection, and in the next five years went through four hardcover and ten paperback editions. Still, reviewers were not altogether pleased although they did acknowledge that part of the novel's value was the fact that "it contains surely the fullest, most authentic, most detailed account of the preparation of a defense case ever to appear as fiction."[11] The novel was filmed in 1959, winning seven Academy Awards.

In 1981, Voelker, at seventy-eight, published *People versus Kirk*, another "courtroom novel" as the *New York Times* reviewer insisted.

In this novel, the defendant in a murder trial is found innocent because he had committed the crime in a state of hypnosis. Reviewers were not impressed. The *New York Times* reviewer said two faults were that "the reader very early concludes that the oppressively glamorous victim will hardly be missed" and that "the accused, a would-be poet who persistently speaks a hyperbolic high-flown migraine-inducing prose, might well do with a life sentence in solitary confinement, guilty of murder or not."[12]

In *Hornstein's Boy* (1962), Voelker left the courtroom scene for big-time politics. In their college days at a downstate Michigan University, Emil Hornstein from the East and Walt Dressler from Chippewa in Michigan's Upper Peninsula had become close friends. Dressler, now a Chippewa attorney, is visited by Hornstein who wants Dressler to run against the incumbent Republican U.S. senator from Michigan, with Hornstein as his manager. Dressler is persuaded; the novel focuses on the consequences of his decision.

In 1983, the Society for the Study of Midwestern Literature awarded Voelker its Mark Twain Award for Distinguished Contributions to Mid-Western Literature.

Janet Polachek (1914–) was head librarian for the new Delta College at Midland, Michigan, when she wrote *Mystery on Wheels* (1960). In this story for high school girls, a teenager dreads a summer-long visit with an older woman, a bookmobile librarian. But then books begin disappearing from the bookmobile, and the girl finds herself involved in rural intrigue and a romance.

Two non-Michiganians, Mary J[ane] Latsis and Martha Hennissart, using the pseudonym Emma Lathen, have demonstrated that in tandem they have a genuine talent for mystery novels featuring John Putnam Thatcher (a senior partner of a major New York City trust company) as a private sleuth.

Their fourth novel, *Murder Makes the Wheels Go 'Round* (1966), is set in Michigan. Because Thatcher's firm is about to purchase 1.5 million shares of Michigan Motors stock, the number four company in the automobile industry, he is sent to investigate charges of corruption in Michigan Motors. Before long, he is mixed up in the murder of one of the company's executives.

The novel takes Thatcher through the business and social lives of Michigan Motor executives in his search for the murderer. Oddly enough, Detroit police hardly appear in the novel.

The novel's chapter titles, "Down Payment," "F.O.B. Detroit," "Merging Traffic," exemplify the kind of cuteness in the prose. And Emma Lathen is too often the typical omniscient mystery writer who sees all and tells most, but what she withholds turns out to be vital information.

Vera Henry's *Mystery of Cedar Valley* (1964) is set in a town in Michigan's dune country that has not only a year-round population and summer visitors but also an art colony, a romantic triangle involving a married couple, and a long-unsolved mystery. A murder and its investigation clears up most of the complications.

Thomas McGuane's *The Sporting Club* (1969) is set at an exclusive club with a vast area of private forests and streams for the use of its wealthy members. (One thinks of Blaney Park or of Henry Ford's fiefdom on Lake Superior.) The Centennial Club is celebrating its one-hundredth year, unaware that the event will also be its final one. Present are the high-toned sportsmen and their wives (and at least one mistress) who are descendants of the original members. Vernor Stanton, a practical joker, has hired a Snopesian Earl Olive as caretaker, unaware that Olive's "friends ride motorcycles and indulge in native American orgies." When Olive is discharged, he hides out in the woods, "blows up a lake, levels the rustic lodge itself, tars and feathers one of the distinguished guests, and shoots Stanton"—but with rock salt. In the end, as he holds everyone at bay with a machine gun, the state troopers arrive.[13]

The Sporting Club was filmed in 1971. The February 27, 1971, *Variety* review was lukewarm. A *New York Times* review on March 1, 1971, was negative, but a later, much longer review praised the film for its achievements but did not overlook its failures.[14]

Thomas McGuane (1939–) was born in Wyandotte, Michigan, the son of an automobile-parts manufacturer, attended Cranbrook School, the University of Michigan, Michigan State University, and Stanford University. Like his Upper Peninsula contemporary, John D. Voelker, he is an avid fly fisherman. He has written other books and screenplays.

David D. Osborn's *Open Season* (1974) is a sadistic tale of three successful businessmen from Ann Arbor who, tired of hunting animals, begin hunting humans. They pick up couples, abuse them, and rape the women. Then, after setting their victims loose in the woods, they hunt them down. But soon they find themselves being hunted, in turn, by a man named Wolkowski who is seeking revenge for his wife's mistreatment at the hands of the trio and her subsequent suicide.

Osborn also wrote the script for the 1974 film with the same title. William Holden, as Wolkowski, is only briefly seen (except for his boots). *Variety* called it a "gamy potboiler"; the *New York Times* said it was "dull sadism."[15]

F. H. Hall's (1926–) *In the Lamb-White Days* (1975) is a murder mystery set on, and adjacent to, Lake Michigan near Muskegon and Holland. It centers on Cricket Crane, a would-be writer, three generations of a wealthy family in the import business, and the murder of the wife of one of them. Agents from the FBI appear, a dog mysteriously dies, there are hints of drug dealings and other strange happenings—all of which Hall manages to untangle or explain just in time for the novel to end. The book got the usual short reviews awarded to many similar novels.[16] It was released as a paperback in 1977.

Edward Keyes's *The Michigan Murders* (1976, reissued 1978) uses the format of Truman Capote's 1965 book, *In Cold Blood*. (The latter work tells of the actual murders of seven members of a Kansas farm family by combining journalistic fact and fictional technique.) In his book, Keyes relates the murders of seven young women in Washtenaw County (on and near the campuses of the University of Michigan and Eastern Michigan University) over a two-year period from July 1967 to July 1969; the ultimate capture of the murderer, an "all-American boy"; and the killer's trial. Like Capote's book, it employs the fictional techniques of the New Journalism genre and comic relief.

Unlike Capote's book, this story uses fictional names for almost all the characters. Keyes was reluctant to use actual names, even though they were a matter of public record. One possible reason was that his semifictional approach allowed the author to compose dialog and create character in a great many situations where information was either not available or would have required considerable effort to obtain. The *Miami Herald* said that "this factual account of each murder, through the conviction of the killer, has all the excitement of a first-rate work of fiction."[17]

In a way, the books by Keyes and Capote represent an ultimate point in literature, beginning with the turn-of-the-century rejection of romanticism, then the advent of realistic fiction, followed by naturalism.

Keyes (1927–), a non-Michiganian, in 1976 won a special award for suspense nonfiction from the Mystery Writers of America for *The Michigan Murders*. He previously had coauthored *The French Connection* (1969).

In 1988, NBC-TV produced a two-part documentary based on Richard Larsen's *Bundy: The Deliberate Stranger* (1980), the story of a young man who murdered several young women in Utah, California, and Florida that closely parallels the case Keyes describes.

With Vern E. Smith's 1974 *The Jones Men*, we come to a new era in Michigan crime novels—the novel of Detroit crime that involves police, gangsters, blacks, and drugs. As Richard Elman noted, these novels are in sharp contrast with "so much current fiction" of the latter half of the twentieth century, " . . . mere *weltanschauung* tethered to a subject (rather than a place or action). So much autobiographical surmise. [One] read[s] the plot as a superficial gloss on the author's aspirations and complaints, his [or her] literary education, his or her psychotherapy; and when [one is] finished the chief consequences of the action in any social setting have become merely the concocting of the novel."[18]

Smith, a Detroit writer for *Newsweek*, had won an award for an article "Detroit's Heroin Subculture." *The Jones Men* portrays the Detroit drug scene in depth. *Jones* has two meanings—it is both street slang for heroin and the craving for it—as in "his jones came on him bad." In the novel, two young men, trying to establish themselves as big-time operators, find themselves in a deadly war with the Big Man in the heroin trade.

S. K. Overbeck responded to criticism of Vern Smith's journalistic style:

> What holds the book together is not fancy literary merit but Smith's unblinking, unsentimental eye. Using descriptive prose as stark as the graffiti slashed angrily on a ghetto wall, he relies almost totally on dialogue—he has perfect pitch for the profane slum poetics . . . his choice of details is also effective. . . . The result is a hard-eyed transcription of a thoroughly unromantic, ruinous subculture described with the richness and rawness the sociologists usually edit out.[19]

Edmund G. Love's *Set Up* (1980) is a more conventional crime story, the type that Newgate Callendar of the *New York Times* calls a procedural. Captain Crowe, a retired Detroit police officer—unhappy because his department has done nothing to solve an armored car robbery and because he has not been able to convict reputed mobster Sam Rancone—investigates the robbery, finds the money, and connects the man who stole it to Rancone. Then discovering Rancone has double-crossed some out-of-state gangsters, Crowe stops, knowing the gangsters will take care of Rancone in their own fashion.

William X[avier] Kienzle (1919–) was a Catholic priest for twenty years, the last twelve of which he edited the *Michigan Catholic*. The year he left the priesthood he married Javan Herman, an editor and researcher. For the next three years, he edited *MPLS-St. Paul* in the Twin Cities; in 1979, he became a full-time author. By 1988, he had written ten procedurals set in Detroit Catholic churches: *The Rosary Murders* (1979), *Death Wears a Red Hat* (1980), *Mind over Murder* (1981),

Assault with Intent (1982), *Shadow of Death* (1983), *Kill and Tell* (1984), *Murder on 3* (1985), *Deathbed* (1986), *Deadline for a Critic* (1987), *Marked for Murder* (1988), and *Masquerade* (1990).

The Rosary Murders set the pattern for most of the series. Father Robert Koesler, the editor of a Detroit Catholic journal who is a priest-detective in each of the novels, becomes involved in a series of Lenten murders that begin on Ash Wednesday and continue on each successive Friday. Alternately, a priest and nun are slain and left with a rosary carefully entwined in one hand. Lieutenant Walter Koznicki and Sergeant Daniel Fallon of the Detroit Police Department turn to Father Koesler for aid in unlocking the pattern all three of them are certain exists. The killer is caught just in time to spare the victim intended for Good Friday.

The Rosary Murders was filmed in Detroit in 1982 with a script by Elmore ("Dutch") Leonard (1925–), but reviewers were not enthusiastic about the film.[20]

Death Wears a Red Hat follows a similar pattern. According to custom, cathedrals that have been the home church of a deceased cardinal hang the cardinal's red hat from the ceiling. The novel begins with a little girl staring at one of these hats and saying to her startled mother, "Mommy, there's a head in that hat."

Kill and Tell focuses on a Detroit executive, his mistress, and his wife. Here, the murderer uses hypnosis to motivate her victim to swallow a poisoned cocktail.

Deathbed is atypical. Although the first paragraph reports that an unidentified person has killed a nun by mistake, no one is murdered until page 241; the murderer is identified on page 242. The novel is set in a small Catholic-operated hospital in Detroit's inner city. In addition to its focus on the attempts of Sister Eileen Monahan to keep the hospital functioning and her problems with three members of the staff, the novel features two comic characters and an unusual amount of specific sexual activities, particularly by a security guard who spends almost as much time in hospital beds with nurses' aides as he does providing hospital security.

There are, of course, other murder mysteries featuring priests— one, for example, is Ralph McInerny's Father Dowling. In Kienzle's *Kill and Tell*, we learn Father Koesler has been reading the Father Dowling stories and thinks that "McInerny [is] the only creator of a fictional priest who truly captured what it was like to be a priest (p. 141)." In *Death Wears a Red Hat*, a nun says that Father Brown, a 1911 fictional creation of G. K. Chesterton, "would have solved" the book's murders by then. To which another nun replies, "It's too early in the book for Father Brown to come up with one of his elaborate solutions (p. 158)."

Kienzle's novels utilize newspaper stories, Catholic ritual and theology, and police department procedures. Priests are often shown as earthy men who drink, play cards, sometimes tell off-color jokes, and use profanity.

Kienzle's *Deadline for a Critic* may be his best. Several murders lead to the killing of a newspaper critic. One critic has said that the novel does not feature the characteristics of previous Kienzle mysteries, no dramatic signature murders, "rather, it is a frightingly insightful examination of how religion may drive one to blackmail, theft and even murder. It bears the former priest's characteristically clear vision of how religion, in particular the Catholic Church, may destroy souls, instead of enriching them."[21]

In *Masquerade*, the Reverend Klaus Krieg blackmails four members of religious orders into attending a conference of mystery writers, then fakes his own murder as a means of implicating them—his goal is to get them to write for his publishing company, which has a reputation for publishing smutty books. Then an actual murder takes place and Father Koesler is once more drawn into a partnership with the Detroit homicide squad to solve the crime.

In Jim Harrison's *Warlock* (1981), John Lundgren—who has recently lost his executive job in Detroit and is married to a nurse with aspirations to become a doctor—has a vision. So, he changes his name to John Warlock and takes a job as a private detective for a Doctor Rabun, a man who claims he is being robbed of his northwoods lumber by a thief *and* of his money by his wife and son in Florida.

Warlock catches the apparent thief in the Michigan northwoods, then heads south to Florida where he discovers it is Rabun who is the real thief. Back home Warlock learns that he is like the young man in Arthur Conan Doyle's "The Red-Headed League." He has simply been gotten out of the way, in this case so that Rabun could conduct a number of sex experiments with Warlock's wife.

Critics thought that the novel should have been closer in length to Doyle's short story. John Buckley, in the *Saturday Review*, said, "It's flawed in its timing, taking forever to start, then no time to end. There is rich irony in [the] ending, but it is less conclusion than punch line."[22]

Detroit newspaperman John Weisman's novel, *Evidence* (1980), features Robert Mandel, a Detroit reporter who covers the narcotics scene and has two rules: "Never write about a friend; never let your emotions get in the way of your thought." Then his friend, Jack

Fowler, a bisexual, is murdered while doing a story about the homosexual underworld in Detroit and Mandel has to break both rules. As one critic says, "very nasty things turn up."[23] *Evidence* has frequent explicit descriptions of homosexual and heterosexual personal and interpersonal activities in street language.

In 1974, John Weisman (1942–) and Bryan Boyer (1939–), the latter also a newspaper reporter, coauthored a book sometimes referred to as *The Headhunters #1: Heroin Triple Cross* and sometimes only as *The Heroin Triple Cross*. Under the former title, the book, intended to be the first in an action series, tells how "an undercover cop fights corruption with flair in black Detroit."[24] An elite unit of the Detroit police is given the task of policing itself and finding the corruption within its ranks. The two central characters are an aristocratic WASP and a black who speaks street dialect. A reviewer thought that the villains were mere comic caricatures, that the plot was "dubious," with too much violence and too little credibility.[25]

Ann Arbor residents Alfred Slote, an author of children's books, and Garnet R. Garrison (1911?–), a retired university professor who was Slote's teacher in the late 1940s, coauthored two crime novels under the pseudonym of A. H. Garnet, *The Santa Claus Killer* (1981) and *Maze* (1982).

In the first, Charley Thayer, an idealistic twenty-nine-year-old Detroit lawyer campaigning for mayor against Jasper McSweeney, "a long-time lush with a glad hand and a greasy palm" becomes the attorney for a mobster, who, in trying to rob a bank to replenish gang funds he has used, kills a woman employee. Charley's girlfriend, Ellie diAngelo, a hard-nosed television reporter, is trying to win an Emmy Award with the gangster's story. To discredit Charley's mayoral campaign, gang leaders help the gangster escape, intending to eliminate him later.

Reviewers liked the story, calling it a well-written "fast-paced mystery" novel, believable even though the plot was an old one, and "a remarkably good first novel."[26]

Maze is a novel about several seemingly unrelated murders on the campus of Mid-East University. A prominent lawyer (a member of the law school's faculty) with a reputation for dallying with the ladies is found well done in the Law Club kitchen's large oven; the coach of the football team is fatally shot during a game; and an English professor dies from a poisoned cocktail as he is about to introduce a woman poet who has offered the school a sizable grant. Cyrus Wilson, an English professor who had done some amateur sleuthing in the first novel, *The Santa Claus Killer*, cooperates with the police on the case.

Critics wondered why the police would "practically turn the case over to" the professor and also complained that several loose ends of the plot were not well resolved.[27]

One of Slote's books for children is *Hang Tough, Paul Mather* (1973), a story about a Little Leaguer with leukemia who comes to the University of Michigan hospital at Ann Arbor for treatment.

Theodore Weesner (1936–), a Flint native, took a 1959 B.A. degree at the University of Michigan and a 1965 M.F.A. degree from the University of Iowa Writers' Workshop with a thesis titled *Three Stories*. In "The Unspeakable," a young man, wounded in Korea, romances a girl whose husband had been killed in that country and who is concerned over what her husband might think about the affair. The "Trainee" is Edward, a new army recruit from Michigan who has trouble orienting himself. In "Edward, His Son," Edward is seen with his father at a lakeside home in Michigan.

In 1970 and 1971, Weesner published three other short stories— one each in the *Atlantic Monthly*, the *New Yorker*, and *Esquire*—that became chapters of his first novel, *The Car Thief* (1972).

In an automobile factory town in 1959, schoolboy Alex Housman is arrested after he has given a young girl a coat he found in a stolen car. She told her parents, and they called the police.

The novel tours through Alex's memory as, sitting in a detention home, he recalls problems with his parents, ransacking school lockers for cash, voyeurism, stealing cars. In the end, Alex joins the army, leaving home for a new life.

Roger Sale in the *New York Review of Books* wrote that the work was "the best American novel [he had] read in some time . . . the prose is sharp, pointed, locking us into each moment." But he was disappointed because of the "gratuitous violence near the end . . . Weesner has been unable to see his story through on its own terms."[28] C. P. Collier said, "in deceptively simple language, [Weesner] has revealed the loneliness and frustrations of his characters, without in any way becoming morbid, depressing, or maudlin."[29] Joseph McElroy commented, "Weesner conveys in a factual rhythm so natural one sees only later that he has evoked the continuum of human growth."[30] Lance Morrow called the novel "an achievement of almost perfect symmetry. One begins caring about Alex."[31]

Weesner's second novel, *A German Affair* (1977), focuses on Billy, a troubled, deprived youth from Detroit, now a U.S. Army private stationed in Germany. In some ways, he is a recreation of Alex Housman.

Mark Smith's (1935–) first novel, *Toyland* (1965), tells of a couple of killers who take two small children they have been hired to kill to the Michigan northwoods. Eventually, Pehr, the narrator, kills Jensen, his accomplice, in order to save the children—who, in the meantime, are lost in a snowstorm. The novel is as much a psychological study of two violent-prone men as it is a crime novel. Mark Smith's 1966 *The Middleman* tells of a family in an isolated lodge on the shore of Lake Michigan and the attempt of a greedy brother to wipe out the group. Again Smith's emphasis is on the psychological elements.

J. Sloan McClean is a pseudonym for two residents of northern Michigan, Virginia M. Gillette and Josephine Wunsch. Their book *The Aerie: A Gothic Novel* (1974) is set on a forested island in the center of Georgian Bay, an arm of Lake Huron that is in Canada. The Aerie is the enormous Brock Harrington estate on the island. A young woman, hired to be the swimming coach for the estate owner's son, arrives at The Aerie and soon encounters an old unsolved murder, two new ones, a highly organized smuggling ring, and other troubles.

In the later 1970s, Jon A[nthony] Jackson (1938–) wrote two procedurals set in Detroit with Detective Sergeant Mulheisen as the central character in each. In *The Diehard* (1977), Jackson's detective is involved not only with an executive of an insurance company who has embezzled $20 million from his firm and hired an assassin to murder his wife in their suburban home but also with the Detroit Mafia and the man it has hired to find the money. Eventually, the story takes everybody but the Mafia to a northwoods cabin where the executive's wife had hidden the money—which she had found in her home. In a shootout, the executive and the assassin are killed and the Mafia's man gets the money. Mulheisen arrives just too late.

In *The Blind Pig* (1979), Mulheisen investigates both prosperous trucker Jerri Vanni and the Mafia man from the previous novel, *The Diehard*. The attraction for both is a truckload of guns stolen from Selfridge Air Force Base, which Vanni hopes to sell to Cuban exiles wanting to start a revolution on that island. The Mafia man gets the guns and the police get several corpses. Critics thought the first novel was the better one.[32]

Although Jackson, who has a B.A. from the University of Montana and an M.F.A. from the University of Iowa Writers' Workshop, has said that he was at work on *Queensleap*, the third novel in this series, so far it has not appeared.[33]

Robert C. Wilson, a Detroit lawyer, is the author of two horror novels set in the Upper Peninsula, an area where Wilson likes to vacation. *Crooked Tree* (1980) has its basis in the bearwalking lore of Upper Peninsula Indians described by Richard Mercer Dorson in his *Bloodstoppers and Bearwalkers* (1952). The spirit of an Indian dead for a hundred years takes over the body of a young Ottawa Indian woman who is married to a white lawyer. She and black bears in the area embark on a murderous rampage; the bears kill people, she cuts out the victims' tongues. Axel, her husband tries to stop the bloody business, but before he succeeds in destroying the evil spirit, he is very nearly murdered by his wife.

Although not widely reviewed, the book became a best-seller with film rights reportedly being sold to two Hollywood producers.[34]

Wilson again turned to the Upper Peninsula for the setting of *Icefire* (1984.) Reuker Stilkes, a psychopath, has been imprisoned in a correctional facility for savagely killing several middle-aged ladies in a ritualistic fashion. For a time, he is kept under control by drugs, but when a psychiatrist changes the prescription, Stilkes breaks out of prison and has to be hunted down. Although the book apparently became a best-seller, reviewers were unimpressed.[35]

William J. Coughlin, a former prosecuting attorney and federal judge, has three criminal fictions to his credit so far: *The Destruction Committee* (1971), *Day of Wrath* (1980), and *No More Dreams* (1982). In the first, a group of ex-army officers is foiled in its plot to take over the government; in the second, a federal judge and his subordinates are held hostage by a terrorist group seeking to free its leaders; the third is set in Washington, D.C.

Wayne State University Professor Richard E. Werry (1916–), in his *Casket for a Lying Lady* (1985), features Jane "J. D." Mulroy, a petite young private detective who, assisted by a former professional football lineman, takes on the task of finding over $1 million in unregistered bonds for a client. Only a fourth of the story is set in the Detroit area; the balance—including most of the action—is set in south Florida. In *A Delicately Personal Matter* (1986), Mulroy, back in Birmingham, Michigan, becomes involved in the affairs of an apparently normal middle-class family man. The books received minimal reviews.

Deerlovers (1987) by E. H. Creeth (1928–) is a novel of a retired high school teacher's efforts to do something about hunters of wild life. During a two-week deer-hunting season in the Michigan northwoods, he tracks and kills a hunter each day. In the following year, his decision to publicize his activities creates complications that he survives. As with Werry's books, the Creeth novel also received minimal reviews.

Creeth (1928–) taught in the English department at the University of Michigan from 1958 on.

Two Major Michigan Crime Novelists

Loren D. Estleman (1952–) had written twenty-six books up to 1990 (some Westerns, others based on Dracula and Sherlock Holmes). At least eleven of the twelve of these that are set in Detroit feature Amos Walker, a black private detective. In *Motor City Blue* (1980), the hero seeks a missing girl; in *Angel Eyes* (1981), a nightclub dancer hires Walker to find her should she disappear (she does); in *The Midnight Man* (1981), Walker seeks vengeance for the shooting of a policeman friend now a vegetable; in *The Glass Highway* (1983), Walker is hired to find the twenty-year-old son of a television anchorwoman— the son is mixed up with a young woman drug addict; in *Sugartown* (1984), a seventy-three-year-old Polish woman hires Walker to find her grandson missing for nineteen years, after the father of the family supposedly killed the boy's mother, a sister, and himself; in *Every Brilliant Eye* (1986) Walker investigates the disappearance of his friend, journalist-author Barry Stackpole.

Lady Yesterday (1987) also takes Walker on a tour of Detroit, including many nightspots featuring jazz; the Detroit La Cosa Nostra lingers in the background. *Downriver* (1988) begins at Marquette, where Walker meets a freed prisoner who insists someone else got the loot for which he served his sentence. A number of Detroit highrolling auto executives appear in this one.

General Murders (1989) is a collection of ten short stories published from 1982 on. In each, Walker meets personal perils as he seeks to aid clients with problems.

In *Silent Thunder* (1989), Walker is hired to help defend a woman who shot her abusive husband, the son of a prominent Detroit family. The husband's hobby was buying weapons—anything from pistols to a howitzer or a Polaris missile. As usual, Walker finds himself the target of several opposing forces, ranging from corrupt police to a hillbilly arms merchant to an FBI man. *Sweet Women Lie* (1990) involves Walker with his former wife; an actress living on her long-past reputation; a Mafia leader whose life depends on a life-support system; the CIA; and a couple of minor Detroit hoodlums. Walker, said a critic, is a "hard-boiled" detective with a "touch of romanticism" that leads him to risk his own life and reputation for the downtrodden.[36]

In *Kill Zone* (1984), Estleman introduced a new character in Detroit hit man Peter Macklin. Eight terrorists, who have hijacked a Boblo Island excursion boat with eight hundred passengers aboard, announce that unless the governor of Michigan releases ten political prisoners from Michigan's state prison, they will blow up the booby-trapped boat (which has a U.S. cabinet member's daughter aboard). With only a knife and a pistol, Macklin overwhelms the heavily armed hijackers.[37]

Macklin was again featured in *Roses Are Dead* (1985). This time a commision from an ex-prostitute to terminate a former male friend produces a complex tale with more characters than a reader can keep in mind—and some even have aliases. The prostitute dies along with other members of the cast. Macklin survives, probably for another book.

Whiskey River (1990) is the first of a projected series of three novels blending actual Detroit history with Estleman's imagined tales of what might have been. *Whiskey River* begins with the 1929 stock market crash, the end of Prohibition, and the start of the 1930s depression. In 1939, Constantine Minor, a newspaper columnist, tells a Detroit Grand Jury his observations of the crime scene in those years, focusing on two fictional figures, Jack Dance and Joey Machine, and their relations with a corrupt Detroit police and judicial system.

Estleman planned to follow this novel with one set in the 1950s and a third set in the 1990s.

Estleman's books focus on the seamy side of Detroit life—prostitution, car thievery, drugs, organized crime, illegal after-hours bars, gang conflicts.

And so we come to Elmore Leonard from Birmingham, Michigan—if not Michigan's best writer in a long time, at least its most popular. Newgate Callendar says Leonard "has a wonderful ear, and his dialogue never has a false note."[38] Richard Herzfelder in the *Chicago Tribune* said Leonard is "a writer of thrillers whose vision goes deeper than thrill."[39] Grover Sales in the *Los Angeles Times Book Review* said "Leonard is an original. His uncanny sense of plot, pace and his inexhaustible flair for the nervous rhythms of contemporary urban speech have caught the spirit of the '80s."[40]

Leonard is a veteran screenwriter and novelist with close to three dozen Western and mystery films and book titles to his credit so far. His first book, *The Big Bounce* (1969), got minor reviews. The film was nominated for worst film of 1969, and even Leonard disliked it. The plot revolves around a young transient farm laborer-housebreaker and his relationship with a young woman with similar inclinations but greater ambitions. She tries to kill him but he survives. The young man's employer also owns a farm in Florida and in 1974 reappears as the protagonist in *Mr. Majestyk;* the story takes place in Florida. The novel was filmed in 1974, but relocated to Colorado. Critics complained that it emphasized violence too much and de-emphasized the migrant labor problems with which the novel was concerned.

In 1974, Leonard also produced his first Detroit novel—*Fifty-Two Pick-up*. (The title refers to $52,000, not to a truck.) The work pits an industrialist against three vicious men. They first try to blackmail Harry Mitchell; failing in that, they kidnap his wife and hold her for ransom. But the industrialist, as tough-minded as the kidnappers, sets the three against each other until only one, the nastiest, is left. Mitchell then persuades the survivor to release his wife for only $52,000 instead of the $105,000 the trio had originally demanded. The briefcase, which supposedly contains the ransom money, is actually a booby trap.

Both the novel and the 1986 movie of the same name—but filmed in Los Angeles, not Detroit, the setting of the novel—were equally well received by critics who were comparing Leonard to Raymond Chandler, Dashiell Hammett, Ross MacDonald, and George V. Higgins.[41] The popularity of both versions (the film's story line varies from that of the novel) may be due in part to the image of American free enterprise taking on the criminal world and defeating it.

Leonard's paperback *Swag* (1976) was reissued as *Ryan's Rules* (1978). It is the story of Frank J. Ryan, a Detroit used-car salesman who persuades a young car thief, Ernest ("Stick") Stickley, Jr., to join him in a career of armed robbery.

Swag's climax comes in an attempt to rob Detroit's Hudson's Department Store of a payroll. Two men are killed and Frank and Ernest are double-crossed—someone else gets the money. But in a succeeding shootout, Frank and Ernest retrieve the money, only to be trapped by the police because Ryan has violated one of his own ten rules for successful criminal behavior.

Leonard's next was *Unknown Man No. 89* (1977, reissued 1984). Newgate Callendar, commenting on this novel, said Leonard utilized a verismo style of speech: "Leonard's characters speak in a way that cannot be reproduced in a family newspaper." Moreover, "Leonard is a moralist. [In his books] Good overcomes Evil."[42]

Unknown Man No. 89 is a complex tale in which a process server is after the money of Robert Leary, Jr. So are characters named Tunafish, Raymond Gidre, Francis X. Perez (who will stop at neither murder nor mayhem to get the money), and Denise, who is first Leary's wife and then his widow. After several shootouts, Ryan, Denise, and Leary's money end up together. Said Newgate Callendar, "Leonard's books are not High Literature nor [do they] pretend to be. Leonard is primarily an entertainer."[43]

The Switch (1978) tells of Mickey Dawson, the self-effacing wife of a dishonest Detroit businessman. She is kidnapped, and her husband, rejecting the kidnappers' demand for $1 million as ransom, flees to the Bahamas with a mistress. But Mickey makes friends with her abductors (who compromise on their demands) and turns the tables on her no-good husband.

Leonard's next Michigan novel, *City Primeval: High Noon in Detroit* (1980), begins with a black Detroit judge charged with misconduct in office; he is mistaken for another man and murdered.

Raymond Cruz, a white officer in Detroit's largely black homicide department, sets out to find the murderer. The action takes place in a Detroit that is primeval in its violence and disregard for mores, morals, and human life—a city, for the most part out to get all it can regardless of the consequences.

In 1982, Leonard produced *Split Images*, a tale of a rich but mentally disturbed industrialist who kills people simply for the pleasure he gets out of the act. With a former policeman, he plans the murder of a woman whose boyfriend is a Detroit policeman. But Leonard is always unpredictable and, in this case, when the woman meets the killer, the unconventional takes place.

Leonard's *Touch* (1987), set in the late 1970s, features a romance between a young faith healer and a young woman who is a previously married publicist. The villain in this story is a right-wing protester. *Touch* is an atypical Leonard story.

In 1988 came *Freaky Deaky*, named for a sexy dance popular in the decade before this story. Chris Mankowski, in the last hour before his transfer from the Detroit Police Department's Bomb Squad to its Sex Crimes Department, is given the task of trying to free a Detroit drug king who has sat down in a booby-trapped chair and will be blown to bits if he tries to get up.

Mankowski lets nature take its course—but in his new job, he comes to grips with two 1960s activists who had dynamited a federal building, served prison sentences, and now plan to blow up a former Ann Arbor classmate who has become one of Detroit's richest citizens. And Mankowski, once again, finds himself involved with explosives.

Leonard's *Killshot* (1989) replicates *Fifty-Two Pick-up*. A pair of criminals (one is named Richie Nix!) select a northern Michigan couple in order to extort money from them. At first, the couple plan to give in but then decide to tough it out. As usual, readers, although they know it is only a story—only words on paper—are hooked once they begin reading *Killshot*. But in this novel Leonard, always a superb storyteller is even more unpredictable than usual.

James Kauffmann says that "maybe the best thing about Leonard is the affection he lavishes on his characters, even the out-and-out crazies and the jerks. Somehow they're all human, recognizable (though not necessarily likable) and always believable."[44]

In 1988, a new writer, Tom Kakonis, "a sharp new gambler in the literary crap shoot,"[45] appeared on the Michigan crime fiction scene with *Michigan Roll* set in Traverse City. The novel focuses on an ex-college professor who, after a prison term for murdering his wife's lover, has become a professional gambler; an attractive woman he has rescued from two professional killers; and the woman's brother, who has stolen some illegal drugs from the pair. Despite the nightmarish events that ensue, all ends well for the professor.

Summary

Those who follow the criminal activities reported in the press and on television may have the impression that criminal behavior in Michigan is limited to Detroit and its environs. Michigan novels about crime, however, prove otherwise. Although they do narrate criminal behavior in Detroit, these crime novels also range across both peninsulas, from farm to town to city, and even onto the Great Lakes around them.

The most popular of the writers in this genre are Elmore Leonard, Loren Estleman, and William Kienzle. We shall surely hear more from them.

CHAPTER XIV

PEOPLE IN MICHIGAN LITERATURE

Let me say "we" for I am not alone in this
desire to live
where the land is neither dramatically flat
nor high, where it snows enough
to keep the world
the bitter white of aspirin.

People with such needs grew up
snow-belted, rust-belted
in towns like mine
—Alice Fulton, "The New Affluence."[1]

Michiganians are at the center of every literary work set in the Wolverine State. However, in the literature discussed in other chapters, it is the settings of the small town, the farm, and the lakes, and it is the themes of ethnicity, crime, and pioneer settlement that receive the primary emphasis. In the works discussed in this chapter, it is the characters that receive the most emphasis. Where the focus between character and other elements has seemed equal, hard choices have been made with which some readers may not agree.

Cavalcade Novels

Some of the fictional works that emphasize Michigan people fall into the cavalcade category—the novel, play, or motion picture that focuses on individuals, families, or groups over a period of years or generations. For a time earlier in the twentieth century, the cavalcade novel was popular with many authors.

Ashes of Yesterday: A Historical Novel (1941) by Del (Dan E. L.) Patch, is a fictional biography of Margaret (Grandma) Withington

Thrillby who was born on January 26, 1837, the first day of Michigan's statehood, and who lived almost a century. As a young girl she sees Thomas Alva Edison thrown off a train because one of his experiments has started a fire; near the end of her life in 1933, she is present at Chicago's Century of Progress when Edison reenacts his invention of the first incandescent lamp.

Patch was chief of police in Highland Park and president of the Michigan Association of Chiefs of Police. He had earlier published *Past Finding Out* and *Aamon Always*.

O Distant Star! (1944) by Mary Frances Doner (1893–) is a two-part novel. In pre-Civil War days, Delia Clune, an Irish servant from South Boston, is courted by a wealthy visitor to a North Boston mansion. Subsequently, she is wrongfully accused of thievery and discharged. Some years later in Marquette, Michigan, married to Dermot Reagan, an iron mine manager, and the mother of two children, Delia renews the affair with her former lover. Discovering this and knowing that a third pregnancy will kill Delia, Dermot rapes her. But she survives until the end of the century.

Wilbur Schramm said that "Delia was a woman's heroine"; Andrea Parke said "it takes only a little mental huffing and puffing to blow [Doner's] make-believe house down."[2]

Alvah C. Bessie's lengthy *Dwell in the Wilderness* (1935) takes the middle-class Morris family through three generations from 1876 to 1925, first in a small town, then from 1917 on in Detroit. Eben, a somewhat ambitious young grocer, joins in "ultra-holy matrimony" with a minister's daughter. Her frigidity and a family atmosphere of almost hopeless frustration create problems for their children. Two sons try to escape through marriage, business careers, and World War I service, but do not quite succeed. A daughter, "the most completely realized character, enters on a vain search for self-understanding and fulfillment."[3]

Bessie (1904–1985) was not a Michigan native. He won an Academy Award in 1946 for the script of *Objective Burma*; in the 1950s he was sentenced to a year in prison for his refusal to answer the questions of a congressional committee about his Communist party affiliations.

Belle Kanaris Maniates's *David Dunne* (1912) was the first of several homespun novels written before illness forced her to quit writing. Despite a poverty-stricken boyhood, David Dunne acquires a law degree. When he becomes a political candidate, enemies railroad him off to South America. But a novel he writes there makes him famous, and he returns home to become a congressman and a governor.

One commentator said that the novel was "the result of observations of political life in Lansing" where Maniates worked in the
capitol building.[4] But the sugar-coated narrative suggests that there
were elements of Michigan politics Maniates either was ignorant of or
deliberately overlooked. Maniates was born in Marshall, Michigan.
She died in Lansing in 1925.

Every once in a while, the urge to seek a copartner and write
books in double harness has infected Americans. Helen Genung
and Caryl May Hayes offer an example in *Valiant Dust* (1936). Their
heroine is Nora Dillon, thirty, who—after her father dies and her
mother scandalizes the Dublin society by marrying eight days later—
marries and emigrates to a stock farm in Detroit's suburbs. There she
raises thoroughbred horses (one of which "tosses her husband into
eternity as carelessly as he had been accustomed to toss off a glass of
Irish whiskey")[5] and concentrates on making "suitable marriages"
for their two daughters and two sons. One of the sons invests in a
"horseless carriage" factory and develops it into a money-making
operation.

Margerie Bonner's *Horse in the Sky* (1947) echoes *Valiant Dust*.
Thurles Dungarvon, whose well-to-do mother had been disowned
after she had eloped with a horse groom, becomes a servant in the
home of a wealthy upper-class family. Later, while riding a horse
she had always wanted and had bought with an unexpected legacy,
Thurles is thrown and killed. Andrea Parke said the novel "is a
strange little tale with a haunting quality and a heroine . . . who
might have wended her stormy way through one of Thomas Hardy's
novels."[6]

Hilda Morris (1888–1947)—author, poet, and artist—wrote *The
Long View* (1937) and *Landmarks* (1941). In *Landmarks*, set in the 1930s,
an artist from the East, researching a Michigan town's past for a mu-
ral, discovers his mother is a descendant of the man who founded the
town about 1850 and learns about his own heritage. "Reading *Landmarks*," a reviewer said, "is rather like rummaging in an attic trunk
filled with souvenirs and symbols of the past, or thumbing through
an album of faded photographs with its dim fragrance of plush and
pressed flowers."[7]

The Long View follows the descendants of the Allan family from
Pennsylvania to southwest Michigan for more than half a century.
Part 3 focuses on Asher Allan who has taken a factory job in Dune
Harbor, his wife Sybil, and their sons, one of whom attends college at
Ann Arbor. To aid the reader, the novel has a genealogical table on its
end papers.

Edith H. Walton said the *The Long View* was a "pleasant book," but in no sense "either brilliant or profound." B. E. Bettinger said that the book was one more example of "literary America . . . becoming root–conscious." He added "the whole story . . . is told with dignity and fidelity."[8]

Joseph McCord's *Dominie's Daughter* (1943) follows the daughter of a stern, selfish minister to several small Michigan towns from the 1890s to 1940. As a child, Marcia McBride lives in the world of her imagination because of her father's strictures; as a young college graduate, she marries the son of one of her father's wealthiest parishioners, only to have tragedy stalk the marriage.

Critics liked the "especially rich and informative account of a vanishing America in this portrayal of small town[s], and of an intensely religious family"—"a rather more pretentious novel" than any of the score of McCord's earlier romances."[9]

Before McCord (1880–1943) became an author, he had engaged in mineral explorations on the south shore of Lake Superior.

Barbara Frances Fleury (1907–) set her second book, *Faith the Root* (1942), on the Saint Clair River. It is (as a reviewer said) two books in one. The first is the life story of Father Germain (Father Jerry); he gave up a romantic interest in a girl to become a priest and ministered in the novel's Algonquin for half a century. The second and deeper story is Father Germain's strong and enduring faith:

> [A] faith which has for three generations heard the same sordid and shabby [confessions] each week, and sees in the fact of their recurrence not the essential evil of man but some unguessed-at failure in [himself]; of a faith which sees in all his "children," the easy and the difficult ones, they are never the good and the bad to him, the inheritors of a divine destiny.
>
> Miss Fleury has taken us inside a soul, and with delicacy and subtle understanding made us the richer for what we found there.[10]

Fleury dedicated her book to a priest who was obviously the model for Father Jerry.

Like *Faith the Root*, Dr. Louis J. Gariepy's *Saw-Ge-Mah* [Medicine man] (1950), set in an Upper Peninsula sawmill town, Ann Arbor, and Detroit, is the fictional life story of a man whose goal is always to help others. From boyhood, Hal Adams, son of a sawmill worker, wants to be a doctor. His first training at Norris (Ferris?) Institute is followed by medical training at the University of Michigan. Back home, his first patient, an Indian, calls him Saw-Ge-Mah. As his career proceeds, the sawmill town becomes a town in transition, then a resort town that outlasts the Great Depression and World War II.

Dr. Gariepy was "an eminent [Detroit] surgeon, author of several pharmaceutical and technical volumes, a researcher into Ottawa Indian lore, and 'a driving force for the social and economic status of the American Indian.' [The novel] was intended both as a case history designed to deter or inspire those who would seek a career in medicine, and as a tribute to a country doctor."[11]

In Helen Hull's *Morning Shows the Day* (1934), *morning* is the time when seven boys and girls are editors of their high school annual; *day* is the next thirty years as they and their town grow—the coming of the automobile, factories, physical expansion, motion pictures and radio, chain stores; the acceleration of those leisurely first years of the twentieth century to the boom of the 1920s, and then the stock market crash, which leads to the Great Depression.

The seven, representative of the town's population, are bound together by chance: born in the same Michigan town at the same time, thrown together in the public school, chosen for the yearbook board. But their lives take differing directions.

Reviewers thought Hull was an excellent storyteller but was too detached from her characters, more like a scientist than an artist, "Hull has handled her large canvas well and told her story with liveliness and warmth. But it adds up to nothing more than 'a story,' neither enlarging nor reinforcing our comprehension of life."[12]

In 1939, Sterling North used Hull's basic theme in *Seven against the Years;* in 1942, Susan Glaspell repeated the theme in *Norma Ashe*.

Hobert and Hubert Douglas Skidmore, identical twins born in 1911, came to Ann Arbor just as the Hopwood awards were initiated. Hobert won a Hopwood Award in fiction (1932) and in drama (1935); Hubert a Hopwood Award in fiction in 1935. Hubert's *Three-a-Day* and Hobert's *Lassitude*, neither with a Michigan setting, were published in *University of Michigan Prize Plays*, Book II (1930).

Of the several novels published subsequently by the two Skidmores, only Hobert's *The Years Are Even* (1952), obviously based on the twins' own lives, is set in Michigan. The novel's two characters are drawn to the graphic arts rather than literature and drama, however. When one is tragically burned to death (as Hubert was), the other offers to replace him in his widow's life, but she accuses him of incest. (Hubert was married to Michigan novelist Maritta Wolff.)

In *The Lie* (1953), Peggy Goodin (1923–) tells of three generations of women—Billie, fifty-six, her daughter, Kate, thirty-four, and Jen, a teenager. The lie of the title is that for years Jen is passed off as Kate's younger sister, even though (and Jen does not know it) Jen is Kate's illegitimate daughter.

For a time, it appears that on Jen's seventeenth birthday, the long-hidden secret will be revealed. But at this point, when readers are expecting "emotional fireworks, ethical challenges, dramatic tension," they get "wisecracks and horselaughs." The story "called for the sensibilities of a [Theodore] Dreiser rather than the sophistications of a Dorothy Parker."[13]

Nineteenth-Century People

The earliest of this group is the Reverend James H. Pitiezel's *The Backwoods Boy Who Became a Minister* (1859), a novel based on the autobiography of the author who was a Methodist missionary to the Upper Peninsula.

Dr. William Ryerson Vis called his *Saddlebag Doctor* (1964) a historical novel, but with no apparent narrative strand, the format is closer to a series of tableaux. The setting is Grand Rapids in the mid-nineteenth century. Two early doctors, a trader, and several Ottawa tribespeople are the main characters, along with Father Frederic Baraga, better known for his work in the Upper Peninsula. Dr. Vis was born in 1886 in Drenthe (now Newaygo, an Ottawa county community) and took an M.D. degree at Ann Arbor in 1916. He practiced medicine in Grand Rapids until he died in 1969.

Rose Elizabeth Cleveland's *The Long Run* (1886) is a brief saccharine tale of a small-town romance between Rufus Grosbeck, resident of Stonewall and a woman visitor that takes place over two summers. At the end of the second summer, Rufus proposes marriage in a personally delivered letter.

Ermina Stray was the author of *The Golden Link; or, The Shadow of Sin* (1891), a book that is about as much a religious tract as it is a novel. A woman who believed she was the daughter of a wealthy iconoclast—a man who believed that "Robert Ingersoll was the smartest man in the United States" (p. 65)—discovers that she and a neighbor were given to the wrong parents at birth. One scene in the novel shows a strike by millhands who want a ten-hour workday. Tract novels such as this were popular with readers who wanted a moral in fictional imitations of life.

Mary Cummisky Bliss's *Dr. Joy* (1899) is a tale of the adventures and misadventures of a Saginaw-area country doctor in the 1890s that may be based on an actual person.

Juell Deming (1901) by Albert Lathrop Lawrence (1865–?) takes place in the 1890s in an imaginary town on the Kalamazoo River. A rural schoolteacher finds an unconscious writer and nurses him back to health. Later, he serves in the Spanish-American War. Too many coincidences and too much withheld information mar the tale.

Agnes Grant's Education by Hope Daring (pseudonym of Anna Johnson) was published serially, then in book form (1902, with several later editions). It was followed by a sequel titled *An Abundant Harvest* (1904).

Agnes Grant, born in a log cabin, becomes a college teacher and college dean. Later, she marries a wealthy doctor. But her rise in social status is accompanied by trials and tribulations, through all of which she is sustained by fundamentalist Christianity. Both books have some of the qualities of religious tracts.

Johnson was also the author of a number of other novels, including *Father John; or, Ruth Webster's Quest* (1907) and *The Furniture People* (1903), republished as *The Woods in the Home* (1927).

Seymour Eaton's (1859–1916) *Dan Black: Editor and Proprietor* (1903) is little more than a short story. Black, a recalcitrant middle-aged editor and printer in a lumbering town is the only one to defend a young waitress when she is charged with theft. Later, the two wed.

Mildred Evans Gilman (1898–?) in *Fig Leaves* (1925) tells the story of a Grand Rapids young woman whose conditioning by her mother, friends, and lover leads to a deep automatic desire for the approval and applause of society. It begins with Lydia Carter seeing an incubator baby at the 1893 Chicago World's Fair, then follows her as she tries to learn the facts of life from patent medicine advertisements and novels about white slave girls. At a university, she joins first a sorority and later a movement to abolish sororities. Finally, she marries a young man who at first seemed odious and who her sorority sisters advised her to drop.

Maxwell Bodenheim (1893–1954), a minor associate of Sherwood Anderson, Theodore Dreiser, and Carl Sandburg in the Chicago Renaissance, set his *A Virtuous Girl* (1930) in the Windy City, Grand Haven, and Kalamazoo at the turn of the century; the book focuses on a Chicago woman and her sexual relationships with several men in the three cities. This is one of several novels in which Bodenheim demonstrates his insights into the problems of women as victims.

Iron Mountain native Rosemary Obermeyer (1903–) was a forty-year-old teacher with a master's degree from Columbia when she won a first prize in the 1943 Avery Hopwood awards for *Golden Apples of the Sun* (1944). Set about 1900, it tells how a gypsy girl and several older friends pretend to be pioneers in a Fourth of July parade to cover up their scheme to drive their covered wagon north to the

Michigan wilderness. Both Hopwood judges and reviewers were charmed by the novel.[14]

Melvin E. Trotter's *Jimmy Moore of Bucktown* (1904, reissued 1970) is a story of an eleven-year-old boy who, after applying to "Der Boss" of a Grand Rapids slum mission for help for his family, sets out to reform the incorrigible residents of Bucktown, a slum area near the city market. Trotter ("Der Boss") was the superintendent of the mission. Its goals were to aid the destitute and to convert them to fundamentalist Christianity.

The novel is unique in that no other Michigan novel shows this aspect of the failure of the American dream. Jimmy's success where adults had failed illustrates the biblical concept that "a little child shall lead them."

The hero of Thomas Enright's somewhat improbable *The King of Nobody's Island* (1909), John Douglass, a young millionaire Chicago stock trader, comes to the wilderness area of lakes and islands on the Michigan–Wisconsin boundary to recuperate. There, he is shot by a man who regards him as an intruder, but the attacker is then killed and scalped by an Indian friendly to Douglass. For a time, the hero's romance with a neighbor is complicated by his discovery that she is the daughter of one of his unfriendly Chicago competitors.

Twentieth-Century People

Edwin Faxon Osborn (1859–1937), a Baptist clergyman who graduated from Kalamazoo College, was the author of several religious books and *Onar* (1909). The heroine, Onar, lives with a black female servant and a dog in a castlelike structure in the jackpine region of Michigan, where she is romanced by two men.

Two Michigan women, writing at about the same time, used similar themes and techniques to produce similar books. The first was Belle Kanaris Maniates, whose *Amarilly of Clothes Line Alley* (1915), earlier written and produced as a play, made its author famous. Amarilly Jenkins, child of a city's slums, progresses from assistant scrub lady at a theater to become a college student.

In 1918, the story was filmed with one of Hollywood's all-time illustrious actresses, Mary Pickford ("America's Sweetheart"), in the title role. As a consequence, one of the first of three Michigan novels ever to be filmed became nationally famous.

The success of the novel in its own right in 1917 led to a sequel, *Amarilly in Love*. Out of college, Amarilly goes to Europe with a party of friends, arriving just as World War I starts. Back home, Amarilly then writes a play.

Mildew Manse (1916) uses the epistolary mode. Joan Lynn writes "quite impossible" letters to her father in Alaska, telling him of her life with the Haphazard family. She also opens a "ridiculous but entertaining business enterprise." A reviewer said "there's a love affair on every page."[15]

In *Our Next Door Neighbors* (1917), Maniates again utilized a family theme—five boys are foisted on a childless couple. The book got miniscule reviews; Hollywood ignored it.

Bessie Ray Hoover (1874–?), a college teacher, began in 1907 to contribute stories of the fictional Flickenger family of her southwest Michigan area to periodicals in the East. These became *Pa Flickenger's Folks* (1909), *Opal* (1910), and *Rolling Acres* (1922).

In the first book (1909), Hoover sets "the [Flickenger's] family's cheerfulness, kindliness and determination to make the best of everything off against the . . . ever pitiless squeeze that attaches to those whose wallets are inconsiderably lean."[16]

Opal (1910) is a novel of the "new woman"—a common type in the first two decades of the twentieth century, a woman striking out on her own, disregarding the old nineteenth-century strictures about women's roles. Opal Flickenger finishes high school—unusual for rural girls at that time—and, despite the Flickengers' wish that she teach school, she marries a well-to-do young farmer.

Caleb Hobson Rutledge (1855–?) in his locally published *Flashes from a Furnace* (1912) tells of a clergyman who attempts to bring temperance to the Copper Country of the Upper Peninsula.

Deepwood (1981) by Walter S. J. Swanson (1917–) is set in the area around Au Sable; the time is from the early 1900s to about 1920. A widow takes in a teenage boy who has been left homeless by a forest fire. When he is twenty-two and she forty, they wed. Later, he has a love affair with a young woman he has met through the widow. Swanson's theme seems to be that life flows along, bringing both hope and despair, good times and bad, life and death. Critics had mixed emotions about the book.[17]

Webb Waldron (1882–1945) was the son of a principal of a public school and an artist mother. He was elected to Phi Beta Kappa and took his A.B. degree at the University of Michigan in 1905. After time out in the West for health problems and a decade as a New York journalist, he began writing articles and books. In 1915, he married Marion Keep Patton, a writer and an illustrator.

Two of Waldron's novels, *The Road to the World* (1922) and *Shanklin* (1925) seem autobiographical. In the first, Stan Hilgert—the son of a teacher and an artist—goes through school, has health problems, takes a degree at Ann Arbor, and becomes a writer.

Shanklin might well have been entitled *Quest*. Mark Shanklin's search for a friend takes him away from his Upper Peninsula home. On one occasion, he rooms with a red-headed novelist, a character probably based on Sinclair Lewis, whom Waldron knew in New York.

Critics praised the two novels with moderation. The *New Republic* said that the first novel is "a book alive with real characters, rather casually drawn, and so full of the American scene that it almost becomes the American panorama."[18] The *Saturday Review of Literature* said *Shanklin* is "romantic, melodramatic, psychical, intuitive, a none too real odyssey of experiences in love, in politics, in business, in self-discovery."[19]

Waldron's nonfictional *We Explore the Great Lakes* (1923), with illustrations by his wife, is a fascinating collection of articles about Michigan people that have a fictional quality about them.

In his first novel based on his "scientific philosophies," *In the Sight of God* (1924, reissued 1976) Dr. Jacob Wendell Clark (1878–?) tells of a supposed daughter of a Copper Country miner who, discovering that she is actually the product of an illicit relationship between her mother and another man, leaves home. Lost in a winter storm, she comes to the home of an ailing self-educated scientist who is trying to apply Mendelian theories to people. When Staggering Smith (named from his ongoing illness) dies, the girl continues his research, and, to prove one of his theories (and Clark's), she has an illegitimate child.

Helen Holman Smith, granddaughter of a Cornish mining captain and publisher of the 1976 reissue of *In the Sight of God*, says that "the original [1924] edition was banned from the company-owned Calumet Public Library and its contents whispered about over the tea tables" in proper homes in the Calumet area.[20]

Lee J. Smits's *The Spring Flight* (1925) follows the son of a Puritan mother and a bumbling father from 1900 to 1920. After affairs with "the looser sort" of women, he marries a "good woman" his Puritan mother would approve of and begins "the dull, safe years of his middle age. Normalcy [sic] as the late martyr [President Warren G.] Harding might have said, is his final and supreme commitment."[21]

Among the extensive reviews of *The Spring Flight*, there was this comment by Harrison Smith, "Smits has added one more to the endless chain of midwestern novels of adolescence . . . youth . . . early manhood . . . and failure. Most of them are intensely autobiographical, stories of young men and women who have made the alarming discovery that they have come out of a slightly different mold from that which produced the machine-made products around them."[22]

Smits, a Detroit resident and the son of a Puritan minister, had little formal education and had worked in lumber camps and newspaper offices.[23] Arnold Mulder said he was one of the "frustration" group of Michigan authors.[24]

Isabella Holt (Mrs. Haldeman Finnie [1893–1962]) was a native of Chicago who moved to Detroit. Her 1939 *A Visit to Pay* is another novel that illustrates close connections between Detroit and Chicago. The book focuses on the two Converse beauties of Detroit and the consequences of their marriages. The novel begins in Detroit, then in the Great Depression moves to a farm near Gooseford. Other parts of the story take place in the Jackson Prison and in Chicago.

Ernest (Miller) Hemingway (1899–1961), born in Oak Park, Illinois, found the sources for some of his early work and best-known short stories in the northern sections of Michigan. From his early childhood on he vacationed with his family in the Petoskey-Little Traverse Bay area of the Lower Peninsula. As a young man, he fished the rivers of the central and northeastern portions of the Upper Peninsula.

From 1925 to 1933, Hemingway wrote several stories about a character named Nick Adams—an obvious projection of himself as a young man. "Of the place[s] where he had been as a boy, he had written well enough," thinks the dying writer in an early version of "The Snows of Kilimanjaro."

In 1925, some Nick Adams stories were published in *In Our Time*—a book with contrasting images of the Michigan northwoods and World War I (in which Hemingway was wounded) that immediately focused attention on Hemingway. In 1927, other Nick Adams stories appeared in *Men without Women*. The best of these stories is "The Killers," a story about two gangsters who take over a restaurant and lie in wait for a frequent customer, intending to kill him. The customer, however, doesn't appear.

"Indian Camp," a story about Nick Adams watching as his father performs a caesarean operation under primitive conditions; "The Three-Day Blow," a tale of two boys in a shanty in the northwoods waiting out an offshore lake storm; "The End of Something," a story presumably based on an affair young Hemingway once had with a young woman; and "Country People," a story of summer visitors in a resort area are all set in the Petoskey area.

"The Big Two-Hearted River" is set in the east-central Upper Peninsula. When Nick Adams arrives in Seney, he finds that the Seney fire has left only stone foundations, nothing else. Nick hikes and fishes along the river that flows through Seney. (In fact, it is the Fox River; for the Two-Hearted River in the title is north and east of the Fox and flows into Lake Superior.) Sheridan Baker in his "Hemingway's Two-Hearted River" furnishes an excellent discussion of the story and its background.[25]

The twenty-odd Nick Adams stories together with related materials were assembled by Philip Young and published as *The Nick Adams Stories* in 1972. *Hemingway's Adventures of a Young Man* (1962), based on these stories, was filmed in and around Ironwood, Michigan. A reviewer for the *New York Times* said Hemingway "would have taken a blowtorch to the film."[26]

Hemingway's *The Torrents of Spring*—subtitled *A Romantic Novel in Honor of the Passing of a Great Race* (1926, reissued 1972)—is set in a pump factory in Petoskey. It is a "hilarious satire" of poet-novelist Sherwood Anderson—whose praise of *In Our Time* had appeared on the dust jacket of the latter book together with blurbs from several other American writers. There are also, as reviewers noted, "sideswipes" at Gertrude Stein, a contemporary of Anderson and Hemingway.[27]

The reviewers of *Torrents of Spring* (William Rose Benét, Allen Tate, and Harry Hansen, among others), although reporting some displeasure with Hemingway's burlesque of Sherwood Anderson and Eugene O'Neill, agreed with the *Little Review* that he was to be "the big man in American letters."[28]

Constantine Cappel's *Hemingway in Michigan* (1966) examines this period of Hemingway's literary history.

Kenneth (O'Donnell) Horan based three books, *Remember the Day* (1937), *Oh Promise Me* (1938), and *Papa Went to Congress* (1946), on the personal experiences and service in Congress of her father, a publisher in Jackson. Although Albert G. Black calls the 1937 book a novel, all three are nonfiction—but with the charm of fiction.

Her non-Michigan novel, *The Longest Night* (1932), was followed by *It's Not My Problem* (1938), a *roman à clef* of a woman writer who turns down a Hollywood job because she does not want her children raised in the movie capital's false atmosphere.

I Give Thee Back (1942) is Horan's best novel, and recounts the story of a woman who is censured by townspeople because she rears the orphaned son of a former lover. With her help, he becomes a doctor, but then he marries a girl with an unwholesome reputation.

Helen Clark Fernald (1888–?) set her *The Shadow of the Crooked Tree* (1965) on the northwest tip of the Lower Peninsula, a place that once had two landmarks for Lake Michigan sailors—a cross on a church erected by Jesuits and L'Arbre Croche (The Crooked Tree), which for years reared its misshapen top above surrounding trees.

The novel tells the story of an Indiana girl who had hoped to teach in a city but instead becomes a teacher of rural students, half of whom are Ottawa Indian children. She finds romance with a conservation officer (who offers to help her find a city school) and an area storekeeper. We know early on what her choice will be.

Fernald was also the author of books for young people.

Charles Louis Severance's (1907–) *Tales of the Thumb* (1972) has eighteen short tales that the author implies were told to him when he was a boy in the Michigan "thumb" area. One is a reworking of the Jack-the-giant-killer theme; another is reminiscent of the case of an Iowa girl who risked her life to flag down a train. Still another story is an account of an Eskimo boy. Readers learn very little about Michigan's "thumb" area from this book.

Harold Waldo, the son of a school superintendent at Ovid, Michigan, in 1919 sent a story entitled "Old Twelve Hundred" to George Horace Lorimer, the distinguished editor of the *Saturday Evening Post*, a magazine then carrying about two hundred pages in each weekly issue and selling for a nickel. The *Post* published the story and Waldo found himself in the November 1919 issue along with Irvin S. Cobb, Albert Payson Terhune, Will Payne, Ben Ames Williams, David Belasco, and Mary Roberts Rinehart—all major popular writers of the time.

In 1923, Waldo inserted that story in *The Magic Midland*, dedicating his novel to the "memory of the glorious time . . . in that brave state of the Lakes and in that magic midland of youth when troubles were trifles and a chap owed hostage neither to care nor sore responsibility nor any alien god whatsoever."

The novel focuses on Lawrence ("Horsey") McGuire and his puritanical father who does not want his son consorting with "low-level fellows" like railroad employees. But "Horsey" has been taken with Old Twelve Hundred, an antiquated steam engine. The novel details "Horsey's" trip in the engine with its engineer and his role as a part-time actor in a local theatrical stock company.

The novel has some good parts, but Waldo was no Mark Twain or Booth Tarkington. The latter, however, praised the novel, "It comes from life itself. . . . Waldo possesses to a most uncommon degree a sensitiveness to exultant moments [and] has the power to picture them to his readers."[29]

Clarence Budington Kelland's "The Girl Who Was a Coward," one of his typical stories, appeared in the *Delineator* for November

1914. A retired Great Lakes skipper refuses to let his daughter marry a sailor because she's a coward, and he does not want any descendants with coward's blood. But, as the sophisticated reader would expect, the girl proves her worth when the "black diptheery" attacks a boy, and she and the sailor are wed.

Sigrid Woodward's *Kathleen* (1929) focuses on Kathleen Walters, daughter of a well-to-do Upper Peninsula mining town family, from her fifth year until she graduates from college. Along the way, there is a train wreck, two romances, a lake storm—all mildly reported— and, finally, near the end of the novel, a slight mystery.

Malcolm Stuart Boylan (1897–) was a Hollywood scriptwriter and producer of silent films. His novel *Tin Sword* (1950) tells the story of Joshua Doty, a precocious thirteen-year-old native of Battle Creek, "a tilter at windmills about midway between those of Cervantes and Booth Tarkington,"[30] in the early years of the twentieth century. For a time, he is a newspaper reporter in his hometown, but he then embarks on a series of adventures that make the Rover Boys seem like stay-at-homes. A critic said the novel seemed to have been "written all in one breath"[31] in a lightly humorous, tongue-in-cheek style, somewhere between Corey Ford and James Branch Cabell.

Boylan was the son of Grace Duffie Boylan (1861–1935), born in Kalamazoo, an editorial writer and an author of numerous books about Michigan natural features and several volumes of verse.

John Herrmann (1900–1959), the son of a well-to-do Lansing family, while still in high school was a school news reporter for a Lansing newspaper. He graduated from the University of Michigan.

Like other members of the group Gertrude Stein called the lost generation, Herrmann lived in Europe in the early 1920s. In 1925, he married Iowan Josephine Herbst (1897–1969), who was to become a more successful writer than her husband. He became a staffer on *transition*, and his first significant stories were published in a French anthology that also included stories by James Joyce, Ezra Pound, and Ford Madox Ford.

His first book, *What Happens* (1926), was published in Paris. In this *roman à clef*, a high school boy flees from his hometown after he is accused of responsibility for a classmate's pregnancy. Later, like his creator, Winfield Payne becomes a seed salesman, a reporter, and a Washington correspondent for a Detroit newspaper.

The U. S. government refused to allow *What Happens* to be sold in this country because of its content, which is quite tame by later standards.[32]

Herrmann's *Summer Is Ended* (1932) is a tale of a Benton [Lansing], Michigan, high school romance that concludes in Paris with the marriage of Carl Yoeman and Charlotte Dale. Charlotte, who has always wanted to have Carl's children, cannot have any; Carl, who never wanted children, will have his way.

Harlan Henthorne Hatcher (1898–)—president of the University of Michigan from 1951 to 1967—in his *The Modern American Novel* (1935) called Herrmann, a "hard-boiled realist," and said of the novel, "The narrative is stark and the expression laconic; it achieves occasional flashes of power and also stretches of the flattest monotony . . . in a too eager effort to be ironic and hard."[33]

In 1932, Herrmann's long story, "The Big Short Trip," was published in *Scribner's Magazine* as one of two award-winning stories; the other winner was Thomas Wolfe. The story follows a jewelry salesman on his last trip—he does not do too well because the Great Depression has caused a market downturn for his wares. Although Herrmann and his wife both had leftist political and literary leanings, his hero in this book is worried that his son is being converted to communism by dippy college professors. Herrmann's last novel, *The Salesman* (1939), also has a protagonist who is trying to make a living in the Great Depression.

Arnold Gingrich (1903–1976), a Grand Rapids native, graduated from the University of Michigan with a Phi Beta Kappa key in 1925 and married Helen Mary Rowe, also of Grand Rapids. He is best known for his career with *Esquire,* which he helped found in 1933, and thus became a friend of many major American authors. He is less well known for his novel *Cast Down the Laurels* (1935) set in the Grand Rapids of his youth, an effort that has been called, "The Book That Shook Grand Rapids."[34]

The first of the novel's three parts is a series of dossiers that an advertising man sends to a friend who is a successful novelist, asking him to write a novel based on the material. The novel, *Apollo's Young Widow,* is the second part—a case history of a Viennese pianist who, sensing he is a failure, opens a music school in a Michigan city like Grand Rapids. There, although married, he romances a young, talented student and his wife subsequently murders him.

In the third part, the writer rejects the case history as a potential novel. Then, we learn that the advertising man played an important role in the actual events.

Reviewers were happier with *Esquire* than with the novel.[35]

Chicagoan Mary Synon's *Copper Country* (1931) might just as easily have been set on Chicago's North Shore as on the Keweenaw

Peninsula. Its subjects, the third generation of Chicago descendants of men who made fortunes logging and mining the area, are the idle rich with too much leisure time. The book is considerably poorer than Synon's *The Good Red Bricks* (1929), a novel with a Chicago setting.

In *The Self-Made Man* (1960), Sylvia Cooper (1903–) focuses on a Detroit businessman (a trucker), who, on his sixtieth birthday, recalls his life—from the day in France in World War I when he rescued a wounded lieutenant to the time when he married the lieutenant's former wife—as well as events of his marriage. The novel seems not to have been reviewed.

Using the pen name, Sylvia Paul Germain, Cooper (1903–) wrote four later novels, none of which are set in Michigan. She was a member of the Detroit Women Authors Club.

Harold Titus's 1924 *American Magazine* story, "The Stuff of Heroes," was filmed in 1925 as *How Baxter Butted In*. A timid young clerk in a newspaper office persuades the publisher to offer a monthly Valor Award for outstanding heroic acts as a means of increasing circulation. It probably came as no surprise to readers of *American Magazine* fiction or viewers of the film that the clerk was the first winner; the story line was commonplace.

The *New York Times* thought the film was "splendid fun"; *Variety* liked it also.[36] But Mordaunt Hall, the *Times* reviewer, was rightly skeptical about the claim that the film was based on Titus's story. The film script was written by playwright Owen Davis who had written *How Baxter Butted In*, a play with the same story line, some dozen years before Titus's story. Davis's play had been performed by stock and repertory companies all over America.

Titus's short story, "The Frame House," appearing in the fall 1931 issue of John Towner Frederick's distinguished *Midland*, tells of a widow who lives her life in a house her husband had built from a shipwrecked Lake Michigan schooner. Frederick said in 1944 that Titus was "one of the very few writers who have [sic] recognized the materials of fiction in American industry and business, and his stories of automobile building and railroading are among the finest in their field.[37]

English author Sir Philip Gibbs's *Reckless Lady* (1924) is set in Michigan only in its latter part. An English adventuress marries the son of a wealthy furniture manufacturer. In Grand Rapids, her affair with another man almost destroys the marriage. But her husband realizes she is having difficulty with the "stuffy midwest culture," and the marriage survives.

Michigan literary historians like to include Lloyd Cassel Douglas (1877–1951) as a Michigan writer; he served the First Congrega-
tional Church for six years (1915–1921), there is a Douglas Memorial
Chapel in Ann Arbor, and he and his wife are buried in Ann Arbor's
Forest Hill Cemetery.

Three of his novels, *Magnificent Obsession* (1929), *Disputed Passage*
(1939), and *Dr. Hudson's Secret Journal* (1939), are said to be clearly set
in Ann Arbor.[38] In the first novel, a wealthy young playboy atones for
his role of inadvertently causing the death of a prominent doctor by
becoming a doctor, curing the doctor's attractive young widow of
blindness, and marrying her. His skills come as much from the moral
principles he has adopted as from his education.

The other two novels carry Douglas's concept of this spiritual
doctrine into philosophical areas less dependent on action. Critics
found the books less than magnificent, but readers carried them out
of bookstores by the thousands.

Philip Freund's *The Evening Heron* (1937) is, said its publisher, "a
study of medievalism in modern life" that begins in Paris in 1927 and
continues on an island in a small Michigan lake. Two brothers, sons
of a wealthy lumberman, become involved in a romantic tragedy.
Edith H. Walton said the novel "is pretentious, stilted and dreary,
shot through with cloudy philosophizing, with labored, tedious anal-
yses of characters and motives." She added that the novel is convincing only when it describes "the wild romantic atmosphere" of the
Michigan wilderness.[39]

Freund (1909–), a Michigan university teacher, wrote several
other novels as well as books of verse.

Stirling Bowen's *Wishbone* (1930) has three stories, each about
one hundred pages in length. In "An Imperfect Crime," a man remains in a small Michigan town while the woman he loves goes to
Detroit, takes part in a botched crime, goes to jail and dies there.
"The Townsman" is a small-town dentist's son who all his life is a
man going nowhere.

"Some Go Away" is the tale of a potential writer who is frustrated by blindness and married to a sighted girl with artistic talent.
One evening while her husband is listening to a reading of one of his
stories, an artist implores the wife to go to Alaska with him. Critics
thought that the husband's "story within a story" was the best part
of the book although they were pleased with the collection.[40]

Edmund G. Love's 1973 *A Small Bequest*, one of his three mem-
oirs that have all the excitement and flavor of fiction, is set in the

Great Depression summer of 1934. Young Edmund Love inherits two sections of Upper Peninsula land. With $25 and his friend George, who lives only for the moment, he sets out in a 1916 Buick to check out the property. In spite of George's devil-may-care attitude and his penchant for spending Love's limited funds, they arrive at the lake. There, they encounter bears, poison ivy, a neighboring property owner who is out to swindle Love of his land, and a girl who swims nude in the lake's icy waters. The undertone of the flavor of the Great Depression years gives this fascinating book an added interest.

Love (1912–1990), a native of Flushing, Michigan, earned B.A. and M.A. degrees at the University of Michigan and became a teacher, historian, and columnist.

Baxter Hathaway (1909–) earned both M.A. and Ph.D. degrees at Ann Arbor where he was a classmate of Maritta Wolff and, like her, won Hopwood awards, his in poetry and fiction. Later, he was a Fulbright scholar.

Hathaway's *The Stubborn Way* (1937) is the result of his school efforts. The plot hinges on Wally Stevenson, who works in a Kalamazoo paper mill to support his mother and sister. Wally is told by a novelist that he should quit his job and become a writer. The novel's characters, like those of Maritta Wolff's, are doomed to menial, unhappy lives; the work is to some extent a proletariat novel, like those discussed elsewhere. But, as a reviewer said, *The Stubborn Way* "is never aflame with the common theme of the proletarian novel, the sickening effects of industrialism upon a group of [workers]." He concluded that Hathaway's contemporaries, Robert Cantwell or Albert Halper or Josephine Herbst would have made the book into a "more emphatic and stirring story."[41]

Jim Houlston, in Irving Bissell's 1937 *A Sow's Ear,* is a Grand Rapids businessman who cannot keep his hands off the wives and daughters of his business and country club associates. When his wife discovers an infidelity, she goes to Europe to reconsider their marriage. He reacts by taking a young salesgirl to his fishing cabin, a fact his far-off wife soon learns.

A critic called the book "cheap fiction."[42] Bissell was obviously not the authorial equal of a distant Iowa relative, Richard Bissell, the author of *Pajama Game* (1954) and books about life on the Mississippi.

Richard B. Erno (1923–), a native of Boyne City, is the author of several books, three of which are set in Michigan. *My Old Man* (1955) takes place in a small Michigan town in one year of the Great Depression. The narrator, sixteen-year-old Joe Burns, despises his alcoholic father, but hates him even more after the father's behavior causes Joe to lose his job in a bank. Resolution for Joe can come only with his father's death.

The Hunt (1959) describes the internal conflicts of a young man who watches his closest friend drown in a Lake Michigan storm; afterward he marries and then divorces his friend's lover. Later, as a guide on a hunting trip to the Upper Peninsula, his conflicts are resolved as he watches one of his clients kill another, because the killer mistakenly thought the victim was the man with whom his wife was having an affair.

In *The Catwalk* (1965), Arnold Bricker builds a catwalk on the roof of his house to watch for a sea monster he insists inhabits the nearby lake and thereby becomes the butt of his small town friends' jokes. The monster does appear, but by that time Bricker has lost his girlfriend and his catwalk has been blown away by a windstorm.

Erno's novels are related by the central character, which means, as a critic said of one novel, that the reader is "confined to the perceptions and blurred visions of an intrinsically limited character." But, this critic noted, readers "emerge from the encounter[s] strangely rewarded."[43]

The best part of Joseph Weeks's *All Our Yesterdays* (1955) is its background, "the golden days of radio" in the 1930s. An unstable Catholic boy, accustomed to bluffing his way through life, becomes an announcer for a radio station in his "one-horse town." Because he is vulgar, dishonest, and basically unlikeable, he loses that job and a later one like it at a Detroit station. At novel's end, with only fifty cents in his pocket, he heads for Chicago.

The novel's only major critic said:

> [Weeks] would seem to have written a type of novel that has long since run its course. . . . [His] thoroughness and honesty recall Dreiser, but when Sister Carrie, Hurstwood and Drouet were being buffeted like tennis balls by the natural forces around them, determinism in the novel was still fresh.
>
> Nowadays the hero as vegetable seems uninteresting, even when one can think of actual human vegetables whom he resembles.[44]

The boat of Kathryn and Glendon Swarthout's *The Button Boat* (1969) is a flat-bottomed, rectangular-shaped scow used for dragging river bottoms for clams whose shells will be converted into buttons.

The time is 1934; Dicksie and Auston, eleven and nine respectively, live in a squalid shack on a riverbank; their alcoholic, ignorant, and cruel stepfather will not let them go to school. Into this dreary picture comes one of the first motorcycle policemen pursuing gangsters who dump their stolen goods into the river. The children's discovery of the loot leads to a deadly conflict from which the policeman rescues them.

Richard Schickel, a *Life* film critic, liked the story, comparing its treatment and development to "the old silent cinema with its broad villains and comics, its fast and endless action, its frequent theme of innocence and innocents imperiled."[45]

The Swarthouts are also the authors of *The Ghost and the Magic Sabre* (1963), *Whichaway* (1966), *TV Thompson* (1972), and *The Whales to See* (1975).

Helen ("Holly") Ann Finegan Wilson's *The Kingpin* (1939) continued the tradition of portraying the American family in comic relief that had become a staple of novels, films, and plays. The book covers about eighteen months in the later years of the 1930s Great Depression. It centers on the Braun family of Lakewood [Marquette], an ore-shipping point and lumbering town. The kingpin is Carl Braun, a man who is always paying off last year's debts with next year's income and always looking beyond the present opportunity for the next one. Wilson's manuscript for this novel received the highest Hopwood Award for fiction in 1938.

Maritta Wolff

In 1940, Maritta Wolff (1918–) first showed she had a talent to become an important Michigan author when she won the major Hopwood Award for the typescript of her *Whistle Stop*. (Incidentally, Jay McCormick was one of her classmates, see p. 125). In 1937, Arthur Miller had won only a minor award; in 1938, Wolff had finished behind Helen Ann ("Holly") Wilson and *The Kingpin*; in 1939, Wolff finished behind Iola Fuller and her *Loon Feather*.

Among Hopwood Award poetry winners in those years were Norman Rosten, John Malcolm Brinnin, John Ciardi, and Robert Hayden. Judges included Oliver La Farge, Martha Foley, Marjorie Kinnan Rawlings, John Marquand, and Helen Hull.

Whistle Stop was "the unexpected hit of the spring season" in 1941—four printings in five days.[46] Reviewers compared it to Victoria Lincoln's *February Hill* (1934) in "shiftlessness, prostitution and petty thievery" and to Erskine Caldwell's 1932 *Tobacco Road*, in its depiction of "a slothful family, who, to say the least, are in the main immoral."[47]

Nine Veeches—among them a racketeer's mistress, a petty thief, and a ne'er-do-well son—and a suicidal old man inhabit the Veech house near the railroad tracks. This grotesque menagerie's collective behavior led Clifton Fadiman to comment that if the book counted as evidence, Wolff did not learn her trade in the classroom. "She knows too many things not discoverable on any campus. She has no right to be so ruthless and mature at twenty-two."[48]

Joseph Hilton Smyth said, "[I]n the academic sense, *Whistle Stop* is not a novel; it has no beginning, no end, no formalized plot . . . it is a cross-section . . . of the indolent life of the Veeches."[49]

Edith H. Walton said that among the many Hopwood Award novels she had read, none had "seemed in any way the equal of this story."[50] Rose Feld wrote "[Wolff] has the lush vitality of Thomas Wolfe [and] the concentration on the unusual among the lowly that characterized Carson McCullers's first novel."[51] *Whistle Stop* was filmed in 1946 with Ava Gardner, George Raft, and Victor McLaglen in the lead roles.

Wolff's *Night Shift* (1942) focuses on three sisters who live in a Michigan factory town in the days just before World War II. One, whose husband is mentally ill, supports three children as best she can, aided in part by the youngest child who sings in a nightclub owned by a gangster and also helps support the third sister, her aunt. Reviewers thought that this book, with half again as many pages as the first, had less to offer.[52] *Night Shift* was filmed in 1946 as *The Man I Love.*

In Wolff's *About Lyddy Thomas* (1947), the war is over, but its consequences are not. When Lyddy tells her returned soldier-husband their marriage is a failure, he attempts to kill her. She is saved by a rooming-house owner, a woman, who kills Lyddy's husband. This novel won a special award in a Metro-Goldwyn-Mayer contest for a book that would make a good film.

Back of Town (1952) tells of a man and his dying wife who return to the town where his former sweetheart lives. The wife dies, but a scheming young woman and other complications prevent him from marrying his former sweetheart.

Victor P. Hass spoke for himself and other reviewers, "If you have read *Whistle Stop* and *Night Shift*, you have in a sense read *Back of Town*. It's the same murky, bleak, rich, coarse, brutal section on the edge of town where life is an unceasing struggle, relieved only occasionally by flashes of softness."[53]

Wolff's final Michigan novel, *Buttonwood* (1962), focuses on a World War II pilot who saw his best friend shot down. Fifteen years later, he calls so frequently on his friend's widow that her teenage daughter asks why they do not marry. At novel's end, his relationship to widow and daughter is revealed in a surprise ending.

Wolff, born on Christmas Day 1918, married author Hubert Skidmore in 1940. After his tragic death by fire in 1946, she married Leonard Stegman, a jeweler, and moved to California.

More Books about Michigan People

Russell Banks, in the *New York Times Book Review* for March 18, 1984, states three times that William McPherson's *Testing the Current* (1984) is set in the book's Grand Rivière, Wisconsin. One hopes that Banks paid closer attention to the rest of the novel's contents; the novel is plainly set in Grand Rivière, Michigan, obviously based on Sault Sainte Marie, the author's hometown.

The novel begins in 1939 when Tommy McAllister is nine; it ends with the well-to-do McAllister's twenty-fifth wedding anniversary celebration. Tommy's mother's ongoing adulterous relationship with a man named Wolfe (!), social affairs at the country club, and a fatal explosion at the McAllister's mill, are all seen through Tommy's eyes. He doesn't see the significance of these events, but the reader does.

Two characters in the novel are Michigan Governor Wentworth and his daughter Bellanova—obviously modeled on Governor Chase Salmon Osborn and his daughter Stellanova.

Banks praised the book in his review, "[I]t is a novel written with great skill, and with love. It's what most good first novels merely aspire to be."[54]

McPherson was educated at the University of Michigan and at Michigan State University but took no degree. He served as an editor at the *Washington Post* and at William Morrow book publishers; in 1977, he won a Pulitzer Prize for distinguished criticism.

The doctor in Mary Frances Doner's *The Doctor's Party* (1940) invites seven randomly selected people he has brought into the world to a party at his home to celebrate the thirtieth anniversary of his practice in Doner's usual small town. Six come. When the doctor asks each one to tell what they have achieved, no one is willing to talk. Then the doctor and his guests receive a message that the seventh invitee has committed suicide. This message is the catalyst that opens the floodgates of confessions.

The brief story, more like a script for an ongoing television soap opera than a novel, does not persuade the reader that six persons, selected at random in a small town, could have had such tangled lives.

Nancy Willard's first novel, *Things Invisible to See* (1985), is set in her home town of Ann Arbor in the 1940s. Twin brothers, one an intellectual, one a mystic, become involved with a mysteriously paralyzed young woman in a series of events that take place in Island Park, a hospital, the black residential section, and elsewhere. The story ends with a baseball game that anticipates the film *Field of Dreams* in its player lineup of baseball luminaries. Susan Fromberg Schaeffer said the novel "has the quality of a fairy tale . . . a paradigm of life as a Manichean conflict between good and evil."[55]

Willard (1936–) has a 1958 B.A. degree from the University of Michigan and a 1963 Ph.D. degree from Stanford. She won major Hopwood essay and poetry awards in 1957–1958. She is the author of eight books of verse and three volumes of short stories.

Jay McCormick's second novel, *Nightshade* (1948), reports the involvement of a young writer and his friend with two women in a small midwestern college town, one the college widow. When the writer's grandmother senses she is losing her control over him, she has him committed to a sanatorium. Trying to escape, he is killed.

Dr. Charles A. Cooper (1906–1972) in *We Pass This Way* (1950) used his experience in the Copper and Iron ranges of the Upper Peninsula to portray a cross-section of life in those locales. But the book lacks a narrative strand; it is more a series of set scenes that reveal the authors' prejudices in favor of his upper-class characters. A mine strike is the subject of one chapter.

Virginia (Lowell) Chase (Perkins) (1902–), in 1940, while a graduate student, won a second place Avery Hopwood Award, finishing next to Maritta Wolff's *Whistle Stop*. Her *Discovery* (1948) focuses on a forty-year-old suburban housewife who is trying to adjust to a life without her children. The novel, said a critic, was written with "penetrating sympathy."[56] In 1953, Chase capitalized on her thirteen years of experience as a Detroit public schoolteacher in *The End of the Week* (1953), a novel that focuses on a Friday afternoon end-of-the-term party for a departing teacher. In turn, the novel looks at the life and point of view of each of the teachers. A critic said the novel had "a ring of authority" and would be "important to parents, teachers and taxpayers alike."[57] A second critic called it a well-balanced book with a "true picture of school life."[58]

Curt G. Knoblock's *Above, Below* (1952, reissued 1988) offers sketches from the lives of Beer Suds Joe, Stumpy Shafer, Captain Jim, Indian Pete, Bullfrog Upton, and other colorful characters of the countryside around Detour, Michigan, where Knoblock lived. The title is the name given by residents to the area above and below the Straits of Mackinac.

Herbert Gold (1924–) is listed as a Michigan author by two reporters, but he lived in Michigan only from 1954 to 1959 when he taught at Wayne State University. Of his dozen and a half books, only part of one, *The Optimist* (1959), is set in Michigan. Burr Fuller, the optimist, has affairs with a sorority member and a town citizen while attending the University of Michigan in the early 1940s. He joins a fraternity despite a humiliating experience at the hands of his about-to-be fraternity brothers, and, in his own opinion, is a success in college. The balance of the novel is set in 1956. Fuller, a married man who, at one point has contemplated suicide, decides to run for Congress.

Although critics generally have looked at Gold as a major figure on the American literary scene, they had misgivings about this novel. Robert Phelps said the book ends "without an adequate answer" for Fuller's psychological problems.[59] Thomas E. Cassidy compared Gold somewhat unfavorably to John O'Hara "at this kind of thing."[60] Granville Hicks said, "[T]here is something Gold has seen and is trying to make [the reader] see, but I just don't get it." Still, he insisted that Gold was "a first-rate novelist . . . if this novel is in some sense a failure, it is the kind of failure only a first-rate man could produce."[61] R. Baird Shumann has an essay about Gold and a list of sources in Gerald Nemanic's 1981 *A Bibliographical Guide to Midwestern Literature* (pp. 229–230).

Jo Valentine (Charlotte Armstrong) (1905–1969), "the *grande dame* of American suspense novelists,"[62] who was born in an Upper Peninsula iron mining town and who wrote some thirty books, two Broadway plays, and several motion picture and television scripts, did not begin writing until about 1940, after the birth of three children.

As Jo Valentine, she set her one Michigan book, *The Trouble in Thor* (1953), in a fictitious Upper Peninsula iron mining town. There are *two* troubles in Thor—one begins when a married woman covets another woman's husband and he covets a young woman; the second involves the whole town as a fatal explosion in an underground mine leads to disaster. *Trouble in Thor* was reprinted in 1971 under Armstrong's own name. Neither edition received the national attention her mystery novels did.

Saginaw native Eugene Lee (Gene) Caesar (1927–) was a machine operator and airplane mechanic until he wrote *Mark of the Hunter* (1953). Marty Jevons, the scion of a family of Detroit industrialists, who had been a combat marine on Guadalcanal, finds campus life at Ann Arbor tame and purposeless. Not caring for the family business but liking hunting and backwoods living, he takes a job as a guide for hunters in the Michigan northwoods. "Here," said Nicholas Monjo, "his passion for hunting [becomes] a compulsion, his pleasure in killing wolves 'almost sexual.' " These drives conflict with his equally strong need for women, which he expresses in barroom brawls and "restless promiscuity." But after he meets a young woman, Pat Brodie, he is able to accept society and even conservative politics, and he achieves release from his compulsive wolf hunting.

Reviewers were pleased with the hunting scenes, but unhappy with the novel's larger philosophical solutions. "When [Caesar] ascribes the dynamics of social dissatisfaction and liberal strivings wholly to sexual motivation in disguise, he robs love and politics alike of their share of will and reason," said Monjo.[63]

After a writing course with Pulitzer Prize winner Dr. S. I. Hayakawa, Caesar became a full-time writer using the pseudonyms Anthony Stirling and Johnny Laredo. None of four later novels are set in Michigan.

In *I'm Owen Harrison Harding* (1955, reissued 1972), James Whitfield Ellison (1930–), following in the footprints of Mark Twain, Booth Tarkington, J. D. Salinger, and William Maxwell, took his turn at immortalizing the American Boy. This one is a Fleming (Lansing), Michigan, boy born as the Great Depression begins and entering high school near the end of World War II. Owen narrates his adventures during his first year of high school: his fear of hazing by upperclassmen, a romance with a somewhat older girl, his problems with his teachers, his alcoholic father's bookselling business, the illness and death of his mother, and the deterioration of some of his friendships.

Critics read this book with one eye on its predecessors. Collectively, they thought that, although the book was valuable for its time period, it was not equal to its literary forebears.[64]

Readers who carried Inez and Loys Cowles 1953 *Ball Four* home, thinking it perhaps might have something to do with the Detroit Tigers, would have been disappointed. This narrative of a bumbling husband (who prefers garage sales to watching the Tigers) reports a summer vacation on the south shore of Lake Superior.

Saginaw native George Lea III won the major 1956 Hopwood Award of fiction for a story that became *Somewhere There's Music* (1958). Mike Logan is the son of a great trumpet player; Mike plays modern cool jazz on a saxophone. His first summer home from the Korean War is a summer of discontent: he quarrels with his father, has two unhappy love affairs, drinks to excess, and finally departs for New York.

Reviewers noted that Lea's book was the twelfth "jazz novel" to appear between 1938 and 1958. Its most favorable review came from University of Michigan Professor Arno L. Bader, "The story is fast-paced, the author excels at description . . . and he has the novelist's indispensable gift for sustained narration. . . . [It is a] brilliant first novel.[65]

Alma Routsong Brodie's *A Round Shape* (1959)—the title is from a Robert Frost poem—is the story of a returned war veteran who discovers his mother has spent the money he sent home for her to save for him. A reviewer said it would be nice if, in her next novel, Brodie "eliminated the gloom and doom and included a little more 'gradual joy.' "[66] The quoted phrase referred to the author's earlier novel.

From the time he was sixteen, Edwin Daly (1936) passed his summers at Mrs. Lowney Handy's Writer's Colony in Marshall, Illinois. Mrs. Handy's first success was with James Jones and his *From Here to Eternity* (1951); Daly's *Some Must Watch* (1957) was her second. Daly was then twenty and a Yale student. Part of the story is set in Illinois, part at a summer resort near Holland, Michigan. Richard Colby's summer of beer drinking, wild parties, and an affair with a married woman ends in tragedy with his father's suicide.

Although James Jones is quoted on the dust jacket as saying that Daly was America's answer to Françoise Sagan (a comment that did not please Daly), reviewers said the work was immature.[67] They were more impressed with Daly's second novel, *A Legacy of Love* (1958), which details the misfortunes of two families in a small Michigan city. Susan Churchill discovers that her father, a high school teacher, is having an adulterous affair with her boyfriend's mother.[68]

Robie (Mayhew) Macauley collected several of his short stories in *The End of Pity* (1957). They tell of a man who, contemplating drowning, instead rescues two women from a sinking boat; of an encounter in the Michigan dunes between a young couple and two prison escapees; of the relations between two women following the death of one's mother; and of the antics of a man who receives an unexpected sum of money. Two stories, set on campuses, feature the sort of intellectual debates that replace sports events in the lives of some professors. Those critics with academic leanings were more enthusiastic about the stories than were other critics.[69]

Henry L. Van Dyke, Jr. (1928–), the son of a college teacher, won a 1953–1954 Hopwood Award for fiction. In 1965, his first novel, *Ladies of the Rachmaninoff Eyes*, caught readers' attention with this opening sentence: "Aunt Harry died near the saltlick on a Saturday

daybreak in August, shortly after she and Mrs.Klein beat Maurice Le-
Fleur almost to death with a stick in a patch of joe-pye weeds."

The story is related in a long flashback leading up to the beating. Mrs. Klein, a wealthy elderly Jewish lady in Allegan, employs
Harrietta Gibbs, a black woman, as her maid. They are visited by Le-
Fleur, who pretends to be a warlock but is actually a jewel thief.
When the women discover his true identity, they beat him. The tale
is narrated by Aunt Harry's nephew, Oliver, whom Mrs. Klein wants
to send to Cornell University rather than "a sensible school right
[here] in Michigan."

The most favorable review of the novel, in the London *Times Literary Supplement*, said the novel was "pithily and wittily written. It
has the extraordinary virtue of dealing with race relations as if they
were ordinary human relations, and thus makes an efficiently quiet
and humorous contribution to this raucous dialogue."[70]

Oliver appears in a sequel, *Blood of Strawberries* (1969), but this
and Van Dyke's *Dead Piano* (1971) are set in New York.

Alfred Kazin said Van Dyke was "one of the most brilliant and
unpredictable of the younger black novelists. . . . His mind is too independent, ironic, and even humorous for messages. He is essentially a novelist of character, of the hidden idiosyncrasies."[71]

Feminist poet and novelist Marge Piercy (1936–), born in Detroit, won Hopwood awards in poetry in 1956 and 1957. Following
graduation from the University of Michigan in 1957, she took a 1958
master's degree at Northwestern. She moved to Massachusetts in
1976; most of her later novels are set on the East Coast.

Piercy's *The High Cost of Living* (1978) is a contemporary romance
focusing on a group of graduate students at a Detroit university who
are assisting a professor in his research project on an aristocratic old
Detroit family. Although the novel presents some details of university life, the emphasis is on the interpersonal affairs of the novel's
chief characters. Pierce says the novel is about "labeling [and] the cost
that attends moving from the traditional working class to the college-
educated working class . . . [its theme] confusing morality and
politics."[72] Some readers might infer, however, that the title refers
to the social and personal costs of a group of homosexuals, and het-
erosexuals adapting to each other.

Her seventh novel, *Braided Lives* (1982), tells of Jill, a lesbian at
the University of Michigan in the early 1950s who becomes romantically involved with a male burglar and Donna, a fellow student.
When Donna breaks off the relationship and marries, the resulting
pregnancy causes her death.

Piercy has been praised for her multidimensional portraits of both men and women and her treatment of contemporary settings.[73]

Walter S. J. Swanson's *The Happening* (1970) is a psychological novel that uses a stream of consciousness technique. A confused and unhappy newspaper writer tells a woman how his relationships with two other women put him in his present condition.

For his 1971 M.F.A. thesis at the University of Iowa, Geoffrey Clark, who had two previous degrees from Central Michigan University, submitted six short stories under the generic title of the first, "My Love Is There." Twelve years later, he published four of these six stories with five others in *What the Moon Said*, the title of one of the new stories. Of the eleven stories, four are set in Clark's Michigan home area, one elsewhere in Michigan, and one in Iowa.

The stories range from the latter days of World War II to about 1970. In some ways, the stories strike the reader as chapters in a novel yet to be completed.

Only five of the stories in Helga Sandburg's *Children and Lovers: Fifteen Stories* (1976) are set in Michigan. One story, "The Goose," is much like her *Joel and the Wild Goose* (1964). One critic wrote, "[T]he themes are all too familiar, and Sandburg's writing is so often completely formulaic that the endings become entirely predictable." But a second critic said the stories were written "with consummate artistry . . . these vignettes of average people confronting the large issues of daily living, bespeak a deep understanding of the American, as well as the human, psyche and the artist's ability to make us all sharers."[74]

Slouching toward Kalamazoo (1983)—one of a score of novels and plays Peter DeVries (1910–) has written—begins in a small North Dakota town in the early 1960s. When precocious Anthony (Tony) Thrasher cannot seem to get beyond eighth grade, his parents turn for help to Maggie Doubloon, twenty-nine, one of his teachers. Soon Tony and Maggie are a couple, and she begins strolling the streets wearing a scarlet *A* on her sweater. When she realizes she is not only an adulteress but also pregnant, she goes home to Kalamazoo. Tony follows her; but he soon transfers his affections to her babysitter, whom he later marries.

On the surface, this seems like a tale not to be taken too seriously. But Thomas Meehan says that "at the heart of [the novel], there is a serious theological discussion—on whether or not man can rationally believe in Christianity."[75] The title suggests this, particularly in its reference to these lines by William Butler Yeats:

And what rough beast, its hour come round at last,
    Slouches toward Bethlehem to be born?[76]

Daniel Curzon (born Daniel Russell Brown) is a gay writer with a Ph.D. from Wayne State. His books, short stories, and one play reflect his interest in bringing this aspect of the human scene to the attention of readers.

Only *Something You Do in the Dark* (1971) is set in Michigan. A young man who has served three years in prison for a homosexual offense tries to heal the long quarrel over his lifestyle with his dying father but to no avail.

Thomas F. Vandeberg's 1969 *Orphans in the Sun* is "essentially a character study of a man in his relationships" with two women that emphasizes his dual personality. A critic said it is "a strange novel which requires much concentration from the reader."[77]

Larry Woiwode's *What I'm Going to Do, I Think* (1969) is set in Michigan, although as Woiwode said, it could have as well been set in North Dakota, his home state. Christofer (Chris) Van Eenanam and Ellen Strohe decide that marriage is a better solution to her state than abortion. But the baby dies in childbirth. At one point Chris contemplates suicide. Critics agreed with *New York Review of Books* that "the novel is impressive, it has certain moments, it contains many fine pages, but it is incompletely realized."[78]

In Woiwode's book of verse, *Even Tide* (1977), he comments humorously on the mispronunciations of his name:

Why wade?
    Wit who, Didi?
    Witty Whitey
    Wee wood
    Woe weed
    A whee ah
    Wide weighed wad
    (And rhyming with load)
    Ah woda wode? . . .
        . . . It's wi-wood-e (with an ending long E) (19)

In *Wolf, a False Memoir* (1971) Jim Harrison (1937–) presents a new tradition in outdoor writing—a novel of contemplation rather than action. In earlier Michigan novels, the central characters had taken to the great out-of-doors to find themselves in action. In *Wolf*, Swanson, the "anti-heroic" narrator, tells "a bittersweet saga of his

Kerouacian-on-the-road wanderings to the ends of the American continent, East and West. . . . [T]he thirty-three year-old inveterate wanderer and traveler has a huge appetite for experience and 'lowlife instincts.' "[79]

This Michigan native travels to the "comparatively vast, the peopleless Huron Mountains of the Upper Peninsula" (p. 18) where he hopes to see a wolf, "the one sign that will reassure him that wild, untamed instinct still survives and can excite fear and admiration in him."[80]

Swanson finds no resolution. He has already been cut off from his family and his past, and sexual experiences have been boring. For him, Nature does not heal, it diverts. Moreover, Swanson has come to care only for "the luminescence we offer each other" (p. 192).

H. L. Van Brunt said that *Wolf* "[is] vulgar, nasty—and for long stretches, exhilarating." But he concluded that the narrator is a "crybaby. Ultimately, his rages against life as it is and people as they are come to sound like the long howl of a timber wolf unable to run with the pack—or perhaps unwilling to tolerate anyone's company except his own."[81]

In Harrison's *Sundog: The Story of an American Foreman, Robert Corvus Strang, as Told to Jim Harrison* (1984), a writer is challenged by a Florida millionaire to write "about someone who actually has done something." Michigan-born Strang, who is vaguely related to "King" Strang, and has worked on major construction projects, has been crippled from an attack of tropical fever and a fall down the face of a three hundred-foot-high dam into a raging river. Strang is living in the Michigan northwoods with a Costa Rican woman, Eulalie. Strang claims she is his daughter. The novel has three narrators: Harrison, Strang, and Harrison's persona; the last narrator relates his efforts to get both his story and his relationships with Strang and Eulalie untangled.

Critics were not exuberant over the novel. It is, said one, a case of "three stories struggling to get out of one slim book," and he found the narrator to be "amusing when facing barmaids . . . and candid when admitting the power sex has over him," but "annoying" when he writes such sentences as "There is nothing so fatiguing as real emotion."[82]

Harrison seemed to attract a different set of "cultists" with each of his works. "Followers of Harrison's poetry [for example] are dismayed he should even consider prose."[83]

Harrison's most recent book, *The Woman Lit by Fireflies* (1990), consists of three novellas. Only the first, "Brown Dog," is set in

Michigan. It is narrated by.Brown Dog (also called B. D.), an Anish-inabe living on the south shore of Lake Superior. He has recovered the frozen body of a long-drowned Indian from the icy waters of the lake and has a scheme for selling it to an anthropologist downstate—if he can only get it there before it thaws.

In 1972, Harrison was living on a small farm near Lake Leelanau, Michigan, and vowing "[S]hould developers move into the area [he would] move to Montana." His philosophy might well be summarized in these lines from his "Drinking Song":

> I want to die in the saddle. An enemy of civilization,
> I want to walk around in the woods, fish and drink.[84]

Ohioan Hannah Green's autobiographical novel, *The Dead of the House* (1972) focuses on a Cincinnati family who spend their summer vacations in the Traverse City area from the 1930s to the 1950s.

Albert Drake (1935–), a Michigan State University English professor and an author of short fiction and poetry, in *Beyond the Pavement* (1981) shows a young man home from college who plans to spend the summer building a racing car. Complications ensue—he has problems getting the parts he needs, his brother's hoodlum friends attack him, he meets a beautiful young heiress whose brother had been killed in a racing accident. But all ends well and he goes back to college.

Drake is also the author of *Postcard Mysteries and Other Stories* (1976). His wife, Barbara Drake (1939–), also a Michigan State faculty member, has published poetry and short stories.

Dean F. V. DuVall, the author of three books on easy ways to make money, was the author of *The Big Dream* (1979), a novel in which an oversexed, hyperactive Michiganian is elected President of the United States in 1980, and then, minutes after the votes are tallied, is shot to death.

Nine of the twelve stories in Janet Kauffman's *Places in the World a Woman Could Walk* (1983) are set in Michigan. Some stories first appeared in the *New Yorker.* The emphasis in most, as the title suggests, is on women. "My mother has me surrounded. I must be hers," says one of Kauffman's characters.[85] The many favorable reviews also emphasized the quality of her writing; "Janet Kauffman brings a poet's sensitivity to her prose."[86]

Kauffman's *Obscene Gestures by Women* (1989) is a collection of stories and sketches with a "quirky collection of characters: a woman who grinds her teeth, a book burner with a megaphone, two farmers who ride a combine by night."[87] Critics particularly liked "The Easter We Lived in Detroit"; in general, they praised her sensitivity and poetic prose even more than her stories.

Kauffman, a teacher and farmer as well as a writer, has lived on a farm near Hudson, Michigan, since 1972. She is the author of three books of verse and of *Collaborators*, a novel that develops some of her non-Michigan stories. In 1985, she received the Rosenthal Award from the Academy Institute of Arts and Letters.

Gary Gildner (1938–) has two degrees from Michigan State University and presently teaches in Iowa. He has won several fellowships and awards for his work: *First Practice (1969)*, *Digging for Indians* (1971), *Nails* (1975), *The Crush* (1983), and other titles.

The Second Bridge (1987) is an outgrowth of a short story, "Burial," in his anthology, *A Week in South Dakota* (1987)—the two books were published at the same time. The novel is set in Michigan, Iowa, and Scotland's Isle of Skye.

When Bill Rau, forty, returns home to Michigan from a writer's workshop in the East, his wife, Jay, tells him about an affair she has had with another man. The two contemplate separation until their daughter's death (the second bridge) helps resolve their situation.

Kesho Scott, Cherry Muhanji, and Egyirba High are the authors of thirty-six short stories based on their own lives in *Tight Spaces* (1987). The collaboration resulted from a shared writing assignment at the University of Iowa where Scott wrote her 1988 Ph.D. dissertation, *The Habit of Surviving: Black Women in America*.

In one story, "The Scales of Superman," Scott wrote "The liquid life of American Black Women is taking no form, like mercury in a broken thermometer splattered all over the bathroom floor." But a critic of the book argued that "depictions of real life in literature do require form."[88]

Three of the seven short stories and part of the long tale that gives the book its name in Sharon Dilworth's *The Long White* are set in the Upper Peninsula. The work won the 1988 Iowa Short Fiction Award.

In "Winter Mines," the wife of a laid-off miner may be setting her husband up for a suicide attempt as a means of ending his cabin fever (a common complaint in the Upper Peninsula), which is a daily irritant to her. "The Mad Dog Queen" tells of an Indian girl who hitchhikes from Marquette to L'Anse to win the Mad Dog Queen wine-drinking contest for the third year in a row. The story implies an ongoing animosity between the descendants of Indians who originally inhabited the L'Anse area adjacent to Keweenaw Bay and the descendants of Finnish immigrants who preempted the Indian lands.

"The Seeney Stretch" presents a jealous husband who obviously has shot and killed a younger man on a deer-hunting expedition. "The Long White" (referring to Upper Peninsula winters) is set in the town of Good Hart (just "below" The Bridge). Three significant characters are involved: an Indian who has murdered his wife and left the area; a young man, member of a local rockabilly band with a national reputation; and the young man's father, a crewman on an ore boat who has drowned searching for the Demon who lurks in the dark, icy depths of Lake Superior.

Dilworth is a graduate of the M.F.A. program in creative writing at Ann Arbor, but her stories hum with life, free from the putrid atmosphere that infiltrates so many workshop stories. As Robert Stone, a writer-in-residence at several major universities, says, "[Dilworth's style is] animated and sympathetic, wry and aware. Her characters are vivid and unpredictable. She is able to convey a sense of life lived in a time and place with great immediacy. The reader senses a complete world in the control of the author's sensibility."[89]

Books about Young People

Naturalist Ernest Ingersoll (1852–1946), a Michigan native, set two of his sixty-six books in Michigan. *The Ice Queen* (1885) tells of three young people adrift on a Great Lakes ice floe. *The Raisin Creek Exploring Club* (1915, reissued 1919) tells of several boys who have an unexpected vacation when their school burns. A critic called the book "a stirring mystery story that tells a great many new and interesting things about woods and woods' folk."[90]

Frances Margaret Fox from 1901 until World War II wrote fifty-two books for young people, most of them set in the area around Mackinaw City where she was born. Her work includes folklore and legends both historical and contemporary. Her better known books include *Betty of Old Mackinaw* (1901), *Janey* (1925), *The Magic Canoe* (1930), and *Little Mossback Amelia* (1939).[91]

Elizabeth Witheridge's *Never Younger, Jeanie* (1965) is set in 1914. Eleven-year-old Jeanie spends a year in Michigan with her grandparents while her parents are in Europe.

From 1955 on, Helen ("Holly") Ann Finegan Wilson, the author of *The Kingpin* (1938), wrote books for girls. Her *Deborah Todd* (1955) uses the theme of ethnic relations between those of Canadian and Chippewa ancestry. *Carolyn the Unconquered* (1956), set in pioneer days at Henry's Bend (Marquette) about 1855, also has Indian characters. *Always Anne* (1957), a story set in northern Michigan, contrasts two high school girls and two cultures—white and Ojibwa. *Snow Bound in Hidden Valley* (1957) shows a friendship between an Indian girl, Onota Leroy, and a white girl, Jo Shannon, who is snowbound at Onota's cabin for a week. *Stranger in Singamon* (1959) is the story of a young girl who finds surprise and suspense in a lumber town that at first seems miserable. *Maggie of Barnaby Bay* (1963), set at the time of the War of 1812, tells of a romance interrupted by that war. In *Double Heritage* (1971), her Indian heritage, the Black Hawk War, and a cholera epidemic seem destined to prevent eighteen-year-old Emily's marriage to the son of one of Detroit's aristocratic families. Wilson's *The Hundred Steps* was published in 1958. Mrs. Wilson said that she preferred writing for younger readers.[92]

Dorothy Maywood Bird (1899–), a native of the Upper Peninsula's Crystal Falls, set two of her three books "for older girls" in her native area. *Granite Harbor* (1944) is the story of a Texas girl who comes to the Upper Peninsula in midwinter. The book's first image recalls a scene from the film *Winter Carnival* (1939) scripted by F. Scott Fitzgerald and Budd Schulberg. At a train window, the protagonist, Terrill, sees a boy come out of the snowy landscape on skis, float through the air, and just as it seems he will crash into the train, the boy touches ground, does a graceful Telemark turn, and then skis alongside the train as it slows for the station.

Terrill, recovering from a recent automobile accident, faces new experiences—fifteen-degree-below-zero nights and an equally chilly reception from the students in her new school. The story has no plot, only a series of incidents that lead to a time a year later when Terrill can once again brace herself for the fun of being a teenager.

In Bird's *Mystery at Laughing Water* (1946, reissued 1963), Phyllis Rockfort comes for the first time to Camp Laughing Water on Lake Superior. She remembers that over a century before, her great-great-uncle and great-great-aunt came from England and had mysteriously disappeared in the area. In addition to enduring a number of initiatory-type experiences at the camp, Phyllis also uncovers the secret of her family's long-ago mystery.

[I]n *The Black Opal* (1949, reissued 1963), Bird used the Albion College campus for her locale. Critics liked all three books.[93]

John Bellairs (1938–), reared in Marshall, Michigan, in the 1950s, calls the town New Zebedee in his three children's novels based on his own childhood: *The House with a Clock in Its Walls* (1973), *The Figure in the Shadows* (1975), and *The Letter, the Witch, and the Ring*

(1976). A young boy, the main figure in the first book, shares his central position with a young girl in the second; she is the main figure in the third.

Bellairs's children are at first the victims of other children's cruelty, but in the end, in part owing to the love, affection, and understanding of their adult peers, they triumph.

William Noone, a thirteen-year-old boy in Neil Faasen's *The Toy Fair* (1963), disgusted with what he thinks is a conspiracy of parents and teachers in his small Michigan town to fit him into their own mold, heads off to Chicago with two girl classmates to find his alcoholic father—and, as it turns out, disillusionment. Critics thought Faasen had relied too much on Holden Caulfield of J. D. Salinger's *The Catcher in the Rye* (1951) as the model for young Noone.[94]

Albert Drake's *One Summer* (1980) tells of a boy just out of grade school, looking forward to the long summer before high school. A reviewer called it a sort of "modern-day 'Pinocchio,' without the cloying sermons of the original" and wondered "What kind of person will this real boy become?"[95]

Kenneth E. Ethridge's *Toothpick* (1985) tells of a teenager, seriously ill with cystic fibrosis, an outcast in her new high school, who finds friends in three male outcasts, and helps one of them with his dream girl. Reviewers were mildly enthusiastic about the book.[96]

Margaret Willey (1950–) has two degrees from Grand Valley State College and teaches in the Grand Rapids area. Her novels *The Bigger Book of Lydia* (1983), *Finding David Dolores* (1986), and *If Not for You* (1986) are written for young adults now finding themselves facing problems their parents did not have to deal with until they were a few years older. Fifteen-year-old Lydia says she is big enough to have sexual relations with a rock band guitarist. In the second novel, thirteen-year-old Arly rejects her mother as she becomes infatuated with a boy who is a high school senior. In *If Not for You*, a girl is drawn into the world of a young woman who eloped with a young man, married him, and has a baby. Reviewers found the books of more than ordinary interest.[97]

Donal Hamilton Haines (1886–1950), the author of some fifteen books for boys, was one of the editors of the *Michigan Alumnus Quarterly Review*, and taught journalism at his alma mater, the University of Michigan. Leon Burgoyne (1916–), a high school basketball coach, wrote three stories about high school athletes. C[aary] Paul Jackson (1902–), using several pseudonyms, wrote some fifty books about young athletes, and Jackson Scholz (1897–) wrote at least a dozen books in the same genre. Though not all of the books by these last four authors are set in Michigan, they focus on youth of high school age and beyond, trying to succeed in some sport, and often, overcoming obstacles to relationships with others.

Summary

Michigan novels have ranged over the whole of Michigan state history, and have ranged in quality from excellent to mediocre.

Of the authors, the most prolific was Helen Hull, although only a few of her books were set in Michigan. The writer drawing the most attention during her publishing period was Maritta Wolff, although she is little read today. Charlotte Armstrong, writing as Joe Valentine, probably drew the most attention during her lifetime—with her mystery novels, none of which were set in Michigan. Steward Edward White was a popular author during his lifetime. Of this whole group, he is the only one with a book in print today—but he would probably be astounded at the reason for keeping it in print.

CHAPTER XV

DETROIT IN LITERATURE
The French City and the Motor City

Historical and romantic souvenirs hang like tattered drapery
around the Fair City of the Straits. These weird tales, quaint
customs, and beautiful traditions have been handed down from
generation to generation as sacred trusts. Originally brought
from their cradle in Normandy, they are still tenderly cher-
ished in the homes of the old families of Norman descent settled along "le Detroit."
                         —Edith R. Mosher and Nella Dietrich Williams,
                         From Indian Legends to the Modern Bookshelf [1]

In 1943, Hal H. Smith (1873–1944) first president of the Friends of
the Detroit Public Library, wrote:

> And why should Detroit not have a Detroit literature? By Detroit
> literature I do not mean only books written in Detroit, though there is
> no reason why there should not be many volumes written here. We
> have a community of two million people. There were only about one
> hundred thousand in Shakespeare's London. If there is any relation-
> ship between population and literary inspiration, we may expect to do
> our part in book production even if we write no *Hamlets*. [2]

As we have seen, there was a Detroit literature—novels and
verse about the Indians, Cadillac, the French settlers, and the British
and the Americans in the area. Still, Smith had a point. By 1943,
many more volumes of verse and fiction had been set in both Chicago
and New York, both admittedly bigger cities—one older than Detroit,
one newer—but both with attractions for writers that Detroit, with its
reputation for being a one-industry city, seemingly lacked.

The French City

Amanda M. Douglas's *A Little Girl in Old Detroit* (1902) is one of at least nine "little girl" books by Douglas, each one featuring a different girl in a different city. Although Douglas was a meticulous researcher, she was not adverse to including some fanciful material in her stories, including this tale of one Jeanne Angelot, a French girl who as a child was left with an Ojibwa woman under mysterious circumstances. The story begins in 1790 and ends with the 1805 Detroit fire.

The novel focuses on the French population. The slight plot has Jeanne fending off several suitors, one of whom kidnaps her and takes her to far off Bois Blanc Island near Mackinac. But she is rescued by her long-lost father and returns to Detroit to marry the son of a wealthy aristocrat.

In 1846, Emma Carra (Avis J. Spenser) wrote *A Tale of the West; or, Life with a Sister*, a grossly overwritten, presumptuously styled novel set in the early nineteenth century that narrates a decade-long romance between a young doctor with a weakness for liquor and poker and a Detroit woman. Reformed after being wounded at the Battle of the Thames (1813), he marries the woman.

Hope Daring (Anna Johnson's pseudonym) set her *Father John; or, Ruth Webster's Quest* (1907) in the French area of Detroit in 1831. A daughter's search for her father is successful. Anna Johnson was also the author of nine other books, several published by the American Tract Society, from 1900 to 1922.[3]

Heart and Soul by Henrietta Dana Skinner (1857–1927)—daughter of Richard Henry Dana and a childhood neighbor of Henry Wadsworth Longfellow—was published in 1901, Detroit's Bi-centenary year. Rodérick (Eric) Frémont grew up in Detroit hating blacks, but one night helps his sweetheart aid a runaway black slave to escape to Canada. The girl dies tragically, but Eric eventually marries her sister. The novel, which traces the careers of Eric and several other Detroit French descendants to the end of the century, utilizes both French folklore and superstitions in developing its story line.

Edward Everett Hale (1822–1909), scion of the distinguished New England family and author of "The Man without a Country" (1863), set one of the poorer of his fifty volumes, *Ups and Downs, an Everyday Novel* (1873), in Detroit. A Harvard graduate operates a carriage-manufacturing firm until the cholera epidemic of the early 1830s forces it to fail. Then he returns east to marry a German girl.

The nineteenth century was a time when newspaper humorists flourished. Among the best known—and certainly the most famous of Michigan humorists—was Charles Bertrand Lewis (1852–1924), who wrote as "M. Quad" for the *Detroit Free Press*. One of his series, "The Lime Kiln Club," focuses on a black self-improvement society; another series features Carl Dunder, a German merchant.

The Lime Kiln essays were collected in eight editions titled *Brother Gardner and His Lime Kiln Club*, and *Gardner's Lime Kiln Club*. Other essays were collected in *Quad's Odds* (1875) and several other miscellaneous titles. Lewis was also the author of plays and several historical stories.

Lewis's essays, often built around stereotypes we now reject, made people smile, but they seldom made them think.[4]

Barbara Frances Fleury's 1936 *Lucky Piece*, set in Detroit in 1879, features an eleven-year-old child who flees an orphan asylum to live with his father. The latter tells him stories about early Detroit. Fleury's ancestors were Detroit pioneers, and she was a Detroit public school librarian.

Nolan Miller set *A Moth of Time* (1946) in the Trumbull Avenue area of Detroit from 1900 to the entrance of the United States into the war in 1917. The novel tells of the deterioration of the three Carmichael sisters, their neighborhood, and their family relationships. Contrasted with this is the personal development of a son of one of the sisters. Business and banking are minor themes.

A reviewer thought the novel was "so penetrating in its insights and so consistently satisfying in its expression that it stands out as a splendid work." Another said it was a "rich and rewarding book," reminiscent of Thomas Wolfe, from whose phrase its title was drawn: "Here, then, is a man, this moth of time."[5]

Mary Francis Doner's mediocre *Chalice* (1936) follows Jane Halloran from 1900 to 1920 as she struggles to become a poet in Detroit. An early unhappy marriage to an older man is a trial, but eventually she finds true love with another.

Ohioan Marjorie McClure (1882–1967) set her *High Fires* (1924) from 1905 through World War I—the years when Detroit became the "automobile city." The novel contrasts the social attitudes of the families of a puritanical Presbyterian minister and an automobile dealer. The minister loves baseball but objects to the Tigers' games on Sunday. At the end of the novel he is churchless, but he and the dealer have become friends, and their children have married.

Comments on the book varied: it was a "well-wrought story" that had "literary excellence," "a thoughtful book [that] will be read with pride by those who are hopeful [for] American literature," "a propaganda novel."[6] The *New Republic* took a satirical stance, "Readers who are shocked and pained by 'Flaming Youth' and *Janet March* will turn to its wholesome pages with relief."[7]

About sixty pages of McClure's *John Dean's Journey* (1923) portray its hero as a newspaperman in Detroit.

Clarence Budington Kelland's *The Highflyers* is a story of the awakening of Detroit to the 1914–1918 "war for freedom." Potter Waite, son of a man who is a millionaire automobile manufacturer and U.S. senator, loves a woman whose father is a wealthy, traitorous German-American, but she remains true-blue, and in the end they wed. Although the city is less war conscious than its East Coast contemporaries, it is the focus of German moles who would like to bomb its factories. A reviewer commented that there were so many of these, the reader wonders "how we were able to produce any airplanes or munitions at all."[8]

Mary Frances Doner's 1946 *Blue River* (a play on the name River Rouge) is an earlier "Dallas." Anne, a woman, whose showgirl mother had deserted her family, marries a man, who, like Henry Ford, builds an industrial complex and a town to house his workers. At the same time, Anne's sister is trying to destroy Anne's marriage through lies and gossip—with some help from Anne who does not always spend her nights in her own bed. Although some reviewers praised the novel for its slickness, its slickness is its major fault.[9]

Midway through the Hoover presidency, Catherine Brody, a New York journalist, wrote a series of factual stories about women—their work, their prospects, their daily routine. In the early 1930s, she toured the United States, working for a week each in twenty cities, to produce a series, "What Happens When a Girl Goes Job-Hunting." In Chicago, she worked in a meat-packing plant, in Detroit in an automobile factory.

Using these stories and experiences, she wrote *Nobody Starves* (1932) about two factory workers from the East in the late 1920s, the era of the two-car-in-every-garage prosperity promised by President Herbert Hoover. They came to Detroit to find a better life. But the Great Depression hits, Mollie is pregnant, Bill loses his job, the bank in which they have their savings fails. Bill, desperate and in love with another woman, murders Mollie.

Sinclair Lewis said *Nobody Starves* was "important." The *New Republic* wrote, "[m]uch of the writing is excellent. . . . It represents exceptionally competent reporting, by a middle-class intellectual, of contemporary proletarian experience. . . . But [the novel] is not a work of art."[10] Herschel Brickell said that Brody had "put on paper one brutal phase of our civilization, in terms of living and under-standable human beings."[11]

Although all the critics agreed that *Nobody Starves* is a proletar-ian novel, written by a proletarian, the novel is not discussed in David D. Anderson's excellent study "Michigan Proletariat Writers and the Great Depression."[12]

Linda Crawford (1938–), daughter of a Detroit foundry owner, earned B.A. and M.A. degrees at Ann Arbor, reported for the *Chicago Tribune* for six years, and then became a free-lance writer. Her second novel, *Something to Make Us Happy* (1978), tells of an immigrant Scotch family that prospers in the foundry business in Detroit. When Rob-ert Clafin dies, Isobel, who has preferred fantasizing about romantic Hollywood stars to normal sexual activities, takes her son to Holly-wood where both survive on the escapism offered by the films. A re-viewer said the novel offers "a healthy mixture of fantasy and reality" to its readers.[13]

Granville Paul Smith's (1893–1947) *Invincible Surmise* (1936) (the title came from a George Santayana poem) portrays an impoverished puritanical minister's son who, after a brief affair with a wealthy girl, moves to Detroit to become a novelist. There, he marries the self-willed daughter of a wealthy industrialist and moves up the management ladder in the industrialist's firm. But the marriage dis-integrates, and he returns to his first love. Critics found the novel's faults, including Smith's too-frequent use of chance meetings, out-weighed its virtues.[14]

William C[losson] Emory's *Love in Detroit* (1934) was published in a limited edition of five hundred copies. It is a "slender account" of the [early] Great Depression years in the Motor City, "permeated with bums, cheap upstairs rooms and violence."[15]

Readers who wish to spare themselves the effort of reading *Myrna* (1943) by Jan Kelson (the nom de plume of Jacob Jankelson), can turn to pages 156–159 where "Myrna" herself—after having been a prostitute, a seducer of other women's husbands, a victim of vene-real disease, and an associate of Detroit gangsters—outlines a story line for a novel. The book she plans is *Myrna*.

Augusta Walker (1914–) won three Hopwood awards as she earned B.A. and M.A. degrees at Ann Arbor, then she became a col-lege teacher and author of short stories. One section of her *A Midwest Story* (1959), written under a *Partisan Review* fellowship, is set in Michigan. It narrates the career of a woman who leaves college to marry a Detroit man, only to discover he is a homosexual. A second marriage also proves frustrating.

David Cornel DeJong's *Somewhat Angels* (1945) is a World War II novel set in a city with an airplane factory (similar to Willow Run) between Detroit and Ann Arbor, owned by the novel's central character, Mrs. Brain. Her three sons are in the army; the wives and the mistress of one son are at home. Reviewers were not as enthusiastic about this novel as they had been about DeJong's three novels of Dutch settlement.[16]

In 1936, Arthur Miller won a Hopwood Award in the drama competition for three plays: *No Villain* (1936), *Honors at Dawn* (1937), and *The Great Disobedience* (1938). Typescripts for all three are at the University of Michigan.

In 1947, Miller's play *All My Sons* (filmed in 1948) depicted a wartime-parts manufacturer (in a city that could be Detroit) who had knowingly allowed a shipment of defective parts to an aircraft assembler. He then stood silently by as his partner was given a prison sentence. Later, he learns his son was killed when one of the planes crashed because of faulty parts.

Glendon Swarthout and Harriet Arnow were specific about the location in their respective novels: *Willow Run* (1943)—written while World War II was in progress—and *The Dollmaker* (1954). Both works are set at Willow Run, the site of the mammoth bomber factory on Detroit's west-central boundary. Each novel dramatizes human problems that were a by-product of the assembly of almost nine thousand long-range B-24 bombers.

The plant, wrote Swarthout, was "immensity. Insane, overpowering immensity." One-fifth of a mile wide, three-fifths of a mile long, it employed 42,000 men and women.

Willow Run takes place during one night shift. Swarthout focuses on seven people, five men and a girl who come to work in the same bus and Joe, a janitor, a kind of Greek chorus. Each chapter has two parallel narrative strands—the airplane assembly process and the interrelationships among the seven.

On the night of the story, the six come to work together, but soon one of them, who is trying to write plays in his free time (Swarthout worked for a year at the plant and wrote the novel in off-hours), is sent home after a quarrel. A second is sent home for violating a plant rule. Pig, the bus driver, murders a third passenger in a quarrel over the girl.

Critics were uneven in their treatment of *Willow Run*. Phil Stong noted that the novel was undeveloped. John Norcross said the novel reflected the hasty, hectic days of the war. The *New York Times* said that Swarthout "gives a word picture, visually, aurally, emotionally, of Willow Run and all its next of kin—the hundreds of great war plants which would seem to dehumanize men who serve them, but which instead only heighten and reinforce their humanness."[17]

After the war, Swarthout enrolled in the University of Michigan, and in the 1947–1948 school year won a Hopwood Award.

Harriette Louisa Simpson Arnow (1908–1986), a Kentuckian, married Harold Arnow, a newspaper reporter she met in Petoskey; in 1944, they moved into a wartime residence project in Detroit where "people of all religious and economic backgrounds and from various sections of the country were poured into the boiling caldron of life in a wartime city."[18] In Ann Arbor in 1951, she began writing her novel of Detroit in wartime, *The Dollmaker* (1954). Unlike Swarthout, who wrote his novel in the heat and fury of wartime, Harriette Arnow had had six years to contemplate her theme of a family uprooted from a remote rural area and resettled in the overcrowded wartime city.

The Dollmaker is the story of a Kentucky hill woman who unwillingly brings her five children to Detroit where her husband has taken a job. There Gertie Nevels, in a culturally shocking social milieu, faces discrimination for the first time: Detroit "went tu hell [when] da hillbillies come" (p. 302). Gertie, a son, and her youngest daughter cannot adapt as the rest of the family do. Cassie dies tragically when, in search of an imaginary friend, she is struck by a train.

The title refers to a section of a tree trunk Gertie brings to Detroit and from which, at odd times, she whittles her own version of a Christ image. In the end, Gertie accepts Detroit, in part, because Cassie is buried there. But in the film version (1984), Gertie (played by Jane Fonda) returns to Kentucky.

Frances M. Malpezzi has described the Detroit of *The Dollmaker* as a "society of the damned." James Seaton says, "Detroit is clearly a hellish place" in the novel.[19] *The Dollmaker* was ranked next to William Faulkner's *The Fable* for the 1954 National Book Award and became a best seller.

Arnow set her second Michigan novel, *The Weedkiller's Daughter* (1970), in a suburban area like the one the Arnows had moved to. It is a tale of Susan Marie Schnitzer, a precocious fifteen-year-old girl whose home is in an area ironically titled Eden Hills.

Like Gertie Nevels, Susan is also an outcast—but in her own home. A liberal, she is at odds with her conservative father—he hates blacks, peace marchers, draft resisters, subversives, *and* weeds with equal fervor. She also has problems with a school psychologist. She finally finds peace of mind in a nearby farm with "The Primitive"—a woman whose Eden-like existence is threatened by the expansion of Eden Hills.

In 1984, Harriette Arnow was presented the Mid America Award for Distinguished Contributions to Midwestern Literature.

"An A in French" in *The Education of Tom Webber* (1977) by Thomas R. Peters, Sr., describes the Belle Isle riots of 1943.

Joseph B. Mullen's *Room 103* (1963), set in the Detroit Public Welfare Department, emphasizes case histories rather than narrative. It focuses on several social workers who interview the thirteen percent of Detroit's population who need help in finding shelter, paying for food, and the like. From time to time, it reports instances of anti-black attitudes and discrimination against blacks, the latter apparently making up a large part of the clientele.

Stephen Dobyns (1941–) set his *The House on Alexandrine* (1990) in a mixed-population area, "the second highest crime area [in Detroit] (p. 10) some six blocks south of the Wayne State University campus in 1973. The characters of this naturalistic novel are men and women residents of a former home built about 1900; the focus is on their uneasy relationships with each other and with Duane, a young farm man from Ontario who has come to Detroit to search for his missing sister. The novel's events are interlaced with crime statistics, including the number of "justifiable homicides"—people shot by police, for example. At the time of writing the book, Dobyns was an English professor at Syracuse University.

Judith Guest (1936–) was born in Detroit and took a 1958 degree at the University of Michigan. Her first novel, *Ordinary People* (1976), set in Lake Forest, Illinois, attracted national attention and was filmed in 1980. Of this novel, Guest said it might have been set anywhere. That is true also of her second novel, *Second Heaven* (1982), which is set in a Detroit suburb.

Both novels deal with family relationships and communication problems in upper-middle-class families. In the second novel, the abused son of a fanatically religious father runs away from home and finds shelter with a recently divorced woman who has as many problems as he has. The father attempts to have the son institutionalized; the novel ends in a melodramatic courtroom scene. Guest has said she wrote a screenplay based on the novel.

Second Heaven got mixed reviews. Novelist Christopher Lehmann-Haupt found the story too neatly patterned. Chicago novelist Harry Mark Petrakis said the novel is an "example of what the art of story-telling is all about."[20]

The Motor City

When you drove a Lincoln, a big yellow Lincoln,
  And I drove a rattling Ford
You tried to 'guy' me as you would pass by me
  But your insults I ignored.
Then you struck a mudhole, a nice mushy mudhole,
  Your motor it raced and roared.
Then I pulled your Lincoln, your big yellow Lincoln,
  At the rear of my little black Ford.[21]

The first automobile fiction was set in Europe in 1903 and 1905. That year Lloyd Osborne published *The Motor Maniacs*, an American collection of short stories. In 1907, Richard Harding Davis's *The Scarlet Car* shared the scene with a third European novel. All these books were popular.[22]

Theophil Stanger's *Mr. Pickett of Detroit* (1916) may be the first Michigan novel to refer to a street crowded with automobiles. Otherwise, the novel is a mixture of polemics, musical events, a romance, early World War I actions in Europe and the United States, and melodrama. There are too many coincidences, and too much information is withheld from the reader until it suits the author's purposes to reveal it.

Pickett, a wealthy Montanan, develops a Detroit housing project with an innovation—each of the twenty-odd houses in this "Little Hague" is inhabited by a person with a different European background.

When we think of Detroit and automobiles, names such as Walter Chrysler, R. E. Olds, John and Horace Dodge, "Engine Charley," and "Electric Charley" come to mind. But America's "Mr. Automobile" has to be Henry Ford (1863–1947) whose inexpensive black Model T put America on wheels and became a permanent part of American folklore.

In 1937, Upton Sinclair (1878–1968), whose 1906 fictional *The Jungle* had savaged the American meat packing industry, produced a slim book, *The Flivver King: A Story of Ford-America*. The 155-page standard edition sold for a dollar and a half. But two hundred thousand copies were also published at Sinclair's own Pasadena, California, press and sold by the United Automobile Workers (UAW) at twenty-five cents each. (The book was reissued in 1969.)

The *New York Times* called the book an example of "pamphleteering"; the English *Times Literary Supplement* said it "was about as much a novel as Henry Ford [was] an historian."[23]

Ford's story is seen through the eyes of Abner, an imaginary boy who lives in the neighborhood where Ford is tinkering with gasoline engines and carriage bodies mounted on wheels. He sees Ford drive his first successful model and later becomes a laborer in Ford's factory. Ford becomes a billionaire; Abner's economic and social status remains unchanged.

The novel's subjects include the attempts of Ford to bring soldiers home from Europe in World War I, his anti-Jewish campaign in *The Dearborn Independent*, the building of the gigantic River Rouge plant, the end of the Model T, Ford's use of Nazi-like tactics to defeat attempts to organize the Congress of Industrial Organizations (CIO), and the building of his Dearborn Museum.

Ford is seen as a literal-minded mechanic whose one talent is driving men and as a hypocrite, preaching one philosophy, practicing another. At first Ford is readily accessible to his employees, at the end he hides behind an army of executives and hired thugs whom he calls the company police.[24] There are, of course, actual biographies of Ford and other studies of his career, including Floyd Clymer's *Henry Ford's Wonderful Model T, 1908–1927* (1955), C. E. Sorenson's *My Forty Years with Ford* (1962), and Mark Sullivan's *Our Times* (1926).

Peter Clark McFarlane (1871–1924) in his *Man's Country, a Story of a Great Love of Which Business Was Jealous* (1923) focuses on an automobile factory in Detroit from its start when it built "horseless carriages" on "a shoestring" in the 1890s to the 1920s when it is worth millions of dollars. Its theme, in McFarlane's words is, "[T]here is a great country, largely inhabited by men, to which most women . . . are strangers. . . . Its name is Business."

A reviewer said, "the best part of the book" was "the building up of [the automobile company.] . . . The history of the automobile business is like a fairy tale."[25]

Newton Fuessle's *Gold Shod* (1921) depicts a Chicagoan who marries a Detroit girl and takes a job in the new automobile business at the turn of the century. Although Fielding Glidden is aware of a "pagan quest for beauty," he stays with the industry. Like other critics, Robert Morss Lovett complained that the novel was all narrative and dialogue and lacked "dramatic action." He thought that Fuessle was "dealing with [great] issues of human life and profounder subtleties of human nature," which demanded greater emphasis.[26]

Faith Baldwin [Cuthrell] (1893–1978), a popular author of conventional romance novels, in *Love's a Puzzle* (1933) concentrates as much on romantic entanglements as she does on the automobile business. In this story, an automobile executive loses his wife, his magnificent home, and his factory in the Great Depression. A minor note in the novel reports the industrial fouling of the river that flows through the executive's estate—it is a "sacrifice to progress."

David D. Anderson has described three novels, one set in a Detroit factory and the other two in Detroit automobile plants, as Michigan proletariat novels. (Geoffrey Dell Eaton's *Backfurrow* is also thus classified.)[27] The proletariat are the members of the working class, the masses, those employed by others—factory workers, field-workers, laborers—usually without a capital investment of their own.

Lawrence H. Conrad's *Temper* (1924), the earliest of these novels, is set in a factory that fabricates metal products.

Paul Rinelli, an Italian-American, who dreams of rising to a position of power either within the factory or outside it, works in a succession of departments, each job less attractive than the one before. Outside the plant he is involved with members of a group of idealistic middle-class people who hope to convert immigrants into "good Americans." But Rinelli is a failure in both situations; finally, crippled by an accident, he can work only as a guard.

During his student days at the University of Michigan, Conrad worked in the Ford factory. At one time he examined biographies of fifty-thousand Ford workers and their families. *Temper*, an outgrowth of this research, was written at Ann Arbor and published in his senior year. Later, he became a teacher at the university and president of the Michigan Authors Association.

New York City journalist Paul Sifton's 1927 play, *The Belt*, was produced in the New Playwright Theater, located outside the theatrical district. The theater had been "the crepuscular scene of ten thousand nose thumbings at modern society."[28] As the play proceeds, the scene shifts from a workingman's living room in the foreground to an automobile production line in the background.

The characters are two women and a man of the working class and the Old Man—obviously Henry Ford—who comes to the home to award the worker a button for a decade of loyal service, a decade that has aged him thirty years because of the Old Man's speedup policies, which have enabled the factory to increase its output by twenty percent.

In 1935, James Steele (a pseudonym for Robert Cruden, 1910–) published *Conveyor: A Novel*. Cruden, once an automobile factory mechanic, became a history professor and contributed articles to liberal magazines and the labor press.

Conveyor is set during the Al Smith/Herbert Hoover presidential campaign. Coolidge prosperity had not trickled down to the factory workers who were also being subjected to a speedup policy that forced them to turn out more automobiles with no increase in pay. When one worker leaves his job to protest unreasonable withholding of part of his weekly earnings, he is blacklisted and no one else will hire him.

David D. Anderson called the novel, "[T]he most clearly proletarian novel to come out of the [Michigan] automobile industry in the [1930s]. . . . [The novel does not depict] a study of degeneration and defeat, however [but] concludes with the note that most clearly marks the proletarian novel of the Great Depression, the identification of the oppressor and the determination to destroy him."[29]

Conveyor was reissued in 1976 in "The Labor Movement in Fiction and Non-fiction Series" (reprints on the subject of labor, unions, etc.) published by the AMS Press.

Wessel Smitter (1892–1951) did some work at Calvin College, took a University of Michigan B.A. in 1922, and worked for two years in an automobile factory before moving to Hollywood and writing the novel *F.O.B. Detroit* (1938). Two men go to work for the Holt Motor Company whose owner's favorite maxim is "Machinery—the New Messiah," (p. 74). Then, in an accident owing to the factory's speedup policy, one man loses both his legs. Recovered, he is assigned to a salvage department to sort out useful metal items from the floor sweepings.

F.O.B. Detroit was more widely reviewed than almost any other Michigan novel and praised by all: literary historian John T. Flanagan, novelist Louis Adamic, *Time, Christian Century, Nation,* among many others. Smitter was hailed as standing "shoulder to shoulder with John Steinbeck."[30]

In 1936, Charlie Chaplin's film, *Modern Times,* presented a satirical treatment of the speedup in a factory. However, it has no recognizable setting.

In the Great Depression years, the federal government established a farm colony of some two hundred financially distressed midwestern families in Alaska's Matanuska Valley. Smitter's *Another Morning* (1941) focuses on a relocated Michigan family enduring its first year. Author Wallace Stegner said, "[T]he novel [is] important because it transplants the typical frontier values from a dead past to a living present and future."[31]

Albert Maltz's *The Underground Stream: A Historical Novel of a Moment in the American Winter* (1940) is set in February 1936. The *moment* is the attempt to unionize automobile workers in Detroit—an attempt that led to the 1936 New Year's Eve sit-down strike at the Fisher Body Plant in Flint and "the battle of the overpass" near the Ford River Rouge plant in May 1937.

Maltz's novel is set in one weekend. "Princey" Prince, an auto plant night shift worker, helping to organize a CIO unit, runs afoul of Harry Greb, the son of a Chicago packing house worker who is personnel manager for "Princey's" employer, and Harvey Kellogg, a ne'er-do-well who has become a leader in "the Black Legion of America," a Nazi-like organization that opposes President Franklin D. Roosevelt, anarchists, Communists, the Catholic hierarchy, aliens, blacks, Jews, and any cult or creed that believes in social and personal equality. When "Princey" refuses to give up his organizing efforts, he is murdered.

The New York Times wrote, "[T]he book has nothing in common with other labor novels. Here is no morbidity, no impressionism, no grim hopelessness. Maltz . . . has built his story around his sure sense of human values, around a knowledge of the things for which men strive. . . . [He] makes a just claim to the calmer and more enduring perspectives of history."[32]

Alfred Kazin offered a balanced judgment, "It is not easy to evaluate The Underground Stream. . . . Its power and harsh excitement do not obscure a certain banality. . . . [But] what Maltz has to say is important, and he says it strikingly."[33]

Jack Salzman's Albert Maltz (1978) has a thorough study of The Underground Stream in chapter five, "An American Winter."[34]

Maltz (1908–), a Phi Beta Kappa graduate of Columbia College and a student of George Pierce Baker at Yale, in the mid-1930s observed firsthand the struggle between labor and management in Flint and Detroit. He described what he saw in "Bodies by Fisher" in the New Masses.[35]

The Hard Rain (1980) by Dimitia Smith [Nasow] contrasts the after-college careers of a college radical who goes to work in a Detroit automobile plant in the 1960s and an apolitical friend who becomes a New York journalist. After Michael has accidentally killed a plant guard with a small bomb he intended as a scare tactic, he flees to New York and asks Luke to hide him. But when the police close in, he kills himself.

Smith is an award-winning television documentary producer.

Inside Detroit was a 1955 film based apparently on attempts to bomb Walter Reuther and his brother Victor in the 1950s. A New York Times reviewer said the film was "low on gas, with a faulty transmission and some of the styling faults of the Model T."[36]

Harold Livingston (1924–), a one-time Detroit advertising writer, set *The Detroiters* (1958) in the automobile advertising scene. The novel focuses as much on advertising executive David Manning's dallying with prostitutes and other men's wives as it does on the promotion of automobile sales.

The novel came soon after John Keats's *The Insolent Chariots*, an exposé of the automobile industry. Meyer Levin said that if anyone were "in search of a second report on what's wrong with the automobile business [she or he] need look no further than" Livingston's novel. "If there are many David Mannings around the motor capital, then it's small wonder the [roads] are jammed with Volkswagens."[37]

Henry B. Hager (1926–), a Yale graduate who became a Detroit advertising man and occasional writing teacher, set his *Fireball* (1963) in the Detroit automobile advertising scene. Like Livingston's novel, it emphasizes sexual adventures as much as it does the deliberations of those attempting to design a promotion campaign for a new model automobile.

John E[dward] Quirk (1920–), a World War II combat pilot, was active in the Detroit automobile industry. The second of his half-dozen books, *The Hard Winners* (1965), focuses on the selection of a new president for an automobile factory. The novel looks, in turn, at the biographies of several potential executives, each of whom is more successful in business than in family relationships.

A reviewer said the book was "overlong, banal"; the characters "know a lot about football and seduction," but they are "squalid and colorless." A second reviewer was slightly more favorable, saying the novel "is effective in a bloodless sort of way."[38]

Edwin Gilbert (1907–1976), playwright and screenwriter, set one of his half-dozen novels, *American Chrome* (1965)—published in the same month as *The Hard Winners*—in the Detroit automobile scene. A reviewer noted that one male character in Quirk's novel was identical to one in Gilbert's novel.[39]

The thrust of this work is the relationship between auto manufacturers and dealers, the latter constantly being pressured into buying more cars than they can sell. A second theme is the role of bribery and corruption within the industry. A third theme, one that seems to triumph as the novel ends, is air pollution, "Farewell . . . to the fumes and furies of the gasoline monsters we all loved to grow up with. . . . with their three-foot-long probosci and four-foot-long assendi all over the place" (p. 441). The novel makes a strong case for the replacement of the atmosphere-fouling gasoline engine by an engine using electrical energy.

The blockbuster novel of the automobile industry is Englishman Arthur Hailey's *Wheels* (1971), the book that alerted us never to buy a car made on Fridays—although it did not tell us how we would know. The novel followed Hailey's *Airport*, part of which was filmed at the Detroit Metro-Wayne County airport on a snowy night in the winter of 1969–1970.

Hailey said that his novels began with an idea that enthused him. Following approval by his wife and publisher, he would then take a year to research the organization and people in depth. In this case, "he was wined and dined by the automobile industry, observed everything, interviewed everyone, from assembly-line workers to General Motors President Edward Cole."[40]

Hailey's method is to take one character at a time, advance him toward his destiny, then put him in a holding pattern and turn to a second character. But the method does not always work. In *Wheels*, we see the General Motors president wondering why his electric blanket does not work—but we never see him again.

Harold Robbins's *The Betsy* (1971) supposedly is about a car of the future (the Pinto?), but it is basically a novel about a Detroit automobile dynasty (the Fords?) from 1930 to 1970.

One reviewer said, "The [Ford] auto dynasty need not worry: [the one] featured in this novel resembles them only in the incredible chutzpah of the author's intentions, not in any of its actual characters. Here we go again; more than five hundred pages of carefully regulated formula sex scenes."[41]

Hollywood waited until 1977 to film *The Betsy*, but reviewers were not happy when they did, "[The director] was in no danger of making a good movie out of *The Betsy*, but he might easily have made a funnier [one. The film] often sags, and a movie this frivolous has no business being dull."[42]

In 1988, Paramount produced a film, *Tucker, the Man and His Dream*, the story of Preston Thomas Tucker, who in 1945 had a vision of an automobile that would be faster, safer, and slicker than any motorcar built before or to be built—at least in the foreseeable future. Tucker did build a handful of cars, but along the way he encountered crooked politicians and opposition from Detroit automobile manufacturers.

Philip Levine's *5 Detroits* (1970)—"for a black man whose name I have forgotten who danced all night at Chevy Gear and Axle"—has five verses that take up fifteen pages: "Detroit Grease Shop Poem," "Saturday Sweeping," "Coming Home," "The Angels of Detroit," and "They Feed the Lion." A half-dozen lines from "Coming Home" will provide an image and the tone of the whole:

A winter Tuesday, the city pouring fire,
Ford Rouge sulfurs the sun, Cadillac, Lincoln,
Chevy grey. The fat stacks
of breweries hold their tongues. Rags,
papers, hands, the stems of birches
dirtied with words. . . .

We burn this city every day.

Detroit native Jim Daniels's *Places / Everyone* (1985) is proletariat poetry, its theme laborers and their manipulation by the automobile industry. Its forty-seven poems focus on Detroit factory workers at work, at home, and on the city's streets. Poems in the first two sections focus on the narrator's grandfather, and on a character, Digger, who is addressed directly by the poet. Daniels's *Punching Out* (1990) might be termed a proletariat poetic narrative. In some sixty unrhymed verse narratives, his protagonist, a young man named Digger, takes the reader through a series of daily work experiences in an automobile factory.

Peter Stitt in the *New York Times* said that Daniels "makes articulate the feelings of inarticulate people . . . through an unusually clear free verse style"; Rochelle Ratner said that otherwise "simple observations are often unexpectedly metamorphosed into a haunting portrait of working-class life."[43]

Daniels wrote his poems from his own and his family members' experiences as automobile factory workers. He took B.A. degrees from Alma College and Bowling Green State University, then became a college teacher. His book won the 1985 University of Wisconsin Press Brittingham Prize in Poetry.

Dan Gerber (1940–), born in Grand Rapids, is the author of *Out of Control* (1974). It is about a young man who achieves a lifetime ambition to become a top race car driver. In *American Atlas* (1973), he tells the story of a young Michiganian who walks out of his father's funeral service, leaving behind his wife, two children, and the Bancroft Pie Company (a family business) to head west in his Porsche with a girl he has picked up, an American Express Card, $5,000 in cash, some Janis Joplin tapes, and a proclivity to write poems.

Three other films with Michigan backgrounds are *Paper Lion* (1968), based on George Plimpton's book about the Detroit professional football team; *Robocop* (1987), set in a Detroit of the future that will at an even more future date become Old Detroit; and *Action Jackson* (1988), about a Detroit policeman's adventures with an automobile tycoon and the latter's mistress and gang of assassins.

Joyce Carol Oates

Joyce Carol Oates, a prolific Michigan author, who has received consideration and praise from most of the major contemporary critics, both popular and literary, lived for several years in Windsor and taught in Detroit. Recently, she has moved to Princeton, New Jersey. To date, she has published more than forty books—novels and collections of verse and short fiction.

Only part of her work is set in Michigan. About the use of local materials she has said, "Regionalism depends entirely upon the writer. Anyone who can write beautifully about anything at all—set anywhere—is a true writer; anyone who must depend upon unusual, eccentric devices, specific more to a region than to a human community is not what I think of as a true writer."[44]

Oates's *them* (1969) is a 508-page novel that begins in Detroit in 1937 and covers about two decades. Its focus is on Maureen Wendall from her sixteenth year, when her brother kills a man he finds in bed with her, until her hyperactive son kills a man.

Oates said that Maureen Wendall was based on the "recollections" of one of her students. Of these, Oates continued, "This must be fiction, this can't be real!" And then she concluded, "This is the only kind of fiction that is real."[45]

Oates's 1971 novel *Wonderland* tells of a boy, who after escaping his father's attempt to murder his family members, is raised by a callous Michigan doctor. Later the young man becomes a doctor, too. Only part of this novel is set in Michigan.

Do with Me What You Will (1973) is the story of Eleanor Ross, a daughter who was kidnapped and brutalized by her father, then forced by her mother to marry a lawyer; she eventually leaves her husband for a second lawyer.

Such simple outlines as these do not reveal the literary qualities that have made Oates a popular author. One critic has called her a "potent myth-maker in the drab guise of a social naturalist [who] releases the stuff of nightmares in the streets of Detroit."[46] But not all of her critics have been happy. An English writer said that although the reader is "struck by Ms. Oates's energy and conviction, (she or he) is alternately numbed and bullied by her resolute handling of language."[47] Another said that the 561 pages of *Do with Me What You Will*, although filled with incident, example, internal monologue, [and] psychological explanation," do not "furnish a clue" to the Eleanor Ross character, and that Ross "is one of the most boring women imaginable."[48]

Oates's *Cybele* (1980) might well have been titled "The Short Un-happy Life of Edwin Locke"—the book has only 204 pages. Locke, an insurance executive, deserts his family to take up with a woman with twins. When he molests one of the twins, he is pursued and mur-dered by a mob, and his body is burned under an overpass. A re-viewer said the book was "strictly for Oates's fans."[49]

Oates's nineteenth novel is *American Appetites* (1989), set in the 1890s. The scene is upper-middle-class suburbia, a favorite target for Oates. Here live writers, architects, academics, and other intelligen-tsia. All seems well in this "sea of plenty" until Oates's favorite ploy, brutal violence, shatters the facade of a group of academics. These people have no moral sense and, as a consequence, their lives begin to unravel.

Summary

The chapter on the French, British, and Indians discussed fic-tion about Detroit becoming a fort, then a settlement, and the strug-gle over its possession. This chapter discusses Detroit after 1815 after it began losing some of its old French appearance and charm and be-came a modern mercantile and industrial city with particular empha-sis on the effects of the development of the automobile. The chapter on crime in the Michigan novel focused on that aspect of our modern day life as it affected the City on the Straits.

And so, as the sun's rays bravely try to fight their way down through Detroit's version of smog, we leave the Motor City, confident that William Kienzle, Elmore Leonard, and others, are still writing (or contemplating writing) more books set amid the sleaze, visible or concealed, that according to these novelists and others, dominates the old French City. What must Antoine Laumet de La Mothe sieur de Cadillac think as he looks down from his Royalist-Jesuit Heaven and sees the present culmination of his vision!

CHAPTER XVI

MICHIGAN POETRY OF PLACE

Land of broad lakes, and many a clear blue stream,
  In which the very heavens seem proud to glass,
So bright, so clear, so tender is their gleam
    When glance the stars adown some wild-wood pass;
    Like lovers topping o'er a forest lass,
Or stately sires that bend with blessings mild,
    The trees lean toward them, and their shadows cast
Free and afar, fantastic, weird, and wild,
Some kisses of the gods bestowed on Nature's loveliest
        child. . . .
    But fairer scenes the startled vision meet:
    A vast and busy city, street on street,
Lit with a thousand lamps, dome, tower, and spire.
                        —Louis Bates, "Detroit"[1]

This chapter, like those that precede it, is limited to items that are clearly set in Michigan, or else refer to Michigan people, places, and events. There have been, and are, many other verses and poems written in Michigan or created by persons who were born, or lived, in the state. These and their subjects seem almost as numberless as the giant white pines that once covered the Michigan northwoods. Although many of these are by poets of great talent, they are beyond the scope of this study. Moreover, any attempt to identify and discuss them would undoubtedly produce a second volume as lengthy as the present one.

Quite early in the Michigan territorial period, poems about the area appeared. A British officer in 1791 published *Miscellanies in Prose and Verse*, using his experiences as his subject mater. A second British officer, Colonel Arent Schuyler De Peyster, commandant at Michilimackinac from 1774–1779, published *Miscellanies by an Officer*.[2]

Referring to emigrants in the Midwest, Iowan Phillip Duffield Stong wrote that these "wildland birds" began singing as soon as they built a nest.[3] This was true of Michigan also; 150 poems appeared in

251

the *Detroit Gazette* during the years 1817 to 1830—the life of that early-day newspaper—and many reflected pride or interest in the new state. Among these were verses by one Damoetas, a pseudonym of Henry Rowe Schoolcraft, and anonymous or pseudonymous verse by Schoolcraft's wife, Jane. "D." (Schoolcraft?) was the author of "Michigan" in 1824. Still other poems were written by James L. Cole who used the pseudonym Adriane; Captain Henry Whiting, whose poetry about Indians has been discussed earlier (see pp. 40, 43); and John P. Sheldon who operated his Detroit Bookstore in combination with a print shop.[4]

Andrew J. Jenner was the author of a fourteen-page *Detroitiad* and W. W. Jennings of a broadside, which included "The Western Pioneer" and "Sale of the Old Farm."

Elizabeth Margaret Chandler (1807–1834), an early nineteenth-century Michigan poet, first attracted attention in Philadelphia with an antislavery poem, "The Slave Ship." Near the town of Tecumseh, Michigan, on the bank of the Raisin River, in a home she named Hazleton, Chandler wrote verses about Michigan that added to her fame. Here is a stanza from her "Indian Camp":

But there was left no relic of them there,
  Save that tradition told of one spot,
Where they had long been sepulchred; it bore
  No stone, no monument, that they might not
Be all forgotten; but the forest bough,
In aged strength bent down above each mouldering brow.[5]

The Burton Historical Collection in the Detroit Public Library has a number of past examples of Michigan poetry of place. Silas Farmer's *The History of Detroit and Michigan* (1884) contains "To the Old Pear Trees of Detroit" by W. H. Coyle and "The Mission Pears" by Louis J. Bates. In the same volume, are James V. Campbell's "Cassina" [The Cass House and Its History] and "Fireside Poem."

W. E. Baubie's *French-Canadian Verse* (1917) has "My Old Canoe"; a river song with its musical score in an essay; "The Old-time Fishing on the Detroit River"; and "A Legend of the Detroit River." The last describes an incident that occurred as Phineas T. Barnum, the famed showman, was moving his circus from Detroit to Windsor by ferry.

Gateway, in its issues for February and March 1904, has M. M. Burnham's "Of the River Kalamazoo"; Ben King's "Benton Harbor, Michigan"; and F. M.'s "Old Saint Joe." (Pioneer Michigan poets of both sexes often concealed their identities behind initials or pen names. Phil[lip] Duffield Stong commented that "it was polite, then, to sign one's verse modestly with initials."[6])

Asa H. Stoddard's *Miscellaneous Poems . . .* (1880) is set in Kalamazoo County. J. L. Gordon's *Legends of the Northwest* (1881) contains "The Sea Gull," based on an Indian legend set at Pictured Rocks National Lakeshore on the Lake Superior shore of the Upper Peninsula.

Francis D. Lacy's *Star Lake Romance: A Modern Poem of Love and Romance* (1883) is a long narrative poem set in Lake County. George Williamson's "The Maids of Detroit" is in his 1894 *Gleanings of Leisure Hours*. Lyman F. Stowe set his *Poetical Drifts of Thought. . . .* (1884) in Detroit; he was also the author of *My Wife Nellie and I* (1895).

Joseph Bert Smiley (1864–1903) of Kalamazoo set his *A Basket of Chips / A Varied Assortment of Poems and Sketches* (1888) in his home county. Frederick H. De Peu's *Poems* (1889) is set in Branch County and also focuses on the Civil War.

Some poems in Frank Hodgman's *The Wandering Singer and His Songs and Other Poems* (1898) are set in Climax. J. W. Bryce's *Random Rhymes* (1899) are set in part in Calhoun County. George Edward Lewis's *Heart Echoes* (1899) is set in Grand Rapids, Traverse Bay, and on Mackinac Island. Charles Musser's *Poems* (1900) is set in Ionia.

Several poems in Will J. Massingham's *Lake Superior and Other Poems* (1904) are set on Lake Superior or in the Upper Peninsula. Scott Woodward's *Life Pictures in Prose and Verse* (1911) is set in Traverse City. Robert Kroodsma's 1913 *Poems: Something for Everybody* is set in Ottawa County.

Earl L. Newton's *Tuneful Tales of Camps and Trails* (1927) are set in both Michigan peninsulas. Some of Marion Frazier Headley's 1927 *Poems* are set in the Ada area.

Gwen Frostic has several volumes of verse including *My Michigan* (1957). The verses in Faith M. Johnston's *Through the Arch of Experience* (1970) are set on Sugar Island and in Leelanau.

Roses That Bloomed in the Snow by J[ames] Fred[erick] Lawton (1888–?) was published in 1959. Lawton was also the author of *"Hurry Up" Yost in Song and Story* (1947), a tribute to the University of Michigan's famed football coach, Fielding H. ("Hurry Up") Yost.

Winfield Scott and J. A. Labadie coauthored "A Jaunt along the River Rouge" in 1908. Samuel M. Leggett in 1878 published *The Legend of Orchard Lake* (The legend of Me-nah-sa-gor-ning), then republished the same poem as *Me-nah-sa-gor-ning: A Legend of Orchard Lake*.

Charles Musser in 1900 published *Poems*, which included "Return to Ionia" and "Night Falls on Ionia." D. C. Nimmo's 1910 *Songs and Tales* includes "Detroit River" and a "Michigan State Song." In 1917, he published his *Detroit Songs*.

One of John J. Snook's 1907 *New Poems and Glad Outings* is set on Mackinac; Ivan Swift's *Fagots of Cedar* was published in 1907—with subsequent editions. Many of Swift's verses were set and written in Harbor Springs, Arkansas.

Andrew Wanless's "Detroit Is the Town for Me," is in his *Poems and Songs* (1872, reissued 1873); George Williamson's "The Maids of Detroit" is in his 1894 *Gleanings of Leisure Hours*. H. Wise was the author of an undated seven-page work, *A Description of Detroit in Rhyme*.

An unusual entry is Mary K. Buck's *Songs of the Northland* (1902), published posthumously. Mrs. Buck (1849–1901) was born Marjánka Knizek in Bohemia and came to Traverse City, Michigan, at the end of the Civil War. She attended college, became a schoolteacher and a contributor to several nationally circulated magazines. She also collaborated with Mrs. M. E. C. Bates on a volume of northern Michigan stories, *Along Traverse Shores*.[7]

Thus, often in pale imitations of better poets, Michigan poetry of place had its beginnings. Although the style and form were imitative, the material was often drawn from actual observations or experiences of the writers.

More current volumes in the Burton Historical Collection are Miriam Heideman Krarup's *Melodies from a Michigan Marsh* (1960), Margaret Collier's *City by a River* [Detroit] (1970), and John Frederick Nelson's *A Frontier Tale of Dolph and Dale* (1971).

Carl E. Burklund has identified many Michigan poets in essays in *Michigan History Magazine*. Among them was Louis Legrand Noble (1811–1882) who, in the early 1840s, began sending verse to literary magazines, including *Graham's Magazine*, where it appeared alongside verse by Henry Wadsworth Longfellow, James Russell Lowell, William Cullen Bryant, and Edgar Allan Poe. Like others of his time, Burklund took nature as his subject with distinct glances back at his formative years in the Huron River valley. One of his poems was "Groves of the River Huron"; his "best and best-known poem is 'To a Flying Swan at Midnight, in the Vale of the Huron.' " Burklund says that "Louis Legrand Noble was a true poet, and fully appreciated the grandeur and beauty of the forest of Michigan."[8]

In 1862, Mrs. Winnifred Lee (Brent) Lyster composed ten verses of a poem that came to be called "Michigan, My Michigan," and, to the tune of the German "O Tannenbaum," became the unofficial state song of Michigan. In 1902, poet Douglas Malloch composed some new verses that are the ones generally used in later years.[9]

Louis J. Bates (1832–1915) was, in Carl Burklund's opinion, among the best of the early Michigan poets, although, except for in William Coggeshall's *The Poets and Poetry of the West* (1860), Bates's verses never appeared in book form.

Bates came with his family to Portland, Michigan, in 1840. About 1849, he became a Great Lakes sailor, but most of his life he was a newspaper writer and editor in Grand Rapids, Detroit, Petoskey, and other places.

His long narrative poem, "Detroit" (1855)—quoted, in part, in this chapter's epigraph—tells of the surrender of Detroit by General William Hull in 1812. Another poem, "Michigan," was also published in 1855.

Three Early Contemporary Michigan Poets

Julia Moore, "The Sweet Singer of Michigan," was one of Michigan's three best-known poets in the nineteenth and early twentieth centuries, her fame (or, perhaps, ill-fame) reaching far beyond the state's borders.

She was born Julia A. Davis, December 1, 1847, in a log cabin in the forests of Kent County north of Grand Rapids. She had little formal education, but she did read a great deal. At eighteen, she married Fred Moore, a farmer, lumberman, and storekeeper.

In 1864, when a neighbor was killed in the Civil War, Moore memorialized him with a poem, "William Upson." Soon after, she wrote the following lines as a memorial on the death of a child:

> We have lost our little Hanner, in a very painful manner
> And we often asked, How can her harsh suffering be borne?
> When her death was first reported, her aunt got up and
>   snorted
> With the grief that she supported, for it made her forlorn.

A. H. Greenly noted that "her verse [was] like much of that period . . . morbid and mournful:

> The period in which she wrote most of her poetry has been referred to as the "dreadful decade," and she has been called its poet laureate. It was then that the [so-called] mortuary poets who extolled the pleasures of dying and death were most profuse. There developed a regular school of this type of poetry. Julia's main source of material [was] the death records of her locale. . . . She wrote her poems in great

seriousness, but . . . the poems that were supposed to produce sadness produced only laughter.[10]

Moore began reading her verse in the Grand Rapids area, earning as much as $50 a night. Ironically, she thought that her listeners came to be impressed, when, in fact, many came to laugh and sneer.

Her first volume of verse, *The Sentimental Song Book* (1876) contained this introductory remark, "Dear Friends: This little book is composed of truthful pieces. All those which speak of being killed, died, or drowned, are truthful songs; others are more 'truth than poetry.' "

This volume was followed by numerous later editions, many published by J. F. Ryder, a Cleveland, Ohio, art dealer. An 1878 edition carried this title, "The Sweet Singer of Michigan. Later poems of Julia A. Moore, together with reviews, commendations, notices, etc., etc., of the Sentimental Song Book."

Among the reviews were many that scorned or ridiculed her work and effort. If Mrs. Moore read these, she apparently misconstrued them. She did not seem to comprehend that people were not taking her seriously. Among those who ridiculed Moore was Bill Nye, a well-known humorist of the time. In his 1881 *Bill Nye and the Boomerang*, Nye said that Moore "took advantage of her poetic license . . . it should have been revoked."[11] Mark Twain, although seemingly supporting Moore, had a different purpose:

> I have been reading the poems of Mrs. Julia Moore again, and I find in them the same grace and melody that attracted me when they were first published twenty years ago, and have held me in happy bonds ever since. "The Sentimental Song Book" has long been out of print, and has been forgotten by the world in general, but not by me. I carry it with me always—it and Goldsmith's deathless story. Indeed, it has the same deep charm for me that *The Vicar of Wakefield* has, and I find in it the same subtle touch—the touch that makes an intentionally humorous episode pathetic, and an intentionally pathetic one funny. In her time, Mrs. Moore was called "The Sweet Singer of Michigan," and was best known by that name. I have read her book through twice today, with the purpose of determining which of her poems has most merit, and I am persuaded that for wide grasp and sustained power, "William Upson" may claim first place.[12]

Moore's verses have continued to draw ridicule. An article in the April 1962 *Esquire* labeled her "The World's Worst Poet." L. W. Michaelson in 1964 singled out Moore's one novel, *Sunshine and Shadow* (published in 1915, after her husband's death, because he had forbidden her to write any more) as "The Worst American Novel."[13]

Moore's reputation did not deter Benjamin Franklin King (1857–1894) from labeling himself "Ben King, the Sweet Singer of St. Joe." Somewhat of a child prodigy pianist as well as a "weaver of dreams," King first attracted public attention in 1893 with a concert in Chicago at the Michigan Building of the World's Columbian Exposition. He was introduced to the Chicago Press Club whose membership included several prominent authors, including Opie Read, author of the humorous and popular *On a Slow Train through Arkansas*.

Read invited King to accompany him on a tour through the South, reading his poems and playing the piano. But on April 7, 1894, King died suddenly. A bronze bust of heroic size marks his grave in a Saint Joseph cemetery.

Immediately after his death, The Chicago Press Club published his volume, *Ben King's Verse* (1894). It contained a two-page "Biography" by Read, and a three-page "Introduction" by John McGovern, a Chicago journalist and novelist. Read said: "Ben King was not only a man of music; he was a poet, a gentle satirist, and a humorist of the highest order. Every man was brightened by his coming, every man felt better for having heard his quaint remarks. There was about him a droll, a charming irresponsibility." McGovern said King was a "genius."

The book was reprinted several times. Its popularity is attested by the fact that in "a quarter of a century more copies of the book were sold than any other single volumes of verse."[14]

One of his poems was "The River St. Joe." Its several stanzas each conclude with couplets such as this:

Oh, give me the spot that I once used to know
By the side of the placid old River St. Joe.[15]

There was also "the immortal Dell Hair," in the early part of the twentieth century, "poet laureate of Shiawassee County," whose books included *Echoes from a Dell* (1921). Although his poetry was of the same poor quality as Julia Moore's, his ill-fame has not traveled as far.

The most popular and most prolific of this group was Will Carleton (1845–1912), Michigan's "poet of the people," the "Eddie Guest of the Seventies."

After graduation from Hillsdale College in 1869, Carleton became a reporter for a local newspaper. One day while covering a divorce case, a part of the testimony led him to write these lines:

Draw up the papers, lawyer, and make 'em good and stout;
For things at home are crossways, and Betsey and I are out.
We who have worked together so long as man and wife
Must pull in single harness for the rest of our natural life.

Never mind that the last line does not scan well—when Ohio's
Toledo Blade printed the story under the title "Betsey and I Are Out,"
it caught the attention of editors of countless newspapers. "It is safe
to say," said Earnest Elmo Calkins, "that these lines eventually became familiar to every literate [American]."[16]

S. S. Coant, editor of *Harper's Weekly*, a major literary periodical,
wrote to Carleton asking for more. The first poem, beginning, "Out
of the old house, Nancy—move up into the new" was based on the
move of the Carleton family from its log cabin home to a new house.
Then came "Over the Hill to the Poorhouse," Carleton's most successful effort in moving readers to tears.

In those years, every county had a poorhouse, a building where
its paupers and mentally unstable residents were confined until they
died. Like the old couple in the 1937 film, *Make Way for Tomorrow*, the
old mother in this poem is unwanted and is being discarded by her
successful children:

Over the hill to the poor-house—my child'rn dear, good-by!
Many a night I've watched you when only God was nigh;
And God'll judge between us; but I will al'ays pray
That you shall never suffer the half I do today.

In 1873, these three and other poems were published by Harper
and Brothers as *Farm Ballads*. The book, illustrated by Harper's best
artists, sold forty thousand copies at $2.00 and $2.50—at a time when
the standard price for a novel was $1.25.

In all, Carleton published some twenty volumes of verse,
among them *City Legends, City Festivals, City Ballads,* and *Farm Festivals.* He toured the United States, Canada, and England reading his
lines and moving his audiences alternately to tears and laughter.

On October 26, 1907, Carleton revisited his boyhood farm
home. Several trains brought visitors, including the entire faculty
and student body of Hillsdale College, to the site. Later, the Michigan state legislature ordered that Michigan schoolchildren should annually observe his birthday.[17]

Today, he is so little known that a recent historian said that he
was born in "western Michigan near the Wisconsin state line [!],"
and entered "Hillsdale College in Wisconsin."[18]

James Norman Hall, the Iowa-born coauthor of *Mutiny on the Bounty* and other books, said that in his hometown of Colfax, Iowa, in the late 1890s, Mrs. Sigafoos's small 'stationery and notions" store, in addition to volumes of poetry by Bryant, Whittier, Longfellow, and Lowell also carried Carleton's *Farm Ballads* and *Farm Legends.* He added:

> I am afraid that his ballads could not be ranked very high as po-
> etry, but they met with my deep approval in boyhood. They had in
> them the same distinctive flavor that one tastes in Edward Eggleston's
> *Roxy* and *The Hoosier Schoolmaster.* I could taste it then, without knowing
> that it was a flavor peculiar to certain inland sections of the [United
> States], and only for a period of two or three decades. Mark Twain pre-
> served it best for us, of course . . . but his humbler assistants, such
> as . . . Will Carleton should not be forgotten. They helped, and it's
> well they did; otherwise the knowledge of that special quality of Amer-
> ican life would be as lost to the world as the flavor of Mrs. Sigafoo's
> chocolate creams.[19]

In 1870, when she was seventeen, Rose Hartwick Thorpe, a Michigan girl, wrote on her slate the lines of "The Curfew Shall Not Ring Tonight." The poem tells of a girl who requested an English town sexton not to ring his nightly curfew bell because her lover, in prison, was scheduled to die when the bell sounded. Although she wrote enough subsequent verse to fill several volumes, none of it ever attracted the attention those few lines did.

Later Poets

Many poems are sooner or later collected in anthologies of one sort or another. An early anthology, *Michigan Poets and Poetry: With Portraits and Biographies*, was compiled in 1904 by Floyd D. Raze of Buffalo, North Dakota, and Warren W. Lamport of Leslie, Michigan. One contributor was Belle Sutfin Moore whose mother, Mrs. M. A. Sutfin, had published *Wayside Gleanings* in 1883. Another was Leila M. Rowan who in 1902 had published a volume, *Trailing Arbutus.* The last poem in that volume, "Me-Noh-Nah, the Chief's Grand-daughter" was obviously inspired by Longfellow's *Song of Hiawatha.*

Eight of the sixteen poets were born in Michigan, but the only two familiar names are those of Carleton and King. The volume's themes are nature and natural objects, death, religion, and rural events. None of the poems deal with city life.

In 1904, Edgar A[lbert] Guest (1881–1959), an English-born ex-change editor for the *Detroit Free Press*, began publishing verse under several pseudonyms in a weekly column, "Chaff," later "Breakfast Table Chat." Still later, responding to popular interest, his poems began appearing daily on the editorial page of the newspaper. Soon they were being syndicated nationally to some three hundred newspapers, and published in book form. In the early part of this century, Guest became one of the country's most popular authors, with more than twenty-five volumes, but he set only one of his verses in Michigan:

> There is no star within the flag
> That's brighter than its brothers,
> And when of Michigan I brag,
> I'm boastin' of the others.
> Just which is which no man can say—
> One star for every state
> Gleams brightly on our flag today,
> And every one is great.

Poetry critics were not happy with Guest's successes. Dorothy Parker, one of the Algonquin Wits, wrote this doggerel verse:

> I'd rather flunk my Wassermann test
> Than read a poem by Edgar Guest.

Guest was a member of the Michigan Authors' Association. Its members in 1918–1919 were mostly newspaper people. Chase Salmon Osborn and Frederick Isham Stewart were among the members. Stewart had been a *Detroit Free Press* reporter, but by 1916 he was nationally famous as the writer of the Broadway play, *Nothing But the Truth*. Its president then was Winfield Lionel Scott.[20] In 1923, its president was Frederic Zeigen, author of three volumes of verse, including *Stardust and Dandelions* (1923), with an introduction by James Oliver Curwood.

Guest, himself, never pretended to be a poet (by an older definition of the term). He said he was merely "a newspaper man who wrote verses." He was a great-uncle of Judith Guest, the contemporary Michigan novelist.[21]

Through the years, there have been other collections of verse that can be labeled poetry of place—that is, verse that refers to specific geographical locations or historical incidents. An early volume was James V. Campbell's *A Legend of L'Anse Creuse*, which refers to the Lake Saint Clair area.[22]

In his 1843 *Alhalla; or, the Lord of Tallega*, Henry Rowe Schoolcraft included this tribute to Michigan's famed whitefish:

All friends of good living by tureen and dish,
Concur in exalting this prince of a fish;
So fine in a platter, so tempting a fry,
So rich on a gridiron, so sweet in a pie;
That even before it the salmon must fail,
And that mighty boone-bouche of the landbeaver's tail.[23]

Other collections are Mary Jane (Wilson) Chamberlin's *Life Thoughts* (1893) with "eulogistic poems" on "lovely Charlevoix" and "beautiful Petoskey"; Dr. Charles Forest Whiteshield's *Cloverland Echoes* (1923), and *Poems of the Northland* (1936); Reverend Joseph Dutton's *Poems of the Upper Peninsula and Songs of the Soo* (1924); Will Prentice's *Songs of the Southland and Other Poems* (1927)—it contains the poem "Michigan"; Dr. William C(harles) S(mithson) Pellowe's *Mirrors of Michigan, a Book of Verse* (1932); Elizabeth Peck's *Frontier Verse* (1938–1939); Flora Slayton Reichle's *Rimes from the Great Lakes*, (1943); F. X. Clifford's *The Beautiful in Time* (1944) [Copper Country settings]; James H. Varty's *In Once across His Town* (1957); Patrick O'Callaghan's *North of Menominee* (1958) [pioneer logging days]; Judith Minty's *Lake Songs and Other Fears* (1973); William Thomas Butler's *Homespun Poetry* (1977); and Peter Thomas's *Poems of Upper Michigan* (1974).

In 1957, Stellanova Osborn's *Beside the Cabin* offered forty-one verses as an "In Memoriam" to her life with Chase Osborn. The first fourteen poems relate to the cabin on Duck Island in the Saint Marys River (an island Osborn owned) where the Osborns spent much of their time and entertained their friends. A second section focuses on Governor Osborn's death.

Lew Sarett's *Many, Many Moons* (1920), *The Box of God* (1922), *Slow Smoke* (1925), and *Wings against the Moon* (1931) contains verses based on his boyhood in Michigan and his sixteen years of service as woodsman, guide, friend to the Indians (he became an adopted member of one tribe) and U.S. forest ranger. Here is one stanza from "Indian Sleep-Song":

Zhoo . . . zhoo, zhoo!
My little brown chief,
The bough of the willow
Is rocking the leaf;
The sleepy wind cries

To you, close your eyes,—
O little brown chief,
Zhoo . . . zhoo, zhoo.

In 1927, the Battle Creek Scribblers Club published *Battle Creek Writers, Poems and Prose*. In the 1930s, Henry Harrison, a New Yorker, published several state anthologies that reflected the interest in regional literature at that time. *Michigan Poets: An Anthology* (1936) contains poems by thirty-six poets (one for each year of the century) and an introduction by Clarence P. Milligan, one of the thirty-six. Milligan said that although "Michigan [is] often referred to as an industrial state,"its educational institutions and its topography offered a "good place for the development and encouragement of the poetic genius." Among the contributors to *Michigan Poets* were Elizabeth Harriet Allen, a Hopwood Award winner in 1932–1933 and 1935–1936, and David Cornel DeJong, who had already published verse in *Poetry*.

In 1940, *New Michigan Verse*, edited by Carl E. Burklund, included poems representing what Burklund considered "the best expression of Michigan talent" in the poetry of that time.[24] In 1960, there were *The Golden Year*, Rachel M. Hilbert's *Michigan Poets*, and a revised edition of *Michigan Poets*, edited by Margaret Elliott. In 1964, there was *Michigan Poets, 1964*, the latter published by the Michigan Association of School Librarians. *Michigan Voices*, a literary quarterly, was published in Saginaw from the summer of 1960 to 1964.

Philip Levine (1928–), one of Michigan's finest poets, was born in Detroit and earned B.A. and M.A. degrees at Wayne State University. He took an M.F.A. degree at the famed University of Iowa Writers' Workshop. Since then he has been a teacher and poet-in-residence at several universities. In his score of volumes and in individually published verse, he has time and again used his Michigan years as the subject of his verses. In 1970, his *5 Detroits* "show[ed] the city reflected in a pool of dirty oil . . . It is angry, controlled and bitter; it is the poet answering the cops and the injustice of it all. [Nevertheless i]t is damn good poetry."[25]

His *Selected Poems* (1984) contains almost two dozen of his Detroit verses selected from ten of his volumes. Here is an excerpt from "You Can Have It":

In 1948 in the city of Detroit, founded
by de la Mothe Cadillac for the distant purposes
of Henry Ford, no one wakened or died,
no one walked in the streets or stoked a furnace,

for there was no such year, and now
that year has fallen off the old newspapers,
calendars, doctors' appointments, bonds,
wedding certificates, drivers' licenses.

The first three lines echo Marge Piercy's *The High Cost of Living* published in 1978: "In grade school we studied all that. Founded by Antoine de la Mothe Cadillac in seventeen-whatever, But you know it's a lie. Henry Ford founded Detroit in the twenties and everything before that is invented" (p. 11).

In 1965, an ambitious volume, *An Anthology of Verse about Michigan's UP,* featured verse about the area written by its people and compiled by two Escanaba teachers, Margaret Gilbert and William J. Finlan. Its authors were lumbermen, farmers, miners, doctors, lawyers, housewives, teachers, and others with "deep roots" in the Upper Peninsula, among them Clarence P. Milligan, Stellanova Osborn, Alice Behrend (Jolie Paylin), Jingo Viitala Vachon, William J. Finlan, and Dr. Charles Forest Whiteshield. Thomas H. Smith has described "Michigan Upper Peninsula Literary Traditions," with particular reference to the verse of T. Kilgore Splake.[26]

In 1968, an Arkansas publisher issued *TEN,* with poems by five black and five white Detroit poets, including Dudley Randall, Oliver LaGrone, Naomi Long Madgett, and Louis J. Cantoni.

In 1969, Albert Drake edited *Michigan Signatures,* which included verse by Dan Gerber, Jim Harrison, Conrad Hilberry, Joyce Carol Oates, Tom Snapp, Radcliff Squires, Linda Wagner of Michigan State University, and John Woods.

Woods was the author of *Turning to Look Back: Poems, 1955–1970* (1972). The volume contained nineteen previously uncollected poems and about seventy reprinted from four earlier volumes.

In 1972, there was *10 Michigan Poets,* edited by L. Eric Greinke, a poet in his own right. Perhaps the best known were Professor Albert Drake and his wife, Barbara. Of the other eight, young Herbert Woodward Martin was to become a distinguished black poet.

Greinke commented that the poems were not necessarily about Michigan although they could have been. However, some poems, such as "Michigan" by John Knapp II, have a Peninsula State flavor:

Leaning into the air
All grip tight to their roots,
Winter comes and puffs out his cheeks against the
Amber reeds.

November, and then
December shaking away the
Orchard from the last plum.
Redmen in
Dinghies have gleaned rice from the lake,
Everywhere whitemen roll collars up against their necks,
     their rifles
Reeking of fresh oil.

Greinke was also the author of *The Broken Lock: New and Selected Poems* (1976).

In 1972, the first issue of *Michigan Hot Apples* appeared with a note indicating that it would be "an annual anthology." It was edited by novelist Jay McCormick, who at the time was teaching at Wayne State University, writing book reviews for the *Detroit News*, and was a member of the board of trustees of the Cranbrook Writers' Guild. Of the forty-odd poets represented in the collection, some are well known today: Joyce Carol Oates, L. Eric Greinke, Albert Drake, Stephen Tudor, Stephen Leggett, Linda Wagner, Barbara Drake, and Conrad Hilberry.

In 1976, Wayne State University Press published *The Third Coast: Contemporary Michigan Poetry* compiled by Conrad Hilberry, Herbert Scott, and James Tipton. Tipton and Robert E. Wegner edited *The Third Coast: Contemporary Michigan Fiction*, a collection of stories by seventeen writers (1982). It was followed in 1988 by *Contemporary Michigan Poetry: Poems from the Third Coast*, edited by Michael Delp, Conrad Hilberry, and Herbert Scott.

Louis J. Cantoni published *Gradually the Dreams Change* in 1980. In 1986, Gerald L. Hall and Jeremy W. Kilar edited *Poems* for the bicentennial of the signing of the U.S. Constitution in 1987.

The Poetry Society of Michigan was formed in 1935 with Carl Edwin Burklund as its president. One of the four editors of the society's quarterly publication, *Peninsula Poets* (begun in 1950), was Joseph Cherwinski (1915–) who served from 1953 to 1975 and who published a half-dozen volumes of his verse. In 1985, the society's golden anniversary, there were some three hundred members. One of Cherwinski's poems was printed in the "official" Michigan highway map in 1972.

In 1945, the group published an anthology, *Convergence*, with Herbert L. Carson as editor. *Golden Song* (1985), its fiftieth anniversary anthology, was assembled and edited by Professor Louis J. Cantoni and Dudley Randall. The first poem in the anthology was David B. Steinman's "Song of the Bridge." Another Steinman poem, also referring to the Straits of Mackinac Bridge, was "Blueprint."

In the 1960s, several poetry magazines were being published in Michigan, among them, *Zeitgeist, Voices,* and *Bardic Echoes*. In August of 1962, the *Michigan Alumnus Quarterly Review,* which had occasionally published short fiction, verse, and reviews of books by University of Michigan alumni and alumnae, ceased publication. It was succeeded by the *Michigan Quarterly Review,* a literary journal, successively edited by Frank E. Robbins, Sheridan Baker, Radcliffe Squires, and, from the Spring 1977 issue to the present, by Laurence Goldstein.

Annually from 1983, the Society for the Study of Midwestern Literature published *Midwest Poetry Festival,* poems read by poets at the festivals held at East Lansing in conjunction with annual meetings of the society.

Black Michigan Poets

James David Corrothers (1869–1917), a black living in Cass County, wrote "To Be a Negro in a Day like This" and other poems that appeared in *Century* and other magazines. Corrothers was also the editor of *The Black Cat Club: Negro Humor and Folklore* (1902). His *In Spite of the Handicap: An Autobiography* was published in 1916.

A Dream and Other Poems by Charles Henry Shoeman of Ann Arbor was published by G. Wahr of Ann Arbor in 1899.

In 1973, Hoyt Fuller, a founding member of the Organization of Black American Culture, said, "[there is a] great black passion for language, the endless molding of it, playing with it, stretching and contracting it, altering it, investing it with fresh sounds and new meanings, using it even sometimes as a shield against overpowering emotion, as a substitute for fury."[27]

The best of the Michigan black poets to date is Robert Hayden (1913–1980) who was educated at Detroit City College (now Wayne State University) and at the University of Michigan where he won the Hopwood Award for poetry in 1938 and again in 1940–1941, and where he later taught. Dorothy H. Lee says that Hayden wrote numerous poems about his growing up in Paradise Valley, then a Detroit slum area.[28]

Dudley Randall was educated in the Detroit's public schools, at Wayne State University, and at the University of Michigan where he took a master's degree in library science. Later, he was both a poet in residence and a reference librarian at the University of Detroit. He became a widely published poet. Among his books are *Cities Burning* (1968), *Poem Counterpoem* (1969)—with Margaret Danner—and *More to Remember, Poems of Four Decades* (1971). However, not all of these poems are poems of place. In *Poem, Counterpoem*, five ("Belle Isle," by Randall, "Bell Isle" by Danner, and "George" by Randall—the last set in a Detroit foundry, "Vacant Lot," and "Ghetto Girls") are set in Detroit; "Winter Campus" and "Ann Arbor" are set in the latter place. His work has also appeared in many collections of poems by black poets.

More important, Randall became a publisher of black poets, both from Michigan and elsewhere, some of whom—like Robert Hayden, Langston Hughes, Jean Toomer, LeRoi Jones, and Gwendolyn Brooks—had established reputations whereas others were having difficulty in finding white publishers to accept their work.

In 1965, he began his Broadside Press in Detroit, publishing broadsides, single sheets, or loosely bound materials. By 1990 the press had published over ninety of these as well as "Broadside Annuals," and also recordings and tapes of black poets reading their own works. Two of these titles are *Broadside Poetry: A Supplement to Anthologies Which Excluded Black Poets* (1969) and *Broadside Memories: Poets I Have Known* (1975).

Publishers Weekly called Randall "a leading Black poet and *the* leading publisher of Black verse in the United States."[29] Leaonhead Pack Bailey's 1974 *Broadside Authors and Artists* identifies many of those Broadside has published, including a number who lived in Michigan: Richard Walter Thomas; William A. Thigpen, Jr.; Harun Kofi and Malaika Ayo Wangara; Cledie Taylor; Hattie R. Steed; Lawrence C. Riley; Robert L. Robinson; Sarah C. Reese; Helen Pulliam; Frenchy Jolene Hodges; Al Ward; Carolyn Thompson; James W. Thompson; and Clarence LaGrone. Other poets published by Randall include Kofi Natambu, who edited a quarterly, *Solid Ground: A New World Journal*, and an anthology, *Nostalgia for the Present*; Aneb Kgositile (born Gloria House), author of *Blood River: Poems 1964–1983*; Baraka Sele (born Pamela Cobb), author of *Inside the Devil's Mouth*; Sarah C. Reese, author of *Songs of Freedom*; Jill W. Boyer (Randall's daughter); and Naomi Long Madgett whose Lotus Press also published verse. Stella L. Crews published black poets through her Thorne Press.

Dorothy Lee has identified other significant Detroit black poets, such as Leisia Duskin, author of *Lights Out in Ten* and Paulette C. White, author of *Watermelon Dress* (1984). The latter's short story, "The Bird Cage," was published in an anthology of short stories by living black women, which was edited by former University of Detroit Professor Mary Helen Washington.[30]

Hayden, Randall, and Madgett are the most significant black Detroit poets. Madgett's books include *Songs to a Phantom Nightingale* (1941), under the pseudonym Naomi Cornelia Long; *One and the Many* (1956); *Star by Star* (1966); *Pink Ladies in the Afternoon* (1972); and *Exits and Entrances* (1978).

Dorothy H. Lee says that such verse, particularly as it applies to Detroit, "is often, like all Afro-American literature, a blues . . . [a] narrative that convert[s] pain into beauty by shaping it into art. . . . Blues is the wail of the forsaken, the cry of frustrated, the laughter of the fatalist. It's the agony of indecision, the despair of the jobless, the anguish of the bereaved, and the dry wit of the cynic."[31]

Upper Peninsula Literary Periodicals

A number of literary periodicals have been published in the Upper Peninsula. Patrick O'Neill published the *Lake Superior Review* in Ironwood, attracting writers from both Michigan and Minnesota. Suzanne Stephens of Michigan Technological University published *Tailings*, a title no doubt inspired by the slag heaps marking former mines in the Copper Country. Michael Felton published the *Chunga Review* in Felch, a community so small it had no post office. Shirley Pratt published *The Upper Peninsula Today* in Munising in the 1970s. For seventeen years (1970–1987) *The Woodsrunner* was published at Lake Superior State College with William Rabe and Peter Thomas in charge.

More recently Elinor Benedict has published *Passages North* at Escanaba. *Above the Bridge* was published at Gwinn by Patrice Oliver Cross, then taken over by Jacqueline Miller and Judith Hendrickson of nearby Marquette. Gary Silver of Iron Mountain edits *The Big Two-Hearted* for the Mid-Peninsula Library Co-operative.

The Upper Peninsula of Michigan Writers Association is now past its thirtieth year. It conducts an annual writers' conference each fall as well as other meetings related to the interests of writers and would-be writers.

Hopwood Award Winners for Poetry

Since the Avery Hopwood Awards were instituted at "the Athens of the Midwest," hundreds of University of Michigan students, both undergraduates and graduates, have won awards for fiction, drama, the essay, and poetry.

Among those who have won poetry awards, these names attract attention: Elizabeth Harriet Allen, 1932–1933, 1935–1936; Baxter Hathaway, 1935–1936; John Malcolm Brinning, 1937–1938, 1938–1939, 1939–1940; John Ciardi, 1938–1939; Augusta Walker, 1941–1942; Rosamond Haas, 1942–1943; Bernice Slote, 1944, 1945; Sidney Corman, 1946–1947; Linda Parker (-Silverman), 1971–1972; James B. Allen, 1972–1973; Gary Kolar, 1977–1978.

Other Michigan Poetry

Asa H. Stoddard, *Poems Read at the Spiritualist Convention* (1878); *Miscellaneous Poems* (1880). Kalamazoo County.

Francis D. Lacy, *Star Lake Romance: A Modern Poem of Love and Rivalry* (1883). Lake County.

Lyman F. Stowe, *Poetical Drifts of Thought* (1884); *My Wife Nellie and I* (1895).

Joseph Bert Smiley, *A Basket of Chips* (1888).

Frederick H. De Peu, *Poems* (1889). Branch County and the Civil War.

Frank Hodgman. *The Wandering Singer and His Songs, and Other Poems* (1898). Climax, Michigan, in part.

J. W. Bryce, *Random Rhymes* (1899). Calhoun County, in part.

George Edward Lewis, *Heart Echoes* (1899). Grand Rapids, Mackinac, Traverse Bay.

Emmaline Smith Bailey, *Crusts and Crumbs* (1899). Coldwater, Michigan.

Charles E. Musser, *Poems* (1900).

Will J. Massingham, *Lake Superior, and Other Poems* (1904); *Old and New Poems* (1924?); *Poems of Life and Love* (1924?).

Robert Kroodsma, *Poems: Something for Everybody* (1913). Ottawa County.

Swift Lathers, *The Yearning Years* (1921). Mears area.

Headley Frazier, *Poems* (1927). In part, set in Ada, Michigan.

Earl E. Newton, *Tuneful Tales of Camps and Trails* (1927). Set in the northern Lower Peninsula.

E[lias] [M]errill Averill, *The Trail of Thirty-Seven, with By-paths in History, Beauty and Philosophy* (1934). Michigan Highway M-37 and the various towns along it.

Gwen Frostic, *My Michigan* (1957), and other volumes.

J(ames) Fred(erick) Lawton, *Roses That Bloomed in the Snow* . . . (1959). University of Michigan. Lawton was also the author of *"Hurry Up" Yost in Song and Story* (1947), about Fielding H. Yost, the famed Michigan football coach.

Faith M. Johnston, *Through the Arch of Experience* (1970). Sugar Island and Leelanau.

Jack Meriwether, *Songs of a Detroiter* (1975).

EPILOGUE

A popular song that helped release the tensions and fears of the early World War II days was "I've Got a Gal in Kalamazoo-zoo-zoo," written by Harry Warren in 1942 with music by Mack Gordon—it was featured in the film *The Glenn Miller Story* (1954).

In 1948, the motion picture *Easter Parade* featured Judy Garland, supposedly entertaining in a New York City nightclub, plaintively singing this verse by that eminent non-Michiganian, Irving Berlin:

I was born in Michigan;
And I wish and wish again
That I was back in the town where I was born.
There's a farm in Michigan;
And I'd like to fish again
In the river that flows beside the field of waving corn.
A lonesome soul am I—
I want to go there, I want to go there,
I want to go back to the farm,
Far away from harm,

With a milk pail on my arm.
I miss the rooster—
The one that used "ter"
Wake me up at four a.m.
(I see your great big city—Very pretty)
Nevertheless, I want to be there, I want to see there
A certain someone full of charm;
That's why I wish again
That I was in Michigan
Down on the farm.

It may not scan as printed, but Miss Garland made it seem just fine.

NOTES

Preface

1. Francis X. Scannell, "The Novelist and Michigan," *Detroit Historical Society Bulletin* 21 (1964), 5.

I. Michigan in Literature

1. Edna Ferber, *Come and Get It* (1935), 3.
2. Marge Piercy, *Parti-colored Blocks for a Quilt* (1982), 162.
3. Kathleen I. Gillard, *Our Michigan Heritage* (1955), 1.
4. Alice Laurine Pearson, *The Upper Peninsula of Michigan in Literature*, M.A. thesis, Univ. of Colorado (1939).
5. Alice Laurine Pearson, "The Upper Peninsula in Fictional Literature," *Michigan History Magazine* 24 (Summer 1940), 329–38.
6. Warren W. Lamport and Floyd D. Raze, *Michigan Poets and Poetry: With Portraits and Biographies* (1904).
7. Arnold D. Mulder, "Authors and Wolverines: The Books and Writers of Michigan," *Saturday Review of Literature* 19, no. 9 (March 4, 1939), 4.
8. Constance Rourke, "Ballads of Songs of Southern Michigan," *New York Herald-Tribune Books* (September 24, 1939), 8.

9. Arnold Mulder, "Michigan's Writing Men," *Michigan History* 35, no. 3 (September 1951), 257–69.

10. Arnold Mulder, "Michigan as a Field for the Novelist," *Michigan History Magazine* 6, no. 1 (1922), 142–55.

11. Lawrence H. Conrad, "Michigan as a Literary Opportunity," *Michigan Library Bulletin* (July 1927), 211–14.

12. Hal H. Smith, *A Detroit Literature* (1953).

13. Arno L. Bader, "Avery Hopwood, Dramatist," *Michigan Alumnus Quarterly Review* 61, no. 21 (Summer 1955), 68.

14. Francis X. Scannell, "The Novelist and Michigan," *Detroit History Society* 21 (1964), 9.

II. Indians, French, and British

1. Allan W. Eckert, *The Conquerers* (1970), 152.

2. Willis F. Dunbar, *Michigan: A History of the Wolverine State* (1973), 35.

3. Ibid., 88–93.

4. "Book Notes," *Michigan History* 50, no. 4 (December 1965), 382.

5. John W[illiam] Tebbel, *Fact and Fiction: Problems of the Historical Novelist* (1962), iii.

6. Thomas L. Kilpatrick and Patsy-Rose Hoshiko, *Illinois! Illinois!* (1979), 105.

7. John T[heodore] Flanagan, "The Middle Western Historical Novel," *Illinois State Historical Society Journal* 37, no. 1 (March 1944), 10–11.

8. G. Harrison Orrians, "Cannon through the Forest," *Ohio History* 71–72, no. 3 (July 1963), 208.

9. Arnold Mulder, "Detroit's First Decade," *Saturday Review of Literature* 20, no. 26 (October 14, 1939), 20.

10. Arthur Pound, "I Was Born in Paradise," *Michigan Alumnus Quarterly Review* 63, no. 18 (May 25, 1957), 197–207.

11. See, for example, "Research and Romance," *Time* 31 (May 23, 1938), 61.

12. See Dunbar, *Michigan: A History of the Wolverine State*, 98, for use of the phrase *Pontiac uprising* and its context.

13. Ibid., 98.

14. Ibid., 115; Howard Peckham, *Pontiac and the Indian Uprising* (1947), 63–67.

15. Dunbar, *Michigan: A History of the Wolverine State*, 122.

16. Robert E. Morsberger, "The Tragedy of *Ponteach* and the Northwest Passage," *Old Northwest* 4, no. 3 (September 1978), 241–57.

17. Kenneth Roberts, *Northwest Passage* (1937) 427, 437–39.

18. Ibid., 438.

19. Flanagan, "The Middle Western Historical Novel," *Illinois State Historical Society Journal* 37, no. 1 (March 1944), 12.

20. Ibid.

21. Peckham, *Pontiac and the Indian Uprising* (1947), 319. Peckham discusses other reports, none of which place Pontiac's death at Detroit in 1763.

22. Edith R. Mosher and Nella Dietrich Williams, *From Indian Legends to the Modern BookShelf: An Anthology of Prose and Verse by Michigan Authors. Prepared Especially for the Youth of the State* (1931), 226.

23. Margaret M. Clark and Judith E. Stromdahl, "Difference of Opinion," review of *War Belts of Pontiac* by William H. Bunce, *Library Journal* 68, no. 6 (March 15, 1943), 251.

24. Rachel M. Hilbert and (Richard H.) Dirk Gringhuis, *Michigan Authors* (1961), 27.

25. Orrians, "Cannon through the Forest," *Ohio History* 72, no. 3 (July 1963), 195.
26. Henry Bedford-Jones, "The Fiction Field of Michigan History," *Michigan History Magazine* 12, no. 44 (July 1928), 451.
27. Lennox Bouton Grey, *Chicago and the Great American Novel: A Critical Approach to the American Epic*, Ph.D. diss., Univ. of Chicago (1935), 103.
28. Hilbert, *Michigan Authors* (1961), 2.
29. Orrians, "Cannon through the Forest," *Ohio History* 72, no. 3 (July 1963), 210.
30. Stella Hargrave, review of *Who Fought and Bled* by Ralph Beebe, *New York Herald-Tribune Books* (May 4, 1941), 10.
31. D. De K., "The War of 1812," *New York Times Book Review* (June 15, 1941), 16.
32. Lawrence R. Dawson, "Captain Henry Whiting: A Poet in Michigan Territory," *Mid-America* 10 (1983), 24–37.
33. Ibid., 34.
34. *National Union Catalog* (listing of pre-1956 books), 96:445, col. 2; and Alice Kahler Marshall, *Pen Names of Women Writers of America* (1985), 58, 112.
35. "Some Michigan Books," review of *Ojibway Drums* by Marion Austin (Waite) Magoon, *Michigan Alumnus Quarterly Review* 63, no. 10 (December 8, 1956), 82.
36. A. O'B. M., review of *Ojibway Drums* by Marion Austin (Waite) Magoon, *Saturday Review of Literature* 38 (August 20, 1955), 29.
37. Flavius Littlejohn, *Legends of Michigan and the Old Northwest* (1875), 5.
38. Carl (Ed) Burklund, "An Early Michigan Poet," *Michigan History* 31, no. 2 (June 1947), 194.
39. Sister Grace McDonald, review of *By Cross and by Anchor* by James K. Jamison, *Michigan History* 30, no. 4 (October–December 1946), 783.
40. Chase Osborn and Stellanova Osborn, *Schoolcraft—Longfellow—Hiawatha* (1942), 76.
41. Ibid., 408.
42. Dawson, "Captain Henry Whiting: A Poet in Michigan Territory," *Mid-America* 10 (1983), 32.
43. John Chamberlain, "A Chronicle of the Old Northwest," review of *The Invasion* by Janet Lewis, *New York Times Book Review* (September 25, 1932), sec. 7, p. 7.
44. Ibid., 7.
45. In the poem, "Nadawatha's" birthplace was "the vale of Tawasentha." Schoolcraft was born in the Tawasentha River valley.
46. Henry A. Pochmann, "Henry Wadsworth Longfellow," *Masters of American Literature* 1, no. 1 (1949), 626.
47. "Burton, Frederick Russell." *Dictionary of American Biography* 2, 342.
48. Ibid.
49. Richard Mercer Dorson, "The Centennial of Longfellow's *The Song of Hiawatha*," *Michigan History* 39, no. 4 (December 1955), 461.
50. Stith Thompson, "The Indian Legend of Hiawatha," *Publications of the Modern Language Association of America* 37, no. 1 (March 1922), 139.
51. Kathleen I. Gillard, *Our Michigan Heritage* (1955), 31.
52. Chase Osborn and Stellanova Osborn, *Schoolcraft—Longfellow—Hiawatha* (1942), 15.
53. Henry Seidel Canby, "Lo, the Poor Indian," review of *Joe Pete* by Florence McClinchey, *Saturday Review of Literature* 6, no. 19 (November 30, 1929), 472.
54. *"Joe Pete" New York Times Book Review* (December 1, 1929), 9.
55. James MacBride, "Rural Guignol," review of *Indian Paul* by John Moore, *New York Times Book Review* (September 16, 1945), 36.
56. Walter Hammond, "A Near Lynching," review of *Indian Paul* by John Moore, *Saturday Review of Literature* 28, no. 41 (October 13, 1945), 87.

57. Arno L. Baird, "*Indian Paul*," review of *Indian Paul* by John Moore, *Michigan Quarterly Alumnus Review* 52, no. 13 (February 2, 1946), 190.

58. Richard Mercer Dorson, "Folklore and Fakelore," *American Mercury*, 70, no. 315 (1950), 335–43. For a more complete discussion of these two terms see Dorson's *Folklore and Fakelore* (1976).

59. "Lew Sarett." *Michigan Authors* (1980), 272.

60. Mary E. Hazeltine, *Authors of Today and Yesterday* (1937), 54.

61. Leo Shapiro, "Lew Sarett and Nature," *Poetry: A Magazine of Verse* 59 (December 1954), 154. Beach's volume is *The Concept of Nature in Nineteenth-Century English Poetry* (1963).

62. Alice Laurine Pearson, *The Upper Peninsula of Michigan in Literature* (1939), 16–18.

III. Settlers Come to Michigan

1. *Detroit Post and Tribune* (February 13, 1881). Cited in *Michigan Pioneer and Historical Collections* 3 (1881), 265, which prints the whole song and similar items.

2. Dorothy Dondore, *The Prairie and the Making of Middle America: Four Centuries of Description* (1926), 221.

3. G. Harrison Orrians, "Cannon through the Forest," *Ohio History* 71, 72, no. 3 (1962–1963), 205.

4. Lawrence R. Dawson, Jr., "James Fenimore Cooper and Michigan: His Novel, Visits, and Attitudes," *Michigan History* 59 (1975) 275–92; Kate Russell Oakley, "James Fenimore Cooper and *Oak Openings*," *Michigan History* 15, 16 (Summer 1931–1932), 309–20.

5. Larry B. Massie, ed., *From Frontier Folk to Factory Smoke* (1987), 17–18.

6. Albert G. Black, *Michigan Novels: An Annotated Bibliography,* (1963), 13.

7. "French Canadians," *New York Times Book Review* (September 2, 1928), sec. 4, p. 16.

8. Willis F. Dunbar, *Michigan: A History of the Wolverine State* (1973), 314–16.

9. Harry R. Warfel, "Helen Topping Miller," *American Novelists of Today* (1951), 202.

10. Michigan Department of Education, *Michigan in Books* (September 1968), 8.

11. Edgar Allan Poe, "Caroline Kirkland," in *The New Literati, Works* 5 (1903), 124.

12. William S. Osborne, *Caroline M. Kirkland* (1972), 81.

13. Caroline Kirkland, *Forest Life* 1 (1842), 5.

14. See, for example, Kirkland's discussion of a Michigan mud-hole in Chapter 1, "Journey into the Interior—Via Mud Holes," in *A New Home; or, Life in the Clearings* (1953), 21–22.

15. Ibid., 18.

16. Larry B. Massie, "Michigan Authors and Their Novels 1832–1941," in *Literary Michigan: A Sense of Place, a Sense of Time*, Michigan Council for the Humanities (1988), 2.

17. William Allen White, in the *Emporia Gazette*, quoted in *Michigan History Magazine* 11, 12 (July 1927–1928), 509.

18. "Elizabeth Howard" in *Current Biography 1951*, 282.

19. Ibid.

20. Society for the Study of Midwestern Literature, *Midwestern Miscellany* 1, 17.

21. May Lambertson Becker, "Books for Young People," *New York Herald Tribune Books* 17, no. 36 (May 4, 1941), 7.

22. "Among the Books," review of *Delecta Ann: The Circuit Rider's Daughter* by Myna Lockwood, *Michigan History* 25 (1940–1941), 257–58.

23. Paul Leicester Ford, "The American Historical Novel," *Atlantic Monthly* 80, no. 482 (December 1897), 721–28.
24. John T[heodore] Flanagan, "The Middle Western Historical Novel," *Illinois State Historical Society Journal* 37 (1944), 10.
25. Bernard DeVoto, "Fiction and the Everlasting *If*," *Harper's Magazine* 177 (June 1938), 42.

IV. Diversity in the Peninsula State

1. Willis F. Dunbar, *Michigan: A History of the Wolverine State* (1973), 351.
2. Richard A. Cordell, review of *Free as the Wind* by Dascomb Atwood, *Saturday Review of Literature* 25 (March 28, 1942), 14.
3. Review of *The Dominie of Harlem* by Arnold Mulder, *The Nation* 97, no. 2524 (November 13, 1913), 460.
4. Alvah C. Bessie, "In Pursuit of a Mirage," review of *Belly Fulla Straw* by David Cornel DeJong, *Saturday Review of Literature* 10, no. 589 (March 31, 1934), 4.
5. Roy W. Meyer, *The Middle Western Farm Novel in the Twentieth Century* (1965), 208.
6. Richard Cordell, "Family of Frustration," review of *Light Sons and Dark* by David Cornel DeJong, *Saturday Review of Literature* 22, no. 33 (December 21, 1940), 15.
7. Edward J. Fitzgerald, "Into a New World," review of *Two Sofas in the Parlor* by David Cornel DeJong, *Saturday Review of Literature* 35, no. 8 (February 23, 1952), 15.
8. David Cornel DeJong, quoted by Harry R. Warfel in *American Novelists of Today* (1951), 116.
9. Alice Beal Parsons, "A Boy's Long Days," review of *Day of Fortune* by Norman Matson, *The Nation* 127, no. 3296 (September 5, 1928), 230.
10. Carl Wittke, "Melting-Pot Literature," review of *Latchstring Out* by Skulda Baner, *College English* 7, no. 4 (January 1946), 192.
11. Reviews of *Here Is My Home* by Robert Gessner: Marianne Hauser, "Hardwood Town," *New York Times Book Review* (November 9, 1941), 20; Milton Hindus, *New York Herald-Tribune Books* (November 16, 1941), 10.
12. Rupert Brooke, quoted by Edith R. Mosher and Nella Dietrich Williams in *From Indian Legends to the Modern Bookshelf: An Anthology of Prose and Verse by Michigan Authors. Prepared Especially for the Youth of the State* (1931), 343.
13. Reviews of *God Head* by Leonard Cline: *Saturday Review of Literature* (November 28, 1925), 147; J(ohn) T(owner) F(rederick), *Midland* 12, no. 2 (1926), 75; Ruth Goodman, "A Self-Made God," *New York Herald-Tribune Books* (November 1, 1925), 11; C. T., "Fiction Notes," *New Republic* 12 no. 576 (December 9, 1925), 93; "A Nietzschean 'Wabbly'," *New York Times Book Review* (December 20, 1925), sec. 4, p. 16.
14. Reviews of *Zip: A Novel of the Left and the Right* by Max Apple: Robert Mauer, "Books in Brief," *Saturday Review* 5, no. 21 (July 22, 1978), 49; *Book list* 74, no. 18 (May 15, 1978), 1473; Dean W. Given, *Best Sellers* 38 (November 1978) 235; *New York Times Book Review* (July 16, 1978), sec. 7, p. 8.
15. Suzann Sherman, "Humorist Spins Tales from Life in Copper Country," *Detroit News* (May 22, 1988), sec. M, p. 1.
16. Aili Kolehmainen Johnson, "Finnish Labor Songs from Northern Michigan," *Michigan History* 31 (1947), 331–43.
17. Ibid., 341.
18. Laurence Goldstein, "The Image of Detroit in Twentieth Century Literature," *Michigan Quarterly Review* 25, no. 2 (Spring 1986), 286.

19. Robert A. Bone, *The Negro Novel in America* (1958), 32.
20. Martin Levin, "Readers' Report," review of *Snakes: A Novel* by Al Young, *New York Times Book Review* (May 17, 1970), 38.
21. Josephine Hendin, review of *Snakes: A Novel* by Al Young, *Saturday Review* 53, no. 24 (August 22, 1970), 56.
22. "Al Young," *Contemporary Authors*, 29R.
23. "*Who Is Angelina?*" *New York Times Book Review* (February 9, 1975), sec. VII, p. 10.
24. Josephine Hendin, review of Barbara Wilson Tinker's *When the Fire Reaches Us* (1970), *Saturday Review of Literature* 53, no. 24 (August 22, 1970), 56.
25. Adele S. Newson, "Terry McMillan's *Mama*: A Great Lakes Version of *The Color Purple*" (Paper delivered at the Annual Meeting of the Society for the Study of Midwestern Literature, May 14, 1986).
26. Will Blythe, "Hustling for Dignity," review of *Mama* by Terry McMillan, *New York Times Book Review* (February 22, 1987), sec. 7, p. 11.
27. Dorothy H. Lee, "Black Voices in Detroit," *Michigan Quarterly Review* 25, no. 2 (Spring 1986), 326.
28. Ron Milner and Woodie King, [Jr.], "Evolution of a People's Theater," *Black Drama Anthology* (1972), viii.
29. Betty DeRamus, "A Man Who Captures Detroit—and Life," in Barbara Nykoruk, ed., *Authors in the News* (1976), 1: 348.
30. Dorothy H. Lee, "Black Voices in Detroit," *Michigan Quarterly Review* 25, no. 2 (Spring 1986), 326.

V. "Timber-r-r-r!"

1. John W. Fitzmaurice, *The Shanty Boy; or, Life in a Lumber Camp* (1889), 10.
2. Stewart Holbrook, *Holy Old Mackinaw* (1938), 72.
3. Ibid., 115. I have not been able to identify the film.
4. Ibid., 137.
5. Fitzmaurice, *The Shanty Boy; or, Life in a Lumber Camp* (1889), 62.
6. Francis X. Scannell, *Michigan Literature in the Sixties* 12, 1 (Summer–Autumn), 7; E[arl "Doc" C[lifton] Beck, *Michigan History* 37, no. 1 (March 1953), 115.
7. F. Churchill Williams, "Red Blood in Fiction," *World's Work* 6 (1903), 3694, 3697.
8. Grant C. Knight, *The Strenuous Age in American Literature* (1954), 70.
9. Lisle Rose, *A Descriptive Catalogue of Economic and Politico-economic Fiction in the United States, 1902–1909*, Ph.D. diss., Univ. of Chicago (1935), 25.
10. John Curtis Underwood, "Stewart Edward White" in *Literature and Insurgency*, (1904), 256.
11. Ibid., 257.
12. John T[heodore] Flanagan, "The Middle Western Historical Novel," *Illinois State Historical Society Journal* 37, 1 (1944), 45.
13. Underwood, "Stewart Edward White," 274.
14. Ibid., 273.
15. Holbrook, *Holy Old Mackinaw* (1938) 120–21.
16. Jean Laming, "Eugene Thwing's Red-Keg: Taming the Competitive Spirit," *Midwestern Miscellany* 13 (1985), 11.
17. Kathleen I. Gillard, *Our Michigan Heritage* (1955), 191.
18. *New York Times*, "Red-Keg Again" (November 4, 1905), 746.
19. Review of *The Man from Red-Keg* by Eugene Thwing, *Literary Digest* 31 (November 25, 1905), 798.

20. Laming, "Eugene Thwing's Red-Keg" *Midwestern Miscellany,* 13 (1985), 10–19; "The Myths and Realities in Thwing's Michigan Novels," *Great Lakes Review* 11, no. 2 (Fall 1985), 58–63.

21. *National Cyclopedia of American Biography* (1910), 14:99.

22. Review of *The Hidden Spring* by Clarence Budington Kelland, *New York Times Book Review* 21 (July 30, 1916), 303.

23. Review of *The Hidden Spring* by Clarence Budington Kelland *Bookman* 43 (July 16, 1916), 539.

24. Louis J. Kern, "Clarence Budington Kelland,"*Dictionary of American Biography,* supp. 7, (1961–1965), 416–18.

25. Edith R. Mosher and Nella Dietrich Williams, *From Indian Legends to the Modern Book-shelf: An Anthology of Prose and Verse by Michigan Authors. Prepared Especially for the Youth of the State* (1931), 284.

26. Ibid., 284.

27. Harold Titus, *Timber* (pp. 216–25). See the Paul Bunyan entries in this book's index.

28. Review of the film, *Hearts Aflame, Variety* (February 2, 1923).

29. Review of *The Manager of the B and A* by Vaughn Kester, *Dial* 31, no. 370 (November 15, 1901), 367.

30. David Garth, in *Current Biography 1957* (1958), 200–201.

31. Walter Havighurst, "Changing the Wilderness," review of *Fire on the Wind* by David Garth, *Saturday Review of Literature* 215 no. 18 (February 24, 1940), 5.

32. Willis Dunbar, review of *White Pine Days on the Tahquamenon* by William Davenport Hulbert, *Michigan History* 34, no. 2 (June 1950), 182.

33. Robert Fries, review of *Between the Iron and the Pine* by Lewis C. Reimann, *Michigan History* 27 (March 1953), 113–14.

34. Robert F. Haugh, review of *When Pine Was King* by Lewis C. Reimann, *Michigan Alumnus Quarterly Review* 49, no. 18, 271–72.

35. Samuel T. Dana, review of *Incredible Seney* by Lewis C. Reimann, *Michigan Alumnus Quarterly Review* 60, no. 21 (August 1954), 361–62.

36. Ibid., 361.

37. Martha Mitchell Bigelow, review of *Hurley—Still No Angel, Michigan Alumnus Quarterly Review* 61, no. 21 (1955), 364.

38. Ibid., 364.

39. Earl "Doc" Clifton Beck, *They Knew Paul Bunyan* (1956), foreword.

40. Walt Whitman, "I Hear America Singing," *Democratic Vistas* (1871).

41. James Cloyd Bowman, "Lumberjack Ballads," *Michigan History Magazine* 20 (Summer 1936), 231–45.

42. Ivan H. Walton, "From Michigan's Lumber Camps," *Michigan Alumnus Quarterly Review* 55 (Autumn 1948), 10.

43. Carl Carmer, "Dudes in the Shanties," review of *Lore of the Lumber Camps* by Earl "Doc" Clifton Beck, *Saturday Review of Literature* 32, no. 20 (May 14, 1949), 50.

44. Alan Lomax, "They Swang Their Axes, Sang Their Songs," review of *Lore of the Lumber Camps* by Earl "Doc" Clifton Beck, *New York Herald-Tribune Books* (April 17, 1949), 1–2.

45. Franz Rickaby, *Ballads and Songs of the Shanty-Boy* (1926), preface.

46. Ibid., xxi–xxii.

VI. Paul Bunyan, Mighty Logger—in Michigan

1. Stanley D. Newton, *Paul Bunyan of the Great Lakes* (1946), 162.

2. Daniel G. Hoffman, *Last of the Frontier Demigods* (1980), 2.

3. K. Bernice Stewart and Homer A. Watt, "Legends of Paul Bunyan, Lumberjack," *Transactions of the Wisconsin Academy of Sciences, Arts, and Letters* 18 (1916), 639.
4. Ibid.
5. Edith R. Mosher and Nella Dietrich Williams, *From Indian Legends to the Modern BookShelf: An Anthology of Prose and Verse by Michigan Authors. Prepared Especially for the Youth of the State* (1931), 194.
6. Susan Hauser, "Paul Bunyan: Just the Facts," *Minnesota Monthly* 21, no. 8 (August 1987), 35; W. B. Laughead, *The Marvelous Exploits of Paul Bunyan* (1935).
7. Stewart and Watt, "Legends of Paul Bunyan, Lumberjack," 639–51.
8. James Stevens, *Legends of Paul Bunyan* (1947), x–xi.
9. Harold Titus, *Timber* (1922), 216–25.
10. Harold Titus, *Michigan Library Bulletin* (May–June 1925).
11. Edith R. Mosher and Nella Dietrich Williams, *From Indian Legends to the Modern Bookshelf: An Anthology of Prose and Verse by Michigan Authors. Prepared Especially for the Youth of the State* (1931), 96–98.
12. John Towner Frederick, "Paul Bunyan in a Tuxedo," *The Midland* 19 (1932), 55.
13. Thelma G. James, review of *Paul Bunyan of the Great Lakes* by Stanley Newton, *Michigan History Magazine* 31, no. 4 (December 1947), 475–76.
14. B. A. Botkin, ed., *A Treasury of American Folklore* (1944), 204–5.
15. Henry Bailey Stevens, *Johnny Appleseed and Paul Bunyan: A Pageant* (1930), presented at Wilton, New Hampshire, May 19, 1935.
16. Arthur Coleman, "Paul Bunyan: Ecological Saint—or Villain?" *Old Northwest* 6, no. 4 (Winter 1980). The quotations are from John C. Frohlicher, "Paul Bunyan and the Forest Service," which are quoted in Harold W. Felton's *Legends of Paul Bunyan* (1961), 309.
17. Richard Mercer Dorson, "A Great Folk Hero, Perhaps," *Yale Review* (Winter 1953) n.s., 42, 298–99.
18. C. Gerald Fraser, "Richard M. Dorson, Historian, Focused on Folklore of U.S.," *New York Times* (September 23, 1961), sec. 4, p. 1.
19. Leo Teholtz, "Ludington's Robert Lyons Stearns: The Mark Twain of Art," *Great Lakes Review* 5 (Summer 1978), 29–41.

VII. "The Great Turtle"

1. Kenneth Roberts, *Northwest Passage* (1937), 463.
2. Robert Price, "Mary Hartwell Catherwood's Literary Record of the Great Lakes and French-America," *Michigan History Magazine* 30 (October-December 1946), 760.
3. Stephen Vincent Benét quoted by Harry R. Warfel in *American Novelists of Today* (1951), 167.
4. John T[heodore] Flanagan, "The Middle Western Historical Novel," *Illinois State Historical Society Journal* 37 (March 1944), 24.
5. Daniel S. Rankin, review of *The Loon Feather* by Iola Fuller, *The Commonweal* 31, no. 20 (March 8, 1940), 438–39.
6. Sheila Dailey, "Little Bear and Other Stories: A Look at the Life and Works of Michigan Children's Author Frances Margaret Fox," *Great Lakes Review* 8, no. 1 (Spring 1982), 25–30; *Michigan Authors 80* lists forty-four titles by Fox.
7. Flanagan, "The Middle Western Historical Novel," 46.
8. Henry James and William Dean Howells quoted by Bartholow Crawford, Alexander Kern, and Morriss Needleman in *An Outline-History of American Literature* (1950), 179.

9. See also volume 3 of Clare Benedict's *Five Generations (1785–1923)*, and Rayburn S. Moore's essay on Woolson in Gerald Nemanic's *A Bibliographical Guide to Midwestern Literature* (1981), 356–58.

10. Mary Ross, "The Michigan Fur Trade," *New York Herald-Tribune Books* 28, no. 26 (February 10, 1952), 4; "Dirk" Gringhuis, review of *Mission to Mackinac* by Myron D. Orr, *Michigan History Magazine* 41 no. 1 (March 1957) 119; Edward Fitzgerald, "Border Fortress," review of *The Citadel of the Lakes* by Myron D. Orr, *New York Times Book Review* 67, no. 5 (February 3, 1952) sec. 7, p. 22; Joseph Grant, review of *The Citadel of the Lakes* by Myron D. Orr, *Saturday Review of Literature* (February 23, 1952), 44.

11. Reviews of *Black Feather* by Harold Titus: *New York Herald Tribune Book Review* 12, no. 20 (January 19, 1936), 15; and *New York Times Book Review* (January 19, 1936), sec. 4, p. 20.

12. Albert G. Black, *Michigan Novels: An Annotated Bibliography* (1963), 25.

13. "Recent Fiction," review of *With the Best Intentions, The Nation* 52, no. 1349 (May 7, 1891), 385.

14. Gay Talese, "The Bridge," *Esquire* (December 1954), 136.

15. *New York Times* (November 1, 1930), 23.

16. Reviews of the film, *Somewhere in Time*: Vincent Canby, *New York Times* (October 3, 1980), sec. C, p. 14; and "Mac," *Variety* (September 24, 1980).

17. Reverend David H. Riddle, untitled poem, in Meade C. Williams, *Early Mackinac* (1987), epigraph.

VIII. The Great Lakes in Michigan Literature

1. William Ratigan, *Soo Canal!* (1955), epigraph.

2. Henry Bedford-Jones, "The Fiction Field of Michigan History," *Michigan History Magazine* 12, no. 2 (July 1928), 452.

3. Ibid., 450–51.

4. Mildred A. Fontaine, "Books for Adolescents," review of *Pirate of the Pine Lands*, by Karl Detzer, *Saturday Review of Literature* 6, no. 17 (November 16, 1929), 418.

5. Reviews of *Stranger on the Island* by Brand Whitlock: William Maxwell, *New York Times Book Review* (March 19, 1933) sec. 5, p. 6; "An Island Tragedy," *New York Herald-Tribune Books* 9, no. 28 (March 19, 1933), 9; *Saturday Review of Literature* 9 (April 8, 1933), 529.

6. Phil Stong, "Hero of Thunder Bay," review of *The Adventures of Captain McCargo* by William Ratigan, *New York Times* (September 9, 1965), 33.

7. Walter Havighurst, "A Vigorous Novel of the Great Lakes," review of *Beckoning Waters* by Robert Carse, *New York Herald-Tribune Books* 29, no. 32 (March 22, 1953), 6.

8. August Derleth, "History of Great Lakes in Lusty Tale," review of *Beckoning Waters* by Robert Carse, *Chicago Sunday Tribune Magazine of Books* (March 22, 1953), sec. 4, p. 4.

9. Michael Bliss, in Alan Sullivan's *The Rapids* (1972) vii.

10. "Our Waterways," review of *The Great Lakes . . .* by James Oliver Curwood, *The Nation* 89, no. 2297 (July 8, 1909), 36.

11. Reviews of *The Lights Are Bright* by Louise Kennedy Mabie: *The Nation* 99, no. 2564 (August 20, 1914), 224; and *New York Times Book Review* (August 16, 1914), 346–47.

12. A. Donald Douglas, "Delicate Light Comedy," review of *The Moth Decides* by Edward Alden Jewell, *New York Tribune* (October 29, 1922), 9.

13. Review of *The Island Mail* by Clarice Nissley Detzer, *Michigan History Magazine* 11–12, no. 3 (July 1927–1928), 510.

14. "Four Adventure Books of the Seas and Lakes," *Chicago Tribune* 96, no. 260C (October 30, 1937), 14.

15. Reviews of *The Cruise of the Gull-Flight* by Sidney Corbett: Margaret Van Doren, *New York Herald-Tribune Books* (October 3, 1937), 10; "A Mystery Cruise," *New York Times Book Review* (October 3, 1937), 10.

16. Review of *Man in an Apron* by Sidney Corbett, *Newsweek* 29 (March 17, 1947), 70.

17. Walter O'Hearn, "Mother Tippett, Smuggler," review of *A Lucky Number* by Vera Henry, *New York Times Book Review* (June 23, 1957), sec. 7, p. 21.

18. "Jay William McCormick," in *Current Biography 1942* (1943), 477.

19. John T[heodore] Flanagan, "Troubles in an Obscure Corner," review of *Bay Mild* by Louis Kintzinger, *Chicago Sun Book Week* (June 24, 1945), 9.

20. Rachel M. Hilbert, "Ruth Barlow," *Michigan Authors* (1960).

21. Reviews of *The Owl's Roost* by Helga Sandburg: William Wiegand, "Allergic to the Pastoral Usage," *New York Times Book Review* (May 27, 1962) sec. 7, p. 30; Fanny Butcher, "The Beauty and Reality of Life Beside an Inland Sea," *Chicago Sunday Tribune Magazine of Books* (April 15, 1962), sec. 4, p. 23: P. E., *New York Herald-Tribune Books* (April 29, 1962), 7.

22. Thomas P. Linkfield, "*An Adolescent's Struggle*," review of *At the Shores* by Thomas Rogers, *Society for the Study of Midwest Literature Newsletter* 11, no. 3 (Fall 1981), 45–51.

IX. The Michigan Farm Novel

1. Arthur Pound, *Once a Wilderness* (1934), 29–30.

2. Willis F. Dunbar, *Michigan: A History of the Wolverine State* (1973), 397.

3. Roy W. Meyer, *The Middle Western Farm Novel in the Twentieth Century* (1965), 227.

4. Reviews of *Once a Wilderness* by Arthur Pound: William Allen White, "Racy of the Soil," *Saturday Review of Literature* 10, no. 38 (April 7, 1934), 607; Phil Stong, "The Good Earth of Michigan," *New York Herald-Tribune Books* (April 8, 1934), 7; Phil Stong, "A Wealth of Plots in One Book," *New York Herald-Tribune* 11, no. 48; *Books* (August 4, 1935) part 7, p. 6.

5. The quotations are from the dust jackets of *Cousin William* (1942) and *The Country Kitchen* (1936). See Lawrence R. Dawson, *Bulletin of Bibliography* 39, no. 4 (1982), 184, 187.

6. Lawrence R. Dawson, "Della Thompson Lutes: A Preliminary Bibliography," *Bulletin of Bibliography* 39, no. 4 (1982), 188–89.

7. "They Ate Like Kings," *New York Times Book Review* (September 27, 1936), sec. 7, pp. 9, 23.

8. Douglas A. Noverr, "New Dimensions in Recent Michigan Fiction," *Midwestern Miscellany* 1 (1974), 9ff.

9. Reviews of *Seedtime and Harvest* by Eleanor Blake: *Times Literary Supplement* (October 10, 1935), 633; Roy W. Meyer, *The Middle Western Farm Novel in the Twentieth Century* (1965), 202–3.

10. Gladys Hasty Carroll, "Workers of the Soil," *Saturday Review of Literature* 12, no. 16 (August 17, 1935), 5.

11. Richard Sullivan, "Proud to Be Alive," *New York Times Book Review* (November 22, 1959), sec. 7, p. 60.

12. Chad Walsh, "Moving Novel of One Day, One Industry, One Family," *New York Herald-Tribune Books* (November 22, 1959), 3; Richard Sullivan, "Proud to Be Alive," *New York Times Book Review* (November 22, 1959), sec. 7, p. 60.

13. Meyer, *The Middle Western Farm Novel in the Twentieth Century* (1965), 171.

14. Nelson Antrim Crawford, "The American Farmer in Fact and Fiction," *Literary Digest International Book Review* 4, no. 2 (January 1926), 101.

15. W. F. Calverton, "Proletarianitis," review of *Backfurrow* by Geoffrey Dell Eaton, *Saturday Review of Literature* 15, no. 11 (January 9, 1937), 4.

16. Meyer, *The Middle Western Farm Novel in the Twentieth-Century* (1965), 88, fn.

17. H. L. Mencken, "The Library," *American Mercury* 5, no. 17 (May 1925), 124. Larry B. Massie, "Literary Michigan" in *The Michigan Connection* (1987) calls it "perhaps the bleakest novel about Michigan farm life" and notes that the publisher, G. P. Putnam's Sons, did not publicize it (p. 7).

18. J[ohn] T[owner] F[rederick], *The Midland* 11, no. 9, 178–79.

19. Delight Ansley, *First Chronicles* (1971), 26.

20. Meyer, *The Middle Western Farm Novel in the Twentieth Century* (1965), 85.

21. N. Brillion Fagin, review of *Green Bush* by John Towner Frederick, *Literary Digest International Book Review* 3 (November 1, 1925), 820.

22. Crawford, "American Farmer in Fact and Fiction," 101.

23. Reviews of *Years of Eden* by Gordon Webber: Richard Sullivan, "Novel Worthy of Becoming Excited About," *New York Times Book Review* (April 1, 1951), sec. 7, p. 5; Florence Haxton Bullock, "A Moving Boyhood Idyll," *New York Herald-Tribune Books* (April 1, 1951), 11; Marion West Stoerr, *Chicago Sunday Tribune Magazine of Books* (March 25, 1951), 3.

24. Reviews of *The Melodeon* by Glendon Swarthout: Diane Haas, *Library Journal* 102 (December 15, 1977), 2524; Edward Guereschi, *Best Sellers* (March 1978), 375; *Publishers Weekly* 212, no. 9 (August 29, 1977), 354.

25. Glendon (Fred) Swarthout, *Contemporary Authors* IR, INR.

26. Meyer, *The Middle Western Farm Novel in the Twentieth Century* (1965), 221.

27. Reviews of *Wheels over the Bridge* by Meindert De Jong: Mary Lamberton Becker, *New York Herald-Tribune Books* (May 4, 1941), 7; Ellen Lewis Buell, *New York Times Book Review* (June 22, 1941), 10.

28. James C. O'Neill, "Madame Bovary in Michigan?" review of *Hilda Manning* by Allan Seager, *Michigan Alumnus Quarterly Review* 63, no. 14 (March 6, 1957), 178–79.

29. Reviews of *Measure My Love* by Helga Sandburg: Doris Betts, "Frame around Faith," *Saturday Review of Literature* 42, no. 19 (May 9, 1959); Richard Sullivan, "Of Earth and Root," *New York Times Book Review* (July 26, 1959), sec. 7, p. 22; Walter Havighurst, "No Recognizable Love," *New York Herald-Tribune Books* (July 26, 1959), 22.

X. The Michigan Small Town

1. *The Indispensable F. Scott Fitzgerald* (1951), 87.

2. Reuben W. Borough, "Saturday Afternoon Town," *Michigan History* 48 (June 1964), 125.

3. G. W. C., review of *Brothers in Kickapoo* by Dan Cushman, *New York Herald-Tribune Books* (April 1, 1962), sec. 7, p. 6.

4. Martin Levin, review of *Brothers in Kickapoo* by Dan Cushman, *New York Times Book Review* (April 29, 1962), sec. 7, p. 47.

5. Theodore R. Kennedy, "Edmund Love's Michigan," review of *The Situation in Flushing* by Edmund G. Love, *Society for the Study of Midwestern Literature Newsletter* (Spring 1985), 8.

6. Ibid., 6–11. Quoted materials will be found in various parts of the essay.

7. Brooks Atkinson, review of "*Morning's at Seven*" by Paul Osborn, *New York Times* (December 1, 1939), sec. 2, p. 26.

8. Christine Birdwell, "Paul Osborn and His Gals in Kalamazoo," *Midwestern Miscellany* 13 (1985), 53.

9. For example: Gladys Graham, "Family Circle," review of *Heat Lightning* by Helen Hull, *Saturday Review of Literature* 8, no. 37 (April 2, 1932), 633.

10. Bernard Duffey, *The Chicago Renaissance in American Letters* (1954), 121.

11. Robert van Gelder, "Neuroses in Athens, Michigan," review of *The Inheritance* by Allan Seager, *New York Times Book Review*, (April 18, 1948), sec. 7, p. 7.

12. Mentor Williams, review of *The Inheritance* by Allan Seager, *Michigan Alumnus Quarterly Review* 54 (July 31, 1948), 24.

13. Warner G. Rice, review of *The White Lilac Tree* by Mrs. Lila M. Burnham, *Michigan Alumnus Quarterly Review* 59 (May 23, 1953), 18.

14. Reviews of *The Center of the World* by Richard Lardner Tobin, Jr.: Mary Ross, "The Tree-Shaded Houses of Sycamore St.," *New York Herald-Tribune Books* (April 8, 1951), sec. 7, p. 5; W. R. Steinhoff, *Michigan Alumnus Quarterly Review* (August 12, 1951) 57, 364; Thomas Sugrue, *Saturday Review of Literature* 34, no. 23 (June 9, 1951), 44.

15. Reviews of *Welcome to Thebes* by Glendon Swarthout: David Dempsey, "Scapegrace's Homecoming," *New York Times Book Review* (June 17, 1962), sec. 7, p. 24; T. B., *New York Herald-Tribune Books* (July 1, 1962), 6; "Improving on Oedipus," *Time* 79, no. 23 (June 8, 1962), 94.

16. Theodore Dreiser quoted in Fred Pattee's, *The New American Literature* (1930), 186.

XI. The Michigan Campus Scene

1. Justin McCarthy, *Dear Lady Disdain* (1875), 207.

2. Basil L. Crapster, " 'New Padua,' Justin McCarthy and Ann Arbor," review of *Dear Lady Disdain* by Justin McCarthy, *Michigan History* (September 1958), 361, fn. 1.

3. Ibid., 361.

4. J[ohn] T[owner] F[rederick], review of *Listen, Moon* by Leonard Cline, *Midland* 12, no. 2 (February 1926), 74.

5. Reviews of *Wings of Wax* by Janet Hoyt: T. P. Brockway, "Depreciation," *New York Herald-Tribune Books* (May 12, 1929), 14; "A College President," *New York Times Book Review* (March 24, 1929), sec. 4, pp. 18, 24; Richard Boys, "The American College in Fiction," *College English* 7, no. 7 (July 1946), 383.

6. Brockway, "Depreciation," 14.

7. Ibid.

8. W. Stock Hume, *Rudderless: A University Chronicle* (1930), dedication.

9. Peter Oppewall, "Manfred and Calvin College," in Arthur R. Huseboe and William Geyer, eds., *Where the West Begins* (1978), 86–98.

10. George R. Stewart, "Big Moose," review of *The Primitive* by Feike Feikema, *New York Times Book Review* (September 18, 1949), sec. 7, p. 37.

11. Paul Corey, "A Wanderer Sets Forth," review of *The Primitive* by Feike Feikema, *New York Herald-Tribune Books* (September 18, 1949), 9.

12. Reviews of *The Merry Innocents* by Nolan Miller: Mary Ross, "Life in a Lively Family," *New York Herald-Tribune Books* (November 30, 1947), 16; Seymour Krim, "Richard II and the Lowrys," *New York Times Book Review* (December 28, 1947), sec. 7, p. 17; John Arthos, *Michigan Alumnus Quarterly Review* 54, no. 10 (December 6, 1947), 92.

13. Reviews of *Why Am I So Beat* by Nolan Miller: James H. Robertson, "Some Michigan Books," *Michigan Alumnus Quarterly Review* 62, no. 21 (August 11, 1956), 363; Kelly James, "Dig That Odyssey," *Saturday Review* 37, no. 9 (February 27, 1954), 33.

14. Reviews of *The Cautious Husband* by Virginia Evans: Marvin Felheim, *Michigan Alumnus Quarterly Review* 55, no. 24 (July 30, 1949), 368; Josephine Lawrence, "Sugar and Spice," *Saturday Review of Literature* 32, no. 23 (June 4, 1949), 28; Marjorie Fischer, "Muddled Adjustment," *New York Times Book Review* (June 26, 1949), sec. 7, p. 18.

15. Caroline Tunstall, "From Wave to Cinderella," review of *A Gradual Joy* by Alma Routsong (Brodie), *New York Herald-Tribune Books* (August 23, 1953), 4.

16. Reviews of *A Gradual Joy* by Alma Routsong (Brodie): Marjorie B. Snyder, "What Critics Cry For," *Chicago Sunday Tribune Magazine of Books*, (August 16, 1953), 7; Tunstall, "From Wave to Cinderella"; J. D. Paulus, "After the G.I. Wedding," *New York Times* (August 23, 1953), sec. 7, p. 18; Charles Lee, "Nice Young Couple," *Saturday Review of Literature* 36, no. 39 (September 26, 1953), 20.

17. H. C. Webster, "Behind Their Masks," review of *Disguises of Love* by Robie Macauley, *New York Times Book Review* (November 2, 1952), sec. 7, p. 6.

18. Rose Feld, "College Professor's Dilemma," review of *Disguises of Love* by Robie Macauley, *New York Herald-Tribune Book Review* (November 2, 1952), 6.

19. Anthony West, review of *Disguises of Love* by Robie Macauley, "Books" / "On the Other Foot," *The New Yorker* 28 (December 20, 1952), 114.

20. Frank E. Robbins, "Take Care of My Little Girl," review of *Take Care of My Little Girl* by Peggy Goodin, *Michigan Alumnus Quarterly Review* 56, no. 18 (Spring 1950).

21. Bosley Crother, review of the film *Where the Boys Are*, *New York Times* (January 19, 1961), sec. 7, p. 26.

22. Arthur M. Eastman, review of *Michigan Memories* by Richard Emmons and Robert Foreman, *Michigan Quarterly Review* 5, no. 7 (January 1966), 343.

23. Reviews of *The Movement* by Norman Garbo: Paul Wagner, *Library Journal* 94, no. 16 (September 15, 1969), 3232; Sara Blackburn, *The Nation* 209 (October 13, 1979), 388.

24. John Wakeman, "Gary Fort, Student," review of *No Transfer* by Stephen Walton, *New York Times Book Review* (February 19, 1967), 45.

XII. Banks, Business, and Mining

1. Robert Barr, *The Victors: A Romance of Yesterday Morning and This Afternoon* (1901), 330.

2. See John Voelker, *About the Historical Novel* (1970), for Voelker's discussion as to how this novel came to be. See *Michigan History Magazine* 28, no. 3 (July–September 1944), 450–55 for more on Charlotte Kawbawgam. See also Russell McKee, *Great Lakes Country* (1966), 182–86 for part of the story; on p. 183 there is a photograph of Marji Gesick.

3. There is a script of Ralph C. Schoonover's *Pageant: Iron Ore Centennial (1844–1944)* in *Michigan History Magazine* 28, no. 4 (October–December 1944), 558–72.

4. Lisle Rose, *A Descriptive Catalogue of Economic and Politico-economic Fiction in the United States, 1902–1909*, Ph.D. diss., Univ. of Chicago (1935), 28–29.

5. John T[heodore] Flanagan, "The Middle Western Historical Novel," *Journal of the Illinois State Historical Society* 37, no. 1 (March 1944), 36–37.

6. Angus Murdoch, *Boom Copper* (1954), 156.

7. Rose, *Descriptive Catalogue*, 161.

8. Reviews of *When Love Speaks* by Will Payne: *The Nation* (November 22, 1906), vol. 83, 441; Cooper, Frederick Taber, *Bookman* (January 1907), 490; *Outlook* 84 (1906), 492; *Dial* 42 (April 1906), 228.

9. Reviews of *The Groper* by Henry G. Aikman: *New York Times Book Review* (August 3, 1919), sec. 7, p. 391; C. M. Greene, "A Canter through the Field of Fiction," *Bookman* 50, no. 2 (October 1919), 190–91; "A Shelf of Samples," *The Nation* 109, no. 2285 (August 23, 1919), 252.

10. Reviews of *Zell* by Harold Hunter Armstrong: L. L., *The Nation* 112, no. 2906 (March 16, 1921), 409; H. W. Boynton, *Weekly Review* 4 (April 20, 1921), 369; R. H., *New Republic* 26 (May 25, 1921), 382; L. B., *Freeman* 3 (June 15, 1921), 334.

11. Reviews of *For Richer, for Poorer* by Harold Hunter Armstrong: *New York Times Book Review* (August 13, 1922), 20; Hunter Stagg, "Marriage Again," *New York Tribune* (August 27, 1922).

12. F. Churchill Williams, "Red Blood in Fiction," *World's Work* 6 (1903), 3694–3700; Grant C. Knight, *The Strenuous Age in American Literature* (1954), 41.

13. Arnold Mulder, "Michigan's Writing Men," *Michigan History Magazine* 35, no. 3 (September 1951), 267.

14. Reviews of *Amos Berry* by Allan Seager: Paul Engel, "Exciting, Richly Loaded Fiction of a Perfect Crime," *Chicago Sunday Tribune Magazine of Books* (March 1, 1953), 9; Harvey Curtis Webster, *New Republic* 128 (June 15, 1953), 21; John Brooks, "Muddled Nemesis," *New York Times Book Review* (March 1, 1953), sec. 7, p. 30; George Miles, "Some Tired Businessmen," *Commonweal* 57, no. 24 (March 20, 1953), 607.

15. "Allan Seager, 62, Author, Teacher," *New York Times* (May 11, 1968), sec. 4, p. 35.

XIII. Crime in Michigan Literature

1. Elmore Leonard, *Freaky Deaky* (1988), 1–2.

2. Mel Gussow, *New York Times* (May 19, 1976) 25:3. See also the *Times* review of the out-of-town opening in Stamford, Conn. (January 10, 1976) 19:1.

3. Frank Nugent quoted by Roger Dooley in *From Scarface to Scarlett: American Films in the 1930s* (1981), 320–21.

4. Reviews of *Loveland* by Glendon Swarthout: Donald H. Cloudsley, *Library Journal* 93, no. 16 (September 15, 1968), 3158; *Publishers Weekly* 194, no. 2 (July 8, 1968), 158; *Kirkus Reviews* 36 (July 1, 1968), 719.

5. Reviews of *Vandameer's Road* by John R[ichard] Humphrey: Richard Match, *New York Herald-Tribune Books* (February 24, 1946), 8; James Sandoe, "Bitter Memories and Broken Minds," *Chicago Sunday Tribune Magazine of Books* (March 17, 1946), 8; Alan Vrooman, "Skulls and Silos," *New York Times Book Review* (February 24, 1946), sec. 7, p. 12; A. L Bader, *Michigan Alumnus Quarterly Review* 52, no. 24 (July 27, 1946), 376; Phil Stong, "With Applique of Fantasy," *Saturday Review of Literature* 29, no. 9 (March 2, 1946), 19.

6. Reviews of *The Mercy of the Court* by Monica Porter: *New Yorker* 31, no. 33 (October 1, 1955), 141. Anthony Boucher, "Criminals at Large," *New York Times Book Review* (October 9, 1955), sec. 7, p. 28. *San Francisco Chronicle* (October 2, 1955), 18.

7. Reviews of *At Last Mr. Tolliver* by William Wiegand: Anthony Boucher, "Man in Dirty White," *New York Times Book Review* (October 8, 1950), sec. 7, p. 29; *New York Herald-Tribune Book Review* (October 15, 1950), sec. 7, p. 24.

8. Albert G. Black, *Michigan Novels: An Annotated Bibliography* (1963), 61.

9. Daniel M. Friedenberg, "The Cross and the Couch," review of *The Treatment Man* by William Wiegand, *New Republic* 142, no. 2 (January 11, 1960), 18–19.

10. Reviews of *A Dream of Falling* by Mary Owen Rank: Marvin Felheim, "Dream of Falling," *Michigan Alumnus Quarterly Review* 66, no. 14 (February 27, 1960), 169; Anne Ross, "Hit Bottom and You're Dead," *New York Herald-Tribune Book Review* (May 23, 1959), sec. 7, p. 41.

11. Reviews of *Anatomy of a Murder* by Robert Traver: Don Mankiewicz, "Before the Trial Begins," *New York Herald-Tribune Book Review* (January 15, 1958), sec. 7, p. 4; Joseph Hitrec, "Courtroom Drama," *Saturday Review of Literature* 4, no. 41 (January 4, 1958), 14.

12. Stanley Ellin, "Murder Forgotten," review of *People versus Kirk* by John D. Voelker, *New York Times Book Review* (November 1, 1981), sec. 7, p. 15.

13. Joyce Carol Oates, review of *The Sporting Club* by Thomas McGuane, *New York Times Book Review* (March 23, 1969), 4.

14. Reviews of the film, *The Sporting Club*: Howard Thompson, *New York Times* (March 1, 1971), sec. 2, p. 22; Whit., *Variety* (February 27, 1971); Stephen Farber, "Did They Give 'Sporting Club' a Sporting Chance?" *New York Times Film Reviews* (March 21, 1971) 11:13:1.

15. Reviews of film *Open Season*: Nora Sayre, "A Film of Dull Sadism . . . ," *New York Times* (November 2, 1974), sec. 3, p. 16; "Murf," *Variety* (August 21, 1974).

16. Reviews of *In the Lamb-White Days* by F. H. Hall: Henri C. Veit, *Library Journal* 100, no. 19 (November 1, 1975), 2073; *Publishers Weekly* 208 (September 8, 1975), 54.

17. Reviews of *The Michigan Murders* by Edward Keyes: Richard Whittington-Egan, in *Contemporary Review* 232 (March 1978), 166–67; Gregor A. Preston, *Library Journal* 101 (September 15, 1976), 1872.

18. Richard Elman, review of *The Jones Men*, by Vern E. Smith, *New York Times* (September 19, 1974) sec. 7, p. 4.

19. S. K. Overbeck, "Dum-dums in Detroit," review of *The Jones Men* by Vern E. Smith, *Newsweek* 84, no. 16 (October 14, 1974), 118.

20. Review of the film, *The Rosary Murders*: *Variety* (May 20, 1987), 45.

21. "Wormwood Scrubbs" [pseudonym of Deborah Cushman], review of *Deadline for a Critic* by William X. Kienzle, *Des Moines Sunday Register* (June 5, 1988), 4C.

22. Reviews of *Warlock* by Jim Harrison: John Buckley, *Saturday Review* 8, no. 10 (October 1981), 76; William H. Roberson, "A Good Day to Live," *Great Lakes Review* 8, no. 2 (Fall 1982), 34–36; John Rohrkemper, " 'Natty Bumpo Wants Tobacco': Jim Harrison's Wilderness," *Great Lakes Review* 8, no. 2 (Fall 1982), 24–26.

23. Reviews of *Evidence* by John Weisman: Newgate Callendar, *New York Times Book Review* (May 4, 1980), sec. 7, p. 24; *Publishers Weekly* 217 (February 1, 1980), 103.

24. Review of *The Heroin Triple Cross* by John Weisman and Bryan Boyer, *New York Times Book Review* (March 10, 1974), sec. 7, p. 24.

25. Review of *The Heroin Triple Cross* by John Weisman and Bryan Boyer, *Publishers Weekly* 205 (January 14, 1974), 96.

26. Reviews of *The Santa Claus Killer* by A. H. Garnet: James A. Phillips, *Best Sellers* 41 (October 1981), 253; MA-L, *Library Journal* 106, no. 13 (July 1981), 1446.

27. Reviews of *Maze* by A. H. Garnet: Anne Marie Stamford, *Best Sellers* 42 (November 1982), 300; *Publishers Weekly* 222 (July 16, 1982), 64; MA-L, *Library Journal* 107, no. 15 (September 1, 1982), 1679. Newgate Callendar, *New York Times Book Review* (December 19, 1982), sec. 7, p. 30.

28. Roger Sale, review of *The Car Thief* by Theodore Weesner, *New York Review of Books* (October 5, 1972) sec. A, pp. 19, 34–35.

29. C. P. Collier, review of *The Car Thief* by Theodore Weesner, *Best Sellers* 32 (July 15, 1972), 197.

30. Joseph McElroy, review of *The Car Thief* by Theodore Weesner, *New York Times Book Review* (June 18, 1972), sec. 7, p. 7.

31. Lance Morrow, *Time* 100, no. 4 (July 24, 1972), 77.

32. Newgate Callendar, review of *The Blind Pig* by Jon A. Jackson, *New York Times Book Review* (March 13, 1977), sec. 7, p. 35.

33. *Contemporary Authors* 81–84, 263–64.

34. Review of *Crooked Tree* by Robert C. Wilson, *Publishers Weekly* 217, no. 8 (February 29, 1980), 131.

35. Review of *Ice Fire* by Robert C. Wilson, *Publishers Weekly* 224, no. 23 (December 2, 1983), 81.

36. Wormwood Scrubbs, "Estleman's *Silent Thunder* Puts Amos Walker to Work Again," [review] *Des Moines Sunday Register* (May 7, 1989), 4C.

37. Review of *Kill Zone* by Loren D. Estleman, *Publishers Weekly* 226, no. 13 (September 26, 1984), 45–46.

38. Newgate Callendar quoted by Robert C. Wilson in "Elmore Leonard," *Contemporary Authors* 12 (*New Revision*, 1984), 268.

39. Richard Herzfelder quoted by Wilson in "Elmore Leonard," 268.

40. Grover Sales quoted by Wilson in "Elmore Leonard," 268.

41. Reviews of *52 Pick-Up* by Elmore Leonard: Wilson, "Elmore Leonard," 26; Newgate Callendar, *New York Times Book Review* (April 4, 1976), sec. 7, p. 34; Janet Maslin, "Screen: '52 Pick-Up' A No-Frills Thriller," *New York Times* (November 7, 1986) sec. 3, p. 40.

42. Newgate Callendar, "Decent Men in Trouble," review of *Unknown Man No. 89* by Elmore Leonard, *New York Times Book Review* (May 22, 1977), sec. 7, pp. 13, 32–33.

43. Ibid., 13.

44. James Kauffmann, "Leonard Gets at the Essentials," review of *Killshot* by Elmore Leonard, *Des Moines Sunday Register* (April 2, 1989), 4C.

45. Reviews of *Michigan Roll* by Tom Kakonis: Marilyn Stasio, *New York Times Book Review* (October 16, 1988), 24; Sybil Steinberg, *Publishers Weekly* 234, no. 4 (July 22, 1988), 41.

XIV. People in Michigan Literature

1. Alice Fulton, "The New Affluence," *Contemporary Michigan Poetry* (1988), 83.

2. Reviews of *O Distant Star!* by Mary Frances Doner: Wilbur Schramm, "Truth or Repose," *Saturday Review of Literature* 27, no. 15 (April 8, 1944), 44; Andrea Parke, "1860 Valentine," *New York Times Book Review* (February 20, 1944), sec. 7, p. 19.

3. Jay Du Von, "Family Novel," review of *Dwell in the Wilderness* by Alvah C. Bessie, *New Republic* 84, no. 1086 (September 25, 1935) 194.

4. Edna R. Mosher and Nella Dietrich Williams, *From Indian Legends to the Modern Bookshelf: An Anthology of Prose and Verse by Michigan Authors. Prepared Especially for the Youth of the State* (1931), 122.

5. Lisle Bell, review of "Valiant Dust" by Helen Genung and Caryl May Hayes, *New York Herald-Tribune Books* (October 18, 1936), 16.

6. Andrea Parke, "Dream-Horse," review of *Horse in the Sky* by Margerie Bonner, *New York Times Book Review* (October 12, 1947), sec. 7, p. 26.

7. Lisle Belle, review of *Landmarks* by Hilda Morris, *New York Herald-Tribune Books* (October 5, 1941), 12.

8. Reviews of *The Long View* by Hilda Morris: Edith H. Walton, "American Generations," *New York Times Book Review* (November 7, 1937), 22; B. E. Bettinger, *New York Herald-Tribune Books* (October 10, 1937), 10.

9. Reviews of *Dominies Daughter* by Joseph McCord: E. J. C., "Fine Midwest Tale," *Chicago Sun Book Week* (May 9, 1943), 12; Charlotte Dean, *New York Times Book Review* (April 18, 1943), sec. 7, p. 37.

10. Clare Godfrey, review of *Faith the Root* by Barbara Frances Fleury, *New York Herald-Tribune Books* (May 10, 1942), 22.

11. Joseph M. Grant, review of *Saw-Ge-Mah* by Dr. Louis J. Gariepy, *Saturday Review of Literature* 33, no. 25 (June 17, 1950), 26.

12. Reviews of *Morning Shows the Day* by Helen Hull: Mary S. Ulrich, "As We Were," *Saturday Review of Literature* 11, no. 17 (November 10, 1934), 257–58; Louis Kronenberger, *New York Times Book Review* (November 11, 1934), sec. 5, p. 6.

13. C. L., "Applesauce Kid," review of *The Lie* by Peggy Goodin, *Saturday Review of Literature* 36, no. 39 (September 26, 1953), 40.

14. Reviews of *Golden Apples of the Sun* by Rosemary Obermeyer: Mary Ross, *New York Herald-Tribune Books* (January 23, 1944), 6; Thomas Sugrue, "Happy Journey," *New York Times Book Review* (January 23, 1944), sec. 7, p. 6; Dorothy Greenwald, *Michigan Alumnus Quarterly Review* 50, no. 15 (February 19, 1944), 182–83.

15. Reviews of *Mildew Manse* by Belle Kanaris Maniates, *New York Times Book Review* (January 2, 1916), p. 21, col. 5; "Midsummer Fiction in April," *The Independent* 86, no. 3514 (April 10, 1916), 66.

16. Review of *Pa Flickenger's Folks* by Bessie Ray Hoover, *New York Times Saturday Review* (September 18, 1909), 549.

17. Reviews of *Deepwood* by Walter S. J. Swanson: JME, *Booklist* 77, no. 9 (February 1, 1981), 747; *New York Times Book Review* (February 22, 1981), sec. 7, p. 14.

18. Reviews of *The Road to the World* by Webb Waldron: *New Republic* 31 (June 7, 1922), 392; Sidney Howard, "Neophytes Three," *Bookman* 55, no. 5 (July 1922), 525.

19. Reviews of *Shanklin* by Webb Waldron: *Saturday Review of Literature* (November 14, 1925), 300; "Quest of the Spirit in a New Novel by Webb Waldron," *New York Times Book Review* (October 18, 1925), sec. 3, p. 8.

20. Helen Holman Smith, *In the Sight of God* (1976), dust jacket.

21. H. L. Mencken, *American Mercury* 17, no. 5 (May 1925), 125–26.

22. Harrison Smith, "In the Pursuit of Nothing at All," review of *Spring Flight* by Lee J. Smits, *New York Herald Tribune Books* (May 3, 1925), sec. 5, p. 4.

23. Joseph Wood Krutch, "Children of the Century," review of *Spring Flight* by Lee J. Smits, *The Nation*, 120, no. 3124 (May 20, 1925), 576.

24. Arnold Mulder, "Michigan's Writing Men," *Michigan History* 35, no. 3 (September 1951), 266–67.

25. Sheridan Baker, review of Ernest Hemingway's "The Big Two-Hearted River," *Michigan Alumnus Quarterly Review* 65, no. 14 (February 28, 1959), 142–49.

26. Bosley Crowther review of the film *Hemingway's Adventures of a Young Man, New York Times* (July 26, 1962), p. 17, col. 1.
27. Lawrence S. Morris, "Frolicking on Olympus," review of *The Torrents of Spring* by Ernest Hemingway, *New Republic* 40, no. 51 (December 22, 1926), 142.
28. Ibid.
29. Mosher and Williams, *From Indian Legends to the Modern BookShelf: An Anthology of Prose and Verse by Michigan Authors. Prepared Especially for the Youth of the State* (1931), 343.
30. "Unpredictable Michigan Boy," review of *Tin Sword* by Malcolm Stuart Boylan, *New York Herald-Tribune Book Review* 27, no. 11 (October 29, 1950), 22.
31. Milton Crane, review of *Tin Sword* by Malcolm Stuart Boylan, *Saturday Review of Literature* 33, no. 50 (December 16, 1950), 15.
32. William McCann, "Lansing's Forgotten Novelist of the Lost Generation," *Society for the Study of Midwestern Literature Newsletter* 11, no. 3 (Fall 1981), 44.
33. Ibid., 45.
34. John Brosky, "The Book That Shook Grand Rapids," *Grand Rapids Magazine* (November 1981), 36–39, 68–75.
35. Ibid., 37.
36. Reviews of the film, *How Baxter Butted In:* Mordaunt Hall, "The Screen: Splendid Fun," *New York Times* (June 23, 1925), 243; *Variety,* (June 24, 1925).
37. John Towner Frederick, *Out of the Midwest* (1944), 40.
38. Shirley W. Smith, "The Shape of Sunday," *Michigan Alumnus Quarterly Review* 63, no. 18 (May 25, 1957), 272–73.
39. Edith H. Walton, "Modern Medievalism," review of *The Evening Heron* by Philip Freund, *New York Times Book Review* (August 15, 1937), 12.
40. Reviews of *Wishbone* by Stirling Bowen: Alice Beal Parsons, *New York Herald-Tribune Books* (February 16, 1930), 4; "Aspiration and Defeat," *New York Times Book Review* (February 23, 1930), sec. 4, p. 7.
41. Stanley Young, "Out of Depression," review of *The Stubborn Way* by Baxter Hathaway, *New York Times Book Review* (October 24, 1937), sec. 7, p. 23.
42. D. DeK., "A House Divided," review of *A Sow's Ear* by Irving Bissell, *New York Times Book Review* (October 17, 1937), 32.
43. James Frakes, "Monster Maker," review of *The Catwalk* by Richard B. Erno, *New York Herald-Tribune Books* (January 17, 1965), 18.
44. Joseph Brooks, "The Hero as Vegetable," review of *All Our Yesterdays* by Joseph Weeks, *New York Times Book Review* (July 10, 1955), sec. 7, p. 16.
45. Richard Schickel, review of *The Button Boat* by Kathryn and Glendon Swarthout, *New York Times Book Review* (October 5, 1969), 34.
46. Malcolm Cowley, "Marginalia," review of *Whistle Stop* by Maritta Wolff, *New Republic* 104, no. 1384 (June 9, 1941), 798.
47. Reviews of *Whistle Stop* by Maritta Wolff: Edith H. Walton, "A First Novel of Distinction," *New York Times Book Review* (May 18, 1941) sec. 7, p. 6; Rose Feld, "Here's a Heady Startling Novel," *New York Herald-Tribune Books* 17, no. 38 (May 18, 1941), 2; Joseph Hilton Smyth, "Wolff . . . " *Saturday Review of Literature* 23, no. 32 (May 31, 1941), 14.
48. Clifton Fadiman, "And Only Just Out of College," review of *Whistle Stop* by Maritta Wolff, *New Yorker* 17, no. 14 (May 17, 1941), 88.
49. Smyth, "Wolff . . . ," p. 14.
50. Walton, "First Novel of Distinction," 6.
51. Feld, "Here's a Heady, Startling Novel," 2.

52. Reviews of *Night Shift* by Maritta Wolff: Florence Haxton, *New York Herald-Tribune Books* (January 22, 1942), 2; *Nation* 155, no. 18 (December 19, 1942), 692.
53. Victor P. Hass, review of *Back of Town* by Maritta Wolff, *New York Herald-Tribune Books* (April 6, 1952), 15.
54. Russell Banks, "End of the Age of Innocence," review of *Testing the Current* by William McPherson, *New York Times Book Review* (March 18, 1984), sec. 7, p. 3.
55. Susan Fromberg Schaeffer, "Playing Ball with Death," review of Nancy Willard's *Things Invisible to See, New York Times Book Review* (February 3, 1985), sec. 7, p. 12.
56. Florence Crowther, "Matriarch, Unemployed," review of *Discovery* by Virginia (Chase) Perkins, *New York Times Book Review* (February 29, 1948), sec. 7, p. 10.
57. Jan Cobb, "Thirteen Heroines," review of *The End of the Week* by Virginia (Chase) Perkins, *New York Times Book Review* (November 1, 1953), sec. 7, p. 28.
58. Review of *The End of the Week* by Virginia (Chase) Perkins, *Booklist* 50, no. 1 (September 1, 1953), 2.
59. Robert Phelps, "Mr. Gold Paints a Portrait," review of *The Optimist* by Herbert Gold, *New York Herald-Tribune Books* (April 26, 1959), 8.
60. Thomas E. Cassidy, "Familiar Search," review of *The Optimist* by Herbert Gold, *Commonweal* 70 no. 8 (May 29, 1959), 236–37.
61. Granville Hicks, "Report on Herbert Gold," review of *The Optimist* by Herbert Gold, *Saturday Review of Literature* 42, no. 17 (April 25, 1959), 12.
62. *Contemporary Authors New Revision Series* 3 (1981), 32.
63. Nicholas Monjo, "Wolf Killer," review of *Mark of the Hunter* by Eugene Lee Caesar, *Saturday Review of Literature* 36, no. 40 (October 3, 1953), 29.
64. See, for instance, Fanny Butcher's "Hardly another *Seventeen*," review of *I'm Owen Harrison Harding* by James Whitfield Ellison, *Chicago Sunday Tribune Magazine of Books* (March 27, 1955), sec. 4, p. 8.
65. Arno L. Bader, review of *Somewhere There's Music* by George Lea III, *Michigan Alumnus Quarterly Review*, 64, no. 21 (August 9, 1958), 362.
66. Review of *A Round Shape* by Alma Routsong Brodie, *New York Times Book Review* (September 6, 1959) sec. 7, p. 12.
67. David Dempsey, "Young Man Grows Up, Not Too Grimly," review of *Some Must Watch* by Edwin Daly, *New York Times Book Review* (February 3, 1957), sec. 7, p. 50.
68. Reviews of *A Legacy of Love* by Edwin Daly: Edmund Fuller, "Second Novel Better," *Chicago Sunday Tribune Magazine of Books* (October 12, 1958), 10; "Susie Churchill's Season in the Sun," *New York Times Book Review* (October 5, 1958), sec. 7, p. 32.
69. Reviews of *The End of Pity* by Robie Macauley: John F. Sullivan, "The Problems of Our Times," *Commonweal* 66, no. 22 (August 30, 1957), 549–50; William Peden, "Stories by Robie Macauley," *New York Times Book Review* (August 25, 1957), sec. 7, p. 8.
70. "Aunt Harry and Mrs. Klein," review of *Ladies of the Rachmaninoff Eyes* by Henry L. Van Dyke, Jr., *Times Literary Supplement* (November 4, 1965), 986.
71. "Henry Van Dyke," *Contemporary Authors* 49, 560.
72. Marge Piercy, *Parti-Colored Blocks for a Quilt* (1982), 30.
73. Kathryn Lee Seidel, *Contemporary Novelists*, 4th ed. (1986), 673–75.
74. Reviews of *Children and Lovers: Fifteen Stories* by Helga Sandburg: Don Halberstadt, *Library Journal* 101 (May 1, 1976), 1144; *Publishers Weekly* 209, no. 8 (February 23, 1976), 118.

75. Thomas Meehan, "Travels of a Lovesick Beast," review of *Slouching toward Kalamazoo* by Peter DeVries, *New York Times Book Review* (August 14, 1983), 7, 20.
76. William Butler Yeats, "The Second Coming," in *Collected Poems of W. B. Yeats* (1958), 185.
77. Guy St. Clair, review of *Orphans in the Sun* by Thomas F. Vandeberg, *Library Journal* 94 (1969), 1164.
78. Review of *What I'm Going to Do, I Think* by Larry Woiwode, *New York Review of Books* 13 (July 10, 1969), 18.
79. Douglas A. Noverr, "New Dimensions in Recent Michigan Fiction," *Midwestern Miscellany* 1 (1974), 12.
80. Ibid.
81. H. L. Van Brunt, review of *Wolf, a False Memoir* by Jim Harrison, *Saturday Review* 54, no. 52 (December 25, 1971), 30.
82. H. C. Greene, "The Man-God of the Michigan Jungles," review of *Sundog . . .* by Jim Harrison, *New York Times Book Review* (July 15, 1984), sec. 7, p. 14.
83. Ibid.
84. Jim Harrison, *Outlyers and Ghazals* (1971). The "Drinking Song" and Montana statement are quoted by Eric Siegel in "A New Voice from the North Country: Portrait of a Prodigal Poet Who Came Home to Michigan," *Detroit Magazine, Detroit Free Press* (April 16, 1972), 19.
85. Ursula Hegi, "At First, Merged with Mother," review of *Places in the World a Woman Could Walk* by Janet Kaufman, *New York Times Book Review* (April 20, 1986), sec. 7, p. 17.
86. Ibid., 19.
87. Doris Lynch, review of *Obscene Gestures by Women* by Janet Kaufman, *Library Journal* (September 9, 1989), 216.
88. "Tight Spaces," *Publishers Weekly* 232 (December 25, 1987), 69.
89. Robert Stone, quoted on the dust jacket of *The Long White* by Sharon Dilworth.
90. Mosher and Williams, *Indian Legends . . .* , 131.
91. Sheila Dailey, "Little Bear and Other Stories: A Look at the Life and Works of Michigan Children's Author, Frances Margaret Fox," *Great Lakes Review* no. 1 (Spring 1982), 25–30. A bibliography of Frances Margaret Fox's books is in *Michigan Authors 80*.
92. Rachel Hilbert, "Holly Wilson," *Michigan Authors* (1960), 65.
93. See, for example, Phyllis A. Whitney's review of *Granite Harbor* by Dorothy Maywood Bird, *Chicago Tribune Book Week* (October 8, 1944), 11.
94. Reviews of *The Toy Fair* by Neil Faasen: Erwin J. Gaines, *Library Journal* 88 (October 15, 1963), 3860; Reader's Report, *New York Times Book Review* (October 6, 1963), sec. 7, p. 40.
95. Ann Jordan, "One Summer," *Best Sellers* (February 1980), xxxix, 400.
96. Reviews of *Toothpick* by Kenneth E. Ethridge: Judith A. Sheriff, *Voice Youth Advocates* vol. 9 (April 1986), 30; Ruth Amernick, *School Library Journal* 32 (December 1985), 99.
97. Reviews of the work of Margaret Willey: M. B. S., *The Bigger Book of Lydia, English Journal* (April 1989), 81; *The Bigger Book of Lydia, Publishers Weekly* 224 (December 9, 1983), 50; Ann Turner, "Finding David Dolores," *New York Times Book Review* (October 12, 1986), sec. 7, p. 37; "Finding David Dolores," *English Journal* 76 (October 1987), 94–95; "If Not for You," *Publishers Weekly* 234 (August 26, 1988), 91.

XV. Detroit in Literature: The French City and the Motor City

1. Edith R. Mosher and Nella Dietrich Williams, *From Indian Legends to the Modern Bookshelf: An Anthology of Prose and Verse by Michigan Authors. Prepared Especially for the Youth of the State* (1931), 37.

2. Hal H. Smith, *A Detroit Literature*, (1945), 5.

3. See "Anna Johnson," *Michigan Authors* (1980), 185–86.

4. James Stanford Bradshaw, "M-Quad—Michigan's Most Famous Humorist," *Chronicle: The Magazine of the History Society of Michigan* 16 (Fall 1980), 14–17.

5. Reviews of *A Moth of Time* by Nolan Miller: Richard Sullivan, "Adolescence," *New York Times Book Review* (June 2, 1946) sec. 7 p. 6; Dorothy Sparks, "Hopeful, Aching Uncertainty of Boyhood," *Chicago Tribune Book Week* (May 26, 1946), 2.

6. Reviews of *High Fires* by Marjorie McClure: S. L. C. *Boston Transcript* (March 26, 1924), 4; Charles Hanson Towne, *New York Tribune* (March 16, 1924), 20; *New York Times Book Review* (March 9, 1924), 8.

7. R. M. L. review of *High Fires* by Marjorie McClure; *New Republic* 38, no. 494 (May 21, 1924), 436.

8. Review of *The Highflyers* by Clarence Budington Kelland, *New York Times Book Review* (March 30, 1919), 159–60.

9. Stephen Stepanchev, "Villainess," review of *Blue River* by Mary Frances Doner, *New York Herald Tribune Books* (June 16, 1946), 10.

10. James Rorty, "Nobody Writes Objectively," review of *Nobody Starves* by Catherine Brody, *New Republic* 62, no. 932 (October 12, 1932), 239–40. Sinclair Lewis's statement is from the dust jacket.

11. Herschel Brickell, "Tragedy in the Machine Age," review of *Nobody Starves* by Catherine Brody, *New York Herald-Tribune Books* 9, no. 5 (October 9, 1932), 8.

12. David D. Anderson, "Michigan Proletariat Writers and the Great Depression," *Mid-America* 9 (1982), 76–97.

13. Phyllis Milder, *Best Sellers* 38, no. 2 (May 1978), 36.

14. Reviews of *Invincible Surmise* by Granville Paul Smith: Margaret Wallace, "Tried Temptations," *New York Times Book Review* (April 19, 1936), sec. 4, p. 17; Samuel Sillen, *New York Herald Tribune Books* (April 19, 1936), 10; J. D., *Saturday Review of Literature* 14, no. 8 (June 20, 1936), 19.

15. Albert G. Black, *Michigan Novels: An Annotated Bibliography* (1963), 19.

16. Reviews of *Somewhat Angels* by David Cornel DeJong: Ruth Page, "War Wives," *New York Times Book Review* (November 11, 1945), sec. 7, p. 3; Rose Feld, "While Home Fires Burn," *New York Herald-Tribune Weekly Book Review* (November 4, 1945), 4; Grace Frank, "Angels Decidedly Unaware," *Saturday Review* 28, no. 46 (November 17, 1945); Elizabeth Hawes, "Satirical Novel of Wives in Wartime," *Chicago Sun Book Week* 4, no. 2 (November 4, 1945), sec. 5, p. 1.

17. Reviews of *Willow Run* by Glendon Swarthout: Phil Stong, "Women at W. R.," *Saturday Review of Literature* 26, no. 24 (June 12, 1943), 17; John Norcross, "Turmoil of Today in Defense Plant Novel," *Chicago Sun Book Week* (June 13, 1943), 10; Rose Feld, "Building a Bomber," *New York Times Book Review* (May 30, 1943), sec. 7, p. 18.

18. Wilton Eckley, *Harriette Arnow* (1974), 42.

19. Reviews of *The Dollmaker* by Harriette Arnow: Dorothy H. Lee, " . . . A Journey to Awareness," *Critique* 20 (1978), 92; Frances M. Malpezzi, "Silence and Captivity

in Babylon . . . ," *Southern Studies* 20, no. 1 (Spring 1981), 84–90; James Seaton, "The Image of Detroit . . . ," *Mid-America* 14 (1987), 137–45.

20. "Judith (Ann) Guest," *Contemporary Authors* New Revision Series, vol. 15, 170–74.

21. Richard Lardner Tobin, *The Center of the World* (1951), 147.

22. Grant C. Knight, *The Strenuous Age in American Literature* (1954), 98, 138.

23. Reviews of *The Flivver King* by Upton Sinclair: "The Story of Ford," *New York Times Book Review* (May 22, 1938), sec. 7, p. 7; *Times Literary Supplement* (March 12, 1938), 172.

24. See Paul H. Douglas's review of *The Flivver King* by Upton Sinclair, *Saturday Review of Literature* 27, no. 3 (November 13, 1937), 11. Douglas also discusses the UAW's role in publishing the 1937 edition.

25. Review of *Man's Country* . . . by Peter Clark McFarland, *New York Times Book Review* (January 21, 1923) sec. 3, p. 19.

26. Robert Morss Lovett, "Workers in Metal," review of *Gold Shod* by Newton Fuessle, *New Republic* 29, no. 366 (December 7, 1921), 18.

27. D. D. Anderson, "Michigan Proletariat Writers," 76–97.

28. [Justin] Brooks Atkinson, *New York Times Book Review* (October 20, 1927), sec. 3, p. 33.

29. D. D. Anderson, "Michigan Proletariat Writers," 92–93.

30. "Wessel Smitter, 59, Novelist, Succumbs," *New York Times* (November 9, 1951), 27 (obituary).

31. Wallace Stegner, review of *Another Morning* by Wessel Smitter, *Boston Evening Transcript* (April 26, 1941), book section.

32. Reviews of Albert Maltz's *The Underground Stream* . . . : Harold Strauss, *New York Times Book Review* (July 7, 1940), sec. 6, p. 7; *New York Herald Tribune Books* (June 30, 1940), 5.

33. Alfred Kazin, "Here Is a Left-Wing Writer Who Can Write," review of *The Underground Stream* . . . by Albert Maltz, *New York Herald-Tribune Books* (June 30, 1940), 5.

34. Jack Salzman, *Albert Maltz* (1978), 54–69.

35. Ibid., 56.

36. M. E., review of film *Inside Detroit*, *New York Times* (January 28, 1956), 10.

37. Meyer Levin, "2-1-0 Means Two in One," review of *The Insolent Chariots* by John Keats, *Saturday Review of Literature* 41, no. 45 (November 8, 1958), 15.

38. Reviews of *The Hard Winners* by John E. Quirk: Frederick Davenport, *Library Journal* 90, no. 8 (April 15, 1965), 1934; *New Yorker* (March 27, 1965), 182.

39. Review of *American Chrome* by Edwin Gilbert, "Tin Lizzie," *Time* 85, no. 12 (March 19, 1965), 112.

40. John Skow, "Round and Round," *Time* 98, no. 15 (October 11, 1971), 112.

41. Review of *The Betsy* by Harold Robbins, *Best Sellers* 31 (December 15, 1971), 427.

42. Janet Maslin, "Cars, Sex, Money and 'The Betsy,' " review of film *The Betsy*, *New York Times* (February 26, 1978), sec. C, p. 5.

43. Reviews of *Places Everyone* by Jim Daniels: Peter Stitt, *New York Times Book Review* (May 4, 1986), sec. 7, p. 22; Rochelle Ratner, *Library Journal* 110, no. 20 (December 1985), 114.

44. Joyce Carol Oates quoted by J. F. Baker in, "On Being a Writer in the Midwest," *Publishers Weekly* 204, no. 17 (October 22, 1973), 79.

45. Joyce Carol Oates quoted by Benjamin DeMott, "The Necessity in Art of a Reflective Intelligence," *Saturday Review* 52, no. 47 (November 22, 1969), 71.

46. Calvin Bedient, "The story of Sleeping Beauty and a Love That Is Like Hatred," *New York Times Book Review* (October 14, 1973), sec. 7, p. 1.

47. "The Heavy Mob," *Times Literary Supplement* (January 11, 1974), 25.
48. Martha Duffy, review of *Do with Me What You Will* by Joyce Carol Oates, *Time* 94 (October 10, 1969), 126.
49. Review of *Cybele* by Joyce Carol Oates, *Booklist* 79 (March 1950), 1348.

XVI. Michigan Poetry of Place

1. Louis Bates, "Detroit" (1855), quoted in *Michigan History Magazine* 32, no. 4 (December 1948), 372.
2. Larry B. Massie, "Michigan Poets and Their Poetry," *Literary Michigan* (1988), 14.
3. Phil Stong, *Hawkeyes: A Biography of the State of Iowa* (1940), 39.
4. Lawrence R. Dawson, "Harps in the Wilds of Freedom; Territorial Verse from the *Detroit Gazette*, 1817–1830," *The Old Northwest* 9, no. 2 (Summer 1983), 182.
5. Carl E. Burklund, "An Early Michigan Poet: Elizabeth Margaret Chandler," *Michigan History Magazine* 30, no. 2 (April–June 1946), 277–87.
6. Stong, *Hawkeyes*, 41.
7. Thomas Capek, "A Forgotten Poetess," *Central European Observer* (April 17, 1936).
8. Carl E. Burklund, "An Early Michigan Poet: Louis LeGrand Noble," *Michigan History Magazine* 31 (1947), 199.
9. Colonel Frederick Schneider, "Michigan, My Michigan," *Michigan Pioneer and Historical Collections* 35 (1907), 157; Willis Dunbar, *Michigan: A History of the Wolverine State* (1973), 455–56.
10. A. H. Greenly, "The Sweet Singer of Michigan Bibliographically Considered," *The Papers of the Bibliographical Society of America*, 39 (1945), 91–118.
11. Ibid., 102.
12. Mark Twain, *Following the Equator* (1897), chap. 36.
13. L. W. Michaelson, "The Worst American Novel," *North Dakota Quarterly* (Autumn 1964), 101–3.
14. Walter E. Banyan, "Ben King Memorial," *Michigan History Magazine* 8, no. 29 (October 1924), 476.
15. *Ben King's Verse*, second ed. (1898), 36, 39.
16. Earnest Elmo Calkins, "The Eddie Guest of the Seventies," *Saturday Review of Literature* 26, no. 30 (July 24, 1943), 22.
17. Ibid.
18. Ibid.
19. James Norman Hall, *My Island Home* (1952), 247.
20. See *Michigan History Magazine* 2, no. 3, 513–17 for a biography of Winfield Lionel Scott and page 523 for a list of members of the Michigan Authors' Association in 1918–1919.
21. For a bibliography of articles about Edgar A. Guest, see *Dictionary of American Biography*, suppl. 6 (1980), 259.
22. See J. V. Campbell, "The Naming of Lake St. Clair," *Michigan Pioneer and Historical Collections*, vol. 3 (1881), 656–65. The poetry was previously printed in *Legends of Detroit* (1884).
23. Kathleen Isabel Gillard, *Our Michigan Heritage* (1955), 193.
24. Carl E. Burklund, *New Michigan Verse* (1940), introduction.
25. Bill Katz, "Levine, Philip," *Library Journal* 95, no. 13 (July 1970) 2489.
26. Thomas H. Smith, "Upper Peninsula Literary Traditions . . . " *Midwestern Miscellany* 16 (1988), 54.

27. Hoyt Fuller, "Blacks Need Black Literature," *Spectator* (University of Iowa Alumni Association, April 1973), 6.
28. Dorothy H. Lee, "Black Voices in Detroit," *Michigan Quarterly Review* 25 (Spring 1986), 315.
29. *Publishers Weekly* (March 15, 1971), 44.
30. Lee, "Black Voices in Detroit," 313–28.
31. Ibid., 313.

INDEX

Titles in the Great Lakes Books Series

Detroit Images: Photographs of the Renaissance City, edited by John J. Bukow-
czyk and Douglas Aikenhead, with Peter Slavcheff, 1989

Hangdog Reef: Poems Sailing the Great Lakes, by Stephen Tudor, 1989

Detroit: City of Race and Class Violence, revised edition, by B. J. Widick, 1989

Deep Woods Frontier: A History of Logging in Northern Michigan, by Theodore
J. Karamanski, 1989

Orvie, The Dictator of Dearborn, by David L. Good, 1989

Seasons of Grace: A History of the Catholic Archidiocese of Detroit, by Leslie
Woodcock Tentler, 1990

The Pottery of John Foster: Form and Meaning, by Gordon and Elizabeth
Orear, 1990

The Diary of Bishop Frederic Baraga: First Bishop of Marquette, Michigan, edited
by Regis M. Walling and Rev. N. Daniel Rupp, 1990

Walnut Pickles and Watermelon Cake: A Century of Michigan Cooking, by
Larry B. Massie and Priscilla Massie, 1990

The Making of Michigan, 1820–1860: A Pioneer Anthology, edited by Justin L.
Kestenbaum, 1990

America's Favorite Homes: A Guide to Popular Early Twentieth-Century Homes,
by Robert Schweitzer and Michael W. R. Davis, 1990

Beyond the Model T: The Other Ventures of Henry Ford, by Ford R. Bryan, 1990

Life after the Line, by Josie Kearns, 1990

*Michigan Lumbertowns: Lumbermen and Laborers in Saginaw, Bay City, and
Muskegon, 1870–1905*, by Jeremy W. Kilar, 1990

Detroit Kids Catalog: The Hometown Tourist, by Ellyce Field, 1990

Waiting for the News, by Leo Litwak, 1990 (reprint)

Detroit Perspectives, edited by Wilma Wood Henrickson, 1991

Life on the Great Lakes: A Wheelsman's Story, by Fred W. Dutton, edited by
William Donohue Ellis, 1991

Copper Country Journal: The Diary of Schoolmaster Henry Hobart, 1863–1864,
by Henry Hobart, edited by Philip P. Mason, 1991

John Jacob Astor: Business and Finance in the Early Republic, by John Denis
Haeger, 1991

Survival and Regeneration: Detroit's American Indian Community, by Edmund J.
Danziger, Jr., 1991